Manning the Margins

Manning the Margins

MASCULINITY AND WRITING IN
SEVENTEENTH-CENTURY FRANCE

Lewis C. Seifert

THE UNIVERSITY OF MICHIGAN PRESS
Ann Arbor

Copyright © by the University of Michigan 2009
All rights reserved
Published in the United States of America by
The University of Michigan Press
Manufactured in the United States of America
⊗ Printed on acid-free paper

2012   2011   2010   2009   4   3   2   1

A CIP catalog record for this book is available from the British Library.

Library of Congress Cataloging-in-Publication Data

Seifert, Lewis Carl.
    Manning the margins : masculinity and writing in seventeenth-
century France / Lewis C. Seifert.
        p.   cm.
    Includes bibliographical references and index.
    ISBN-13: 978-0-472-07058-9 (cloth : alk. paper)
    ISBN-10: 0-472-07058-4 (cloth : alk. paper)
    ISBN-13: 978-0-472-05058-1 (pbk. : alk. paper)
    ISBN-10: 0-472-05058-3 (pbk. : alk. paper)
        1. French literature—17th century—History and criticism.
    2. Masculinity in literature.   3. Sex role in literature.
    4. Homosexuality in literature.   I. Title.
PQ245.S45   2009
840.9'33521--dc22   2008051140

for Andrew and Patrick

Acknowledgments

I HAVE INCURRED MANY DEBTS while researching and writing this book. I wish to thank Brown University for providing essential logistical support: research funds from the Office of the Vice-President for Research, a faculty fellowship from the Cogut Center for the Humanities, and sabbatical leaves from the Office of the Dean of the Faculty. My colleagues and students in the Department of French Studies at Brown University deserve my deepest gratitude for creating a congenial and stimulating environment in which to teach and to conduct research. At the University of Michigan Press, my sincerest thanks go to Alexa Ducsay, Marcia LaBrenz, and Alison Mackeen for their cheerful responses to my many queries and their expert handling of the manuscript.

This book would never have been completed without the advice and encouragement of many people, including Réda Bensmaïa, Michel-André Bossy, Dominique Coulombe, Erika Gaffney, Ben Labonte, Charley Labonte, Stephanie Merrim, Gretchen Schultz, Domna Stanton, Catherine Velay-Vallantin, and Abby Zanger. My warm thanks to Faith Beasley, Beth Goldsmith, Michèle Longino, Jeffrey Merrick, Jeff Peters, and Pierre Saint-Amand for reading and commenting on portions of the manuscript. With her usual warmth and generosity, Virginia Krause provided invaluable advice all along the way. Todd Reeser, my collaborator in French masculinity studies, helped to give conceptual shape to this book in more ways than he may realize. Many years ago, as an undergraduate, Rebecca Wilkin assisted me in compiling an initial bibliography on masculinity; more recently, as a colleague, she gave me many insightful suggestions for this project and helped me arrive at the title. Last but certainly not least, this book owes its greatest debt to Catherine Gordon-Seifert, whose passion for seventeenth-century France and whose uncommon love fill my life with joy. All of the aforementioned individuals have made this book much better than it would have been without their help. But the weaknesses that remain are obviously my own.

Portions of chapter 5 appeared in slightly different form as "Masculinity and Satires of 'Sodomites' in France, 1660–1715," in *Homosexuality in French*

History and Culture, ed. Jeffrey Merrick and Michael Sibalis (Binghampton: Harrington Park Press, 2001), 37–52, and "Boisrobert's *Cabinet* and the Seventeenth-Century Closet," in *Intersections,* Biblio 17, no. 161 (Tübingen: Gunter Narr Verlag, 2005), 261–70. I am grateful to the Hayworth Press/ Taylor & Francis and to Narr, Francke, Attempto Verlag, respectively, for kind permission to reproduce this material. I would also like to thank the John Hay Library at Brown University for photographing and granting permission to reproduce the "Carte de Tendre," and the Bibliothèque Nationale de France for permission to reproduce the engraving *Un Homme marchant de face.*

Contents

Note on Translations   *xi*

Introduction   *1*

PART ONE   Civilizing the Margins

ONE   The Chevalier de Méré's Quest for Honnête Masculinity   *21*

TWO   Effeminacy and Its Meanings from Court to Salon   *57*

THREE   Vincent Voiture and the Perils of Galanterie   *98*

FOUR   Madeleine de Scudéry's Tender Masculinity   *117*

PART TWO   Sexuality and the Body at the Margins

FIVE   Writing Sodomy: Satire, Secrets, and the "Self"   *151*

SIX   Border Crossings: For a Transgendered Choisy   *207*

Afterimage   *246*

Notes   *251*
Bibliography   *305*
Index   *323*

Note on Translations

Because of space limitations, I have included only English translations for French sources, with the exception of poetry, for which both the original French and the English translation are provided. For passages where only the English translation is given, I include as necessary difficult-to-translate French words or phrases in parentheses. A number of key French terms studied in this book (notably *galant, galanterie, honnête,* and *honnêteté*) are retained and not translated because of their semantic complexity. Unless otherwise indicated, all translations are my own.

Introduction

ORGON:

Mon frère, vous seriez charmé de le connaître,
Et vos ravissements ne prendraient point de fin.
C'est un homme ... qui, ... ha! un homme ... un homme enfin.

IN ACT 1, SCENE 5 OF MOLIÈRE'S *Le Tartuffe*, the blindly obstinate Orgon illustrates some central truths about masculinity. When his family assails Tartuffe, whose deceit and hypocrisy he is unwilling to see, Orgon is only able to muster a stuttering defense: "He's a man ... who ... ah! ... a man ... a man, you know."[1] Enraptured with Tartuffe, Orgon attempts to enumerate his purported qualities only to fall back on the signifier "man" *(homme)*. Conscious that he needs to provide particularizing details but unable to do so—in large part because he is so smitten with him—Orgon opts instead to single out Tartuffe's gender, as if that alone provided irrefutable proof of the accused's innocence, as if the word *man* required no further explanation. Even as Orgon's defense provokes the derisive laughter of spectators and readers, it also encapsulates the logic that cultures have often applied to masculinity. By assuming it is a self-evident, unmarked, and universal category, they seek to preserve masculine power and privilege, much as Orgon does for Tartuffe and, of course, himself. Or at least as he does for a time. In the end, of course, Orgon's clumsy defense is woefully and predictably inadequate, and Tartuffe is revealed to be the imposter he has been all along. Even if Orgon's familial authority seems to be reinstated at the end of the play, it is not because of his own efforts, but rather because of the deus ex machina intervention of an offstage, seemingly transcendent king. In the here and now of the play, Orgon's attempts to assert self-evident privilege for both Tartuffe and himself contrast sharply with the vulnerability of these two characters. Just as they are both fundamentally at odds with their prescribed roles as paterfamilias and confessor, so too men can find themselves either deliberately or unwittingly marginalized from the normative masculine roles they are expected to fill.

The irony of Orgon's plight in this scene and throughout much of the play illustrates the central tenets of this book. Orgon's reliance on the term *man* begs the question about what *sort* of man Tartuffe really is, revealing that the meanings of the signifier *man* are not stable, univocal, and transparent, but rather variable, multiple, and contingent. The claim to power that Orgon makes here and elsewhere is in the long run ineffectual, just as the exercise of masculine authority by any single individual is always inherently unstable. Orgon's marginal position within his family, a microcosm of society at large, is a reminder that men can indeed be relegated to the periphery of social structures, notwithstanding the expectation of dominance that patriarchy lays out for them. And the latent homoeroticism in Orgon's attachment to Tartuffe recalls that cultures use sexuality to distinguish among different masculinities, privileging some and marginalizing others. Most fundamentally, though, since Orgon's appeal to masculine authority through the exclamation "a man, you know!" is framed as a failure, the play in effect invites us to consider how arbitrary his assertion of a "natural" masculine being really is. In this moment, the play implicitly performs the sort of interrogation of masculinity that is the raison d'être of this book. As Molière does through the example of Orgon, my study highlights some of the profound uncertainties that surround masculinity. When it comes to the gendered subject *man*, what we think we can take for granted, as Orgon illustrates, turns out to be anything but certain. Thus, I contend that, in contrast to the image of stability painted by patriarchal ideologies (and assumed by Orgon), masculinity is always potentially at risk of being destabilized precisely *because* it occupies the dominant position within the sex/gender system. I argue furthermore that it is through positions of marginality, such as the one occupied by Orgon, that we perhaps best see how normative and dominant masculinities function, how they define what is and is not "masculine," and how these distinctions are made to serve radically asymmetrical power relations *between* men and women, but also *among* men.

The questions raised by Orgon's exclamation "a man, you know!" are among the most important to have been addressed by the burgeoning field of masculinity studies. An outgrowth of feminist inquiry, this field comprises heterogeneous disciplines and approaches that nonetheless strive for similar political goals, namely, the critique of sexist social structures and the philosophical and symbolic traditions that undergird them.[2] At the same time, masculinity studies sets as one of its foremost objectives the difficult task of putting into question the stable and univalent masculine subject upon which feminist thought has often relied in its critique of women's oppression. If masculinity studies occupies an uncertain position vis-à-vis feminism,[3] it has at the very least succeeded in demonstrating that masculinity, like femininity, is a contingent and relational construction and that one cannot be considered without the other. This field has also demonstrated that, no less than femininity, masculinity is not solely the product of the two-gender binary, even if that binary is a central defining feature. Accordingly, scholars have been diligent in pointing out the intersections of masculinity with categories such as class, ethnicity, race, nationality, and sexuality. If the bulk of the work in this field concentrates on contemporary North American masculinities, historical studies have explored the changing norms and models for masculinity, the "crises" of masculine authority, and marginal masculinities, among other things. Tracing genealogies of masculinity is a crucial task if the promise of this field is to be fully realized. For, to grasp the variability of masculine identities as well as the persistence of masculinist hegemony, an understanding of their forms over the long term is essential.

At first glance, seventeenth-century France would appear to be a significant and fruitful period for such a larger genealogical project. On many different fronts, the so-called Grand Siècle has long been enshrined as a bastion of male privilege. After all, this was the century of Descartes and Pascal in philosophy, Corneille, Molière, and Racine in literature, Richelieu and Louis XIV in politics, all figures (among many others) who seem to mark the period as one of supreme masculine dominance. But scholarly work on this period over the past thirty years at least should invite us to arrive at a more complex and nuanced conclusion. To be sure, masculinity per se is only beginning to become an explicit frame of analysis, and it is my hope that this book will accelerate work on this as yet nascent topic of inquiry.[4] Still, trends in scholarship in several different fields indicate not only what this topic contributes to our understanding of the period but also what masculinity in seventeenth-century France offers for the broader fields of gender and specifically masculinity studies. For instance, in philosophy, the consequences of (so-called) Cartesian dualism for gender difference are the subject of considerable debate, putting into question the common assumption that the "modern" subject is inevitably masculine.[5] Work on the representations of Louis XIV has pointed to their reliance on the king's masculinity, making important symbols of his virility and his metaphorical fatherhood.[6] And, in the history of early modern science, the question of how the sexed body was (re)conceptualized during this period and how (or even if) one might consider a history of the male body has provoked considerable interest.[7]

But it is without doubt in relation to feminist scholarship on this period that the study of masculinity holds the most immediate promise. In contrast to the image of a century dominated by men such as Louis XIV, feminist scholars have demonstrated the important contributions of women in artistic, philosophical, literary, musical, political, and religious life of the period.[8] If it is true that prominent figures such as Marie de Médicis, Anne d'Autriche, Marie-Madeleine de Lafayette, or Marie de Sévigné were never completely absent from traditional historiographical accounts, it is also true that women's overall influence was significantly obscured by a masculinist perspective that concentrated on "great" men and, more generally, did not adopt gender as a category of analysis. Scholarship concentrating on the history of women and women's artistic and literary production has brought into view their increased participation in the cultural sphere during this period as well as the significance of their contributions in general. By restoring to critical prominence the role of certain women, such as Madeleine de Scudéry and Marie-Catherine Desjardins (Madame de Villedieu) in the literary realm, this work has demonstrated that their production is all the more remarkable given the gendered constraints under which they lived. To emerge onto the cultural scene, as scholars have shown, women had to overcome lack of formal education and strictures of "feminine" propriety, among other things.[9] If, ultimately, this scholarship is providing a more and more nuanced understanding of the sociohistorical realities of women's existence and the contours of feminine subjectivity during the seventeenth century, it paradoxically risks reducing the complexity and variability of masculinity to an amorphous and monolithic patriarchy. To be sure, it is important *not* to minimize the masculinist violence against women in this (or any) period. But we must also recognize that masculinity too involves constraints and that masculine privilege is contested among men if we are to get a more complete picture of the relational tensions not only *between* women and men, but also *among* women and *among* men. Thus, for instance, to fully understand the reasons and the significance of women's increasingly prominent role in the literary field, conceptions of masculine authorship must be brought into sharper focus.[10] In short, work on women in seventeenth-century France has arrived at point where the study of masculinity has become imperative.

As an integral part of seventeenth-century French culture, then, masculinity necessarily touches on multiple disciplines and requires diverse fields of competence to be studied in a comprehensive way. The perspectives I adopt here reflect my conviction that masculinity cannot be reduced to a single model for this or any other period. Hence, I resist an explanatory scheme that would purport to sum up all forms of masculinity in seventeenth-century France. I also avoid a strictly chronological organization that would give the impression that there is a straightforward "evolution" of masculinity over the course of the century. To be sure, there are inevitable and important trends, as I point out at various moments in the following chapters. But my focus here is rather on one aspect of masculinity that persists across most periods and cultures, namely masculine dominance not only over women, but also over men alienated from normative masculinity and the authority it confers.

Masculine Domination

Throughout this book, I concentrate on how seventeenth-century French masculinity is defined by tensions between submission and dominance. The theoretical model I rely upon is inspired largely by Pierre Bourdieu's landmark *Masculine Domination* (1998), which insists on the agonistic construction of masculinity.[11] In this model, the binary of the *dominant* and the *dominated* functions on both the level of the social, though interpersonal relations, and the level of the individual, through the gendered *habitus*, the largely unconscious dispositions acquired through experience in social interactions. Thus, gender positions are constructed relationally within various social fields, but these positions become naturalized as the habitus, which is experienced through and as the body. The masculine habitus, according to Bourdieu, strives for a relation of domination within social interaction, which is by definition a site of struggle. Consequently, some men are successful, while others are not. What this means is that masculine domination, especially in its bodily form, must be continually reaffirmed, not only in relation to women but also—and even more so—to other men. For individual men, the masculine habitus is always unstable, and dominance, once achieved, can easily be lost.

What is at stake here is not only the struggle for dominance in social interaction, but also *within* the masculine subject. For Bourdieu, this is true first of all in the well-known sense of domination requiring submission to its strictures: "Structure imposes its constraints on the two terms of the relationship of domination, and therefore on the dominant themselves, who can benefit from it while being, in Marx's phrase, 'dominated by their domination'" (69). Even though the domination of the dominant (so to speak) yields rewards, it also entails a constant oscillation between hegemony and nonhegemony.[12] The masculine subject occupies the positions of dominant and dominated and thereby applies to himself a structure that is homologous to the asymmetrical gender opposition "masculine" versus "feminine."[13]

Hence, the relational construction of masculine subjectivity occurs not only in the mixed-gender and same-gender interactions of the social field, but also, by homology, within the psyche of the masculine subject. In sum, the constraints and instabilities to which masculinity is constantly exposed and which masculine domination must continually negotiate occur simultaneously on the levels of both inter- and intrasubjectivity.

Ultimately, the understanding of dominated masculinity provided by Bourdieu's model has the advantage of accounting for multiple variables that are often treated separately.[14] Dominated masculinity is produced by interactions within the social field as well as by the psychic and bodily effects of the masculine habitus, and it results from asymmetrical power arrangements between men and women, but also *among* men. In addition, Bourdieu's model addresses at least two concerns central to the field of masculinity studies that has developed in English-speaking cultures. First, there is a recognition that masculine positions are multiple and hierarchically situated among themselves. To speak of masculinity is in fact to speak of masculini*ties*. And second, Bourdieu's model provides a different way of approaching the "crises" of masculinity, a recurrent theme of much work in the historical and cultural branches of masculinity studies. If the "crisis" model emphasizes the variability of masculine roles and identities over time and gives nuance to the image of a monolithic patriarchal masculinity invoked in some feminist work, it also tends to imply that masculinity is "in crisis" at certain times, and *not* at others, and ultimately ignores the persistence of masculinist oppression. Bourdieu's theory of masculine domination provides a corrective on both counts. According to this model, masculinity is perpetually in crisis, although this fact is not overtly acknowledged by the masculine habitus; and yet, in spite of this fact, masculine hegemony remains in effect across cultures and time periods.[15]

This book begins with the recognition that the risk of submission—of being dominated or of losing a position of dominance—drives the elaboration of most masculine ideals. Accordingly, my focus throughout is to show how dominant masculinity creates positions of submission—and thus positions of marginality—so as to (re)affirm its own hegemony. However, I also concentrate on the constant movement of oscillation within dominant masculine subjectivity. Following Bourdieu's model, the dominant masculine subject incorporates within himself the dominated position, not only as a subject who submits to the dictates of a norm, but also as a subject who, in the midst of this sort of submission, must always consider the possibility of not measuring up to that norm, and specifically, of being confined to the realm of dominated men, who, with women, are confined to the margins of social power structures. In short, assuming a position of dominance always involves putting oneself in a position of submission, and this latter position always threatens to undo the hegemony that the dominant masculine subject assumes is "naturally" his own. But this threat is not (always) explicitly articulated, and my analyses tease out the signs of this threat within discourses that seek to establish a masterful dominance by ostensibly banishing any traces of submission and thus marginality. Put another way, this book uncovers how dominant masculine subjectivity "mans" the margins of its own dominance, how it attempts to use these positions of submission to (re)affirm its own hegemony. The margins are "manned" in the sense that they are occupied by the dominant subject position seeking to avert the submission that lurks within it and threatens to destabilize it, not unlike the way a soldier "mans" a post, awaiting omnipresent but unpredictable threats. But also like the soldier, the dominant masculine subject can be overwhelmed by these same threats.

The analyses in *Manning the Margins* are informed by Bourdieu's understanding of masculine domination, but they do not endeavor to "apply" this model in an explicit way. Instead, I use the notion of a dialectic between dominant and dominated masculinities as a general lens through which to explore specific instances of marginal masculinities in seventeenth-century French culture. Overall, my concern is to foreground and articulate this complex dynamic in three general discourses where masculinity emerges as a problem within the cultural and literary imaginary of seventeenth-century France: the discourses of civility, sexuality, and the gendered body.

Civility and the Margins

Part 1 considers some of the consequences for men and masculinity of discourses of civility (conceived broadly as both etiquette and courtliness, and called such things as *civilité*, *honnêteté*, and *galanterie* in the seventeenth century). Work to date on civility in this period has for the most part neglected to focus on gender—and especially masculinity—in a central way, privileging instead its aesthetic, ethical, and sociopolitical ramifications.[16] This neglect is all the more surprising given that the vast majority of texts about civility are specifically addressed to men and codify *masculine* conduct. The gender of intended addressees is made clear in the titles of such works as *L'Honnête homme ou l'art de plaire à la cour* (Nicolas Faret, 1630), *Traité de la*

fortune des gens de qualité et des gentilhommes particuliers (Jacques de Caillières, 1658), *Instructions pour un jeune seigneur ou l'idée d'un galant homme*
(Trotti de la Chétardie, 1683), and *Le Portrait d'un honnête homme* (Jacques
Goussault, 1692). Although prescriptive conduct literature has a long history,
going back to the *Miroirs des Princes* and the *Contenances de Table* in the Middle Ages (not to mention antecedents in antiquity), the seventeenth century
witnessed an unprecedented popularity and publication of such texts under
the influence of Castiglione, Della Casa, and of course Montaigne. To these
works should be added the pastoral and heroic novels and much of the poetry
of the first half of the century, whose role in defining "refined" conduct for
both women and men was significant.[17]

At first glance, it is difficult to measure how the seventeenth-century discourse of civility influenced gender norms, especially if we take our cue from
Norbert Elias's notion of the "civilizing process," which purports that a
gradual reduction in interpersonal aggression resulted from increasingly
stronger internal constraints on the individual level and a growing monopoly
on violence at the level of the state. At best, gender is a latent category in
Elias's work, which devotes almost no attention to gender-specific behavior
and seems to approach the changing norms observed in conduct literature as
applying unequivocally to both men and women, in spite of an explicitly
masculine purview.[18] Still, his descriptions of the civilizing process as an internalization of external constraints that often induces inner conflict are useful for uncovering the dynamic of masculine subjectivity within the discourse of civility, especially when considered alongside the dialectic of
dominant versus dominated positions.[19] Civility offers the promise of dominance (within prescribed limits, to be sure), yet the attainment of that
promise is predicated on a submission to rules that results in a constant struggle, both with others and with oneself. Within the broader discourse of civility, it is no doubt true that a similar submission and thus struggle apply to
women. But both the positions of dominance they may envision and the submission to which they are subjected are qualitatively different than those
foreordained for men, first and foremost because of the prevailing structure
of masculine domination.

Beyond emphasizing the category of gender in the discourses of the civilizing process, my objective is to highlight the persistence of aggression or
struggle within them. This is to say that the discourse of civility required aggression in the form of the oscillating tension between dominant and dominated positions, whether or not Louis XIV succeeded in "pacifying" the nobles at court (by restricting the traditional aristocratic right to vengeance, for

instance). To aspire to the recognition accorded polite refinement is to overcome the risk of social debasement, which theoretically is always—indeed, must always be—a possibility. For male nobles (and even for bourgeois men), this oscillation meant that an *intra*subjective aggression would persist, even if aggression were no longer a readily available option in the realm of interpersonal physical combat such as the duel. And if it were (as Stuart Carroll's recent work on "vindicatory" violence in early modern France seems to show),[20] this self-subjected violence existed alongside, and at odds with, an interpersonal, physical violence. Contrary to the assumption or even the appearance that the civilizing process resulted in a reduction in anxiety and aggression, quite the opposite was true. Of course, seventeenth-century moralists such as La Rochefoucauld and La Bruyère were keenly aware of this, noting that the *paraître* of docile refinement could mask an *être* of cold and calculating ambition. And, closer to our own time, the aggression at the heart of *honnêteté* is one of the central arguments of Domna Stanton's seminal *The Aristocrat as Art*.[21]

But the more fundamental point I want to make here is that the inner conflict induced by the discourse of civility had particular consequences for ideals of elite masculinity in seventeenth-century France. This is true first of all because the inner struggle required by this discourse is inseparable from intersubjective relations. The quest for the dominant masculine positions envisioned by civility involves a dialectical struggle with dominated masculine *and* feminine positions—both a distancing from them in social exchange and an internal oscillation between dominance and submission. Thus, for instance, Faret's *honnête homme* had to aspire to the glory won on the battlefield but, doing so, had to avoid resembling, among many others, the "blowhard" *(fanfaron)* who speaks of nothing else but his martial prowess[22] and the "overdressed man" *(homme trop ajusté)* whose preoccupation with his appearance supposedly resembles women's (93). To gain the prestige of the "profession of war" required not only visibly distancing oneself from these and other marginal masculine positions, but also interiorizing the risk of resemblance with them and oscillating between the dominant *honnête homme* and the marginal *fanfaron* or *homme trop ajusté*. But if dominant masculine positions, such as the honnête homme, must confront their marginal others, it is because these latter are produced by the discourse of civility. And, by producing them, this discourse makes them available as weapons in an arsenal that can be deployed in the struggle for "civilized" masculine dominance. For example, the honnête homme can attempt to assert his status as such by qualifying other men as *fanfarons* and *hommes trop ajustés*.

Over and beyond providing for an agonistic masculine ideal, the seventeenth-century moment of the civilizing process placed particular importance on heterosocial (male-female) relations. In a reiteration of a commonplace from courtly love and Petrarchanism, men were enjoined to seek out women's refining influence, through conversation and love. And this recurring imperative was a fundamental justification for men's participation in the mixed-gender salons that flourished throughout the century. After describing the beauty, difficulty, and benefits of conversation with women, Faret tells his would-be honnête homme he must "go into the city to see which noble Ladies are deemed to be the most honnête women and in whose homes are the most beautiful salons *(les plus belles assemblées)*" (90). Ostensibly, men's interaction with women in sociable settings required a reversal of the usual power differential among the sexes. At least for the duration of salon meetings or the courtship ritual, men were to defer to women's authority in matters of cultural taste and love.

Many scholars take these injunctions at face value, arguing as Benedetta Craveri and Claude Habib have recently that this discourse cleared the way for increased agency by women and greater exchange between the sexes.[23] Although these claims are not entirely without merit, they overlook the consequences of masculine civility.[24] Thus, against an idealized view of male-female sociability that pervades much scholarship on this period, I will contend that there is more to this dynamic than meets the proverbial eye. In both theory and practice, the posture of submission that men were to adopt frequently became a cover from which men were able to reassert their own authority over women. But at the same time, the ostensible submission to women carried the marginalizing risk of effeminacy: bowing to women's taste could be—and was—perceived as becoming *like* women, as renouncing the dominant for the dominated position. As prescribed by the discourse of civility (if not the actual interaction of the salons), women's room for maneuver was by definition constrained; but so too was men's. This does not mean that women and men were on an equal footing within the bounds of male-female sociability. But it does indicate that there is reason to seek a nuanced middle ground between what are sometimes two extreme visions of seventeenth-century salon life in particular. Neither a utopia for women and heterosocial relations nor a locus of conservative reaction, salon meetings entailed constraints on both women and men.[25] Considering how the discourse of civility sought to regulate heterosocial relations so as to preserve masculine domination brings into focus the broader tensions within elite masculine subjectivity.

These tensions are the focus of the first four chapters of *Manning the Margins*. Chapter 1 examines perhaps the most prominent masculine ideal of seventeenth-century France, the honnête homme, or honorable gentleman, who is only rarely treated as a gendered construct. Concentrating on the writings of the preeminent theorist of honnêteté, Antoine Gombaud, chevalier de Méré, I argue that this decidedly masculine ideal necessitates a process of approximation and rejection of both masculine and feminine models so as to gain the upper hand in mastering the *art de plaire*, the art of captivating others. But this goal is elusive, I argue, and the only sure means of managing all the contradictions of honnête masculinity is to be endowed with the *je ne sais quoi*, the transcendent sense of the sublime that appeals to an ideological ruse.

Chapters 2, 3, and 4, as a group, turn to the dynamics and risks of salon masculinity. The benefits men, and especially male writers, stood to gain from participating in salons were considerable; yet salon masculinity was often equated with effeminacy because of the allegience owed to women and their tastes. Each of these chapters highlights different aspects of the inherent instability of salon masculinity. Chapter 2 begins with an overview of the signs and "causes" of early modern effeminacy before moving on to the uses of this satirical charge in relation to court and salon culture. I then examine the aesthetic and sociable ideal of *galanterie*, prized in most seventeenth-century salons, and argue that it exposes the destabilizing effects of civility's attempts to refashion the relations between men and women. This chapter then concludes with a consideration of satirical reactions to salon culture and traces how the figure of the *précieuse* comes to absorb anxiety about effeminacy, but also how this anxiety reappears in the *petit-maître* at the very end of the century.

Chapter 3 pursues the exploration of salon masculinity by concentrating on the legacy of Vincent Voiture, the quintessential *galant homme* whose posthumous works became a vade mecum for male salon-goers. The rhetoric of galanterie he employs both reiterates and complicates the neo-Petrarchan stance of the submissive lover, but the subtlety of this posture was easily misconstrued. I show how male writers hostile to his legacy derided its effeminizing effects, while those more hospitable to it sought to reconceive it as a refinement that retains "feminine" elegance while conveying "masculine" strength.

Chapter 4 considers the model of masculinity developed in Madeleine de Scudéry's novels *Le Grand Cyrus* and *Clélie* and apparent in the archival record of her salon, the *Chroniques du Samedi*. Effeminacy is not a primary concern for Scudéry, who concentrates on the *lack* rather than the *excess* of masculine submission and refinement. Her vision of ideal masculinity, which I call "tender masculinity," entails a reiteration of the neo-Petrarchan topoi of male submission, suffering, and sensitivity; an innate "tenderness" *(tendresse)* or extreme form of empathy; and melancholy, a sign and affect of tenderness. I then turn to the gendered role playing in Scudéry's salon, which extends the ideals elaborated in her novels but modifies them as well. The men and women of the *Samedis* were self-conscious actors who used the ideal of tenderness to scrutinize the distance between the gender dynamics of the salon and the outside world.

Sexuality and the Body at the Margins

In part 2 of this study I consider how sexuality and the gendered body were used to produce marginal masculinities in seventeenth-century France. That is, I explore how masculine domination was put in tension with male same-sex desire on the one hand and with cross-dressing on the other, resulting in marginalized positions that were products of the evolving regulation of sexuality and the body by broad mechanisms of power.

The seventeenth century has often been seen as a key moment of rupture or transition in the "production" of modern sexuality and the body.[26] In *History of Madness*, for instance, Michel Foucault describes what he calls the "Great Confinement," the surveillance and incarceration of a broad range of "deviants" in seventeenth-century France, as evidence of a "new" preoccupation by church and state alike. As he concludes, "confinement was an institutional creation peculiar to the seventeenth century."[27] The working poor, the unemployed, the mentally ill, the physically frail, and the sexually "deviant" increasingly became objects of concern on secular rather than religious grounds, and were increasingly deemed to represent a threat to "order" and "reason," which became justification for their confinement. In the first volume of his *History of Sexuality*, Foucault uses a different conceptual frame to pursue his reflection on the emergence of this regulatory intervention, showing its effects on conceptions of sexuality and the body. But, once again, he situates the seventeenth century at the threshold of a new era, when a period of supposed discursive freedom gave way to one of expanding discursive control, especially through Tridentine confessional practices, and when the state's "right of death" began to transform into the "power over life" (or "bio-power").[28] For Foucault, these changes in regulatory practices were central to the seventeenth century and mark it as a period when sexuality and the body were increasingly probed and interrogated so as to produce the "truth" of the subject. If later periods witnessed other crucial developments in the "incitation to discourse" that characterizes "modern" sexuality, the seventeenth century remains something of a terminus a quo for Foucault, even as he recognizes that its own regulatory practices were the result of long-term continuity. "This scheme for transforming sex into discourse had been devised long before in an ascetic and monastic setting," he says. "The seventeenth century made it into a rule for everyone."[29] No matter how imprecise and undeveloped, the importance of the seventeenth century within Foucault's genealogical project makes it a useful starting point for the study of sexuality and the body in this period.

Although the place of gender within Foucault's project is not at all clear, as feminists in particular have noted,[30] I follow the lead of promising work applying Foucauldian paradigms to gender and especially to masculinity so as to sketch out genealogies of male same-sex sexuality and the male body in seventeenth-century France. But at the same time, I also foreground the relationality of power along the lines of Bourdieu's model of masculine domination. For, in spite of diverging understandings of power, Bourdieu's model of the tensions between dominant and dominated positions accounts for a gendered specificity that is otherwise missing from Foucault's narrative of the power relations subtending the discourses of sexuality.[31] My contention is that being attentive to the dialectic of masculine domination within any genealogy of sexuality and gender brings into focus the marginal positions produced by normative discourses of gender and the body. Adopting this perspective means uncovering the mechanisms by which those positions of marginality are created, as well as the parameters of their conflict with normative discourses.

Specifically, then, I explore how the masculinity of the (elite) sodomite and male cross-dresser in seventeenth-century France was or was not marked and what was or was not perceived to be threatening about each. As I will show, there are both differences and similarities with our own contemporary expectations about the masculine positions that such sexual and gendered desires produce. I am as interested in the differences that these positions present as I am in the continuities with our own understandings of sexuality and gender. And, accordingly, I side neither with those who wish to emphasize the historical ruptures between past and present sexualities nor with those who, on the contrary, accentuate the continuities.[32] Instead, I wish to exploit something like the ambiguity that marks Foucault's own account of seventeenth-century sexualities, which he variously characterizes as similar to our own (in the multiplication of discourses, for instance) and yet as different (in the regulation of sexual acts rather than desires, for example).[33]

Of particular interest to me is the extent to which the sodomite and the male cross-dresser could affirm his desires in the face of considerable constraints. To do so, of course, is to assert the possibility of an agency and a resistance that both Foucault's and Bourdieu's models of power would seem to render difficult if not impossible. I do not contest the claims by both theorists that resistance is made possible by the hegemonic power being resisted and that resistance often ends up reiterating that power. At the same time, however, I argue that the cases of Théophile de Viau (chap. 5) and the Abbé de Choisy (chap. 6) nonetheless suggest how positions of masculine marginality can sketch out, if only tentatively, alternatives to the predictable dynamics of masculine domination. Thus, I go beyond the dialectic between submission and domination among and within masculine subject positions in order to consider how dominated men, at the margins of the sex/gender system, sometimes reject the telos of hegemony and assert their submission as a telos in its own right. What these chapters consider, then, is how men who are unable to exert masculine dominance (attempt to) affirm masculinities that seek something other than dominance.

The broad outline of this scenario has been the object of important work by queer theorists, who from different methodological perspectives have sought to account for the process by which marginalized sexualities may be affirmed in the face of social oppression. Specifically, I am thinking here of models that describe how subjectivity formed through social stigma can exist and, further, affirm its existence. Particularly useful for my purposes is the theorization of gay "abjection" by David Halperin, who rejects the psychoanalytic understanding of this notion in favor of a dynamic, dialectical process that is not buried in the unconscious, but is partially if not fully intentional.[34] Halperin's theory gives us a way of seeing how subjected populations (and not only those stigmatized because of their sexuality)[35] might search for release from the pain of domination—a search for indifference to its effects—through a process equivalent in many ways to religious ascesis. Through this search, they might even transform their suffering, shame, or humiliation into pleasure, pride, or elevation. The result, Halperin concludes, is that one becomes "unfindable" to one's oppressors through a sort of reversal of power relations (76). Rather than being controlled by the oppressor, the oppressed control the pain directed toward themselves and channel it into self-affirming uses.

As it has been deployed within queer studies, the model of a self-affirming stigmatized subjectivity applies first and foremost to *sexual* subjectivity. In chapters 5 and 6, I do indeed consider the question of sexuality—that is, same-sex sexuality—and the subjective positions it entails among selected writers. But my objective is also to explore the links between sexuality and masculinity and to show how a stigmatized sexuality creates a stigmatized masculine subject position, which certain writers then (attempt to) affirm and transform in ways reminiscent of Halperin's account of abjection. Referring once again to my title, I would contend that these writers, specifically Théophile de Viau and the Abbé de Choisy, "man" the margins of masculinity, affirming their own stigmatized positions as *masculine* alongside the dominant and normative positions.

In chapter 5 I consider the tensions between normative masculinity and male same-sex desire in seventeenth-century France. To highlight these tensions and to avoid a simplistic narrative about the "emergence" of the homosexual or the repression of same-sex activity, I focus on three distinct moments in reverse chronological order. The first section examines the satirical discourse on sodomy (to use the terminology of the period) in a group of manuscript songs and poems from the second half of the century (1660–1715) and traces a shift from politically motivated satire to an ambivalent fascination and disgust with sodomy that aims to give consistency to a distinctly heterosexual masculine norm and to counteract the fluidity of same-sex and different-sex desires prevalent until this period. The second part of the chapter examines two scandals that concerned François Le Métel de Boisrobert (1592–1661), a prolific poet and playwright in the entourage of the Cardinal de Richelieu. The first, more traditional, was motivated by retribution for court intrigue, but the second, more recognizably modern, had no other reason than to draw attention to his perceived sexual inclinations. The third section then moves to the highly unusual expression of what I call a sodomitical "self" in the prison writings by Théophile de Viau (1590–1626). Tried for free-thinking and sodomy, the poet defended himself by creating a sodomitical persona that can emerge for public view only to the extent that it rejects fixed sexual roles and embraces contradiction, but in the private correspondence addressed to his close friend Jacques Vallée Des Barreaux after his partial acquittal, he develops an ideal of male friendship in terms not unlike Michel Foucault's call for a new "way of life" transforming relations among men and society as a whole.

Chapter 6 takes a fresh look at the cross-dressing narratives of the Abbé de Choisy, both his autobiographical *Memoirs of the Abbé de Choisy Dressed*

as a Woman, and a novella, "The Story of the Marquise-Marquis de Banneville." Unlike most critics who interpret the cross-dressing in these texts as
either pathological (as a psychological disorder or a cultural symptom) or exclusively performative (as drag), I argue that it should instead be understood
as transgendered experience. In the *Memoirs,* I contend that Choisy questions
his self-identity as a masculine subject by insisting on the pleasure of his feminine personas and the ease with which he "passes" as a woman. I show how
in the novella, about a boy raised as a girl, the Marquise de Banneville, who
only learns of her/his "true" sex after falling in love with a cross-dressed
young man, Choisy departs from literary convention by allowing the couple
to retain their adopted genders at the end of the story, all the while enjoying
the benefits of heterosexual desire. Ultimately, this chapter asserts that in
both his *Memoirs* and his novella Choisy is caught in between genders, striving for womanhood but tied to manhood.

Studying civility, sexuality, and the body tells only part of the story of masculinity in seventeenth-century France. In this book, I do not cover every
possible aspect of even these topics, and in no way do I provide an encyclo-
pedic overview of the many forces upon and manifestations of masculinity in
this period. Similarly, I do not engage every single social category (such as
race, class, ethnicity, and nationality) with which masculinity is necessarily
imbricated. To give such a narrative, assuming it were possible, would demand a much longer study and preclude the sorts of close readings of texts I
rely upon in this book. This said, I do seek to integrate as many other questions and categories of analysis as possible and as necessary. But there remain
other points of entry into this topic, and I do not in any way claim to have
covered all of them. In particular, the place of masculinity in medical discourse, political history and theory, nonelite culture, religious discourse, and
French colonial expansion are all subjects I regret not having been able to address in an extended way. Hence, their absence should not be interpreted to
mean that they are unimportant (quite the contrary is true); it is instead the
consequence of my efforts to construct a study with a relatively limited and
cohesive focus.

As for what I *do* in this book, I have already made clear my debt to work
on women and especially women's writing in seventeenth-century France.
My study builds upon this (now considerable) body of scholarship and extends it, inviting readers to consider women and their writing along with men

and *their* writing. But it is my hope that *Manning the Margins* will make a further contribution by charting one course (among others) for moving beyond the binary understanding of gender that work on women in early modern France has often promoted. Thus, rather than relying on a conception of women and femininity as "marked" categories opposed to men and masculinity, the "unmarked" universal, I show that men too can be and *are* "marked" and how this status shaped masculine subjectivity and relations among men and between the sexes. Now, this is not to deny the important fact that in the broader sex/gender system women are indeed the "marked" category and that masculine domination works to obscure its own historical and structural contingency, as Bourdieu for one insists.[36] Still, my aim here is to encourage ways of thinking about masculinity *and* femininity as categories that are multiple, dynamic, and constantly in flux. In other words, although the gender binary has obvious political relevance, it needs to be understood in conjunction with the complex tensions within and between each of its terms. Considering the struggles *among* masculinities and *among* femininities and the links *between* these struggles helps us to see the binary itself as a constantly evolving structure. Reconceiving the study of gender along these lines has particularly important consequences for the field of seventeenth-century French studies, which must constantly struggle against the ossifying effects of monumentality. For gender and culture more generally are dynamic, and the so-called Grand Siècle was no less so than any other period.

Finally, two features of this book warrant special mention. First, in several chapters I examine the links between an author's work and her or his biography. But my approach is decidedly not that of positivist literary history, with its emphasis on the now much-scorned *l'homme et l'œuvre*. I do not reduce the meanings of the texts analyzed to the lives of their authors; on the contrary, I am interested in the ways that their texts exceed their lives and presumed intentions. More specifically, I endeavor to draw out the often implicit and unacknowledged gendered meanings an author's writing might assume over and against the context of her or his life and its connections to literary and social practices. Such an approach is all the more justified, I believe, because the distinction between life and work we rely upon today was largely inoperative for the period and texts I study here. The aesthetic of galanterie so central to Voiture's letters and Scudéry's novels and salon writing, and the autobiographical references in Théophile's and Choisy's texts foreground the interpenetration of life and work, but without making the work the "authentic" replica of the life.

Second, many of the authors and texts I examine might be considered "minor" when set against the traditional canon of seventeenth-century French literature. Besides the many well-known problems of reading practices beholden to the notion of a canon, it should be noted that almost all of the authors in this study were anything but minor figures in their day, and several of them have seen a dramatic renewal of critical fortune in recent years. Still, it is perhaps fitting that a study focusing on marginality includes authors and texts that are, in the main, "marginal" by the standards of a restrictively canonical view of this period. Although it is not my primary objective here to contest such a view, central to my approach, as I have already made clear, is the belief that the "marginal" has much to tell us about the "dominant," something as true for literary canons as it is for gender ideologies. For what the marginal reveals is so often a central truth that the dominant works to obscure.

PART ONE   🌿   Civilizing the Margins

ONE

The Chevalier de Méré's Quest
for Honnête Masculinity

IT WOULD BE DIFFICULT TO IMAGINE a concept more central to seventeenth-century French culture and literature than *honnêteté*. This aesthetic, ethical, and social discourse of ideal comportment was the period's most visible form of what Norbert Elias called the "civilizing process," the codification and internalization of constraints on behavior that gave rise to the concepts of "civility" and "civilization."[1] Anything but an emblem of marginality, honnêteté aimed to confer cultural distinction and social domination. From its origins in treatises addressed to aspiring courtiers, it became during the course of the century the sociable ideal that allowed polite urban circles to constitute themselves into a prefiguration of the next century's bourgeois public sphere. Throughout the seventeenth century, writers of many different stripes (including many of the most canonical, such as Molière, Pascal, La Rochefoucauld, and La Bruyère) explored the modalities and meanings of this notion, which was not a stable doctrine but rather a fluid and shifting set of principles. For scholars of this period, honnêteté has provided a means of examining changing conceptions of the heroic, problems of so-called moralist literature, the relation between civility and literature, the evolving appropriations of ancient Greek and Roman culture, the boundaries between the noble and the nonnoble ethos, the opposition between court and city life, and the aesthetics of writing itself, among others.[2] But amid all the attention given to it, surprisingly little has been made of honnêteté as a *gendered* construct. With only a few notable exceptions, critics treat it as an unmarked, quasi-universal notion, even if its preeminent incarnation was the honnête *homme* (roughly, the urbane and honorable man).[3] In some ways, as we will see, this gesture simply reproduces a posture taken by many writers during the seventeenth century, who suggested that the honnête homme was somehow a model for both genders. But to approach honnêteté in this way is to reinforce the sort of patriarchal logic that equates the unmarked and the universal with the masculine. In this chapter, I work against this logic by positing that honnêteté was a gendered discourse that sought to undergird masculinist privilege by confronting the relationality and contingency of masculinity.

Although critical attention has focused overwhelmingly on the honnête homme (albeit without foregrounding the figure as gendered), from the beginning of its history in the French language, the adjective *honnête* was used to modify both *homme* (man) and *femme* (woman). In his dictionary entry for the adjective *honneste*, for instance, Pierre Richelet cites as examples La Rochefoucauld's famous bon mot: "The *honnête homme* is a man who doesn't boast about anything" and then gives "she is an *honnête femme*."[4] However, the precise qualities denoted by this adjective were hardly the same for men and women, and this tendency was only accentuated by the peculiar interest seventeenth-century writers displayed for this notion. As Jean Mesnard has observed, for both men and women, being honnête designated the ability to accommodate others through a balanced dialogue, emphasized the importance of one's merit over one's birth, highlighted one's virtue, and implied more generally an uncommon mastery of the self. But for women, honnêteté denoted strict limits on sexuality, an emphasis on moral purity (rather than on masculine courage), and constraints on domestic and public freedom and education. Such characteristics are certainly echoed in an example from Furetière's definition of *honnêteté*, which draws a stark contrast between its feminine and masculine variants. "The honnêteté of women is chastity, modesty, decency, and restraint. The honnêteté of men is a way of acting appropriately, sincerely, courteously, obligingly and civilly."[5] But while it is true that this period recognized two different ideals of honnêteté—one masculine and the other feminine—defining the honnête homme was given far and away greater priority. Even a cursory glance at the titles of seventeenth-century conduct manuals (many more of which concern men than women) suggests that setting the standards of honnête masculinity was a pressing, even obsessive concern for writers at the time.[6] From Nicolas Faret's *L'Honnête homme ou l'art de plaire à la Cour* (1630) to Jacques Goussault's *Le Portrait d'un honnête homme* (1692), numerous were the volumes that, over the course of the seventeenth century, specifically focused on honnêteté as a *masculine* ideal. In sum, the discourse of honnêteté was above all a discourse of masculinity.

Many different factors explain why this discourse became prominent at this time: the "civilizing process," sociopolitical reorganization, topical aesthetic questions, and the configuration of the literary field.[7] Although I do not want to diminish the importance of these questions, the central purpose of this chapter is to examine not the *why* but the *how* of honnête masculinity.

Instead of the context that made this discourse possible, my interest here is to read the dynamics of masculinity at work in a group of texts by Antoine Gombaud, chevalier de Méré (1607–84), the foremost theoretician of honnêteté. As the author of the most voluminous writings on the subject, Méré developed in greater detail many of the problems also treated by other writers at the time.[8] Like his contemporaries, the chevalier admitted that honnêteté was an elusive ideal that could never be fully set forth in language. And yet this is precisely what he and others who wrote about honnêteté attempted to do. Méré illustrated this paradox more than any of his contemporaries. The sheer volume of his work suggests an intense struggle to codify the seemingly uncodifiable. What I contend here is that Méré's discursive struggle to define abstract aesthetic qualities is also—and quite centrally—a struggle to define the contours of an ideal masculinity.

Like all proponents of ideal social types, Méré endeavors to set honnête masculinity apart from—and especially *above*—its Others. That is, Méré strives to distinguish the honnête homme from other social types—both masculine and feminine—in a quest to confer on him a exclusive and dominant status. And yet this status was anything but self-evident. As I will argue, within Méré's writings, the honnête homme ideal exists in a tenuous relationship with its Others—the overly ceremonious man, the provincial, the professional bourgeois, the courtier, the warrior, the galant homme, and especially, women. In some ways, the honnête homme is always at risk of resembling these types too closely; but at the same time, he must carefully distance himself from them. My contention is that the dialectic between resemblance and differentiation is a precarious one that leaves the honnête homme on unstable ground. Mastery of this dialectic is the essence of honnête masculinity, but this mastery can only be acquired and maintained by recourse to the *je ne sais quoi*, the (purportedly) inexpressible quality to which the elite appealed so as to preserve its exclusivity.[9]

DEFINING THE HONNÊTE HOMME

What precisely *is* an honnête homme? To address this question, Méré and his contemporaries relied on a long and varied tradition hailing back most immediately to Castiglione and Montaigne, but ultimately to ancient Greek and Roman thought as well.[10] The ideal of the Greek philosopher in the mold of Socrates or Plato, unquestionably virtuous but also preeminently sociable, is a frequent point of reference for Méré. More specific semantic influences, though, are found in an array of ideals from ancient Rome: the Senecan notion of *honestus* (the utmost good deriving from virtue and honor); Quintilian's goal of *urbanus* ("the total absence of all that is incongruous, coarse, unpolished and exotic, whether in thought, language, voice or gesture")[11] and his emphasis on the appearance of a "natural" expression that hides all effort; Cicero's conjunction of *honestum* and *decorum* and his insistence on moderation in all things.[12] In Méré's (and others') appropriation of the classical Greek and Roman *paideia* (the tradition of forming men to achieve perfection and excellence), the overriding consideration was the aesthetic fashioning of the self and in particular the elegant and seductive use of language along the lines of the ideal rhetor conceived by Cicero and especially Quintilian. Of course, these intertexts had been synthesized and reworked by Castiglione and Montaigne, both of whom proposed models that were the immediate precursors of the honnête homme. Castiglione's courtier, preoccupied more with his own refinement than with his service to a prince, gave enormous impetus to the development of conduct literature in sixteenth- and especially seventeenth-century France. More specifically, the courtier's seemingly natural grace, or nonchalance *(sprezzatura)*, and verbal seductiveness in conversation were to have the greatest influence on theoreticians of honnêteté.[13] But by the time Méré and his contemporaries were giving form to the honnête homme, Castiglione's model had been extensively filtered and diffused, most notably and prominently by Montaigne. Invoked as the "breviary of honnête people," the *Essais* were a crucial model for the seventeenth century. As Domna Stanton has argued, it was "[Montaigne's] views on professionalism, pedantry, education, and conversation, his brand of stoicism and epicureanism, his comfortable distance from religion and independent attitude toward established codes . . . even more . . . his vision of a select society devoted to the beautification of life, and, above all, his representation of self as art that determined the substance of seventeenth-century honnêteté."[14]

In keeping with the tradition popularized by Montaigne, Méré offers a much less pragmatic vision of the honnête homme than do earlier seventeenth-century theorists, notably Nicolas Faret, who are concerned with the mechanisms for winning favor at court. Instead, Méré concentrates on the means for ensuring an elusive superiority in the vaguely defined realm of *le monde* (society). In this sense, Méré's reflections on honnêteté consecrate a shift away from the traditional signs of aristocratic prestige—birth and rank, or the means of compensating for the lack thereof—toward the more general definition of the honnête homme provided by Bussy-Rabutin: "a refined man who knows know to live."[15] By the end of his life, when some of his most important works were published, Méré's conception of honnêteté was increasingly overshadowed by the dual perspectives of traditional aristocratic reaction (e.g., Joachim Trotti de La Chétardie, *Instructions pour un jeune seigneur ou l'idée d'un galant homme*, 1683) and an increasingly prominent Christian moralist revision (e.g., Armand de Gérard, *Le Caractère de l'honnête homme*, 1682; Jacques Goussault, *Le Portrait de l'honnête homme*, 1689). Yet Méré's conception still constituted the *summum* of the honnête homme as worldly and sociable ideal, key elements of which would be integrated into the eighteenth-century figures of the *libertin galant* and of course the *philosophe*.[16]

From his earliest to his latest writings, Méré was preoccupied above all else with defining what it means to be an honnête homme. In concert with other writers of the time, he sees the happiness of the group as the overriding objective for the honnête homme. "Honnêteté . . . is only to be desired to the extent that it makes those who have it and who approach it happy," he writes.[17] As a result, there is nothing more important for the honnête homme than "pleasing" his audience, the exclusive circle to which he belongs. A key (even fetishized) notion in seventeenth-century aesthetics, the *art de plaire*—quite literally, the art of captivating, enrapturing, enchanting others[18]—implied, in Méré's understanding, the ability to excel "in all that concerns the beauties and proprieties *(bienséances)* of life" so as to engender "the most perfect and most agreeable interaction among people." So doing, those striving for honnêteté "spread joy everywhere, and their greatest care is but to deserve esteem and to make themselves loved."[19] "I believe that one can never be too captivating *(on ne sçauroit trop plaire)*," says Méré (*OC*, 2:33).

When contrasted with the courtier, the figure who precedes and competes with the honnête homme, the importance of the *art de plaire* is unmistakable. Instead of being guided by his place within a rigid hierarchy, cut off from the rest of society, and forced to cultivate appearances that mask his true intentions, as the courtier must, the honnête homme, in Elena Russo's words, "develops a decentered self that has less as its objective power than pleasure and harmonious coexistence with others. To the quest for success, the honnête homme prefers the quest for happiness—his own—which he can only obtain by assuring that of others."[20] To be sure, this is an accurate statement of the goals that Méré prescribes for honnêteté when it is contrasted with the ethos of the courtier or the later libertine.[21] But when viewed within the larger dynamic of Méré's oeuvre, the emphasis on the honnête homme's investment in collective happiness and exclusive group identity risks overlooking what is at stake in the *art de plaire*. This is not only because ensuring the happiness of others is tantamount to *captivating* them, holding sway over them and thus exerting a power over them. It is also because the honnête homme's interests are not reducible to those of the exclusive group he attempts to win over. Rather, his own honnêteté is paramount, and his obligation to captivate others presupposes a position of dominance. He must have about him "a certain something noble and exquisite *(je ne sçay quoy de noble & d'exquis)* that puts one honnête homme above another" (Letter 6, *L*, 58.). To maintain and display that "certain something" involves an internalized struggle with the self and with others, a struggle that is by and large coded masculine in Méré's writing. In sum, then, the collective ethos of honnêteté is founded upon an agonistic masculine stance within the group (not in spite of, but rather *because* of the *art de plaire*), and this stance requires first of all a struggle within the honnête homme himself.

Scholars have long noted the quest for self-mastery required in honnêteté. Not unlike the ascesis of Stoicism and the Christian ascetic tradition, the honnête homme must give himself to rigorous training, self-discipline, and self-restraint.[22] The end goal is *ataraxia,* a feeling of inner peace and happiness that results from mastering the art of captivating others. With its valorization of pleasure, this doctrine also incorporates Epicureanism, which is amalgamated with Stoicism.[23] Of course, it is highly significant that honnêteté has at its core these two philosophical discourses, which were often used to fashion ideals of masculinity from antiquity through the early modern period. And connected as they are to these discourses, the ethical and aesthetic principles to which Méré's honnête homme aspires are likewise gendered masculine in important ways.

Foremost among these and consistent with the intertextual models Méré reworks (notably Cicero) is his "virtue." "I can conceive of nothing under the heavens that is above honnêteté: it is the quintessence of all the virtues" (*OC*, 3:71), he says. Here as elsewhere, Méré's understanding of virtue is not only that of ethical morality, but also that of the masculine strength and energy denoted by the Italian notion of *virtù,* wisdom leading to control over oneself and thus over fate. But what makes honnêteté the "quintessence of all the virtues" is that it enables one to be well received by "persons of good taste" (*OC*, 3:71). Unlike its meaning in conventional ethics, this virtue is a means to an end and not the end in and of itself; it is a necessary—but not a sufficient—component of honnêteté, which must be supplemented with aesthetic discernment. "One could be a very virtuous man and a very bad honnête homme," Méré contends. "One only needs to be equitable *(juste)* to be a virtuous man, but to be an honnête homme one must know about all sorts of *bienséances* and know how to put them into practice" (Letter 110, *L*, 429.). More difficult than the equity required of the "virtuous man" are the knowledge and practice of the *bienséances,* the codes of propriety or social decorum required of the honnête homme.[24] Méré even asserts that virtue is *produced* by the *bienséances:* "to be really virtuous or at least to be so with grace, one must know how to put the *bienséances* into practice, to judge everything soundly, and to favor excellent things over those that are merely mediocre" (Letter 12, *L*, 87–88.). Created by the *bienséances* just as it creates them, virtue has a purpose that is far more aesthetic than ethical. But the point I want to make here is that, by subordinating ethics to aesthetics, Méré also reconceives the wisdom and self-control connoted by virtue (in the sense of *virtù*) as a properly *masculine* mastery of the *bienséances.*

Key to this mastery for Méré was the *justesse* (accuracy or precision) with which the honnête homme was to judge his surroundings, and consequently, his own behavior. "I don't have any other term to explain more clearly this inexpressible wisdom and agility that recognize propriety *(la bien-séance)* everywhere, that do not tolerate letting one do too much or too little for something that needs to be big or small, and that make one feel the bounds one must respect" (*OC,* 1:96), he writes.[25] As this quote makes clear, *justesse* involves the ability to find that elusive middle between excess and lack, a topos of ancient and early modern ethics and aesthetics.[26] The golden mean *(juste milieu)* and the qualities of being moderate *(moderez)* or temperate *(tempéré)* are central to honnêteté, which "shuns the extremes," as Méré puts it (*OC,* 1:75). The effect one has on others must hit the happy medium, and in order to achieve this end, one must control one's bearing, actions, and language so that they are neither deficient nor excessive. In both instances, hitting the happy medium is very difficult. Of the "temperament" best suited to the honnête homme in conversation, Méré writes that "when things are seen as they are, the effects they produce are recognized quite well, but the right temperament *(le juste temperamment),* which is very dependent upon the subject matter and the occasion, always seems very elusive" (*OC,* 3:146). But as difficult as it is to achieve the golden mean of honnêteté, it is presumably less so for men than for women, even though Méré twice suggests that the qualities of the honnête homme and the honnête femme are the same.[27] In the many discourses of which it was a guiding principle—ethics, civility, medicine, conjugal love, politics, to name but a few—the mean as a goal to which one should aspire applied to both genders. However, a long tradition (harking back to Aristotle) held that men were incomparably better able to achieve the mean than women. By their physical composition, so explained a tradition reinforced by humoral medicine in particular, men were more likely to be endowed with reason and moderate self-control, whereas women were given to passion and excess. And beyond medical discussions, the early modern period resounds with the refrain that women were prone to extremes, against which men had to be vigilant in order to set their foreordained examples of moderation and temperance.[28] Since Méré never refutes these cultural presuppositions and since he relies on male role models and constructs an explicitly masculine ideal, it is hardly a stretch to place his doctrine within this misogynist tradition. But even if the honnête homme is better able to reach the middle than women, he is still faced with a formidable challenge. The *juste milieu* of honnête masculinity is as elusive as it is exclusive.

Achieving the golden mean makes possible yet another crucial feature of the honnête homme—the ability to display a seemingly intuitive elegance. In his actions and his judgment, the honnête homme was to display an ease and grace that eschewed any suggestion of effort. "I believe . . . that one's way of living and acting should be free and unhampered and that one should sense nothing forced about it. So, in order to show an extreme grace in the things one does, one must execute them as would an excellent Master. And one's actions must be precise, unrestrained, elegant *(de bon air)*. . . . One must make them appear natural" (*OC*, 2:13–14). At work here is a paradox that can be traced back to Castiglione's notion of *sprezzatura*, which Méré like others before him reiterates: artifice must pass for nature and effort must appear to be effortless.[29] In other words, if he can *appear* to be a "master" *(maître)*, the honnête homme will *be* one. Since the primary target for this injunction is men, for Méré as for Castiglione and others, the domination in question concerns first of all that of a *masculine* refinement. In effect, then, Méré and all the early modern invocations of *sprezzatura* simply make explicit—without condemning it—the logic of masculine domination, which seeks to present itself as natural. Still, this self-conscious recognition paradoxically works to cover over contingency by making aesthetic mastery the "natural" sign of masculine dominance.

Faced with a myriad of tautologies and paradoxes, Méré nonetheless asserts the superiority of honnête masculinity, and to do so, Méré grants himself the pedagogical role of *maître* (master/teacher) or *gouverneur* (preceptor), a person he recommends for all those who aspire to honnêteté (*OC*, 3:71). Observations about his contemporaries and commentaries on writings both ancient and modern all form what is intended to be a prescriptive discourse that empowers readers to aspire to honnêteté, and particularly honnête masculinity. In a sense, then, Méré leads by example, demonstrating for his readers the role of *maître*, whose mastery of self and others begins with the emulation of models. "It would be very difficult to perfect oneself in anything at all without referring to the best models," he says (*OC*, 3:71). And yet, emulation is not the only or even primary means to achieve perfection. Rather than concentrating solely on what he *should* be, the aspiring honnête homme must scrupulously study those persons and those traits that are found lacking. "One must have so many rare qualities to become a perfect honnête homme that it is easier to say what one must shun than those things one must observe, and I believe that by avoiding those faults and several others one can make good progress in honnêteté" (Letter 6, *L*, 58.). Repeatedly, Méré bemoans the lack of models for honnêteté. Placing himself in the position of supreme judge, he explains that even Socrates and Julius Caesar, his recurring points of reference, fall short:

> I've seen very few people in society or in history who were entirely to my liking. I am only speaking about the qualities of the soul, for the assets of the body may be wished for but should not be revered; but those of the heart and the mind are above all the rest and should be called true greatness *(la véritable grandeur)*. And, to my mind, no one surpassed in that respect Socrates and Caesar, who would also be the two men of antiquity I would admire the most if only the first had been a bit less of the Philosopher he was and if the second had been content to become master in the mold of a noble Conqueror. (*OC*, 3:140–41)

Perfection in honnêteté would seem to be impossible. No one has surpassed Socrates and Caesar, and yet even they have shortcomings, which pertain to the very things they are best known for—philosophy and the art of war. If even these honnêtes hommes *avant la lettre* are not entirely pleasing to Méré, presumably no one can be. So, in the end, honnêteté is a never-ending quest for an elusive goal, and honnête masculinity is never entirely achieved. It is a masculinity that is always becoming, never finished. To be sure, as Pierre Bourdieu (among others) has famously noted, masculine domination is by definition elusive: "Everything combines to make the impossible ideal of virility the source of an immense vulnerability."[30] And such domination is always fraught with conflict, external as well as internal.

THE OTHERS OF HONNÊTE MASCULINITY

Honnêteté is intrinsically relational: just as the mean cannot be defined without reference to its extremes, so too the honnête homme can only be described by comparison with other people and character types. It is by observing others that the honnête homme is best able to gauge his own thoughts and actions. For Méré, of course, evoking historical examples and "types" makes it possible to prescribe the perfect middle course he envisions for honnêteté. And this relational construction of the honnête homme (the relational component of his ascesis) is precisely what reveals the hegemony of masculinity within the discourse of honnêteté. The comparisons and contrasts Méré makes between the honnête subject and other subject positions privilege the masculine: not only are the majority of his examples (and counterexamples) men, but the consummate final product is a *man,* distinct from other men and from the most honnête of women.

In the relational networks that appear in Méré's writings, some of the most frequent points of comparison are Alcibiades, Alexander the Great, Augustus, Caesar, and Socrates, and their failings (which Méré details and occasionally invents) are all the more instructive because their accomplishments in so many domains were incontrovertible. But Méré also includes less lofty models. In his "Discours de la vraïe Honnesteté" (Discourse on True Honnêteté), for instance, he describes how young men might be prepared to remain captivating in the midst of "people so disagreeable and so naturally inclined to be unpleasant that it is difficult not to be disconcerted in their company":

> One must be prepared for it and seek that noble and steadfast way of acting that does not waver. Heroes of antiquity and even the adventurers of the old romances can be very useful for this purpose. At the very least one almost always finds marks of extreme valor in their deeds. Examples from one's family are not to be neglected. A father or a relative covered all over with wounds who never hears about a cowardly action or one unworthy of a brave man without roaring like an old lion impresses on a soul that is still young and tender feelings of honor that time can never efface. (*OC,* 3:98)

Of course, Méré is not recommending that young men aspire to be like the Knights of the Round Table or the battle-wounded, lionlike relative who roars at cowardly actions. Rather, he is interested in the feelings of honor and valor such examples supposedly inspire:

> This initial upbringing seems crucial to me, and I believe that the best one for giving a refined manner to young men, no matter what profession they are destined for, is to raise them for the court and for war. Those who are not trained for these, no matter how intelligent and meritorious people find them to be, are felt to be lacking this upbringing in their countenance and actions, and this is always unsuitable for them. (*OC*, 3:98–99)

If the "heroes of antiquity," the "adventurers of old romances," and the "examples from one's family" are excessive as models of actual conduct, they nevertheless provide an "upbringing," the lack of which is sensed by those who are "in the know." In the end, Méré prescribes a middle ground between fictional and real-life warriors on the one hand and those untrained in court life and military service on the other.

More often than models to be imitated, Méré uses counterexamples to define the contours of honnête masculinity and reinforce the difficulty of attaining perfection. The honnête homme does not transcend his Others, whether they be models or countermodels. He is never an autonomous subject whose dominance is somehow stable and self-sufficient. Rather, he is very much dependent upon the Others that give meaning to the middle ground of his honnêteté. Méré the *maître* and the honnête homme he imagines must repeatedly, and obsessively, conjure up the excessive and deficient extremes against which the dominance of well-balanced honnêteté is defined.

COUNTEREXAMPLES

For Méré, certain character types are so completely antithetical to honnête masculinity that rejecting them is an obvious necessity. They are so far removed from the ideal as to be seemingly incompatible and irreconcilable with it. And yet, they are not so distant as to be unintelligible or unuseful for the honnête homme. Using these counterexamples, Méré gives, by negation, greater relief to the ideal he proposes; yet, with them he also identifies significant qualities of honnêteté.

L'homme formaliste

Few traits are more opposed to honnêteté than an excessive attachment to social customs. Méré makes this clear when he writes about the Roman general
Scipio (Publius Cornelius Scipio Africanus Major, 285–183 B.C.E.): "I find
Scipio to be so legalistic *(formaliste)* and tense that I would never have sought
him out as a man of good company. There are few occasions in which so
much virtue is necessary, and in all other times minds of a human bent are
horrified by it" (*OC*, 3:91). It is not Scipio's virtue that is in question, but
rather his interpretation of ethical dictates and social mores. Scipio was, as
Méré puts it, *formaliste*, meaning "legalistic" but also referring to a "ceremonious and affected man who desires that others have great respect for him."[31]
Being *formaliste*, then, implied being self-possessed and self-interested, and
thus what bothers Méré are the constraints individuals such as Scipio place on
others. In contrast to the Roman general, he says, "I would like an honnête
homme to be more gentle and affable than stern and severe, to enjoy insinuating himself in a way that is enticing and comfortable for all sorts of people,
just as Socrates did" (*OC*, 1:91). Associated with *formaliste* are a bitterness
and severity that are diametrically opposed to the gentle, gracious, and ac-
commodating demeanor equated with Socrates. On the one hand, rigidity
and self-righteousness; on the other, adaptability and altruism.

For all Méré's protestations to the contrary, though, Scipio still possesses
qualities that his ideal honnête homme must necessarily have. In a letter to
Guez de Balzac, he writes, "If [Scipio] hadn't been so legalistic and such a
meticulous observer of the customs of his country, which betrays a mind of
limited breadth, I would count him among the most excellent men" (Letter
66, *L*, 270.). Wishing to include Scipio among the most excellent men and yet
unable to do so, Méré cites as a shortcoming something that elsewhere in his
oeuvre is an oft repeated, undeniable, even indispensable quality—Scipio
was a "meticulous observer of the customs of his country. . . . Propriety requires infinite study; one must observe it incessantly, both in solitude and at
court" (*OC*, 3:144). In other words, the honnête homme must indeed be a
"meticulous observer," thereby resembling Scipio, albeit only partially, for he
must be an observer without being legalistic. Méré makes this clear by stating
that "it is not sufficient to know things by rules or instructions; one must try
to make them natural so as to practice them easily and gracefully" (*OC*,
3:144). Observation leads to a firm grasp of the "rules" and "instructions" of
the *bienséances*, but they are not sufficient in and of themselves. Honnêteté re-

quires that one assimilate this knowledge to the point of making these rules (appear) intuitive.

But there is an irony in Méré's treatment of "rules" and "instructions," for whereas the honnête homme is to eschew Scipio's example—that is, to follow the *bienséances* intuitively and implicitly—the master of honnêteté himself makes this principle into a conscious and explicit rule. The supple, graceful, nearly unrecognizable adherence to propriety has become a blatant rule in its own right, and Méré in effect assumes a persona not unlike Scipio's. However, the honnête homme is supposed to internalize the master's rule so as to avoid Scipio's rigid demeanor. The Roman general's vigilant observation of the *bienséances*, as filtered by Méré, is indeed a model for the honnête homme, but a model to be internalized and not realized in social interaction. As distant as the "legalistic and tense" man is from the nuanced application of rules and instructions, he is not—indeed *cannot* be—rejected. The honnête homme must keep him at the ready within himself as observer and arbiter. But he must also take pains to prevent the Scipio-like inner self from high-jacking the outer persona.

Le provincial

No one could be more antithetical to either Scipio's rigorous observation of social customs or the honnête homme's "natural" embodiment of them than the closed-minded provincial. An occasional appearance in Méré's oeuvre, the provincial evokes a difference where geographical and spatial distance from Paris and the court expresses a lowly position in the social hierarchy of the *bienséances*. To be sure, antiprovincial sentiment was widespread in seventeenth-century France, but Méré spends little time reiterating this commonplace and instead promotes its obverse. Speaking of eloquence, for instance, he asserts his conviction that "style can never have too much of the court and high society *(le monde)* about it" (*OC*, 3:129). In linguistic as in aesthetic matters, the court and *le monde* are incontrovertible points of reference. But of greater concern to Méré is the facile reliance upon court and worldly fashion *(la mode):*

One should also note that following fashion and going about it elegantly aren't everything. Most important is knowing an infinite number of things that have nothing to do with fashion, by which I mean that they are neither *of* fashion nor *against* it. Rather, some things succeed in society and others are not well received. On this depends the great secret for living well and becoming enticing *(agréable)*.[32] (*OC*, 3:100)

Rejecting the argument of *The Courtier* and its avatars, Méré does not view life at court as the sine qua non of honnêteté, which emanates not from any particular external locale but from the inner space of the self, and less from social interaction than individual superiority and self-mastery. "When one is even more of an honnête homme in private *(en particulier)* than in public, this is an infallible sign that one is not so in just a mediocre way" (*OC*, 3:93). As a result, the honnête homme is capable of exerting his seductive prowess wherever he finds himself: True honnêteté "is universal, and its manners belong to all the courts from one end of the earth to the other, although they do not belong more to courts than to country retreats *(Deserts)*" (*OC*, 3:93). Going even further, Méré disrupts the aesthetic hierarchy that keeps the provincial at the bottom: "I believe that [honnêteté] is not dependent upon time or place and that he who can succeed in being an honnête homme in his shack would have been so in all the courts of the world" (*OC*, 1:76–77). Hardly someone to be shunned, the lowly country dweller becomes a model for the universality of honnêteté and above all for those at court, and the provincial, ostensibly incompatible with the honnête homme, can become his ultimate embodiment. In the self-reflection that is his self-fashioning, he should put himself in the place of the "honnête homme in his shack" all the better to hold sway at court. Made honnête, the provincial man moves from being rejected to being introjected. And once again, a figure who at first sight is an Other is integrated into the self-image of the honnête homme.

L'homme de métier

Alongside the provincial, men who foreground their professional activities—especially those of nonnoble birth—are likewise alienated from honnêteté, and Méré considers them all to be of the same cloth. Of the faults the honnête homme must never display are the "uncouth and unnoble manner" and more precisely the "manners *(air)* that reek of the tribunal, the bourgeoisie, the provinces, and serious matters" (Letter 6, *L*, 57.). Besides provincials, then, lawyers, merchants, financiers—in short, all those whose social identity is defined by their profession—are doomed to fail at honnêteté. For Méré, the honnête homme transcends any one particular profession, art, craft, or trade. With a knowledge that is quasi-universal in scope but unspecialized in practice, his primary objective is decidedly nonutilitarian. As a group, *honnêtes gens* (honnête people) "have hardly any other goal than to spread joy everywhere, and their greatest care inclines only toward meriting esteem and making themselves loved. . . . Thus, being an honnête homme is not an occupation, and if someone were to ask me what honnêteté consists of, I would say that it is nothing other than excelling in everything that concerns the *agréments* and the *bienséances* of life" (*OC*, 3:70). A nonprofession, being an honnête homme is in fact closely allied—although not identical—with the aristocrat at court. Suggesting that the term can be traced to the French court of the past, Méré makes this connection quite explicit: "There have always been certain lazy men without occupations *(certains Faineans sans métier)* but who were not without merit and who only dreamed of living well and presenting themselves elegantly. It is perhaps from these sorts of people that came this so very essential word" (*OC*, 3:70). By linking the honnête homme to the "lazy men without occupations," Méré reasserts aristocratic privilege.[33] But his is not a defense of the aristocracy in a collective sense. Instead, like all theorists of honnêteté, Méré sets out the parameters for an elect within the aristocracy; in short, an aristocracy within an aristocracy.

However, the primary condition for admission into this elite of the elite is not birth, but *le mérite*, a position that inverts the period's dominant understanding of aristocracy and harks back to earlier definitions.[34] And thus, at least theoretically, nonnobles too are eligible for admission into the body of *honnêtes gens*. But ultimately, Méré maintains that both birth and education are required for honnêteté, even if what he means by "birth" is less than straightforwardly obvious:

> I've sometimes seen it debated whether this ever so rare quality comes principally from a fortunate birth or from an excellent upbringing, and I believe that in order to acquire it in its perfection nature must contribute to it, and art, as in everything else, must complete what nature has begun. The heart must be noble and the mind docile, and then they must be put onto the right paths. (*OC*, 3:70)

Clearly, the honnête homme is born with a propensity toward excellence, but this propensity must be cultivated. Nature requires nurture. However, by figuring nature as the heart, Méré dodges the question about whether "fortunate birth" is indeed aristocratic birth. A topos of ancien régime political symbolism, the nobility of the heart was considered to be an ideal for the highest born, but was not denied to those of nonnoble birth.[35] Whether the heart in question is exclusively noble or not and whether or not "noble" is synonymous with "aristocratic" or instead signifies "excellent," the crux of the issue remains the acquisition of honnêteté through learning. But since this learning had to be concealed as such and instead presented as innate and intuitive, the notion of a superior aristocracy is not at all subverted, but rather displaced, as Michael Moriarty has argued.[36] From the perspective of masculine subject formation, though, the possibility that the man of lower birth might come to resemble the man of a higher station has a cautionary function for the latter. Since the true honnête homme avoids all signs of a specialized occupation and, further, any suggestion of work, he is in effect tantamount to a landowner, or *rentier*.[37] To avoid being confused with or surpassed by a man of lower rank requires extra vigilance and redoubled efforts so as to conceal the process of learning that was necessarily involved in becoming honnête. By evoking as he does the "uncouth and unnoble manner" of the lawyer and the bourgeois, then, Méré reminds his aspiring honnête homme of his own vulnerable position. He cannot simply rely on birth; he must *demonstrate* his superiority. A counterexample to be rejected, the professional man is still part of the honnête homme, a figure he must paradoxically keep in view in order to keep it at a distance.

MODELS

If the honnête homme must paradoxically remain closer to his countermodels than it would at first seem, the opposite is true of the relation to his models. From all appearances, he is closely associated with the courtier, the military hero, and the galant homme, each of whom embodies important qualities of honnêteté. And yet Méré goes to great pains to draw distinctions that seem minimal at first but quickly become crucial. In other words, his honnête homme creates a distance where one is difficult to discern. Not unlike a skillful painter, then, he must manipulate perspectives in order to bring closer what is far away and to distance what is in the foreground. But in this dizzying trompe l'oeil, the honnête homme, unlike the painter, never finishes his creation. The perspectives are always in danger of being misperceived by the honnête masculine subject and being all too accurately viewed by what Méré calls "le grand monde," an imagined elite that sits in judgment of honnêteté.

Le courtisan

Of all the models of honnêteté, the courtier is perhaps the most obvious. In the speculative genealogy Méré sketches for the honnête homme at the beginning of "De la vraie Honnêteté," for instance, he immediately evokes court life as the prefiguration of honnêteté (*OC*, 3:70). But rather than the person of the ideal courtier, he focuses on the court as an assembly of men and women that exudes an "air," a manner of acting, speaking, and living that is superior to all others and that, consequently, must be imitated.[38] Spending time at court and being well received by its inhabitants are highly advantageous, according to Méré, and success at court is a goal to be sought after.[39] If the honnête homme has a "talent for society *(le monde)*," he says, "he will be highest at court, at least for his reputation" (*OC*, 3:152). The court is a goal and a destination because it is a superlative judge whose approbation is success in and of itself. Thus when Méré entertains the question of how to instill in young men the "refined manner" *(le bon air)*, it is hardly surprising that he proposes the model of the court (*OC*, 3:99).

But he must also see *through* and *beyond* the court, and he must not equate honnêteté with the existence of the courtier. Indeed, there is a profound ambivalence toward this site and this figure in much of Méré's writing, so much so, in fact, that critics have often argued his brand of honnêteté is incommensurable with the court.[40] Méré recognizes that it is insufficient as a model: "Most people are persuaded that to be an honnête homme it is sufficient to see the court. . . . Those who only judge things as they are practiced in a court, however great it may be, do not recognize all that is good and bad. And the most enlightened who do not go beyond this only have a mind of limited breadth" (*OC*, 3:73). While he sees the court as "the most suitable place for perfecting oneself in the *agréments* and *bienséance*," he insists that success among "the most honnête men and the most galant Ladies at court" requires something more, namely reflection on what is most appropriate for any particular occasion (*OC*, 2:27). Arduous deliberation about aesthetic matters and not slavish observation of court fashion is what is required.[41] He cannot simply rely on the model provided by the court, but must seek out *le grand monde*, a sort of "supercourt." Speaking of the court of France, he intones:

> This court, although the most beautiful and perhaps the greatest on earth, still has its faults and limits. But *le grand monde* that extends everywhere is more perfect and, as a result, for those ways of living

and acting that one likes, one must treat the court and *le grand monde* separately and not be unaware that the court, either by custom or by whim, sometimes approves things that *le grand monde* would not tolerate. Whoever wants to judge things of *le grand monde* and even those of the court must ascertain what the most honnête people of all the courts, if they were assembled together, would say about them in order to recognize their true value. (*OC*, 2:111)

Le grand monde is a standard that the honnête homme must imagine based on what the "most honnête people of all the courts" would dictate. In the midst of the real court he must act as if he were in a court that is more perfect because universally elite. If it is true, as Moriarty insists, that honnêteté supports a "feudal-absolutist" ideology and the "real social authority" of the court,[42] it is also true that the honnête homme must not let himself be bound by the examples he witnesses in the actual court of France. Modeling himself at least initially on the courtier, the honnête homme seeks to become an idealized but real courtier by viewing the real through the ideal and by using the ideal to create a distance from the real.

Le conquérant

Closely allied with the courtier—and often one and the same person—is the warrior. Much scholarship has rehearsed the mixed fortunes of the warrior aristocracy in early modern France.[43] While it now appears that scholars (especially literary scholars) have long exaggerated the "emasculation" of the nobility and specifically the obsolescence of their military roles during the sixteenth and seventeenth centuries, it is generally accepted that the high nobility underwent a process of "curialization." Even if this process did not (always) reduce nobles to utter passivity, it was nonetheless marked not only by allegience to the king, but also by increased attention to codes of behavior. Méré's honnête homme illustrates the tensions of this class, at once a courtly nobility and a warrior aristocracy, by taking the conqueror as a model for what is an aesthetic and a worldly ideal.

Among the conquerors of antiquity cited by Méré (Alcibiades, Alexander the Great, and Pompey, among others), it is Caesar who garners the most admiration. In the portrait that concludes *Les Conversations*, Caesar is presented as "the greatest man in the world . . . as much for the wonders of his life and destiny as for the greatness of his genius and virtue" (*OC*, 1:88). Granted, Caesar's grandeur is not tied to his military success alone, yet his superiority stems from being one of the "masters of the world" (*OC*, 1:89), which was made possible by his conquests. A "surprising conqueror" *(conquerant admirable)*, Caesar did not view war as an end in itself, but rather as a means to gaining the upper hand: "although he was so great in war, he did not love it so much for itself but rather as a means of putting himself above everything" (*OC*, 1:90). In the end, his superiority as a general was the result of his superiority as a person. Of his character, Méré notes that Caesar was born with two "violent passions: glory and love" (*OC*, 1:89) and that he was generous, grateful, proud, and forgiving (*OC*, 1:90). Of his physical appearance, Méré writes admiringly that he was "tall, of a graceful and handsome stature and a healthy countenance," that he was "skilled in all the techniques of combat and a good horseman," and that he had "a white and sharp complexion, black, fiery, and keen eyes" (*OC*, 1:90). He was destined to greatness, so much so in fact that what would wear others down had quite the opposite effect on him: "It is said . . . that he kept his health by neglecting it and that by dint of training he made himself indefatigable" (*OC*, 1:90). Virtuous, handsome, a pillar of strength, Caesar was also a master of aesthetic taste, especially in the sartorial domain: "He loved beautiful clothes, and his attire always made him stand out, principally on a day of battle" (*OC*, 1:91).

Most remarkable of all is the way Caesar conjoined seemingly antithetical qualities: "I would not be surprised by the extreme bravery of a brute who knows neither pleasure nor pain and who does not know the difference between being dead or alive. But for a man with such a perceptive and refined temperament and such a subtle and great intelligence, that seems very rare to me" (*OC*, 1:91). No matter how unusual it is to combine bravery with perspicacity, refinement, subtlety, and intelligence, doing so is crucial for the honnête homme, who is far less concerned with winning on the battlefield and much more with winning the hearts and minds of those he encounters in all other walks of life. That Méré prefers the verb *gagner* (to win) over *vaincre* (to conquer) when speaking of the honnête homme as conqueror is significant, as Stanton has observed.[44] It underscores just how much the military hero can indeed provide a model of assertiveness and domination for the honnête homme so long as those qualities are expressed as refined seduction. Applying the lessons of Caesar to realms other than war, he must master the art of sending mixed signals, in short, the art of the oxymoron. Thus, when in the company of women, the honnête can never be too "brazen" *(hardi)* "provided one is no less modest" (*OC*, 3:160). In conversation, he must display gentleness *and* piquancy, soften disagreeable subjects, and state things indirectly (*OC*, 1:62, 2:125–26). Bent on conquest, he conceals his utilitarian telos in a refined demeanor that appears to be its opposite, all the more so because it was equated with the "feminine." Being sensitive, suave, subtle, gentle, and indirect, among other things, were all qualities that men were presumed to learn and perfect in the company of women. The honnête homme was to resemble the conqueror insofar as he was a "surprising conqueror" in the mold of Caesar, whose model he was to assimilate by inflecting it with what would appear to be its antithesis. His "feminized" demeanor distances him from the uncouth warrior, and his persuasive, self-assertive goals differentiate him from women. But in order to acquire such "feminine" traits he must come to terms with yet another model.

Le galant homme

Just as closely related to the honnête homme as the courtier and the warrior is the galant homme. In a multifarious body of mid-seventeenth-century writing, the galant homme was the masculine manifestation of *galanterie*, an ideal of comportment and sociability.[45] As we will see in the next chapter, although *galanterie* and *galant/e* could have pejorative meanings, the most prominent of which denoted transgressive amorous relationships, these words also had positive meanings, which many seventeenth-century writers attempted to highlight. While the adjective *galant* could refer to professional competence, it was primarily linked to the notions of urbanity, politeness, and courtliness and was often seen as overlapping honnêteté. Unlike his contemporaries and consistent with his own rigorous definition of honnêteté, Méré, though, draws a distinction between the two by deploying a series of binaries, such as playful/serious, surface/depth, and worldly/retiring. "It seems to me," says the Chevalier in *Les Conversations*, "that a galant homme is a fixture in social settings and certain *agréments* are found in him that an honnête homme does not always have. But those of an honnête homme are very profound, even though he makes himself less visible in society" (*OC*, 1:18). To these binaries he adds another: "the galant homme is more outgoing and the honnête homme more reserved" (*OC*, 3:140). Ultimately, however, galanterie is fleeting, whereas honnêteté is eternal: "the status of galant homme, which captivates young men, passes like a flower or a dream. . . . But if someone is loved because he is an honnête homme, he will always be loved" (*OC*, 1:18).

All things considered, it is clear that the honnête homme is superior to the galant homme; and yet, like all binaries, the two form a signifying relationship with each other. Nearly identical and virtually indistinguishable, they still have respective differences that set them apart. Among these are the inherent risks of galanterie, which is subject to "true" and "false" iterations. "Ordinarily galanterie is false," writes Méré (*OC*, 2:43). Prone to superficiality if not hypocrisy, galanterie must instead be "natural," come from the heart, and be practiced with "dexterity" *(adresse)* and "wit" *(esprit)* in an refined and uncommon way (*OC*, 2:43). If the components of galanterie bear a striking resemblance to honnêteté, so too does its principal objective: "it must captivate people who know how to judge, for the goal of galanterie is to captivate and, what's more, with a surprising twist. And when it does not captivate at all, we can conclude that it is false" (*OC*, 2:43). Distinguishing between true and false galanterie and, especially, practicing the true form requires the ability to appeal to the select few. Like honnêteté, galanterie is reducible to an *art de plaire*.

Yet, galanterie remains distinct from honnêteté, and the honnête homme must learn to adopt the persona of a galant homme when it serves his interests, and specifically with women. "One derives great advantage from being able to be one and the other as one deems appropriate, and I have seen honnête men be very awkward with the Ladies and who did not know how to engage in conversation with them even though they had things of good sense to tell them" (*OC*, 1:20), explains the Chevalier of *Les Conversations*. The honnête homme should not *become* a galant homme, rather he should extend himself *into* galanterie (he should be "one *and* the other"). Speaking in idealistic terms, the Chevalier explains that "a galant homme is nothing other than an honnête homme who is more scintillating and lighthearted than he is ordinarily and who knows how to come across well in everything" (*OC*, 1:20). The honnête homme combines the solidity and durability of honnêteté with the outward, seductive graces of galanterie.

Between Heterosocial and Homosocial Exchange

Among all the models of honnêteté, women are just as significant as the courtier, the warrior, and the galant homme. Through pleasurable interaction with women, the honnête homme seeks to acquire many of the qualities they (supposedly) possess innately—refined manners, good taste, and grace. But the relationship between the honnête homme and women is both more complicated and more vexed than that with the courtier, the conqueror, or the galant homme. These latter are, on the whole, static and largely abstract models who can be emulated and assimilated without personal exchange.

Women, however, are dynamic and for the most part concrete models with whom the honnête homme must have sustained contact. But interaction with women is not straightforward, and it is not the only type of required or even desired social interaction for the honnête homme. In fact, Méré situates his honnête homme ambiguously between two types of exchange—male-female (heterosocial) and male-male (homosocial). As I will argue, this ambiguity is heightened by the conflicting heterosocial and homosocial *desires* that Méré, at different moments in his writing, posits as crucial for men aspiring to honnêteté. Further still, Méré's honnête homme confirms Eve Kosofsky Sedgwick's assertion that the heterosocial and the homosocial exist on continuums with hetero*sexual* and homo*sexual* desires respectively. The uncertain place the honnête homme occupies in relation to these desires reveals some of the destabilizing roles of femininity and sexuality within honnête masculinity.

Fundamental to honnêteté is what Stanton has called the "'female' principle," the refined manners and speech that women were deemed to possess innately.[46] Reiterating a commonplace of early modern conduct literature that can be traced back to Petrarch, if not the medieval courtly ideal of *courtoisie*, Méré asserts that to acquire "feminine" refinement a man must be or act as if he were a courtly lover. Motivated by desire, he will seek to please his beloved in every possible way and so doing will learn the *art* of captivating—not only his beloved, but all those whom he encounters. "[He] who accustoms himself to the ways [of the Ladies]," says Méré, "finds that the desire to acquire their good graces forces him to take on a more insinuating manner and renders him altogether different, for it is from love that most of the truest *agréments* are born" (*OC*, 3:75). "Imagine how much a young man who falls in love with a woman who is knowledgeable about what is fitting socially and who knows how to put it into practice can become an honnête homme with her. For love naturally bestows ingenious means for captivating the person whom we love. And if this Lady discerns everything justly, only exquisite merit and noble manners can win her over" (*OC*, 2:80). In this scheme, then, male heterosexual desire is channeled into a "civilizing" function: the desire for the (judicious) female object is simultaneously desire for her most prized qualities. The honnête homme seeks to possess his beloved and to resemble her—to possess her by resembling her.

What men desire to possess is women's ability to captivate others. "Ordinarily men do not have as much grace in their actions as women do, and . . . women have a finer knowledge than men about doing things well, either because the capacity to captivate others comes more naturally to them or because sensing that it's their specialty, they make it their occupation from childhood on" (*OC*, 1:18). Endowed with the gift of captivating, women are, after Méré himself, the supreme arbiters of honnêteté. Thus, men must make every effort to captivate women in order to captivate *like* women. In their presence, as the Mareschal tells the Chevalier in a conversation, the honnête homme must master "refined manners, sparkling and lighthearted conversation, an agreeable and somewhat flattering deference, that inexplicable spiciness and that deftness at being playful with women without making them feel awkward, that practice of *le grand monde* that envelopes everything, that bold and modest practice that has nothing lowly nor malicious about it, only things that have the scent of honnêteté" (*OC*, 1:20). If he is able to manage all of this, then, the honnête homme is sure to be captivating to women. However, the Mareschal warns, "one must remember that the more these sorts of things are pleasing when well executed, the more they disgust when they are not" (*OC*, 1:20). It is not just a matter of engaging in the "things that have the scent of honnêteté," it is also necessary to do those things *well*. Even then, according to the Chevalier, "this very scintillating way of living" *(cette façon de vivre si brillante)* should only be displayed sparingly: "Most women do not like it much; at the very least one can be sure that so much éclat and eagerness will tire them in the long run" (*OC*, 1:20–21). Captivating women requires a delicate balance between excess and lack that women themselves are best able to discern, so men must cede to the judgment of women while seeking to emulate their *art de plaire*.

And yet, for all of their advantages, women are not models the honnête homme can appropriate wholesale. Women may be able to discern the pleasing "middle" to which he aspires, they may be able to please more easily than he can, and they may be able to inspire in him those qualities most needed to succeed in honnêteté. But they do not possess the honnête mean because they are burdened by the corporeal. Again and again, Méré gives examples of women's obsession with their physical beauty, which in his view is founded on the superficial and the ephemeral. Thus, to describe the difference between the *beau* and the *agréable*, he writes:

> The Ladies who dream more of becoming beautiful *(belles)* than enticing *(agréables)* are poorly advised. When this happens, it is the worst possible way of making themselves loved for the long term. For as soon as one possesses something beautiful, usually one does not value it as much. . . . But it is not so with something enticing. Indeed, when one loves a woman because she is beautiful, this love sometimes passes very quickly. But when true and profound *agréments* are the

cause of affection, one does not turn away from it in that fashion. (*OC*, 2:37–38)

The materiality of physical beauty, to which women seem to be drawn, does not lead to the lasting pleasure and happiness that are the ultimate goals of honnêteté. Only the "true and profound *agréments*," which transcend the corporeal, offer such hope. Overall, in Méré's writings, women are to the honnête (masculine) "middle" what beauty is to the *agréments*. They approximate it, but remain distinct from it.

The Honnête Homme as Courtly Lover

In spite of these shortcomings, the honnête homme must still seek out women, and to do so, he must adopt the stance of a courtly lover by enacting two general principles of honnêteté. He must first of all engage in social exchange and welcome the rivalry that ensues. For Méré, individual merit, no matter how superlative, can only blossom into an excellent reputation by contact with others, albeit a select happy few. Withdrawing from society is not an option for the aspiring honnête homme, for only through social exchange *(le commerce du monde)* can he demonstrate that he is able to "live well and . . . comport himself gracefully, by his speech and his actions" (*OC*, 3:142). However, social exchange generates envy, which must in turn be instrumentalized for one's own benefit. When conversing with others, for instance, "one cannot give enough thought to saying only what people one esteems the most would want to have said, and in the same way. In this consists the greatest secret of communicating with grace" (*OC*, 3:132). Knowing how to inspire envy in others is the key to graceful interaction, verbal and otherwise. At the same time, inspiring envy requires the ability to imagine oneself in a triangularized web of rivalry if one's attention is directed to a specific person, and all the more so if the person is of the opposite sex:

> He who only thinks of making himself enticing to the woman who captivates him, even if he is good looking and a very galant homme, is still not assured of winning her over, because she does not want to love someone who is loved by no one (for an example in those things can go a long way) or because someone else has taken the initiative, or finally because her inclination leads her to other thoughts. What I say about men can be observed in women. They are the same feelings. (*OC*, 2:25–26)

Being graced with advantages all one's own is no guarantee of success in the *art de plaire*. The honnête homme (and the honnête femme as well) must take into account his (her) rivals. If how one should react depends on the reason for the object's resistance, it is nonetheless clear that the subject (the honnête homme or femme) must be desired by others and that she or he is in a struggle with rivals for the affections of the beloved. Through this insight, Méré recognizes the fundamental truth of the theory of mimetic desire proposed by René Girard and revised by Eve Kosofsky Sedgwick, namely that "the bonds of 'rivalry' and 'love,' differently as they are experienced, are equally powerful and in many senses equivalent."[47] Desire for the beloved is not only indissociable from the envy of rivals, but requires it. Contrary to what Méré affirms in the passage just quoted, however, there is not a symmetry between the honnête homme and the honnête femme. Throughout his writings, the courtly lover wooing his beloved is in fact the preponderant model of desire.

The other principle of honnêteté apparent in the courtly lover scheme is that, for both women and men, heterosocial is preferable to homosocial interaction. Deprived of the company of women, men among themselves become overly direct—"without affectation and without ceremony" *(sans manière et sans façon)*—and too narrowly focused on their ambition (*OC,* 3:74). When confined to all-female groups, Méré contends, women are prone to boredom, jealousy, and vicious backbiting (Letter 146, *L,* 535–36.). In what appears at first glance to be a perfectly symmetrical complementarity, each gender serves as a "civilizing" regulator for the other. Heterosociality would seem to save each gender from its purportedly innate impediments to honnêteté. Yet, indirectly and allusively, Méré suggests still another reason for the superiority of heterosociality: it guards against the ambiguously erotic potential of homosociality. "Galant compliments *(les tendresses galantes)* are out of place *(pas dans leur place)* between one man and another or one woman and another. They are too affected" (*OC,* 3:75). Beyond the supposed reason for this proscription—affectation—the expression "tendresses galantes," with its simultaneously amorous and sociable connotations in seventeenth-century usage, evokes the decidedly homosexual. Men paying "galant compliments" to other men and women to other women—what would be honnête homosociality—are "out of place" because of the proximity to same-sex desire. This homoerotic potential is made even more explicit in a variant of this observation that ends with a traditional Latin proverb condemning excessive flattery: "Displays of affection *(caresses)* are appropriate between a man and a woman and between a woman and a man; but from a man to another man, it is as if *asinus asinum fricat* [the donkey rubs against the donkey]" ("Divers," 1925: 72). By using the Latin proverb to condemn compliments between men, Méré transforms a commentary on flattery to one about the gender of the flatterers. Through this proverb, male homosocial compliments are equated with the evocative metaphorical image of the two donkeys, whose physicality becomes the consequence of a man showering another man with compliments. Even if it is disguised by the animal proverb, the specter of the homosexual is evoked by the homosocial. To avoid being equated with homoerotically suggestive donkeylike behavior, men must keep their "galant compliments" and their "displays of affection" within the bounds of heterosocial and heterosexual desire.[48]

But all the while insisting on the merits of heterosociality, Méré actually undermines his occasional suggestions that men and women stand in a symmetrical relationship to each other. More often, women are described as having a utilitarian function for the honnête homme. Stanton has observed that "[women] are not inaccessible subjects to which the honnête homme slavishly submits, but to the contrary, objects used in the elaboration of his own poetic text" (139). To be sure, women are the arbiters and pedagogues of good taste in polite (heterosocial) company. As the Chevalier in Méré's *Conversations* asserts, women have

> a finesse of the mind *(une délicatesse d'esprit)* that is not so common among men. I have even observed that in many places and throughout the social ranks ordinarily men do not have as much grace in what they do as women, and that women have a more exquisite understanding of how to do things well. . . . Consequently one is never entirely an honnête homme . . . unless the Ladies have had their say. (*OC*, 1:17–18)

And yet women, as social actors, play a lesser role than do men. "The role of a man is of greater breadth than a woman's. A man has to extricate himself from quarrels, be a good judge of things, be enticing, know society, be witty, etc." ("Divers," 1924: 494). By virtue of succeeding in the masculine social sphere (extricating himself from disputes, knowing *le monde*), a man seemingly takes what are otherwise "feminine" qualities (being enticing and witty) to a higher, more expansive level. When judged against this standard, it is perhaps not surprising that Méré is said never to have seen a woman whose demeanor totally satisfied him ("Divers," 1924: 494.). Nor is it surprising that he contradicts his own advice that the honnête homme take his cue from women by liberally dispensing advice to his female correspondents. With the women in his own life, Méré was clearly the master of honnêteté.[49]

With more social power and thus greater sociable prowess, men have an asymmetrical advantage over women.[50] But in order to acquire "feminine" refinement, the honnête homme must still interact with women, albeit in ways that conceal his dominance as the submissiveness required of a courtly lover. With the objective of insinuating—as opposed to forcing—himself into women's company ("s'insinuer parmi les Dames" [*OC*, 3:157]), the honnête homme must adopt a resolutely theatrical frame of mind. Hence, although he is fully capable of being lighthearted and outgoing, Méré contends that "a modest and restrained air . . . seems to me to be more appropriate for insinuating onself among the Ladies, who are concerned about their reputations" (*OC*, 3:157). Being modest and holding back even though he has much to offer, the honnête homme is able to be all things in all situations. By contrast, it seems, women *are* the qualities they exemplify. They are not actors on the social stage; they are, quite simply, themselves. If the honnête homme is the master of appearances, women are nothing more and nothing less than *being*. Thus, the apparent complementarity of honnête heterosocial exchanges is in fact rooted in a radical asymmetry between men and women. The honnête homme qua courtly lover and the honnête femme qua beloved are not equal. But as Eve Kosofsky Sedgwick has famously established, heterosexual erotic triangles are never symmetrical.[51]

Homosociality

This, however, is not the only asymmetricality in Méré's vision of honnête masculinity and femininity. For all of his theoretical pronouncements in favor of heterosociality (and against homosociality), there are many positive examples of male homosociality throughout his writings. The most prominent of these is found in Méré's first published work, *Les Conversations* (1668), a series of six conversations between a Mareschal and a Chevalier about the best course of education to offer a young prince (who is none other than the Dauphin) so as to instill in him the final goal of honnêteté. At the same time, between themselves, the Mareschal and the Chevalier (who is also the narrator) illustrate this goal by their own example. Their exchanges are marked by numerous mutual compliments through which the two interlocutors present themselves as masters of honnêteté.[52]

The very first conversation between the Mareschal and the Chevalier underscores in striking fashion Méré's ambivalence toward heterosociality. When, after dinner, a group of women decide to play card games, the Mareschal and the Chevalier opt instead to retire to a different room for private conversation. The Mareschal opens the dialogue by expressing his desire to learn things from the Chevalier, so as to resemble an unnamed lady: "I am cherishing even the slightest things you tell me about Socrates, and I hope that one of these days I will be heard citing the divine Plato, following the example of a Lady who is very witty and who enjoys speaking about everything" (*OC*, 1:9). From the Mareschal's self-avowed wish to emulate the Lady, the conversation shifts to women, their supposed "finesse of mind" (*délicatesse d'esprit*) (*OC*, 1:18) and its potentially formative effect on the honnête homme. The focus changes, then, from the Lady as the object of desire and emulation to women as the object of discourse. And with this shift, the two male interlocutors stake out their own distance from—and mastery over—women. After rejecting those who claim that women are incapable of intelligence, the two men discuss whether it is better to expose the young prince to "lighthearted women" or "clever women" (*OC*, 1:17). Finally, they outline the qualities necessary for "winning them over" and especially the difficulty of achieving that goal. "Most often," claims the Chevalier, "one begins badly with them because one does not realize that they are won over in the same ways that we are and that they are likewise lost in similar ways" (*OC*, 1:21). In the midst of their musings about the shortcomings of men's seductive powers, the women who had been playing cards ask the two speakers to mediate a dispute that had arisen among them. The Mareschal seems to welcome the opportunity, commenting: "This could not have happened more fortuitously . . . and we could not have done better than to have opened at that very moment the chapter on the Ladies. For if we want to keep them all from complaining, we need to muster everything possible to judge them" (*OC*, 1:21). If, initially, the rationale for considering women was for the young prince's benefit, in the end their discussion benefits themselves. After describing and praising women's "good sense," "finesse of mind," and "grace" (*OC*, 1:17–18), the two men use this knowledge to enhance their position vis-à-vis women. The heterosocial/heterosexual desire expressed in these moments of male homosocial exchange enhances the two men's asymmetrical advantage over women.

At times, though, women's role in the cultivation of honnêteté is almost entirely obscured and attributed instead to male homosocial desire. One example is found in an account of a trip Méré and a male friend purportedly took with Pascal. At the beginning of the journey, they found Pascal to be "a great mathematician who knew nothing more . . . who had neither good taste nor feeling" (*OC*, 2:86). But after several days of patient listening and self-critique, Pascal began to resemble his honnête travel companions: "He said almost nothing that was not good and that we would not have wanted to say ourselves. Frankly, he had come a very long way. And, to tell the truth, the joy he showed us at having taken on a completely different frame of mind was so visible that I do not think it possible to feel a greater one" (*OC*, 2:87). This transformation was not effected by the heterosexual desire to possess and thus emulate women, but rather by Pascal's careful and methodical observation of the two men with whom he was traveling. (After two or three days, Méré notes, "He was somewhat distrustful of his feelings, and limiting himself to listening or asking questions so as to understand the subjects that came up, he had notebooks that he pulled out occasionally to write down some comments" [*OC*, 2:87.]). The homosocial context nonetheless allowed Pascal to blossom into the honnête homme that his mathematical mind-set had heretofore prevented him from becoming. So successful was he that his models came to wish that *they* had uttered the things their informal pupil said. The bond of envy and desire that inspires Pascal to emulate Méré and his friend in the first place comes full circle.[53]

Extending this logic further, Méré even intimates that honnêteté is compatible not only with male homosociality, but with male same-sex desire as well. If only allusively and by reference to historical personages, he displays a consciousness of the continuum that exists between the homosocial construction of honnêteté and male homosexual desire. Of course, this consciousness does not necessarily indicate enthusiasm on his part, but it does at least reveal his understanding of this link. His manuscript *Divers propos*, for instance, contains several statements about sodomy. Sometimes cited as an example of "bad tendencies" ("Divers," 1922: 92, 1925: 433), it is also recognized to be part and parcel of the "things that are done": among the types of questions posed by ignorant and stupid people, he cites "How can he like boys?" ("Divers," 1922: 90). The *Divers propos* also contain numerous passages that defend Théophile de Viau's works. Thanks to a trial at the end of his life, Théophile had an established reputation as a sodomite, and he remained a controversial figure throughout the seventeenth century.[54] Although Méré does not overlook what he considers to be his improprieties— both stylistic and personal ("I am aware of what was bad about him" ["Divers," 1923: 526.], he states, doubtless referring to sodomy)—he also contends that Théophile's works appeal to the *honnêtes gens* ("Divers," 1923: 84) and, further, that the author was one of only two men from the time of Louis XIII he would have liked to have met, precisely because he possessed "something excellent" ["Divers," 1923: 526]).[55]

A similarly allusive recognition of the compatibility of honnêteté and male same-sex desire can be detected in the praise Méré offers for Alcibiades. Known as Socrates' *eromenos* (younger male partner of an older man [*erastes*] in ancient Greece), Alcibiades famously addresses a passionate hymn of love to him in Plato's *Symposium*. It is precisely this discourse that Méré cites as an example of the "style of the *honnêtes gens*" (*OC*, 3:116). And he is even more explicit in his praise when he quotes Cornelius Nepos's assessment of Alcibiades: "'I assure you . . . that I have noticed nothing in his speech or his actions that did not please me greatly and that of all the men I know he is the one I would most like to resemble.'" Agreeing, Méré adds: "Perhaps . . . he would not be a bad model for young men to imitate, for with such beautiful qualities he was still very brave. He had to have had, as one says, that galant manner, in which so few people succeed" (*OC*, 2:42–43). Granted, if Alcibiades is a model to be emulated it is not because of his love for Socrates. Yet that love, and Méré's oblique allusion to it, do not disqualify him as a paradigmatic honnête homme.

A Confluence of Desires

Méré's consciousness of the continuum between homosociality and male homosexual desire is most explicit in a letter from his published correspondence (Letter 195) that is all the more fascinating because it illustrates how male homosociality, heterosociality, and heterosexual desire all contribute to honnêteté and, further, how Méré's *theoretical* preference for *heterosociality* can be reconciled with his *illustrations* of male *homosociality*. Writing to an unidentified woman, Méré begins with a historical litany of "extraordinary events . . . that have been observed concerning love" including a "great lord" who tires of women and pursues only men; a Roman empress who desires only whipped and beaten slaves and gladiators; Henri II, who falls in love with his father's mistress, Mme de Valentinois; a prince who murders the woman he loves above all others; and Seleucus, who divorces his wife so that his son-in-law can marry her. But most of the letter is devoted to an anecdote whose veracity Méré guarantees by what may be a self-reference ("a quite unusual adventure to which I can attest as if I had had it myself" [*L*, 676.]). He then tells of a husband and wife whom he knew well. Each was remarkable, but not without faults. The wife was as appealing for her physical appearance as she was for her mind, yet she was overly severe and reserved.[56] The husband was even more attractive than his wife, in fact, more perfect and captivating than anything painted by Apelles or Mignard, says Méré. Endowed as well with a keen mind, he had but two failings: "His constitution seemed to be too delicate, and . . . he captivated certain men more than a man should wish to" (*L*, 677). In addition to the wife's severe reserve and the husband's "constitution," the couple had been married so young, explains Méré, "they had become accustomed to giving each other nothing more than children's hugs" (*L*, 677).

The anecdote then turns to the remedy the couple finds for their individual failings and their inability to consummate their marriage, which is nothing other than a ménage à trois. The husband had a close friend from whom he kept no secrets and was rarely separated (*L*, 678) and for whom the wife developed a "tendre inclination" she was unable to extinguish. When the husband noticed this state of affairs, he approached his friend, who in turn acknowledged his feelings for the wife and proposed to cut off contact with both of them. But the husband immediately rebuffed this suggestion and instead declared his devotion to his friend: "Could you live without me? I swear to you on our friendship that I would abandon Helen and Cleopatra to follow you to the end of the world" (*L*, 679). He then offered to share his wife with his friend, an offer that both his friend and his wife eventually accepted. In the end, declares Méré, "It would be very difficult to conceive the extent of the happiness they had achieved" (*L*, 681). Happiness, indeed: the wife overcame her severity and her reserve, and the friend retained his friendship with the husband all the while pursuing his feelings for the wife. What the husband derived from this arrangement is explained in particular detail. When he initially made his offer to the friend, he disclosed that he could only desire his wife by conjuring up the image of his friend and his wife together: "I assure you as well that I only have pleasure with her by imagining that you hold her in your arms and that without this sweet and alluring sort of rivalry I would not be moved by her any more than by a beautiful statue. I want, I implore you to consent that all will be common among the three of us" (*L*, 680). By imaging his friend as rival—by using his friend's desire for his wife as proxy—the husband in turn is able to "enjoy" *(avoir plaisir avec)* his wife.

At first glance, the threesome described in this letter seems to resolve the ambivalence between heterosociality and homosociality in Méré's other writings. Heterosocial, heterosexual, homosocial, and homosexual desires are all affirmed, and they all lead to the happiness that is the ultimate goal of honnêteté. After settling on their arrangement, concludes Méré, "to the utmost of their felicity . . . never have three persons enjoyed more enticing conversation and all of their pleasures were filled with wit" (*L*, 681–82). He further explains that, to endure, this happiness requires not only physical expression but also the "wit" and "refined manner" of honnêteté:

It is true that if the person one loves is but a well-formed idol, the deepest happiness of love begins more pleasurably than it ends. . . . But when the graces of wit and a refined manner accompany a beautiful body, love never displeases. A pleasure that passes away is followed by another pleasure, and the more we interact with people who captivate us in this way the more we love them. (*L*, 682)

In this concluding commentary, Méré seems intent on making the point that physical love alone is ephemeral. And yet the example of the husband proves quite the reverse. Possessing an "exquisite mind" *(esprit fin)*, he is unable to love his wife physically and, thus, experience lasting pleasure without the mediation of his friend. Thereafter, all three partake of the unrepresentable happiness to which Méré alludes. In the end, such happiness is made possible at once by heterosocial *and* heterosexual desire, and at the same time it subsumes the homosocial desire of the two men and the homosexual desire of at least the husband. However, while the heterosexual takes precedence over the homosexual, it does not negate it (as the ambiguous "that all will be common among the three of us" seems to suggest). Rather, it is necessary so that the heterosocial/heterosexual can emerge and be maintained as such. The happiness of this ménage à trois is rooted first of all in male-male desire and then by extrapolation and projection in male-female desire.

In a broader sense, the solution that allows the husband to desire both his friend *and* his wife foregrounds the wider function of homosocial desire within honnêteté. Sedgwick has noted that the exchange of women among men involves considerable risks, and that for a man "success in making this transaction requires a willingness and ability to temporarily risk, or assume, a feminized status. Only the man who can proceed through that stage, *while* remaining in cognitive control of the symbolic system that presides over sexual exchange, will be successful in achieving a relation of mastery to other men."[57] Seen in this light, the instances of male homosociality throughout Méré's writings would seem to counteract the risk of being "feminized" or "objectified." Not only do they establish men's control of the traffic in women as sexual property and as aesthetic value, these examples also involve men defining or living out that key component of honnêteté, a "relation of mastery" to other *honnêtes gens*. Indeed, in several of Méré's anecdotes (such as the one about Pascal), the exchange of women is circumvented altogether. Amongst themselves, men seemingly reproduce the heterosocial dynamic necessary for the blossoming of honnêteté. They are able to exchange those prized "feminine" attributes without the intervention of actual women. With or without them, men's quest for honnêteté necessitates a desire to possess those qualities of the "female principle" as they are embodied and enacted by other men.

Still, in Letter 195, the husband's erotic desire for his friend (who is described as being "very much an honnête homme" [*L*, 678.]) is not straightforward and illustrates an exceptional version of the emulation that is imperative for all men in honnêteté. In one sense, Méré envisions an honnêteté that genuinely relies on both heterosociality and homosociality and that seems to put male-female and male-male relations on a equal footing. In another sense, though, the homosocial and the homosexual exist on an uninterrupted progression of influences and desires that reinvigorate and recast the social position of the honnête heterosexual male. It is as if Méré dares to imagine something beyond the masculinist and heterosexist logic of honnête masculinity, but without being able to renounce this logic.

THE *je ne sais quoi*

"To become an honnête homme, one can never follow the best models too closely" (*OC*, 3:75), says Méré at the outset of his "Discours de la vraie Honnêteté." But even the "best models" are imperfect in one way or another, as Méré repeatedly and insistently shows. Whatever his model or countermodel, the honnête homme must maintain the distinction between self and other. Thus, it is not difficult to see why Méré resorts to the theatrical metaphor to explain the frame of mind required of the honnête homme. "I am persuaded that in many situations it is useful to consider what one does as a play and to imagine that one is acting a role on stage" (*OC*, 3:158), he says. Taking the theatrical illusion to the next level (by *imagining* that he is an actor), the honnête homme negotiates between his authentic being and his social persona, thus isolating him from the emotional minefields of social exchange.[58] "This thought prevents one from taking things too seriously and, further, affords a freedom of language and actions that one does not have when troubled by fear and anxiety. What I like even more about it is that one is hardly debased at all by disgrace and one is not inflated too much by prosperity" (*OC*, 3:158). Acting on the stage of the world, the honnête homme achieves that goal of classical philosophy, the moderation of the passions, which in turn guarantees his lasting happiness. But this goal ultimately reveals just how little the honnête homme resembles the dramatic actor. Whereas the latter only needs skill *(adresse)*, the honnête homme must apply both his heart and his mind because "acting in society *(l'action du monde)* always has some true feeling about it and is not a vain appearance like acting on stage" *(OC,* 3:158). No matter how much he distances himself from the roles he plays, then, he cannot help but identify with them. He plays his part with his heart and his mind, and at the same time he keeps an actor's distance from himself all the better to *be* the role he *plays.*

As if this difficulty were not sufficient, Méré adds yet another. For, the honnête homme, unlike the dramatic actor, must be able to play any role whatsoever. "One sees that actors who are good at certain roles do not succeed at others . . . but the character of an honnête homme encompasses everything. He must transform himself with the agility of his genius as the occasion demands" *(OC,* 3:157). Adaptable to seemingly any situation, the honnête homme is an inimitable actor. Not only must he be able to be self and other at the same time, he must also transform himself at will, as the situation warrants. Méré concedes that this ability is rare: "It is a very rare talent to be a good actor in life. One must have much intelligence and precision to find perfection" *(OC,* 3:157). But this perfection demands something other than the skill acquired by learning and practice. It demands an elusive quality that is unexplainable, ineffable, and quasi-magical.

To confront the difficulties of being a "good actor in life," the honnête homme must ultimately seek refuge in the quality that goes to the heart of who he is and what he does—the *je ne sais quoi.* The very essence of what honnêteté represents, the *je ne sais quoi* is, in Méré's words "something inexplicable that is recognized better by seeing it practiced than by explaining it." It is impossible to capture in words; yet those who see it and those who feel it are convinced of its presence. They *are* so convinced because this quality is "a certain something noble *(je ne sçai quoi de noble)* that enhances all good qualities and that comes only from the heart and the mind. The rest is but its escort and baggage" *(OC,* 1:77). It is, in other words, the quality that assures one will always be captivating. With it, everything else falls into place.[59] But unlike descriptions of the *je ne sais quoi* as a force of nature or a stroke of passion in philosophical discourse, Méré's usage is a means for a social elite to preserve its hold on distinction and exclude those it deems unworthy of inclusion within its ranks, as Richard Scholar has shown. A "collective fabrication," the *je ne sais quoi* as Méré evokes it is an "artificial sign of quality" for the *honnête gens.*[60] And in the end, it is a "subtle artifact" rather than "a truly inexplicable occult quality."[61]

Even so, the appeal to the *je ne sais quoi* complicates Méré's attempts to codify honnêteté because the *je ne sais quoi* enables the honnête homme to become so exceptional and so superlative that he paradoxically gains license to transgress, if not redefine the mean as it is commonly perceived. Such is the case in a brief anecdote about the Duke of Buckingham that concludes the "Discours de la conversation" (Discourse on Conversation). On a visit to the French court in 1625, Buckingham attended a ball where "one could hardly imagine a more beautiful and scintillating gathering" and where "there wasn't a single outfit that wasn't fashionable" (*OC*, 2:131). Pushing the envelope of diplomatic protocol, Buckingham appeared "in a Persian outfit with a velours hat completely covered with feathers and jewels, and breeches so tight fitting that they showed not only the whole outline of his legs, which were handsome, but also far above his knees" (*OC*, 2:131–32). Greeted at first with ridicule, the duke succeeded in playing his part and dancing "so elegantly" *(de si bon air)* that mockery quickly gave way to admiration and, as Méré observes, "with his bizarre and astonishing attire he outshone *(effaça)* the French fashion and those who were most galant at court" (*OC*, 2:132). Buckingham's fashion statement triumphed in spite of its audacity (Méré qualifies it as "extremely bold and risky").

Beyond the malleability of the *je ne sais quoi*, Buckingham's example demonstrates the ambiguity between the corporeal and the noncorporeal within honnête masculinity. The duke wins over the French court because of his intangible *bon air;* but at the same time his performance highlights his own body, and tellingly "not only the outline of his legs . . . but also far above his knees." If his *bon air* is primarily a noncorporeal quality, it nonetheless complements and accentuates his male body. Similarly, in Méré's theory of honnêteté, the inexplicable *je ne sais quoi* ensures that the honnête homme either achieves or redefines the golden mean, something the male body alone cannot do. But since men are presumed to have an advantage over all others in honnêteté, the *je ne sais quoi* attempts to attribute a transcendent meaning to their corporeality. The honnête homme's sublime ability to achieve the mean betrays—even as it attempts to remedy—the limits of biological sex. Hegemonic masculinity can never simply appeal to the body but must always employ ideology in order to justify its domination. Or, as Jeffrey Peters has written in an analysis of Boileau's *Art poétique:* "Men are men not because their semiotic design corresponds to a natural essence, but because they artfully—sublimely—*are* that essence."[62]

In spite of all the writings Méré the *maître* leaves us, in spite of all the rules and maxims he formulates, the essential quality of honnêteté could not be captured in language or rational thought. It was always shifting as the *honnêtes gens* closed ranks to ensure they remained a select few. As a result, the necessarily fluid *je ne sais quoi* left the honnête homme with no sure footing, neither among his models nor his countermodels, neither in heterosociality nor in homosociality, neither in the body nor the intangible *bon air*. The honnête homme, like all those in a position of domination, had to submit to the constraints of that position—he had to be dominated by his own domination. Aspiring to the "certain something" that is honnêteté, he had no choice but to strive for what amounted to a ruse, with no certain outcome. Buckingham may have succeeded in the end, but the court's initial mockery could just as easily have been confirmed as transformed. The ability to define and embody a collective sense of the *je ne sais quoi* was as unexpected for Buckingham as it was rare for the honnête homme. No matter how much he tried to stand apart from and above his Others, the honnête homme had no lasting assurance that his grasp of the *je ne sais quoi* would translate into masculine domination. And he had no guarantee that he would not, in the end, become indistinguishable from his Others.

TWO

Effeminacy and Its Meanings from Court to Salon

IN A SONNET ENTITLED "Le Pousseur de beaux sentiments" (The Babbler of Sweet Nothings), Georges de Scudéry depicts an effeminate salon man who in many ways resembles the twenty-first-century "metrosexual," defined by the Merriam-Webster dictionary as "a usually urban heterosexual male given to enhancing his appearance by fastidious grooming, beauty treatments, and fashionable clothes":[1]

Au sortir de son lit, ayant quitté ses gands,
· Décordonné son poil, défait sa bigotere,
Pinceté son menton, & ratissé ses dents,
Il prend un bon boüillon, & va rendre un clistere.

Le voila bien muny tant dehors que dedans,
C'est pour un grand dessein, pour une grande affaire,
C'est pour aller pousser de ces beaux sentimens
Dont les Godelureaux font un grand mystere.

Il paroist vers le soir, poudré, frisé, lavé,
Exhalant le jasmin, de canons entravé,
Dont un seul pese autant que la plus grosse botte.

Il va chez quelque Dame, où d'un ton de Coquet
Il lit un Bout-rimé sur defunt Perroquet
Cette Dame l'admire, ô le fat! ô la sotte![2]

[Once out of bed, having taken his gloves off, / Untangled his moustache, undone his *bigotère* [accessory for curling moustaches], / Plucked his chin, and scraped his teeth, / He drinks some broth, and gives himself an enema. // Now he is ready on the outside and the inside, / For a great plan, for a great affair, / To babble those sweet nothings / Which young dandies make such a big fuss about. // He appears toward evening, pow-dered, hair curled, washed, / Exhaling jasmine, hampered by *canons* [lace around the knee], / A single one of which weighs as much as a big boot. // He goes to some Lady's house where in a flirtatious tone / He reads a *bout-rimé* [poem] about a dead parrot / This Lady admires him, oh the impertinent fellow! oh the idiotic woman!]

In spite of the many historical details that mark this sonnet as a seventeenth-century text, its insinuation of effeminacy remains strikingly relevant for our own time. Then as now, to be effeminate is to become like a woman, to blur the boundaries between the male and the female, the masculine and the femi-nine. But being effeminate does not erase all traces of these boundaries. The dandy in the sonnet, like the metrosexual of today, still wears men's clothing and takes pride in his male body, after all. No matter how much like women they would seem to be (in the eyes of observers in the ilk of Scudéry, at least), they are both still identifiable as men—but as men who occupy an unstable midpoint between masculinity and femininity. The dandy and the metrosex-ual apply a "feminine" care to enhance their male bodies and masculine cloth-ing. Appropriating for masculinity what is supposedly the domain of femi-ninity, effeminate men figure the ontological impossibility of the simile: they are *like* women, but they are *not* women because they retain indelible signs of being men.

In seventeenth-century salon circles as in contemporary urban centers, ef-feminacy is not a naturally occurring phenomenon, but is deliberately defined and staged. Scudéry's satirical sonnet like the numerous media re-ports about the metrosexual frame these figures in ways that underscore their departure from conventional masculinity. Of course, what is meant by "con-ventional masculinity" is vastly different in early modern France and twenty-first-century Western societies, and thus much of how effeminacy is defined and staged also differs in these two time periods. But in spite of these differ-ences, effeminacy remains a matter of perception, which is to say that it is defined first and foremost by those who, like Scudéry or critics of the metro-sexual, deride certain men and certain forms of masculine conduct and ap-pearance. This is not to deny that some men may deliberately endeavor to be effeminate, as Scudéry claims of his *pousseur de beaux sentiments* (and as is the case of certain gay men today, for instance). But in order for them to do so, they must themselves understand what that entails in the culture in which they live and in which effeminacy as a "code" has been predefined and widely accepted as such.

To say that effeminacy is defined first of all by those who distance themselves from it points to the multiple ways that it helps us to reflect on the broader constructions of masculinity. For effeminacy exposes what normative understandings of masculinity often attempt to repress or sublimate. Most fundamentally, effeminacy lays bare the relationality of masculinity, both with respect to women and to other men. As Pierre Bourdieu has pointed out, masculine domination requires the subjection not only of women but also of seemingly lesser forms of masculinity itself. Emphasizing, by negation, that dominant masculinity contrasts with both femininity and other forms of itself, effeminacy thus reveals the fundamentally constitutive divisions within normative masculinity. Seen from this perspective, effeminacy—along with femininity and other marginal masculine positions—is in fact crucial to any dominant masculine ideal. Effeminate masculinity must necessarily be evoked in order to give consistency and stability to its noneffeminate other. It must be evoked all the better to be rejected. But, of course, that process, by definition, can never be completely accomplished. The specter of effeminacy haunts the noneffeminate or "virile" ideal in order for this latter to exist. What this means, though, and what effeminacy further makes clear is that the attainment of a normative masculine status is the result of arduous cultural work.

In early modern France (as in many other periods), part of this work involved determining precisely what *was* and what was *not* effeminate. There was a broad consensus in this period about what constituted the effeminate man in his most satirical form. But there were other forms of masculinity, which I will be calling "soft" masculinities to distinguish them from their satirical counterpart, that could be considered effeminate—or *not* effeminate—depending on the perspective adopted. Just as effeminacy is always in the eye of the beholder, so too is soft masculinity. What some observers denounced as "effeminate" in the conduct of courtiers and male salon-goers, for instance, was not always perceived as such by others, and particularly by other members of the court and salons (although even in these venues there was not necessarily unanimity of opinion). And what was prized as refined or soft masculinity by some was derided as effeminate by others.

This chapter first examines how effeminacy was defined and used in early modern France and then explores the ambivalence between effeminacy and soft masculinity, which, I argue, is indicative of masculinity's conflicted relation to femininity in this and any period. Throughout the early modern period, treatises of courtliness and civility insisted that interacting with women made men graceful and refined, which is to say that it allowed men to acquire those qualities that (elite) women demonstrated "intuitively" and "naturally." As we saw in the previous chapter on honnête masculinity, although this commonplace at first glance valorizes women and certain prized "feminine" qualities, in the end it turns out to be something altogether different by enabling men to wrest the "civilizing" role from women. In the present chapter, I contend that the problem of effeminacy provides yet further confirmation of this interpretation of the "female principle," but from a different perspective. Focusing on the stakes of men's participation in the heterosocial settings of the salons, I demonstrate how effeminacy becomes an indictment of (what was perceived as) women's potentially dangerous influence on men and masculinity in general. The critique of effeminacy thus denounces not only what it casts as an excessively close resemblance to women, but also those "womanlike" qualities assumed by certain men. Effeminacy, in its satirical and moralistic modes, is an epiphenomenon of misogyny. Even in its "soft" ideal form, effeminacy turns out to be as much about dominating women and femininity as it is about dominating certain marginal men and forms of masculinity.

Signs of Effeminacy

In early modern Europe, there was a fairly broad consensus about the core traits that made a man effeminate from the satirical and moralistic perspectives. To be sure, not all representations necessarily include every element I discuss in what follows. But the composite portrait that can be sketched of effeminacy is a remarkably coherent one in which the various characteristics slide almost effortlessly from one to the next and in which one "sign" of effeminacy connotes multiple other signs. This is not to imply that effeminacy signified uniformly across differences of class, profession, or social situation, for instance. Yet at the core of early modern effeminacy is a set of signs that can be inflected in various ways.

There is no more fundamental principle—and sign—of the effeminate man than excess. In appearance, clothing, and manners, he always aims to be and he always invariably *is* "over the top." Of course, his most egregious error is to be found in his excessive similarity with women. But indissociably linked to excess is, of course, its opposite, lack. By displaying *excess* in his appearance, manners, or resemblance to women, he necessarily renders himself lacking in other vital ways. Above all, he shows himself to be incapable of the self-restraint and self-mastery that are the hallmarks of the gentleman and the honnête homme. What is at stake in effeminacy, then, is once again the ideal of the golden mean. If, as we saw in the previous chapter, honnêteté displayed the rewards to be gained from mastering the elusive nuances of the mean, effeminacy, on the opposite end of the spectrum, exposes (often flamboyantly) the ridicule, if not worse, of missing the mark, or more precisely of going beyond it. In seventeenth-century prescriptive conduct literature, the ideal of moderation inherited from a tradition extending back as far as Aristotle continues to be evoked, even if it has lost some of the prominence it had in the sixteenth century.[3] Thus, Nicolas Faret repeatedly urges his aspiring honnête homme to seek the middle path between, among other things, ignorance and erudition,[4] prodigality and avarice (44), insensitivity and volatility (68–69), obsequiousness and brashness (79), disinterest and overinterest in fashion (90–93). For Faret as for later theorists of civility and courtliness, the principle of the golden mean remained an obvious, if conventional touchstone. But no matter how self-evident, this principle had a crucial role in framing effeminacy, the signs of which all emanate from excess or its necessary corollary, lack.

Perhaps the most prominent of these signs are those with the interrelated semes of softness, weakness, and passivity. Few signifiers are as frequently used to designate effeminacy as *mou, mol,* and *mollesse,* especially at a time when neo-Stoicism provides a prominent ideal for masculinity.[5] At once moral, physical, and psychological, the notion of softness denoted both a lack, an inability to carry out the military and moral duties expected of men, but also an excess, an attention to all that distracts from the obligations of "hard" (or muscular and resolute) masculinity. Thus, on the education boys should receive, Pierre Charron states: "One must expel from him all softness and refinement in clothing, sleeping, drinking, eating. Raise him harshly with pain and toil; accustom him to heat, cold, wind, even to chance; strengthen and firm up his muscles and ligaments (as well as his soul) with labor and beyond that sadness. . . . All this promotes not only health, but also serious matters and public service."[6] If hardness ensures both physical and social health, as Charron asserts, softness, on the contrary, indicates a reversal of the gendered order of things. In Molière's *Les Femmes savantes,* it is the notion of *mollesse* that Ariste invokes when blaming his brother Chrysale for the "disorder" of his gynocentric household:

> N'avez-vous point de honte avec votre mollesse?
> Et se peut-il qu'un homme ait assez de foiblesse
> Pour laisser à sa femme un pouvoir absolu,
> Et n' oser attaquer ce qu'elle a résolu?
>
> (2.9.659–62)[7]

[Aren't you a bit ashamed to be so placid? / And can a man be quite so weak and flaccid / As to bow to his wife in word and deed / And never dare attack what she's decreed?][8]

Chrysale's weakness and passivity as both father and spouse—his *mollesse*—puts him in the feminine position and his wife in the more properly masculine role. As Chrysale's case shows, then, the consequences of *mollesse* are not simply individual, but also familial and social. Softness is the sign of all that is disorderly about effeminacy.

Mollesse and its associated semes are frequently tied to a penchant for pleasure that distracts a man from his obligations. And so writers of various persuasions warn against the dangers of *volupté* (intense or sensuous pleasure) in particular. Typical is what Nicolas Pasquier tells aspiring gentlemen: "Since in intense pleasure *(volupté)* resides the corruption of the body and the soul and since things dishonorable to do are not honorable to say, he must never allow himself to become enslaved to that cowardly, soft, and effeminate pleasure nor to bend under the force of his passions by fixing his eyes on reason."[9] That *volupté* is by definition "cowardly," "soft," and "effeminate" makes clear the risks it entails, especially for noble men, for whom military service was an expected duty of their rank. As Guillaume Colletet reminds a young prince:

> Grand prince, . . .
> Une langueur oisive est indigne de gloire,
> Et l'on n'a jamais veu qu'un prince efféminé
> Ait eu de verds lauriers le front environné.[10]

[Great prince, . . . / A leisurely languor is unworthy of glory, / And one has never seen an effeminate prince / Have his forehead encircled with green laurels.]

"Leisurely languor," the effect of pleasure, is incompatible with princely and more fundamentally masculine glory. It is yet another sign of effeminacy and its dangers.

If softness and pleasure primarily emphasize the passivity of effeminate men, many other signs emphasize their activity. Following logically from their inability to achieve the golden mean, they are passive when they should be active and active when they should be passive. Foremost among their active qualities is a flamboyant extravagance in everything they do, from choice of clothes to gestures to conversation. Such manifest effort given to self-presentation immediately becomes affectation, a fault roundly excoriated by theorists of courtliness and civility alike. Paraphrasing Castiglione's famous definition of *sprezzatura*, for instance, Nicolas Faret implores his honnête homme to "flee as if it were a dangerous precipice that miserable and importunate affectation that tarnishes and defiles the most beautiful things, and . . . employ everywhere a certain negligence that hides artifice,"[11] and then he immediately illustrates this point by denouncing "made-up women" *(les femmes fardées)* whose affectation and desire to appear beautiful "cause even our eyes to suffer when watching them and show clearly that the grace they study is a lesson that can only be learned by those who seem to want not to know it" (21). Citing "made-up women" as the prime example of affectation in a text written for men, Faret thus implicitly codes it as effeminate. Later in his treatise, when explaining how men should go about dressing so as to please women, Faret suggests that less attention to one's appearance is actually better than too much: "A more studied art is more harmful than helpful, and one often sees a man appear more enticing to the eyes of a group of Ladies, all tanned as he is and covered in sweat and dust after battle or hunting, than those men of wax *(hommes de cire)* who never dare to show themselves in the sun or approach the fire too closely for fear of melting" (93). Excessive concern about one's appearance underscores one's softness and weakness. And set against Faret's critique of the affectation of the "made-up women," the "men of wax" are clearly effeminate. In short, to be affected is to be womanlike, effeminate.

But to be affected is also to be self-satisfied and narcissistic, as the satirical portraits of so many seventeenth-century effeminates make abundantly clear. Trissotin and Vadius in *Les Femmes savantes* or Acaste and Clitandre in *Le Misanthrope* are among the best-known examples of this phenomenon. But writers of prescriptive texts also frequently equate affectation and narcissism with effeminacy. Writing at the end of the century, for instance, the Abbé de Bellegarde is mockingly incredulous of this phenomenon:

There is nothing more impertinent *(fat)* than a man who perpetually applauds his complexion, who is among the first to speak of it, who plays the role of the enticing and handsome man *(qui fait l'agréable et le beau)*, who wants others to praise him for his handsome figure and his beautiful teeth. Women who let themselves be taken in by this bait must be utterly stupid. How can they tolerate a man who has all the little mannerisms and all the affected ways of the *Précieuses*, whose clothing, air, speech, sentiments, actions have nothing of a man about them, about whom everything seems effeminate, the demeanor, the winking, the movements of his head, the tone of his voice?[12]

Berating both the men who take pleasure in appearing enticing and handsome *as well as* the women who are seduced by them, Bellegarde uses a term, *fat*, that becomes a leitmotiv for effeminacy in the second half of the seventeenth century and throughout the eighteenth century.[13] To be *fat* is to be stupid, impertinent, and self-satisfied. As Bellegarde makes clear, the impertinence of the self-applauding *beau* makes him—or at least *should* make him—an outcast on numerous counts. But at the root of his disorder is his effeminacy, which our *moraliste* quickly (and not surprisingly) uses to condemn the women seduced by the self-congratulating male avatar of the *précieuses*.

The narcissism that signifies effeminacy vaunts any number of self-perceived qualities, artistic, literary, and martial, among others. But representations of effeminacy attach particular importance to physical appearance, as the examples already cited demonstrate. The effeminate man in satirical texts is obsessed with his clothing (as we will see in a moment) but more generally with his own beauty. If Bellegarde equates such an obsession with femininity, to the point even of suggesting that *women* are responsible for it, what troubles many other observers is the explicitly visible self-consciousness betrayed by such an obsession. As Faret puts it, "A man who is overdressed is worse than another who is underdressed. This sort of diligence is only fitting among women, and a man is never handsome except when he believes he isn't."[14] For a man to be conscious of his beauty is to negate it, according to Faret, because he does not abide by the honnête homme's requisite modesty, but also because he resembles women. Implicitly, then, women have a tendency toward immodesty that men must avoid. What amounts to a call for (feigned or real) obliviousness exposes a discomfort with male beauty that could be interpreted in several different ways.[15] But it is this very discomfort that the effeminate man fails to make visible, and this lack is a telltale sign of resemblance to women.

An inappropriate comfort with one's beauty leads to an ostentatious self-display that is regularly mocked by observers. Most immediately exhibited and most readily observed are the clothes of the effeminate man, and it is his subservience to fashion that commentators highlight over and over. In a famous *caractère,* La Bruyère depicts the effeminate Iphis who goes to church sporting new shoes only to discover they are already *passé* and who then retreats to his room in shame for the rest of the day.[16] Appropriately named (Iphis is the cross-dressed heroine who falls in love with another woman, Iante, in one of Ovid's *Metamorphoses* and the subject of a 1637 play by Benserade),[17] La Bruyère's effeminate is obviously a victim of fashion; but in the misogynist logic of this *caractère,* this outcome is inevitable given his resemblance to women. After dwelling on all the ways that Iphis is indistinguishable from fashion-conscious women, La Bruyère ends with a sarcastic *pointe:* "It is also true that he wears breeches and a hat and that he has neither earrings nor a pearl necklace; consequently, I have not put him in the chapter on women."[18] The few signs of Iphis's masculinity amid what is otherwise his feminine demeanor make his enslavement to fashion all the more ridiculous, so the *moraliste* wants us to believe. Of course, other observers saw far more serious consequences of men's obsessive interest in fashion. In his diatribe against fashion in its multiple guises, Fitelieu denounces the threat such an interest poses for the king's army. Speaking to a generic fashion-conscious soldier, he intones: "The king does not need women in his army. He only wants soldiers like himself, and I am astounded that he allows you to approach him and that he gives you duties since you reek of woman."[19] But most preoccupying for Fitelieu and other commentators of his ilk is the moral depravity that is signified by the subservience to fashion: "[A] vain heart, as Saint Bernard says, manifests itself through clothes, and the vanity that possesses his soul shows itself through the superfluity one notices. Those exterior and fashionable ornaments portray for us an effeminate and evil mind, for if one had not abandoned the care one must have to enrich the soul with the virtues, one would not be devoted to decorating the body in that way" (355). Attention to the exterior self, the body, comes at the expense of the interior self, the soul. Adorning the soul rather than the body would keep men from becoming effeminate, Fitelieu contends. And yet, the body and its coverings remain the sign par excellence, be it for virtue or for vice.

Alongside sartorial display and the body, the narcissism and ostentatiousness of the effeminate man are also manifested in his use of language. Often portrayed as a chatterbox or a babbler, he typically spends his days running from one house to the next so he can "with his cold sweet nothings tire high

society," as Boileau quips about a galant homme.[20] A peripatetic victim of lo-
gorrhea, his *parole* is antithetical to (what is assumed to be) the naturally
refined elegance of women's speech. Instead, it is the linguistic equivalent of
affected mannerisms, and thus is characterized first and foremost by its self-
conscious ornamentation. The error of the typical man who attempts to sway
women, says the satirist Félix Juvenel de Carlincas, is to think that he must
"give a dazzling turn of phrase to things said."[21] Attempting to imitate the
style of novels and compiling collections of his own verse will only result in
proving his ignorance: "Little by little he will become a skilled man among
the coquettes, but at the same time he will pass for an ignoramus among
scholars and reasonable men" (223). Privileging form over content, his
speech is not only rhetorically deficient, it is also devoid of reason and substance. But, like his body and clothes, its form is deliberately ornate, "an
abundant language embellished and ornamented with assorted flowers," as
Pasquier puts it.[22] Still, however superficially pleasing this language appears
to be, it is ultimately motivated not by graciousness, but on the contrary by
maliciousness. Effeminate speech is shown to contradict its apparent objective, barely concealing the speaker's true intent. Molière gives us memorable
portrayals of this phenomenon in the famous scenes with marquis and *beaux
esprits* in *Le Misanthrope* and *Les Femmes savantes*.[23] At bottom, the effeminate man relies upon hypocrisy to achieve his ends, as Juvenel makes clear in
ironic advice he gives men who court coquettish women: "The galant who is
courting a coquette is allowed to say as many malicious things about others as
he wants. But he is not allowed to praise in the same way either in private or
in public. He must only consider the charms of other beauties so as to attribute them subtly to the coquette whose heart he wants to win."[24]

Softness, affectation, narcissism, ostentatiousness, and idiosyncratic
speech are all familiar "signs" of effeminacy to us today. However, from our
own vantage point, one particular and obvious characteristic would seem to
be missing from the portrait I have sketched up until now. Beginning in the
nineteenth century especially, effeminacy became virtually indissociable
from homosexuality such that a contemporary inventory of the signs of effeminacy would doubtless place same-sex attraction at the top of the list (and,
more frequently, assume that effeminacy is a "sign" of homosexuality). But
the close association of the two is not nearly so clear for early modern conceptions of effeminacy. Granted, there are specific instances in which allegations of effeminacy are conjoined with accusations of sodomy, specifically in
the pamphlet literature attacking Henri III and his mignons in the period

leading up to his assassination in 1589[25] and again, later, in some of the *mazarinades* that attack Cardinal Mazarin during the Fronde (1648–52).[26] There are also a few, rare occurrences of this conjunction in other, non-politically motivated texts, such as a dialogue by Jean-François Sarasin, in which Gilles Ménage is made to denounce the obsessive attention to self-display by salon-goers. They are, "Ménage" purports, "preoccupied, like women, with doing their hair and getting dressed, and with such an indecent sensuousness *(mollesse)* that they would leave us to wonder not only if they are men, but if they aren't looking for other men."[27] However, on the whole, the explicit association of effeminacy with homosexual desire is infrequent in seventeenth-century France. Instead, it is excessive heterosexual desire that is more often at issue, and this, as David Halperin has noted, since at least the ancient Greeks and Romans.[28] Still, if homosexual desire is not yet firmly conjoined with effeminacy in this period, *homosocial* desire certainly is. And effeminacy often evokes the ambiguous contiguity of the homosocial with the homosexual.

"Causes" of Effeminacy

If the signs of effeminacy were noted and glossed more frequently, its causes were still an object of concern in the early modern period. And if the signs were numerous, and, on the whole, widely accepted, the causes varied, depending on the perspective adopted. For Christian moralists, effeminacy was one of many possible outcomes of the sinful propensity toward pleasure, or more precisely "concupiscence," which amounted to a rejection of spiritual and social obligations. Thus, distinguishing three degrees of what he calls "mollitude" early in the century, the Franciscan theologian Jean Benedicti defines the first as "a weakness and laxity that is opposed to the virtue of perseverance, as if someone were so indolent and so effeminate that he neglected what is necessary for his salvation. It is a type of sin of laziness."[29] Of course, in such a general meaning, "mollitude" might theoretically apply to women as well as to men, but "mollitude" and its French derivative *mollesse* were far more frequently associated with effeminate men. Through the theological understanding of *mollesse*, effeminacy was frequently explained through its putative connection to pleasure. And, as such, it could only be avoided by repentance, penitence, and ultimately the gift of God's grace through salvation. The religious understanding of effeminacy was obviously part of a broader theological preoccupation with spirituality, which was undergoing a renewal under the auspices of post-Tridentine Catholicism.

In a different register, the most specific medical explanations for effeminacy in the seventeenth century were provided by Galenic humoral theory.[30] In France, the leading exponents of this theory, Jacques Ferrand and Marin Cureau de la Chambre, saw in (heterosexual) love an important cause of effeminacy. Under its influence, men, who were naturally disposed to be hot and dry, could literally become like women, who were ordinarily cold and wet. When afflicted with erotomania, men could become sad, pensive, taciturn, pale, thin, weary, haggard, insomniac, and they could be reduced to hallucinating, speaking haltingly and staring at all women, Ferrand asserted.[31] (For women the effect of love would often be the reverse: "Love has such power over us that it changes and metamorphoses women into men," making them grow hair on their faces and bodies, deepening their voices, and even rendering them physically courageous.)[32] But the most dramatically effeminizing effects could result from the ostensible remedy for erotomania: sexual intercourse. The physical union with a colder and wetter being could easily result in transforming a man into something more like a woman. The more frequent the contact, according to this theory, the more pronounced the symptoms. And ultimately, as Ian Moulton has summarized: "The consequences could be dire—weakness, loss of physical strength, loss of rational control. And if a man engaged in such practices often enough, his humoral balance could be permanently altered—he could become moist and cold himself: he would be effeminate."[33] Moulton further observes that this take on sexual contact with women put men in something of a double bind. The physical possession of women was considered to be a natural and even necessary role for men, and yet that very act had the real potential to weaken—to effeminize—them.[34] Mark Breitenberg has noted the deep paradox in the humoral explanation of male (hetero)sexual desire:

> [I]f the generation of semen (heated blood) is the most quintessentially masculine moment, it is also, finally, just a moment. Thus ejaculation represents the supreme moment of masculine disempowerment *and* vulnerability—a literal and figurative "emptying out" of the masculine principle. Put simply, masculine erotic desire generates the material of masculinity but also destroys it. Orgasm threatens masculine agency and self-control in part because it represents a "feminine" inability to regulate the flow of one's fluids: a struggle represented in the double entendre senses of "will" as volition and desire.[35]

But this paradox might also be considered an ideological contradiction within the Galenic understanding of masculinity. On the one hand, men are presumed to be superior to women because of the predominance of hot and dry humors. On the other hand, they are extraordinarily vulnerable to women and specifically to their cold and wet humors. Thus, women, or more precisely their bodies, hold the upper hand in determining if men will be men in the properly physiological and humoral sense. Men are supposedly endowed with superior physical and mental prowess, and yet women possess a power that is no less considerable. Men are both strong and weak, as are women. The risk of effeminacy brings to the fore the very tenuous superiority of men and highlights their inevitably fraught connection to women within the humoral theory of the body.

In other secular, but nonmedical explanations of effeminacy, women are also made to bear the brunt of the blame. Although it is difficult to assess whether humoralist theory may have influenced thinking on this point, it is widely assumed in the early modern period (and indeed well before) that heterosexual love and even frequent contact with women was effeminizing. When Rousseau quipped that "women make us women," he was reiterating (albeit within his own perspective on "civilized" culture) a widely and long-held commonplace about the pernicious effects women had on the attainment and retention of masculine identity.[36] The clearest occurrences of this commonplace are found in texts that target young men who, while courting women, go to extraordinary lengths to make themselves pleasing to them. As the predictably vitriolic Fitelieu describes the scene: "You see those poor effeminate men on two knees wooing those immodest women, feeling themselves fortunate to be able to serve them and sacrificing their wealth and scruples at their feet. They cannot be satisfied by kissing two ornate fingers of those putrid corpses and calling them their 'dear heart' even though they are their executioners and punishment. They are caught in these traps and probably can never get out except to go to the devil."[37] Women's tyrannical power affects all aspects of their suitors' lives, thoughts, and being. As Juvenel contends: "They are not content to become the mistresses of their wealth and their freedom and to decide the course of their lives; they work to subject to their power the reason of their suitors, those miserable slaves who are not permitted to call a thing good or bad if it is not approved or disapproved by these coquettes."[38] The consequences, he explains, are disastrous not only individually but also collectively: "It is the coquette, boldly deciding what is good and beautiful, who engages men into this dangerous conduct and often obliges them to abandon honorable professions and tasks in order to follow her impulses and obey her whim" (227–28). In a less overtly misogynist vein, René Le Pays nonetheless reiterates the commonplace fear that love renders men inapt for official duties. In his "Dialogue de l'Amour et de la Raison" (Dialogue of Love and Reason), Reason tells Love: "You are an impulsive youth who strikes without realizing what you are doing, who considers neither honor, nor duty, nor justice, and you make yourself enemies of everything that opposes your pleasures."[39]

Other explanations did not render women so directly responsible for effeminacy; and yet women's influence on culture is nonetheless called into question, if only indirectly. Novels, plays, operas, songs, and other art forms that focused on love and that were championed by women were from time to time attacked for their supposedly effeminizing effects.[40] One of the best-known examples of these attacks is Boileau's "Dialogue des héros de roman" (Dialogue of the Heroes of Novels), a frontal assault on the seventeenth-century novel and its supposedly passive heroes and heroines. The dialogue foregrounds Pluto's growing frustration as he calls upon historical conquerors to defend Hades, only to discover that they are incapacitated by lovesickness and unable to think or speak of anything else. They are, as Diogenes tells Pluto, "pretty . . . I've never seen anything so dashing *(dameret)* and galant."[41] And when Pluto asks Cyrus to go into battle, the erstwhile conqueror of the Medes responds, sighing, that he must instead listen to the story of Aglatidas and Amestris, two lovers in Georges and Madeleine de Scudéry's *Artamène ou le Grand Cyrus* (1649–53). Of all the characters in this dialogue, though, one in particular is singled out for special scrutiny. Sapho, the pseudonym of Madeleine de Scudéry, is described as being "the craziest of all of them" and having "ruined all of the others."[42] Making Scudéry responsible for a supposedly ridiculous literary genre, Boileau specifically highlights the effeminizing effects of her work. Her novel *Clélie* (1654–60), he says in the preface to the dialogue, "represents all the heroes of the early Roman Republic . . . occupied only with tracing geographical maps of love, proposing galant games and enigmas for each other, in a word, doing everything that is the opposite of the heroic character and gravity of those first Romans" (9–10). Aiming to discredit the novel as much as Scudéry herself, Boileau's satire does not explicitly detail the genre's effects on its readers.[43] Still, the perceived effeminization of its heroes was clearly cause for concern—and ridicule—for him, and the fact that the novel was championed by women in this period certainly did nothing to allay those concerns, especially given Boileau's misogynistic stance in other writings. But a basic premise of the "Dialogue des héros de roman" is that, whether through personal interaction or representation, love and the entanglements with women it provokes present a real risk of effeminacy.

Once again, then, effeminacy exposes fundamental contradictions within early modern ideologies of gender. That heroes of ancient Greece and Rome could be so easily reduced to weakness and passivity proves the imperious power of women, especially through the love they inspire.[44] Even when mediated through representation, the guiles of women expose the weakness to which men only too readily fall victim. The effeminate man is hardly exempted from ridicule; and yet Boileau like so many others in this period and beyond is quick to shift the focus and to put the blame on women. Men's virility would be indomitable and ubiquitous . . . were it not for the power of women.

Effeminacy and the Court

As a satirical construction, effeminacy was (and is) used in many different contexts and against men of a variety of sociocultural backgrounds. As we have already begun to see, however, two particular contexts and the masculine figures associated with them dominated the seventeenth-century discourse of effeminacy: the court and the salon, and the courtier and the salon man. This is not to imply by any means that the boundaries between the two venues were impermeable. Courtiers could be salon men as well (although not all were, of course, nor were all salon men courtiers). The terms used to designate effeminacy (along with other traits, to be sure) often apply to both figures. If *marjolet, marquis, mignon, muguet,* and *plumet* were employed more often for courtiers, many others designate men irrespective of their affiliation with court, such as *Adonis, beau fils, blondin, coquet, dameret, damoiseau, délicat, doucet, galant, galant de profession, gentil, godelureau,* and *précieux.*[45] But the distinction between the two contexts and their respective masculine "roles" is useful when considering the genealogies of effeminacy in early modern France. Since court culture had existed long before salons were formed, attacks on the effeminacy of courtiers can be seen as the direct predecessor of those on male salon-goers. In part, the effeminacy of the salon man was a recycling of an image already used against courtiers. But there are important differences between the two as well, and a heuristic distinction between the court and the salon will help us to gauge these.

Attacks on the effeminacy of court culture have a long history, going back at least to the Middle Ages. Raoul Glaber's *Chroniques* note the effeminate behavior of troubadours and courtiers in eleventh-century France. And in the twelfth-century England, John of Salisbury's *Policraticus* often denounces courtiers past and contemporary, whose immoderate indulgence in court entertainment, culinary and sexual pleasure, and dress are branded as "effeminate" and impediments to the fulfillment of moral and political duties.[46] In no way, then, does the early modern period "invent" the attack on effeminate courtiers. Many of the complaints about courtiers in the eleventh century, for instance, are identical to those in the sixteenth century, at least on the surface of things: complaints about womanlike clothing, jewelry, makeup, perfume; criticisms about court entertainment, poetry, music; and especially accusations that such pleasures detract from the divinely ordained duties of the nobility. This said, attacks on the effeminate courtier were significantly reinvigorated across Europe by the appearance in 1520 of Castiglione's immensely popular, but also controversial *Book of the Courtier*. From the outset, Castiglione juxtaposes his ideal courtier against an effeminate extreme. Thus, the count prescribes: "I don't want him to appear soft and feminine as so many try to do" before concluding of these womenlike courtiers that "since Nature has not in fact made them the ladies they want to seem and be, they should be treated not as honest women but as common whores and be driven out from all gentlemanly society, let alone the Courts of great lords."[47] The courtier envisioned by the count is both "neither too small nor too big," able to master all traditional physical games of court life and at the same time able to "imbue with grace his movements, his gestures, his way of doing things and in short, his every action" (65). Both "manly and graceful" (61), Castiglione's ideal courtier eschews extremes and follows a middle path that is only open to a chosen few. In the political realm, the corollary principles of temperance and accommodation allow him to influence and even mold the prince whom he serves. Attempting to win over the prince's trust and confidence, the courtier puts himself in a seemingly subservient position all the better to assert his virtuous strength.[48]

The nuances of the graceful middle path and especially the subservience to the prince were viewed with much suspicion and often branded as "effeminate" in sixteenth-century France.[49] Motivated by a general resentment of Italian influence, numerous writers assailed Castiglione's ideal for its emphasis on the courtier's submission and its putative moral ambiguity.[50] Within such attacks, effeminacy became one leitmotiv among others to demonstrate the excesses to which this conception of the courtier would supposedly lead. He could be reduced to impotence on the battlefield; and thus, in his *L'Esperon de discipline* (The Spur of Discipline, 1532), Antoine Du Saix claims that the French courtier of his day, far from being willing to endure hardships such as sleeping with his armor on, as Alexander did,

> se desguise & transforme,
> Et tellement à son plaisir survient,
> Que qui est homme, en brief, femme il devient.[51]

[disguises and transforms himself, / Sustains his pleasure so much / That he who is a man, in time, becomes a woman.]

All the attention the courtier gives to love would cause him to abandon his manly virtues and preoccupy himself with feminine *mignardises,* as Philibert de Vienne calls them in *Le Philosophe de court* (The Court Philosopher, 1547), opining that "there is nothing less fitting for a man than not being a man."[52] During the reign of Henri III, enemies of the king inherited and amplified what were by then commonplaces of the anticourtier discourse, and the charge of effeminacy hit its shrillest pitch yet. In their portraits of Henri III and his favorites as hermaphrodites and sodomites, polemicists were motivated by a myriad of religious and political concerns. But shared widely was an anxiety about the new ideals of the courtly aristocracy, who prized artistic, musical, literary, and other decidedly nonmartial pursuits. Even this very group of courtiers was disquieted, according to Michael Wintroub, "[F]or the ideals through which it sought to valorize itself were closely associated with womanly pursuits. It therefore sought to deflect these associations by redirecting them at the courts of which they were a part and at the king whom they served."[53] By depicting Henri III as a "woman king or man queen" *(roy femme ou homme Reyne)* and his favorites as sexually ambiguous *mignons,* the new courtly aristocracy of late sixteenth-century France seemed to be militating against suspicions of effeminacy in addition to attacking royal policy per se. It found itself in a sort of double bind: even as this aristocracy adopted a "softer" masculine ideal emanating from "feminine" courtly culture, it resisted the charge of effeminacy by projecting it onto the king. It attempted to fashion itself as a moderate but nonetheless virile alternative to an effeminate extreme, all the better to keep from being perceived as indistinguishable from that extreme. Like Castiglione, this new courtly elite sought to find a middle way between the traditional feudal ideal and the caricature of the effete courtier.

In time, this moderate ideal became the dominant model for the masculine courtly aristocracy. Unlike the sixteenth century, the seventeenth century embraced Castiglione fully, although more or less silently. Faret's *L'Honnête homme ou l'art de plaire à la cour*, the century's most popular and most influential treatise on masculine courtliness, relies heavily on *The Book of the Courtier*, lifting entire passages and paraphrasing many others. The popularity of Faret's text reveals just how mainstream the ideals of his Italian precursor had become (and, arguably, were quickly becoming even in the second half of the preceding century). No longer would the suspicion of effeminacy automatically linger over the courtier as it had during the reign of Henri III. To be sure, effeminacy was still a risk for him, as we have already seen. All in all, though, Faret places much greater emphasis on teaching his honnête homme how to please women through his appearance and much less on warning him about the excesses that lead to effeminacy. Faret's approach is emblematic of the evolution toward a softer courtier ideal during the reign of Louis XIII and, indeed, much of the century.[54] If the figure of the effeminate courtier appears regularly in the satirical literature during the first half of the century, overall it is less frequent and less virulent than before. And in prescriptive literature after Faret, effeminacy becomes a much lesser preoccupation than it had been in the anticourtier literature of the sixteenth century. It is not insignificant that Antoine de Courtin's *Nouveau traité de la civilité qui se pratique en France parmi les honnêtes gens* (first edition, 1671), a treatise with broad popularity over and beyond the court, makes virtually no allusion to effeminacy even as it continues to rely upon the keystone principle of moderation.

However we might account for the less explicit reliance upon effeminacy by the time of Courtin's treatise, the important point is that the softer courtier ideal had garnered a fairly wide consensus. Much of the advice given by Faret (and reformulated from Castiglione in particular) about the need to frequent women and to please them in all one says and does becomes commonplace in similar treatises thereafter, for instance.[55] Robert Muchembled more or less follows Nobert Elias's thesis about the curialization of the warrior nobility in the early modern period and identifies the first third of the seventeenth century as the pivotal moment in this process.[56] With the urbanization of the courtly elite and their exposure to the Counter-Reformation religious fervor, male aristocrats adopted an ideal of conduct that contested the primacy of the feudal warrior ethos and promoted instead a less aggressive form of masculinity. Whether or not male aristocrats were actually any less physically violent than they had been before this time is a point of debate.[57] But in prescriptive literature and other modes of representation the dominant *model* for elite masculinity indeed became less aggressive, on the surface at least, and more "feminized" in the sense of being more attentive to the sociocultural influence of women.[58] Evidence of this change can be found in the shift away from defining nobility as a profession (feudal warrior) and toward birth and "culture."[59] But even those nobles who continued to bear arms attested to the more general change in attitudes about what it meant to be an aristocratic man by attempting to preserve aspects of court life, such as fine dining, dancing, and reading, while on military campaigns.[60] Granted, there were many competing models, notably for bourgeois, robe, and sword publics; yet they all converged around the value of an urbane refinement derived from courtly ideals that promoted subservience to women and the monarch alike. And, in the wake of Faret's treatise, the courtier lost ground to the vaguer, less socially specific ideal of the honnête homme,[61] whose reliance on and appropriation of women's influence we have already seen.

At first blush, the evolution I have been describing might be considered to be part of what has often referred to as the "emasculation" of the nobility, particularly after 1661, when Louis XIV assumed power. However, this notion, perpetuated to a certain extent by Elias's otherwise useful concept of the "civilizing process" and its emphasis on the internalization of external constraints, has been widely critiqued.[62] If it is true that the seventeenth century witnessed a general centralization of power in the hands of the monarch, it is also true that this process was only made possible by the development of a system of incentives for nobles who worked under the king. Far from "emasculating" the nobility, then, the so-called absolutist monarchy of Louis XIII and his son Louis XIV developed new ways of conceiving and benefiting from aristocratic identity. These newly defined benefits came at the price of a certain traditional autonomy, to be sure; but to speak of "emasculation" is to adopt a highly reductive and misleading understanding of the aristocracy's role in the monarchical regime during this period. What on the face of things would appear to be its utter subservience to the king was in fact a means by which it preserved a certain number of its own rights and privileges. Accordingly, it would be more than a little problematic to attempt to connect the evolving masculine ideals of the courtier or the honnête homme to the supposed "emasculation" of the courtly elite. Instead, as I will be arguing, attempts to reduce aggressivity and to project a softer image within these ideals are anything but an abdication of patriarchal power. In fact, it would be possible to speak of a homology between the *appearance* of political subservience of the aristocracy and the soft or "effeminate" masculinity of the courtier and the honnête homme. In both cases, what is at first glance submission and even passivity often masks—and *is*—a new form of dominance and activity.

Yet, the courtiers' relationship to the monarch was more than one of political subservience. After 1661, especially, the supreme model of polite masculinity was Louis XIV himself, and this according to contemporaries (including those, such as Saint-Simon, who were restrained in their praise of
him).[63] All the while respecting the king's authority and his exceptional status, courtiers were expected to take their cue from him in general matters of
conduct, fashion, and protocol. Of course, Louis XIV was not the first to dictate such emulation from nobles at court, and indeed in the abstract this was a
commonplace of "absolutist" political philosophy, which made the king the
model for male and paternal authority generally.[64] And before Louis XIV,
Henri III had imposed a more codified system of conduct by courtiers with
himself at the pinnacle.[65] Louis XIV's reign marked a return to a more strictly
regulated code of etiquette and protocol, but, significantly, it also met with
far greater success than his predecessor's attempts. Specifically, the model of
masculinity that Louis XIV sought to project was one of contrasts: refined
and elegant in manners, yet strong and forceful in politics and war.[66] To polish this image even further and to ensure the king's virile credentials, his
brother, Philippe, was said to have been deliberately cast as effeminate. Alluding to his childhood friendship with Philippe, the Abbé de Choisy claims
that "his waistcoat was taken off so he could put on women's coats and skirts;
and all this was done by order of the cardinal, who wanted to make him effeminate, fearing that he might harm the king, as Gaston had done to Louis
XIII."[67] Whether or not Mazarin or others actually ordered or intended that
Philippe be treated in this way is unclear.[68] But what is not in dispute is that
royal propaganda and wide public perception saw in the king and his brother
two contrasting models, a right way and a wrong way to embody refined
masculinity. In Louis, courtiers were to perceive refined virility, but in
Philippe effeminate excess.[69]

To emulate the king with the required dose of subservience, courtiers
were enjoined to model their conduct on that of a suitor courting his beloved.
In *The Book of the Courtier*, for instance, Ottaviano famously draws just this
parallel in his discussion of the courtier's obligations toward his prince.[70] And
yet the two situations were also understood to be inextricably linked. As
Gerzan puts it in his 1646 treatise, *La Conduite du courtisan* (The Conduct of
the Courtier): "I believe true the maxim of Henri III, king of France, 'whoever is unfaithful to his mistress is also unfaithful to his master.'"[71] Infidelity
to one's beloved equals infidelity to one's prince and, implicitly, being faithful to one's mistress proves that one is faithful to the king. That such a maxim
is attributed to Henri III, widely portrayed as effeminate during his reign,

and that it is taken seriously by Gerzan, are testaments to the lessening of anxiety about "soft" courtly masculinity in mid-seventeenth-century France. At the same time, it indicates how crucial the courtier's connection to women at court has become by this period. Gerzan cites Henri III's maxim in the middle of a passage in which he insists upon the pivotal role women play for any man hoping to succeed at court.[72] So important are they, Gerzan affirms, that even the courtier who is not inclined to love should pretend he is anyway "because it is from *them* that one learns to be an *honnête homme*, and whoever is not in the good graces of this *sex* cannot be in those of the *other sex*."[73]

Getting along well with women has other advantages too, though. In advice that some of the courtiers in *La Princesse de Clèves* would have done well to heed, Gerzan explains that "living well" with one's beloved gains the respect of her cabal of female friends and even the grudging esteem of their enemies. Furthermore, such conduct puts the courtier on the right side of the master/prince, who will not suspect him of trying to steal his own love interests, "misfortune that caused the fall of an infinite number of great favorites" (45); it provides the courtier with a ready-made excuse for refusing inopportune or unwanted invitations; and it makes him a virtuous example for others to follow (46). In sum, Gerzan notes, "There are so many advantages to this sort of life that one could write entire volumes about it" (46). "This sort of life"—courting women and negotiating their cabals, finding one's way in the world of women at court—turns out to be a key to the courtier's success. If it is a *key*, though, it is precisely because it has countless advantages for him. It is because it puts him in a position of strength even as he puts himself in a position of apparent subservience.

EFFEMINACY AND THE SALONS

But it was not only at court that men were enjoined to bow to the authority of women. The salons that began to flourish early in the century were also places where men were to put aside their real-world dominance and allow women a measure of control over them, at least ostensibly. As the prominence of the salons became clear to observers, treatises addressed to courtiers explicitly encouraged them to seek out the company of women away from court in the *assemblées, alcôves, cercles, réduits,* and *ruelles* (as salons were called in the seventeenth century) of the city.[74] Caillières says of the "*ruelles* of noble Ladies" that "their approbation often contributes to our good fortune, and I believe it is necessary for an honnête homme to come off well in their conversation."[75] Caillières's statement makes clear the instrumental value of frequenting the salons. Success at court obligated men to seek out the company of women beyond the walls of the king's palace. Thus, abiding by the conventions of salon interactions—and notably adopting a stance of submission toward the hostess—had very real benefits for the aspiring courtier. From women he would learn not only *la bienséance* but more broadly "knowledge of society" *(la science du monde)*, Caillières assures his readers.[76] And armed with these qualities, he would be all the better prepared to return to court.

But the importance of the salons goes far beyond serving as an informal training ground for men aspiring to make an entrée on the stage of the court. As work by both historians and literary critics over the past thirty years has demonstrated, the seventeenth-century salons were crucial venues for a fairly broad cross-section of women, providing them with access to a wide range of cultural production (art, literature, music, philosophy, and scientific work) otherwise denied to them, and giving them opportunities to engage in this production for themselves.[77] Indeed, from within the salons, women were able to contribute to what Joan DeJean has called "salon writing"—poetry, novels, criticism (among other things)—that made its way into print and onto the public stage.[78] Through these settings, they played a crucial role in the development of *mondain* literary criticism, as Faith Beasley has shown.[79] And several of the *assemblées, alcôves, cercles, réduits,* and *ruelles* of the period opened the doors of philosophy for them (albeit only partially, according to Erica Harth). Broadly speaking, then, there is no question that the salons were a strategic means by which women not only gained access to culture but also influenced it, resulting in what Alain Génetiot has called "a feminization of society and taste,"[80] if by "feminization" we mean the wide diffusion and acceptance of aesthetic and social values associated at the time with women, whether or not women actually created or promoted them.

Ironically, though, much of the groundbreaking work that has uncovered and revalorized women's roles and influence in and through the salons has tended to obscure the roles and influence that men too had in and through these venues. But the *assemblées, alcôves, cercles, réduits,* and *ruelles* were by definition places where women *and* men would interact, sites for heterosocial sociability.[81] Failing to account adequately for the presence of men, salon masculinity, and the salons' relation to male-only institutions such as the *académies* skews our understanding of the meanings of salon life for women and their places within broader seventeenth-century society.[82] Even recent work that has resisted the more euphoric strain of some scholarship on women and the salons ends up begging the question about men's participation.[83] Granted, a broad history of seventeenth-century salons and the places of both women *and* men within them is obviously beyond the scope of my discussion here. Instead, my contention is that salon men and the specter of effeminacy that often surrounded them are key pieces of the puzzle for that yet-to-be-written history.

What roles, then, did men play in the salons of seventeenth-century France? The answer to this question could vary from *ruelle* to *ruelle,* and it is difficult to make blanket assertions. At the beginning of the century, for instance, three prominent Parisian salons (those of Madame d'Auchy, Madame des Loges, and the Marquise de Rambouillet) each had a distinct focus, with differing expectations for conduct by the men who frequented them: d'Auchy's aspiring to serious philosophical and literary reflection, des Loges's balancing such reflection with sociable entertainment, and Rambouillet's, by comparison, inclining more toward entertainment.[84] In sum, seventeenth-century salons were not homogeneous and, consequently, did not uniformly promote the same sort of interaction among participants, and specifically between women and men.[85] Surviving documentation frequently confirms this point. For instance, the lighthearted banter using courtship metaphors found in the partial record of Scudéry's salon, the *Chroniques du Samedi,* bears little resemblance to the far more restrained and austere character of the correspondence emanating from Sablé's salon adjoining the walls of Port-Royal.[86]

Still, one common principle cut across all the differences in tone and subject matter of the conversations in various types of salons: while all participants were indebted to the hostess and were constantly to display their respect for her, men assumed a qualitatively heavier debt than women. It was on the condition of submitting themselves to the agenda (at least ostensibly) set by the hostess and her female friends that men would be allowed admission into their company. While it is true that salon interaction was considered to be looser and freer than that at court, men recognized that very specific "rules" applied to them. Writing to Godeau, a fellow male participant in Rambouillet's salon, Chapelain complains: "I know from experience that in the company you find yourself in one cannot do as one pleases . . . its orders are absolute, if not to say tyrannical."[87] But such a statement should not cause us to forget that men enjoyed many freedoms unavailable to their female counterparts in the salons. Most notably, as Erica Harth reminds us, they could attend male-only *cabinets* or even the *cabarets*, where they could set their own literary and intellectual agenda without abiding by the conventions of mixed-gender conversation.[88]

Given these options, it might seem strange that so many men willingly, even enthusiastically chose to accept the constraints of salon interaction. However, even though other motivations could also intervene, the salon held an appeal that was unparalleled by other settings that derived from conversation, which, as Harth describes it, "served as both a social equalizer for the participants and a badge of superiority vis-à-vis the uninvited."[89] It is well known that salon settings allowed men and women of different social ranks to mingle and, within certain limits, to efface hierarchical distinctions among themselves. Carolyn Lougee's study of the salons argues that such intermingling contributed to "misalliances," marriages of noble and nonnoble partners. For a less than financially secure nobleman, the prospect of finding a wealthy *roturière* to marry was conceivably a strong incentive to frequent the *alcôves, assemblées, cercles, réduits,* and *ruelles* of the capital. And conversely, the possibility of marrying into nobility could have attracted well-appointed *bourgeoises*. This said, the precise role of the salons in facilitating these matches is difficult to assess.[90] Far more visible is what Pierre Bourdieu would call the "distinction" that was to be gained by rubbing elbows with the cultural and political power brokers within the salons, especially for those of lesser social status. Thanks to the salons' practice of exclusive self-enclosure whereby the assembled *ruelle* cut itself off from the outside world, participants constituted themselves as elites who were removed (for the time of salon conversation at least) from the hierarchies and the contingencies of everyday society.[91] It was in this way that salons could encompass both real-world and would-be elites, seemingly erasing most signs of difference in social rank. It was also in this way that the real-world strictures of gender difference could be muted or disguised, although certainly not abolished. Specifically, women could have a voice that, outside the salon, would most likely have been denied to them. And they could have a semblance of authority over men that would most surely have eluded them outside the protected spaces of the salons.

For men to be able to gain admission into these feminocentric spaces in the first place required specific qualities, especially within the salons that dominated the period 1630–60. In his *Grand dictionnaire des précieuses* (1661), an ambiguous work that purports to chronicle salon-life while often satirizing it as well, Baudeau de Somaize lists numerous men who attended salons (he calls them *alcôvistes*), and he repeatedly indicates that they were admired by women because of their ability to be witty and to write verse, whether or not they had a love interest at stake. Of the otherwise fairly inconspicuous Abbé du Buisson (given the pseudonym "Barsinian"), Somaize writes that he is "a gentleman who is as witty as one can be; he writes verse with great ease."[92] These two qualities (being witty and writing verse) point to the importance of both conversation and writing for salon men. Within the discursive spaces of the *ruelles*, writing could be both a prelude to conversation and its trace. But either way it was a crucial skill. If Somaize's account is to be trusted (and a review of midcentury poetry collections suggests that it probably is, on this point at least), a great many salon men dabbled in poetry, whether to woo a specific woman or to make an impression on the entire group.[93] And, as is widely known, men who had more serious ambitions within the emerging literary field used the salons as staging grounds for their work and their careers.[94] Of course, the prominence of male writers within these venues is a well-known fact, even if it is has remained on the whole underanalyzed in recent feminist scholarship. Alongside the hostess, one or several writers typically helped to give a *ruelle* its cachet: Malherbe and later d'Aubignac in d'Auchy's salon, Balzac and Voiture in Rambouillet's, Pellisson, Ménage, and Sarasin in Scudéry's, La Fontaine in La Sablière's, La Rochefoucauld in Sablé's, and so on.[95] This is not to downplay the writing of several of the hostesses themselves—such as that by Scudéry and Sablé, for instance—but rather to emphasize that, even in the period, salons were identified by the male writers who frequented them *as well as* their hostesses.

In almost every instance, the relationship between the male writer(s) and the hostess was a complicated and fundamentally ambivalent one. In accordance with the conditions of admission into the salon, the male writer paid homage to the hostess and devoted himself to her "service," which in some instances meant playing a supporting role for her own writing. At the same time, however—and Scudéry's example notwithstanding—the hostess derived much of her cultural authority from the writer(s) she assembled, with the risk of being overshadowed by men intent on making their mark beyond the walls of the salon. At best, the relationship between the salon hostess and her favored male writer was a symbiotic one in which he provided her with a cultural capital that had been denied her because of her gender and that allowed her to make a mark all her own, through her reputation in *mondain* circles or through her own writing.[96] At worst, the hostess (and other salon women besides) found herself co-opted or pressured to take sides in often nasty disputes among rival male writers (such as those between Godeau and Voiture or Chavaroche and Voiture in Rambouillet's salon or between Conrart and Pellisson or Chapelain and Ménage in Scudéry's entourage).[97] To be sure, it was possible for the salon woman to successfully negotiate such conflicts as well as the constraints placed on her access to the public sphere and on her interactions within the *ruelles*. But such an outcome meant coming out from under the shadows of the male writer(s) with whom she conversed, exchanged poetry or other writings, and perhaps even collaborated. It is important to keep in mind that this was not an easy or straightforward task for salon women, which makes those who succeeded in doing so all the more remarkable.

For the male writer, the ambiguities and stakes of his relationship with the hostess and other salon women were quite different. Gaining the admiration of respected *salonnières* (salon women)[98] increasingly became an obligatory step in a writer's attempt to secure a position in the literary field of seventeenth-century France. To do so meant not only playing by all the rules of salon interaction with women (including the profession of subservience to female authority and "feminine" taste) but also and simultaneously vying for the attention of these women, parrying the blows of other male writers within the salons and finding respect within all-male venues. The male writer's relationship to the hostess and other salon women was only one part of his professional trajectory, but it was a crucial part and one that had to be carefully weighed against his relationships with other men both inside and outside the *ruelles*.[99] Of course, integral to this balancing act was the male writer's—and indeed any salon man's—appropriation of the "femininocentric" culture of salon interactions. Conforming to the rules of comportment and adopting as one's own the values defined by (or attributed to) the *salonnières* potentially had very tangible benefits for him. But in many salons it also had very real risks, not least among which was the perception of effeminacy.[100]

In the entry devoted to "Valère" (Voiture) in his *Grand dictionnaire des précieuses*, Somaize touches on some of the ambiguities that surrounded salon men. After praising the success Voiture's works had had with women (and specifically those he terms "précieuses"), the self-appointed chronicler of midcentury salon life lists the reasons men frequent the *ruelles:*

> For men, it is an absolute truth that there are none among those I have spoken of who are not inseparable from the *précieuses* because they are of the same sentiments or because they speak as they do or because they love them and make a public spectacle of galanterie or else because they owe them the esteem they have in society.[101]

Referring to the men he has listed in his dictionary, Somaize mentions not one single, but a variety of motivations for their participation in the salons. Whether because of feelings, language, love interests, or reputation, what is common to all of them, in spite of these differences, is the fact of being "inseparable from the *précieuses*." Even though Somaize does not explicitly encode his description as satirical, it would not be difficult to read it in this way and thus to see these men's inseparability as a sign of their indeterminate or unstable masculinity. Those observers not favorably inclined toward salon culture would certainly have construed this inseparability as a failure to fulfill expected duties of the masculine sphere. And this is precisely what some of them did. Writing in 1671, Chalesme warns his intended male readers that devoting too much time to women's conversation is a "a sort of interaction that gives more reason for fear than hope."[102] "Discussion with Ladies must only be regarded as a pleasant amusement or a school for politeness," Chalesme asserts. "A man who devotes his whole life to it would quickly be scorned even by the people he saw assiduously. What else could be the result of his greatest efforts than knowing how to choose a wig or a handkerchief? ... Going from *ruelle* to *ruelle* with no other intent than to tell and hear silly jokes is a pitiful life" (200–201). The peripatetic salon-goer, obsessed with little else than women's "silly jokes" or his own "individual love affair," is at great risk of becoming a laughingstock of the very people he seeks to please. "The people who make up the *assemblée* almost never fail to cast their eyes on him so as to have something about his gaze and his countenance to smirk at among themselves" (202). Still, Chalesme insists, frequenting "the Ladies" is useful, even necessary for the aspiring honnête homme. He simply has to go about things differently, avoiding the excesses of what other writers term the *galant de profession* and, especially, relying on the advice of other men. And so, "perhaps he could share his opinion about a madrigal or even a play provided that he had heard a man who was more an expert than himself talk about them" (201). In other words, he may engage in the sort of prototypical salon conversation promoted by and pleasing to women on condition that he buttress his opinions not on those of women, but rather those of other men. To avoid the ridicule that results from the company of women, he must seek out the company of men, all the better to succeed in the company of women. If the *ruelle* is indeed a "school for politeness," it seems that Chalesme prefers that his young honnête homme be taught not by a salon woman, but by another man.

Observers whose intent was more satirical than prescriptive delighted in underscoring the ridiculous excesses to which male salon denizens supposedly fell victim. Writing to Mme de Brégy in 1656, Queen Christina of Sweden expresses impatience and indignation at the frivolity of French men, who perform linguistic and corporeal pirouettes for women instead of distinguishing themselves on the battlefield:

> Most Frenchmen are better able to make graceful pirouettes and be dazzling with the belles than to distinguish themselves on the fields of Mars or in the honor of their fatherland. I have seen only a few men here who inspire respect and admiration. All the others seemed to me to be jesters, frivolous, crazy. This is a people of pretty dolls whom one must see often so as to laugh at them and make them one's playthings. Men who spend their lives chatting, making pirouettes and reverences, and who perfume themselves from daybreak to sundown.[103]

Neglecting their country's interest for their own, and privileging the superficial, the corporeal, and the sensorial (over the substantive and the reasonable, one presumes), the Frenchmen Christina describes earn her disdain but also her mocking laughter. They are nothing more than mindless "pretty dolls," easily manipulated for the amusement of all-wise observers such as Christina herself. Other observers likewise derided men whose sole purpose in life consisted of preening themselves and spouting "beautiful nothings" for women. In the sonnet with which I opened this chapter, Georges de Scudéry, much like Christina, focuses attention on the visual spectacle of the caricatural salon man, the *pousseur de beaux sentiments.* So too does a text attributed to Charlotte de Brégy that includes a chapter denouncing fashionable *coquets,* the male counterparts of the *coquettes.* Rather than pursuing Socratic wisdom and neo-Stoic resolve, the coquets devote themselves instead to seducing women with "ridiculous appearances and effeminate attire," reading novels "so as to learn how to say sweet things," and "following *la mode . . .* and taking normal attire to an extreme."[104] Consistent with Scudéry's portrait, Brégy targets the three sorts of "effeteness" *(afféterie)* of the *coquets:* their "way of dressing," their "softness *(mollesse)* of speech," and their "delicacy" *(délicatesse)* or pampered lifestyle.[105] That both Scudéry and Brégy were salon insiders suggests that satires of effeminate salon men were not the sole province of observers hostile to the *ruelles.* Within these circles, this figure perhaps served a sort of self-policing, defensive function whereby *salonniers* and *salonnières* could preemptively disown a vision of salon masculinity all too readily associated with their groups.

By far the most extended satire of salon men is found in the novelist and critic Charles Sorel's *Les Lois de la galanterie* (The Laws of Galanterie; 1644, expanded 1658). A possible intertext for Molière's *Les Précieuses ridicules*,[106] this text details seventeen mock "laws" for galant hommes aspiring to be accepted in Parisian *mondain* circles. Throughout, Sorel pokes fun not only at salon men but also at the burgeoning literature of conduct manuals and the refined behavior it codified. To these ends, Sorel invokes numerous signs of early modern effeminacy, ironically promoting rather than condemning them. At the core of his satire—and true to the putative ethos of effeminacy—is the principle that *paraître* is *être:* "[The true galant] must have specific virtues, which are sumptuousness, magnificence, and flattery in a high degree."[107] Virtue and the merit it makes possible are to be found in nothing other than the ostentatious self-display of the galant homme. Accordingly, Sorel omits any discussion of ethical concerns, central to most writers of conduct literature, and instead enjoins his readers to be preoccupied with such matters as keeping their boots free of mud, staying scrupulously clean, following the vagaries of *la mode*, and choosing the right ribbons and *mouches* to set off the whiteness of one's skin. That attention to such details might be perceived as effeminate by some is explicitly recognized—and dismissed—by Sorel: "If critics think they are right to condemn us for imitating women, we will really astonish them when we answer that we could hardly do better than to follow the example of those whom we admire and adore and even that doing so is to follow the doctrine of Plato, who says that 'the lover must if he can be transformed into that which he loves'" (319). In an obvious caricature of the commonplace injunction to seek out the refining influence of women, Sorel claims that his galants desire nothing other than to become wholly like them. By invoking Plato, however, he introduces a possible further layer of irony. For, in contrast to the Neoplatonic interpretation of the quote given by Sorel as a heterosexual phenomenon, the original context of this allusion is the discussion of the Greek man-boy love ideal in the *Symposium*. Whether or not this double irony is intentional is, of course, impossible to determine. Still, later, Sorel-the-lawgiver underscores the ambiguity between homosociality and homoeroticism for his satirical salon man. After reiterating that the galant's primary goal is to "show himself" *(se faire voir)* especially to women, and that "it is the ladies whom one wishes to please the most, only making other men envious" (320), he describes how the galant should act in the presence of women: how to bow, to hold one's hat, to remove one's gloves, to comb one's hair, to display one's handkerchief . . . the point of all these gestures clearly being to draw to oneself not only the attention of women, but also—and especially—of other men:

Take care to repeat these actions with reasonable frequency and to do them only when you are at least somewhat relaxed, for varied countenances please the ladies greatly and even become a way of speaking without saying a word because the galants watch each other often to see who has the most graceful gestures, and the ladies are also pleased by such a spectacle. (322)

Preoccupied with an ever-changing sequence of empty gestures, Sorel's galant ends up being just as interested in mimetic rivalry with other galants as in the admiration of the Ladies. Both the subject *and* the object of spectacle, he would seem to usurp the very role of the women he had come to honor. And in the end, his narcissistic ostentatiousness works at cross-purposes with his purported goal, for by striving to resemble women to excess, he actually effaces the real women who were not only his models but especially the intended beneficiaries of his efforts at self-display. Such, at least, is the logic of Sorel's satire, developing as it does the familiar topoi that were the stuff of attacks on effeminacy at court and in the salon. But by focusing on the galant, *Les Lois de la galanterie* presents a troubling image of salon culture, implying that it is ill conceived or, more specifically, that ideal interaction between men and women in these venues was well-nigh impossible. At the very least it makes masculinity the central problem of salon interaction, just as it shows women to be both the cause and the victims of this problem.

GALANTERIE AND GENDER

By its very title, Sorel's satire highlights the sociable and literary aesthetic of galanterie, identifies it with salon circles, and draws attention to salon men as its practitioners. Sorel's satirical objective notwithstanding, galanterie was a much prized ideal, as a growing body of recent critical work by Delphine Denis, Claude Habib, Alain Génetiot, and Alain Viala in particular has emphasized.[108] Although this scholarship has made a significant contribution by restoring galanterie as a central notion within seventeenth-century culture, it has also by and large presented an overly idealized and simplistic vision of the strategic gender positions within this aesthetic and specifically its centerpiece, which I call the ideal of soft masculinity. Rather than taking this ideal at face value, as have most critics, I argue that it was highly ambivalent and allowed men to assume contradictory positions vis-à-vis women.

But what is this ideal? The model of masculinity constructed by galanterie—the galant or galant homme—overlaps in important ways with the honnête homme, as we already saw with Méré in chapter 1.[109] At least as early as the 1640s, the adjective *galant* had become synonymous with civility, courtliness, and sociable refinement.[110] As Vaugelas put it, it was "a blend of a certain something *(du je ne sais quoi)*, refined grace, the air of the court, wit, judgment, civility, courtesy, gaiety, all of that without constraint, affectation or vice."[111] And at the end of the century, Furetière explicitly evokes a parallel with honnêteté, but points to differences as well. For the noun *galant* Furetière gives three meanings: (1) "a man who is honnête, polite, knowledgeable about matters of his profession"; (2) "a man who has the air of the court, enticing manners, who attempts to captivate, and particularly the beautiful sex"; and (3) "a suitor *(amant)* who devotes himself entirely to the service of a mistress."[112] Beyond the word *honnête* in the first definition, Furetière incorporates the courtly "air," enticing manners, and the *art de plaire* that are so central to honnêteté, but he also insists on the heterosexual love paradigm. In addition, galanterie places more of a premium on *enjouement* (lightheartedness), good humor, and ludic pleasure than does honnêteté. Finally, galanterie highlights the benefits of conversation, as honnêteté also does, but with particular attention to heterosocial dynamics modeled on the courtly love scheme.[113]

Whether in salon conversations or writings designed to enrich and prolong them (published dialogues and conversations, salon poetry, novels), galanterie had as its most basic premise that the male suitor submit himself to the authority of his beloved. With origins in medieval culture but especially in neo-Petrarchanism, which flourished in sixteenth- and early seventeenth-century Italy and influenced much of the love poetry produced in France during the same period,[114] this ideology of male-female relations stipulated that the man owed the woman absolute and unwavering respect all the while suffering the torments of a long and difficult quest for her love. It would not be far off the mark to say that the masculine subject in this scheme is masochistic and narcissistic: he actively seeks out and exhibits a pain that is pleasureful, and he is obsessed above all with himself. The imagery used to describe the male lover's emotional state evokes at first glance qualities stereotypically associated with femininity more than masculinity. Stricken with love, the male suitor is timid, tearful, and physically weak, and his beloved is strong, assertive, often impassive. Frequently, galant love poetry, like that of the entire neo-Petrarchan tradition, depicts this gender reversal with metaphors of war and bondage: the lover is a victim (and not a conqueror), he is wounded by love, enslaved to his beloved, and often on the verge of death.[115] As Jean-Michel Pelous pointed out, the lover's state is "intransitive" since it has no object other than itself: "It is as if the most important thing was to stop passion in its inevitable evolution toward a conclusion that can only destroy it."[116] In this scenario, the lover is in a state of unending suffering and actually strives for nothing more. His passivity and torment became prized signs of the galant masculine ideal.

Closely allied with these signs is what rhetoricians called *suavitas* in Latin, or *douceur* in French. Opposed to the forceful rhetoric of oratory, for instance, this "sweetness" and "softness" sought to give the appearance of being "natural," simple, and effortless—and thus elegant—even though it was to be just as carefully prepared and executed. From antiquity through the seventeenth century, this *douceur* was regularly coded as "feminine," especially in contrast to the "virile" rhetoric of oratory.[117] And although such gender codings were traditional metaphorical comparisons, *douceur* was taken to be quite literally feminine in seventeenth-century France, as women's supposedly "natural" eloquence, in prose particularly, became a point of reference, and first and foremost for men. In this sense, the galant lover, seeking to give the impression of *douceur* by expressing his interminable suffering at the hands of his beloved, appropriates for himself what is initially posited to be feminine. He adopts a deliberately "soft" masculine stance that is purported to be pleasing to his beloved because it is "feminine."

Noting this soft masculinity, several recent studies have made the claim that galanterie marked a significant shift in gender positions by establishing if not social equality at least mutual respect between men and women.[118] Claude Habib in particular has argued that galanterie promoted a new form of heterosociality *(mixité)* that removed barriers to contact between the sexes.[119] As a result, she contends, winning the esteem of women became a goal as important for (elite) men as glory on the battlefield, service to the king, or the perpetuation of one's family line (113). But in order to earn women's esteem, men had to allow them a certain autonomy in the domain of love, which in turn meant imposing constraints on their own behavior and attitudes. A galant, Habib says, is a man "who renounces the use of force to win over women and is obliged to seduce them on their own terms, following the rules they establish" (66). Consequently, "the intensity of masculine desire was not measured by violence; it was demonstrated by *douceur*. In this way galanterie allowed masculine and feminine desires to be harmonized, metamorphosing power into refinement *(délicatesse)*" (433). Ultimately she asserts that galanterie had as its aim "to make love liveable" for women and men alike (350).[120]

As a description of the gender positions promoted by galanterie, Habib's thesis is mostly accurate. But as an analysis of those positions, it is highly problematic because it fails to consider that male self-interest, homosociality, and thus aggression can persist within galant masculinity. In other words, unlike Habib and others, I would argue that within galanterie male self-interest is not abolished in favor of an altruistic relation to women, but actually reaffirmed; that male homosociality coexists alongside the heterosocial courtly love paradigm and at times even upstages it; and that, as a direct result of homosociality-qua-rivalry, a form of male aggression persists, even if physical violence is proscribed. At the crux of the issue is the nebulous boundary between soft masculinity and effeminacy created by galanterie. For within this aesthetic are the seeds of male self-interest and homosociality that work at cross-purposes with the ostensible male submission to female authority that Habib and others have taken as the watchword of galanterie.

In the final analysis, the soft masculinity of galanterie can all too easily reiterate several of the topoi of (early modern) effeminacy, and this ambiguity can be traced to the theatrical role the galant salon man had to play in his writing, speech, or actions. This role-playing, which emphasized manner over content, used the rhetoric of neo-Petrarchan love as the metaphorical signifier for the respect and admiration men owed women. This rhetoric was not only a staple of galant poetry, but was also the code for sociable interaction between men and women. Adopting the *stance* of the long-suffering, submissive lover, salon men would lavish women with praise, asking in return for their recognition and esteem. And what had the trappings of a courtship ritual was in fact more often the strategic and self-interested deployment of well-worn poetic conventions, the rhetoric and comportment expected of any man hoping to succeed in salon circles.

This ambivalence, even duplicity is evident in the most prominent rhetorical figures inherited from the neo-Petrarchan tradition and recycled in much galant poetry: antithesis, oxymoron, hyperbole, paradox, and syllepsis, among others.[121] Use of such figures was intended to express the intensity of the lover's passion for his beloved, but they also had the effect of bringing attention to the lover himself. The exaggeration, even affectation, indicative of these figures were distinguishing characteristics of the galant homme. His language was to exhibit itself as spectacle—to be *brillant* (shining, dazzling). Adroitly used, it proved his status as a *bel esprit*, someone capable of captivating others with a sharp wit and contributing to the joyfulness of the group, and someone recognized by others as such. Aspiring to be a *bel esprit*, the galant homme put himself in the service of the women he purported to woo and the group he aimed to entertain. But to do so, he necessarily had to primp himself and his language in ways that drew attention to the facade he adopted, thereby putting the spotlight squarely on himself and at least potentially taking it away from the women he professed to serve. At the same time, by putting the focus on the form of his language and his actions, by privileging ("feminine") form over ("masculine") content, he exhibited one of the most prominent traits of early modern representations of effeminacy—ostentatious self-display. In other words, the metaphorical and self-conscious stance of galant masculinity allowed men to use softness for their own benefit. Exploiting the etymological playfulness at the heart of the word *galanterie* (derived from *galer,* to play or amuse oneself), men could be duplicitous, "serving" the ladies of the salons lightheartedly (and without usually forming amorous ties), feigning love and yet avoiding real submission, serving the ladies of the salon while negotiating the homosocial bonds with other galants.

A striking illustration of the ambivalence of galant masculinity is found in the famous "Journée des madrigaux" (Day of Madrigals), an improvised poetry competition among members of Madeleine de Scudéry's salon that took place on 20 December 1653. From the account left by Paul Pellisson, we get a glimpse of how the gendered dynamics of galanterie animated this most famous salon.[122] This day of frenetic creation was sparked by a gift, accompanied by a madrigal, from Valentin Conrart to Jeanne Aragonais, who then asked Pellisson to respond on her behalf. The opportunity to provide the obligatory "countergift" quickly came to be dominated by Pellisson and Sarasin, who wrote not only on behalf of Aragonais, but also to each other and to other members of the group. The madrigals offered to Aragonais created the possibility of giving "gifts" to other salon members, who then responded with "countergifts" of their own.

While it is certainly true that these exchanges glorified the exclusivity of the group as a whole, no less important is the individual ambition of the male participants, who dominated the *journée* by far (of all the women present, only Scudéry contributed madrigals). From the outset, Pellisson and Sarasin squared off in a poetic duel that, by the end of the day, hit a fevered pitch as each tried to best the other by improvising madrigals in praise of Marie d'Aligre (Aragonais's daughter), Scudéry, and Marie Le Gendre. Finally, as Pellisson's account puts it: "The invincible Polyandre, surpassing all the others as much by the fecundity of his mind as by the beauty of his verses, created two more madrigals in addition to the others" (180). He had outdone Pellisson and was recognized by the group as having won "the honor of this combat"

(181). The word *combat* in Pellisson's account is noteworthy because it is one of repeated comparisons of the madrigal competition to a chivalric tournament. Ostensibly motivated by the desire to show their *esprit* for the women of the salon, in reality the men seem just as preoccupied with their male rivals, addressing as many madrigals to each other as to the women of the salon. What begins as a galant ritual of masculine "service" to a "lady" quickly becomes the occasion for men to "serve" first and foremost their *own* interests. The playful heroics of salon-bound chivalry allows Scudéry's knights to display their verbal/viril prowess among and for each other. And then afterward, Pellisson memorialized this tournament in the *Chroniques du Samedi,* a carefully preserved archive of Scudéry's salon, thus putting this exercise in homosocial bonding at the center of a text often cited as the epitome of the galant aesthetic.

What the Day of Madrigals suggests is that galant masculinity was a highly ambiguous proposition for the salon man. Submitting to the dictates of women in the *ruelle* much as a courtly lover would to his lady potentially led to a gendered indifference between women and men that exposes the tenuous relationship of masculinity to femininity within galanterie. Yet, the ludic self-consciousness of this ideal could and did enable men to reassert their dominance, under the guise of a soft masculine stance. But for some observers (such as Charlotte de Brégy, Christina of Sweden, Georges de Scudéry, and Charles Sorel), this same deliberate attention to form could and did transform would-be knights into *pousseurs de beaux sentiments.* So, paradoxcially, the soft masculinity prescribed by galanterie was not necessarily incompatible with masculine domination. And it was potentially perceived and even enacted as an effeminacy that blurred the difference between this ideal and its satire, that allowed men to "serve" women without losing sight of their own interests.

Précieux AND *Petits-Maîtres*

Concurrent with the ideal form of galanterie elaborated by Scudéry's salon and others was its obverse, which Viala has called "libertine galanterie."[123] Disdainful of the "serious" conventions inspired by Neoplatonism and neo-Petrarchanism, this attitude was evident in much salon writing from the period and was even adopted by some of the same participants who claimed to espouse the serious brand of galanterie.[124] Often blatantly misogynist, this version of galanterie expressed cynicism about the outcome of love, promoted *enjouement* and inconstancy over suffering and fidelity, vaunted the immediacy and physicality of pleasure over deferral and transcendence, and made no pretense of upholding truthfulness among lovers. The unfavorable positions for women within this strain of galanterie were in fact motivation for Scudéry's own theories of sociability, which we will see in chapter 4. As the most prominent champion of ideals that were the very antithesis of this sort of galanterie, Scudéry and her writings were obvious targets for satirists. Through allegorical maps and narrative geographies, writers such as d'Aubignac, Boileau, Tristan L'Hermite, Somaize, and Sorel either explicitly or implicitly rewrote the *Carte de Tendre,* exposing what they portray as its fundamental hypocrisy. Rather than a quest for friendship or at most Platonic love, such writers protest, the conduct idealized by Scudéry and many salon women is nothing other than a coded invitation to sexual license.[125] In this satirical disfigurement, the salon woman becomes little more than a coquette, enticing men with erotic pleasures while claiming to uphold traditional feminine modesty.

But of all the attacks on Scudéry and salon women generally, the most significant took the form of the satirical *précieuse*. While the sociohistorical reality of the *précieuses* is uncertain at best, what is not in question is the considerable body of literature that uses the word *précieuse* to denigrate women of the *ruelles* immediately after the Fronde (1648–53) and until the majority of Louis XIV.[126] Attempts to explain the appearance of this satirical figure almost without exception stress attitudes toward women's relation to various forms of power in the post-Fronde era. Pelous highlights the growing hostility toward women within the cynical strain of galanterie; Stanton emphasizes the anxiety toward women's political power during the regency of Anne d'Autriche and the Fronde; and Myriam Maître concentrates on male writers' defensive reaction to the growing number of women readers and especially women writers.[127] As suggestive as these interpretations are, one aspect that they do not address is the relation the satirical *précieuse* had to salon masculinity. Granted, each of the foregoing interpretations presents this satire as the product of a certain masculine subjective stance, that is, the creation of a masculine subjectivity threatened by (what is perceived to be) an ascendent femininity. But the *précieuse* as a satirical fiction was largely the creation of salon insiders, and of both men *and* women (although far more were written by men than by women, it is true).[128] Thus, we need to consider what this satire reveals about changing attitudes toward the figure of the salon man. For, if it is true, as the dictum goes, that satire tells us more about the satirist than it does about the satirized, then it is significant that the vast majority of the satirical representations of the *précieuse* were penned by men who were themselves connected to salons. My hypothesis, then, is that this figure channeled anxieties not only about the cultural and political authority of women, but also about men's participation in the salons, which is to say, salon masculinity.

It might at first seem counterintuitive that the satirical depictions of the *précieuses* concern both femininity *and* masculinity. After all, it is the purportedly ridiculous posturing and language of certain salon *women* that are the central focus of these fictions. At first glance, salon *men* seem to escape completely the brunt of the satirical wrath meted out on the *précieuses*. But closer examination reveals that salon men did indeed come under fire, notably in the figures of the *pousseur de beaux sentiments* or the *précieux*, both of which connoted effeminacy. Still, as satirical fictions, these two figures never gained the sort of traction that the *précieuse* did.[129] Mid-seventeenth-century satirists were not unaware of this disparity. "All one talks about is the *précieuse* without a word about the *précieux*," says Melanire to Gelasire in the Abbé de Pure's novel, *La Prétieuse* (1656–58). In response, Gelasire claims the *précieux* do in fact exist, that they are secretive, and that "the male of the *précieuse* species is called a Jansenist," referring to the Augustinian Catholic movement of the time.[130] But such affirmations notwithstanding, Gelasire fails to give the detailed description one might expect, explaining, "I don't know enough about this topic yet" (2:158–59), and in the end the "*prétieux*" remains even more enigmatic than the *prétieuse* who, in de Pure's novel, is the "mystery of the *ruelles*." Other texts go so far as to claim that the *précieuse* has no male equivalent whatsoever. To the question "Can't both sexes be endowed with the quality of preciousness *(la qualité de prétieux)*?" the "Catéchisme des prétieuses" (Cathecism of the *Précieuses*) stipulates as the response, "No, because the *précieuses* find with each other enough to satisfy themselves, and besides since men do not have sufficiently pure sentiments, they can't even be admitted as poor brothers."[131] Insinuating that the *précieuses* are hypocrites since they practice same-sex love but also uphold a Platonic-like idealism, the "Catéchisme" excludes men from its satirical aim and suggests with its mocking condescension that they are somehow victims of these women, excluded from their ranks and their love. Once again, then, the salon man seems to disappear from the satirical gaze as full attention is given to his female counterpart.

What in fact occurs, I would argue, is that anxiety about the effeminate salon man is projected onto the figure of the *précieuse* with a corresponding marginalization of her male counterpart. This is even the case in Molière's

Les Précieuses ridicules (The Ridiculous *Précieuses,* 1658), in spite of the fact
that the farce takes aims at the two would-be *précieux* (or, more precisely,
galants), Mascarille and Jodelet, as much if not more than the two *précieuses,*
Cathos and Magdelon. But what might appear to be a gendered symmetry in
satirical intent turns out to be asymmetry since the status of the two men
within the overall economy of the play is quite different from that of the two
women. Whereas Cathos and Magdelon lack self-conscious distance from the
ridiculous personae they embody, Mascarille and Jodelet are valets playing
the roles assigned to them by their masters, La Grange and Du Croisy, who
seek revenge for being rebuffed by the two *précieuses.* As actors of a play
within a play (and very enthusiastic actors, it should be noted), Mascarille
and Jodelet actually shield real salon men from the sort of satirical attention
given to Cathos and Magdelon. For even if, in Molière's words, the two
women "imitate [the true *précieuses*] poorly,"[132] they are still closer to their
"true" counterparts than are the two valets. Although provincial, the *précieuses* are still *bourgeoises,* as were many salon women, and, with their references to Scudéry's novels, they display a knowledge—no matter how mis-
guided—of the sort of literature read and discussed in those circles.
Mascarille and Jodelet, on the other hand, are in fact domestic servants, who
would never have been eligible to attend a salon. More importantly, their behavior is the very antithesis of that required of men in mixed company and
very much at odds with the caricatures of effeminate salon men I discussed
earlier. Even if they are obsessed with their outward appearances, Mascarille
and Jodelet are more prone to display uncouth hypervirility than excessive
refinement. They make sexually allusive jokes about the two women, they
discuss their experiences in the army, and they show Cathos and Magdelon
their battle wounds—all examples of behavior explicitly proscribed in conduct manuals of the period (scene 11, 53–58). In terms of personal and sociable elegance, then, they are beset by a lack, whereas the stereotypically effeminate salon man is more often taxed with excess. But the distance between
the two valets and real salon men comes into sharpest relief when La Grange
and Du Croisy return to put an end to their farce within a farce. Beating and
disrobing their valets, the two masters expose them for who and what they
are. They are not to be confused with the galants who frequented the real salons outside the theater, the galants who never set foot in the ersatz salon improvised by Cathos and Magdelon. Most of all, the *mise à nu* of the consciously played farce by Mascarille and Jodelet serves in turn as a *mise à nu* of
the unwittingly performed farce by the two *précieuses.* The onus quickly
shifts from the two valets to Cathos and Magdelon, who are made responsible

for the "dirty trick" *(pièce sanglante)* that La Grange and Du Croisy subjected them to. "Yes, it's a dirty trick, but one that you brought upon yourselves with your impertinence, despicable fools" (69). At the very end of the play, as Mascarille and Jodelet exit the stage, they alone remain to face the wrath of Gorgibus, who, even as he rails against the "novels, verse, songs, sonnets, and sonnetlets" (70) that have lead his daughter and niece astray, insinuates that women are incapable of rational discernment and self-control.

Not only are the two *précieuses*—and *not* the two valets playing salon men—the "problem" the play sets out to solve, but Cathos and Magdelon have also absorbed the anxiety that previously surrounded salon masculinity. This phenomenon is perhaps best illustrated in the language Molière attributes to the two women. Roger Duchêne has astutely noted that Cathos and Magdelon, and *not* Mascarille and Jodelet, illustrate the (satirical) principles outlined by Charles Sorel in *Les Lois de la galanterie,* a major source for Molière's farce.[133] For instance, among Sorel's mock "laws" for his galants is a prescription that aptly describes the linguistic mind-set of the two *précieuses:* "If there are recently coined words that people enjoy using, they are the ones you should have on the tip of your tongue at all times. You should do as you would with new clothing styles, which is to say you should display them shamelessly, no matter how bizarre they might be and even if grammarians and scribblers criticize them."[134] Taking on the language Sorel had ascribed to salon men, Cathos and Magdelon are made responsible for the linguistic aberrations of salon culture. The two women have come to embody the sort of excesses that had previously been attributed to men.

In the way it shifts responsibility to the *précieuses* and obscures that of the would-be *galants* and more fundamentally, in the way it obfuscates the very existence of the salon man, *Les Précieuses ridicules* can be seen to indicate a broader cultural tendency to focus attention away from the effeminacy associated with salon culture. This is not to say that the preoccupation with the supposed effeminacy of salon masculinity or even less with effeminacy generally disappeared after the figure of the *précieuse* came on the scene. As I will discuss à propos of Voiture's legacy in the next chapter, the aesthetic of galanterie, closely associated with salon culture, was taken to be potentially and inherently effeminizing, and this to the very end of the seventeenth century. And yet the salon man and the masculinity promoted by salon culture became less problematic or at least less preoccupying overall when the focus was placed on (salon) women. Thus, the attempts to exorcize the effeminizing potential of Voiture's model evoke the salon man only indirectly. What is at stake is a literary and sociable ideal that is extrapolated from a body of writing derived directly and indirectly from salon interaction. Accordingly, the distance of this anxiety from the real men who continued to frequent salons throughout the period is significant. It is as if the role of the salon as a locus for ambiguously confirming and reconfiguring masculinity becomes less troubling. And in this case, the parameters of effeminacy seem to have changed.[135]

Indicative of the evolving status of both the salon man and effeminacy are the *petits-maîtres* who populated the satirical and theatrical imagination beginning at the very end of the seventeenth and continuing well into the eighteenth century. Although the specific contours of this figure changed from the 1690s to the 1750s, the term *petit-maître* designated young men who frequented not only salon circles but also theaters and cafés among other settings, who were obsessed with the latest fashions, who took it upon themselves to pass judgment on cultural production of all sorts, and who were arrogant and ill-mannered. But fundamental to this satirical image, like that of the salon man from the first half of the seventeenth century, was his association and resemblance with women. A "feminized being"[136] according to Charles Gaudet, who authored a book-length essay on this figure, the *petit-maître* was frequently depicted seeking out women's company if not their affections and, especially displaying their (supposed) obsession with outward appearances. Yet the charge of effeminacy in the figure of the *petit-maître* is melded with connotations that it had not had or had had in only latent form in earlier times. In his multiple guises, the *petit-maître* is portrayed as boasting of his military *bravoure,* as being conceited and foolish, as flaunting homosocial (and by implication homoerotic) bonds, or as espousing radical philosophical thought.[137] By metonymy, the *petit-maître's* effeminacy comes to signify much more than resemblance with women. This is so much the case, in fact, that this figure at times distances himself from real women. In one strain of this satirical tradition, the *petit-maître* is shown as rebuffing or mistreating women, and in another, the ambivalent homosocial/homoerotic bond among *petits-maîtres* virtually sidelines the heterosocial/heterosexual social dynamic.[138] In these cases, their supposed resemblance with women coexists with a nonassociation, and the *petits-maîtres* compete with women for the cultural position of the "feminine." And yet, in the satirical logic that governs this figure, women are ultimately to blame for the ridicule it attracts. According to Gaudet, "If it is true that women make men what there are, then society should make them responsible for making *petits-maîtres*! How glorious it would be for them to correct this futile and contemptible lot who only aspire to please them and will not hesitate to become reasonable if it were possible to please them with reason."[139] By extension, the very cornerstone of heterosocial salon sociability is itself to blame, opines Gaudet, who elsewhere attributes the arrogance of the *petits-maîtres* to "politeness" *(politesse)*.[140] Women turn out to be heart of the "problem" of the *petit-maître*, and since women cannot be "pleased" with reason, there is no solution, or so we are left to conclude.

If Gaudet's misogynist logic is extreme for its rejection of women's role within salon culture (salons were flourishing in mid-eighteenth-century France, after all, and the philosophes were flocking to them), it nonetheless points to a recurring feature within effeminacy, during the early modern period and beyond. Effeminacy is above all produced by a normative sex/gender system intent on enforcing rigid boundaries between men and women and between the masculine and the feminine. When seventeenth-century salons elaborated a new model for heterosocial interaction, dominant masculinity was faced with the prospect that gender boundaries would become blurred. The effeminate salon man was thus a means of counteracting that threat and of reestablishing impermeable barriers, at least as those barriers were understood at the time. As we will see in the next chapter, even those salon personalities who resisted efforts to deliberately efface difference nonetheless aligned masculinity more closely with femininity than had been the case before. Still, effeminacy remained a potent weapon for the cultural policing of gender. At a time when the anxiety surrounding the softness of salon masculinity had subsided, the *petit-maître* emerged as a new threat, or rather as an old threat in new clothing. Of course, this figure was by no means the last used to (attempt to) give consistency to masculinity. As long as normative masculinity defines itself in opposition to femininity—as long as it casts femininity as the threatening Other—then the specter of effeminacy seems likely to persist in our collective gendered imaginary.

THREE

Vincent Voiture and the
Perils of Galanterie

For much of his lifetime and until at least the end of the seventeenth century, Vincent Voiture (1598–1648) was the consummate example of a galant homme. A fixture in the salon of the Marquise de Rambouillet, he was made famous thanks to his correspondence (and to a lesser extent his poetry), which became the incontestable model for galant writing, behavior, and conversation. It is not surprising, then, that while attempting to promote the posthumous fortunes of his friend Jean-François Sarasin over those of Voiture, Paul Pellisson admitted he had to contend with the prevailing opinion that Voiture was "the one and only original of things galant."[1] From all appearances, that belief was widespread, as Vaugelas's entry for the words *galant* and *galamment* testifies. Referring to the new fashion for *lettres galantes*, he writes in a transparent allusion to the *épistolier* that

> in this sort of letter, France can boast of having a person above all others. Neither Athens nor even Rome, with the exception of Cicero, has anyone to rival him, and I can say so boldly, since such a refined genre of writing was hardly even known to them. Thus, all those with the most exquisite tastes take great delight in his letters as well as his verse and his conversation, which are no less enchanting.[2]

For Vaugelas as for many of his contemporaries, the "delight" provided by Voiture extended beyond his letters and his verse to his conversation—and thus his very being. *L'homme* was so inextricably bound up with *l'œuvre* that the work became a veritable vade mecum for the men of the salons. But they were not the only ones to admire Voiture's writings: it is well known that Sévigné, for instance, had great admiration for his letters.[3] Still, Voiture's example had particular significance for salon masculinity precisely because it was the touchstone for galanterie and the roles men were to play in this *mondain* ideal, at once a sociable ethos and literary aesthetic. But over and beyond defining the galant homme, Voiture's example also came to embody the ambiguities that galanterie held for male salon-goers and writers. In subtle but nonetheless distinct ways, his legacy and seventeenth-century discussions about its meaning brought to the fore cultural expectations about men's interactions within salons and their gendered relation to writing. The uncertainties about Voiture's posthumous legacy concern nothing less than seventeenth-century men's status as gendered writing subjects within the evolving literary and social fields of their time.

If Voiture's writing and his biography are just as intertwined today as they were for his contemporaries, it is because his life was in many respects incongruous for the time and fascinating both then and now. The son of a wealthy wine merchant, he pulled off a meteoric rise to the upper echelons of society, becoming the pivotal denizen of Mme de Rambouillet's salon, of course, but also the *Introducteur des ambassadeurs* and *Gentilhomme ordinaire* in the entourage of Gaston d'Orléans and later *Maître d'hôtel ordinaire du roi*, among other official appointments.[4] The fascination with Voiture's biography likely also stems from its many paradoxes: the son of a wine merchant, he was said to drink only water; a *roturier* whom aristocratic men and women sought to imitate; a prolific writer who published virtually nothing during his lifetime; an inveterate suitor of women for whom the art of courtship trumped physical possession. But this preoccupation with Voiture's life is due also, of course, to the fact that so much of his writing is to a great degree *personal*. In his poetry and letters, addressed to women and men at the Hôtel de Rambouillet and at the courts of Gaston and Louis XIII, Voiture celebrates not only these individuals, but also himself and most crucially the social nexus that connected them. In this, to be sure, he was hardly unusual. What makes him stand out is the credit contemporaries gave him—and particularly his wit—for embodying galanterie. Typical are pronouncements by Chapelain, who described him as aspiring to "the royalty of galanterie,"[5] and Donneau de Visé, who called him the "acknowledged master of galanterie."[6]

This ideal came to be defined more by the posthumous reception of Voiture and his oeuvre than by the writer himself. Galanterie affirmed that life and art respect the very same tenets and that they are mutually interdependent. Thus, it is not at all surprising that Voiture's life and works were invoked together and presented as inseparable by seventeenth-century theorists of galanterie. Such is certainly the case in the "Eloge de Voiture" that prefaced the first edition of his collected works (1650). In what amounts to a manifesto, the writer's nephew, Martin Pinchesne, details his uncle's "advantageous talents in social exchange *(le commerce du monde)*" as well as the "very great flair" of his writing.[7] Voiture's person and letters especially privilege sociability, specifically the art of conversation, in the broadest and richest sense of the word. According to Pinchesne, his uncle's singular success in that art was due to his ability to "accompany everything he wanted to do and say with an extraordinary grace" (1:2) as well as "a suavity *(douceur)* and polite civility with which he was able to negotiate judiciously through high society" (1:3) Possessing grace, suavity, and civility, Voiture (and his work) sought above all the ludic pleasure of his interlocutors and readers, be it in the general form of *enjouement* or more precisely, *la belle raillerie,* which aimed to "enticingly turn the most serious discussions into a game" (1:3), all the while displaying impeccably good judgment with others, something all the more important because they were his social superiors. In his writing, Pinchesne insists, Voiture was careful to maintain variety ("extremely varied material, figures, and words" [1:13]) so as to ward off fatigue and boredom. Ultimately, so adept was he at conversation that he was inimitable: "He is only comparable to himself, and . . . since he surpassed everyone who came before him, it will be difficult to find anyone who can conduct himself with nearly as much grace after him" (1:14).

The most central element of galanterie and the most crucial reason for Voiture's success, according to Pinchesne, was the interaction between men and women in *mondain* circles. As we have seen in chapter 2, it was a long-standing commonplace of the period that men could only hope to become "civilized" if they submitted to the refining influence of women, who possessed an innate sense of aesthetic judgment. Voiture, claims Pinchesne, was a master at conforming to the dictates of women's better instincts: "This sex has the most exquisite taste for the refinement of thought, and one must take exacting measures to be always read or listened to favorably in the *cercle* or the *cabinet*. In this, Voiture was a great master" (1:6). To curry women's favor, men needed first of all to celebrate and compliment them—to learn the *art* of the "galant compliment," which involved simulating the stance of a chivalric or Petrarchan lover addressing his beloved. But this simulacrum required above all a transformation of men. As Génetiot puts it, "The man required by galanterie must . . . in addition to his virile qualities, possess the gifts of beauty, suavity, and politeness reserved heretofore to the ladies."[8] Pinchesne claims that such "feminine" qualities were exemplified by Voiture and, to justify his claim, cites the authority of women at the Hôtel de Rambouillet: "They judged that he came very close to the perfect qualities they thought necessary to cultivate the man the Italians describe as the perfect courtier and whom the French call a galant homme" (1:8). The women of the Rambouillet salon pronounce judgment on Voiture based on criteria that they supposedly control ("the perfect qualities"). It is their authority and their judgement that confer upon him the title of "galant homme," according to Pinchesne.[9] In short, what Voiture purportedly mastered, and what galanterie required of any man, was an appropriation and display of the "feminine." By seeking out the company and the affection of women, he came to resemble them.

And yet, in the drive to make his uncle a model, Pinchesne complicates this claim considerably. At the end of his "Eloge," he addresses "a sex [Voiture] always honored":

> I ask it to carry on after his death the many elegant graces he was able to obtain during his lifetime. For, concerning the refinement of taste of the ladies and the extreme politeness they require in writing and conversation, he was always fortunate to captivate them and to win them over. And since this beautiful half of the world, along with the ability to read, also has that of judging just as much as we do and is these days master of the glory of men as much as men are themselves, it is to this half that I have resolved to address myself in conclusion. Suffer, beautiful sex whom he at all times wholly respected, that I conclude with a request I wish to make of you to preserve the glorious benefit of your esteem and that, after having left men the freedom of their opinions, I curry the favor of your own. Grant him your approval and your applause. Look on the works that came from his hands with as kind an eye as that with which he saw in you the most beautiful creation that came from the hands of nature. Courageously defend his cause against those who would criticize him, and never say anything about him except that which is to his honor, since he never wrote anything that was not for your glory. Confess with me that all manner of love and grace was born with him and if they did not live on in you, they would have died with him. (1:14–15)

After calling upon women to continue his uncle's legacy (his "elegant graces"), which meets the standards of taste and refinement they demand, Pinchesne then equates Voiture's works with women, urging them to appreciate these writings as if they *were* women, as if they were "the most beautiful creation that came from the hands of nature." Over and beyond its metaphorically homoerotic implications (women admiring Voiture's writings as *he* admired women, and particularly their bodies), the imperative Pinchesne gives to women also suggests that these writings are "naturally" feminine, that they, like women, are masterpieces of nature. Just how much (or even *if*) Voiture may have had to work to *imitate* women remains unclear; but in the end, the process is reversed: women are to imitate *him*. In the space of a few sentences, then, Voiture goes from seeking women's favor to being the model and even the creator of women's "love" and "grace." Accordingly, so Pinchesne implies, they should defend him as they would themselves. And even more importantly, since his writings *are* women and women *are* his writings, women must perpetuate his existence, something they alone can do.[10]

Through his hyperbolic praise, Pinchesne ends up positing as much or even more of a difference as a resemblance between Voiture and the women he sought to please, as much of a position of dominance for Voiture as one of submission to women. In this, Pinchesne's rhetoric was not entirely off the mark. For, in spite of Voiture's (and Pinchesne's) profession of subservience and resemblance to women, he occupied a commanding role among them. In Rambouillet's salon, for instance, he was often the spokesperson for women, writing letters on their behalf to husbands and male friends away from Paris.[11] He also inaugurated salon games, such as the writing of rondeaux, the vogue of *métamorphoses,* and poetry *en vieux langage,* which women enthusiastically adopted.[12] His, then, was an ambiguous role. Purporting to be submissive to the women of the Rambouillet salon, he also stood apart from them and, on many occasions, *over* them, even orchestrating their interactions. On the one hand, he was just another male devotee at the Hôtel de Rambouillet pledging his "obedience" and his "service" to the women of the salon; on the other, he occupied a position unlike that of most of the other men there. He was, after all, a *roturier,* a fact that his contemporaries often noted. Yet, for them, his bourgeois origins made his success all the more noteworthy. As seventeenth-century observer René Le Pays puts it, "Although Voiture was of low birth, his beautiful qualities earned him the friendship of the highest born of the kingdom and put him on familiar terms with princes and princesses."[13] It may very well be that Voiture's unambiguously bourgeois origins explain a good part of his unusual position in this salon. Surrounded by women and men whose social rank was far higher than his own, he had to make a place for himself not only by adopting aristocratic mores (e.g., his penchant for gambling and dueling), but also by deliberately accentuating his differences from other salon men, directing attention away from his own social origins and onto his galant performances in conversation and writing. Granted, it is important not to exaggerate the negative perceptions the Rambouillet circle may have had of Voiture's bourgeois origins. Thanks to his *charges,* he became exceedingly wealthy, and like many other bourgeois writers in *mondain* circles, he made every effort to conform to an aristocratic ethos.[14] Still, the galant ideal he defined and embodied was doubtless one piece of a strategy to blend into a group of aristocrats, becoming along the way even more aristocratic than aristocrats themselves. Galant masculinity, as advocated and performed by Voiture, most likely allowed him to overcome (or to attempt to overcome) the hindrance caused by his social origins, especially at the beginning of his time at the Hôtel de Rambouillet. In any event, throughout his writings, Voiture's gendered persona figures more prominently in the ideal world of the salon than does the deficiency of his social status in the real world.[15]

SELF-CONSCIOUS GALANTERIE

In his letters and poetry, Voiture uses the posture of a galant homme to stake out his difference not only within the salon of the marquise de Rambouillet, but also from the stereotype of the languid courtly lover vulnerable to charges of effeminacy. These writings develop a rhetoric that constructs a simultaneous proximity and distance between the masculine writing subject and his female addressees. As Micheline Cuénin, Odette de Mourgues, and more recently Sophie Rollin have demonstrated, Voiture recycles Petrarchan topoi, but at the same time frames them with a gently mocking irony.[16] So doing, he underscores a desire for women's approval and affection even as he pokes fun at the stance of the submissive lover. Paradoxically, then, he "serves" his female interlocutors by making light of the traditional topoi about the male suitor's service to his beloved. Ambiguously distancing himself from that stance, he nonetheless aims to please—to "serve"—the women for whom and to whom he writes. And all the while he projects a self-consciousness of his persona as galant homme that makes his own self-mastery obvious to all.

In one of his first and best-known letters, Voiture formulates the praises conventionally owed the beloved in ways that call attention to the artistry with which he manipulates the topoi of courtly and Petrarchan love. The story behind this missive is almost as implausible as its contents. After writing a letter to Madame de Saintot, a member of the Rambouillet salon, Voiture had it printed and bound in a copy of Ariosto's *Orlando furioso,* which he then presented to her.[17] As was often the case with correspondence in *mondain* circles, this epistle was carefully staged not only for its addressee but also and especially for a larger audience. And whatever effect Voiture might have hoped that his letter would have on Madame de Saintot, the effect it had on his unnamed collective addressees was by all accounts momentous: it is credited with nothing less than opening the doors of the Hôtel de Rambouillet for him. In what is a hybrid of a love letter, a dedicatory epistle, a personalized preface, and a novella, Voiture imagines the ecstasy of Roland encountering Madame de Saintot: "Madame, here is probably the most beautiful adventure Roland ever had. And when, all alone, he defended the crown of Charlemagne and wrested scepters from the hands of kings, he did nothing as glorious for himself as having the honor of kissing your own hands at this moment" (1:17). Using syllepsis (invoking "Roland" as both the character and the book in Madame de Saintot's hands), Voiture melds fiction and reality as he envisions Ariosto's hero deviating from his foreordained plot and leaving his beloved: "[I] am certain he will become wise in your presence and will forget Angelica as soon as he sees you" (1:18). Voiture also blends fiction and reality when he contrasts Madame de Saintot's beauty with the magical décor of Ariosto's novel and the *Amadis de Gaule:* "To tell the truth, crystal rooms and diamond palaces are much easier to imagine, and all the enchantments of Amadis that seem so incredible to you are not nearly as much, by any means, as your own" (1:18). Beyond layering hyperbole upon hyperbole, Voiture draws upon fictional examples that defy verisimilitude such that Madame de Saintot's "enchantments" become quite literally fictional and unbelievable. The intention here is certainly not to call into question his addressee's beauty, but the references to the magical décor in *Orlando furioso* and the *Amadis de Gaule* become comical, poking fun at these fictions and the topoi of feminine beauty. Ultimately, of course, the pretext of this letter focuses attention on Voiture's epistolary "I." And that focus becomes clearest when, in closing , the "I" imagines Roland impatiently waiting to tell his adventures to Madame de Saintot:

> This knight who is not accustomed to relinquishing his privilege to anyone is becoming irritated at leaving me so long in your presence and is approaching to tell you the story of his many loves. That is a favor you have refused me many times. And yet without jealousy I will allow him to be happier than I since, in exchange, he promises me to present this note from me and to have you read it before anything else. (1:19)

All the while maintaining a lighthearted tone (afforded by the syllepsis of "Roland"), Voiture incorporates the topos of the indifferent beloved who refuses to receive protestations of love from her suitor(s). But far from conveying a serious tone of suffering, the use of this topos here is likewise good-natured and ludic, even as the *épistolier* affirms that his addressee will still not want to listen to him and even as he proceeds to tell her of his "passions" anyway.[18] Anything but a submissive and languorous lover, Voiture invokes that stance while distancing himself from it, aiming to delight his (named and unnamed) addressees.

In yet another oft-cited letter, Voiture makes it clear once again that he is not the dupe of the rhetorical and poetic conventions he relies upon. Writing to Julie d'Angennes, the daughter of the marquise de Rambouillet, he recycles the Petrarchan topos of death by love, amplifying its improbability, while conferring upon her the role of the indifferent beloved. "Mademoiselle, no one has died yet because of your absence except me, and I am not afraid to tell you so baldly since I believe you will hardly care."[19] Evoking the traditional signs of the suffering caused by the absence of one's beloved, Voiture insists that his is not just a figurative but in fact a literal death: "Since last Wednesday, which was the day of your departure, I no longer eat, I no longer speak, and I no longer see. And thus the only thing that remains to be done is to bury me" (1:337). Later, he makes his addressee complicitous with the playful intent of his epistle before imploring her to have pity on him: "Moreover, I beg you, Mademoiselle, not to laugh when you read this. For, in all seriousness, it is very impolite to make fun of the deceased. And if you were in my position, you would not be pleased to be treated in that way. So, I implore you to pity me, and since you can do nothing more for me, to care for my soul. For I assure you that it is suffering terribly" (1:337–38). But, as the letter continues, Voiture's purported suffering becomes less and less obvious as he concentrates instead on the humor of his metaphorical death made literal to the point of being grotesque. "I was determined to send you my body by courier, but it is in such a pitiful state that it would have been reduced to pieces before reaching you. And then, I was afraid that the heat would ruin it" (1:338). The conventional suffering of the male lover during the absence of his beloved becomes the stuff of the *enjouement* with which Voiture the galant homme seeks to entertain the Hôtel de Rambouillet. More specifically, though, the imagined spectacle of his corpse neatly encapsulates the theatricality of the galant rhetoric throughout his oeuvre. He strives above all to make himself the center of attention, and in this sense, he is not unlike the narcissistically inclined serious Petrarchan lover he distances himself from.[20] But while putting the focus on himself (with the striking fantasy of his decomposing body), he also makes clear that his is a self-conscious posture: he is at once actor and director on the galant stage of his writing.

This self-consciousness comes to the fore in another letter that plays on meanings of the words *discrétion* and *galant*.[21] Having lost a bet with Julie d'Angennes during a game of "discrétion" (the winner of which could impose a wager at her/his discretion), Voiture writes a missive to accompany the twelve English "galants" or ribbons he owed her.[22] Of course, it is hardly surprising that he exploits the polysemicity of these words, and so, after an initial acknowledgment of his wager and the debt he owes Mademoiselle de Rambouillet, he speaks of the "galants" as if they were suitors for the affections of his addressee and attributes to them a "discretion" unusual for such men. "You who have refused to accept even one galant, do not be afraid to take a great number of them," he advises her. "For I assure you that you can have confidence in them and that they will be sure to be discreet about the favor you will give them" (1:250–51). Voiture then shifts the focus back to himself, alleging the difficulty of finding discreet galants: "Whatever glory there is in receiving your favors, it is hardly insignificant to have found so many with this disposition at a time when they are all so full of vanity. Consequently, they could only be found far away and brought from overseas" (1:251). Implicitly denouncing the vain and indiscreet galants of France, he also posits a more ambiguous relationship with the English galants. He is their secretary, so he claims, and so he must imitate their style of speaking even though it is foreign to him:

> I am talking a lot for a man who is paying for a discretion. But consider, if it pleases you, that a short letter is not too much for twelve galants and that the ones for whom I write, at least those of their country, have such a strange way of making themselves understood that they seem to be speaking about love when they are only making compliments. Do not find it strange that, as their secretary, I have in a way imitated their style. And rest assured that if I only had to speak for myself I would have been happy to say that I am, Mademoiselle, with all due respect, your, etc. (1:251–52)

The relationship Voiture establishes between himself and the metaphorical English galants here closely parallels the ideal of galant masculinity he sought to exemplify throughout his oeuvre. Respecting the discretion seemingly so foreign to his compatriots, he submits to the expectations of the women he "serves." But imitating the English galants—and becoming their spokesman to boot!—leads him to adopt a language that is not his own, a language whose signifiers are easily misunderstood. Even if he claims to be closer to the English than the French galants, he is actually in a class all his own. He is not vainglorious and indiscreet, like the French, but he also would prefer not to use the language of love to give compliments, as the English do. Instead, by pointing out that he is the secretary for the English galants and that he must necessarily follow their "style," he once again inscribes his distance from the conventions he recycles. He certainly is not to be confused with the galants ordinarily found around Paris, nor is he to be mistaken for their counterparts across the Channel, even if he resembles them. His brand of galanterie stands alone and is characterized by an explicitly self-conscious manipulation of conventions that, in the end, are foreign to him. Voiture's galanterie requires readers to see a difference that might not be self-evident. That he is not the sort of galant homme he may seem to be is the message he seeks to communicate throughout his writings. But a galant homme he was, no matter how much he qualified that distinction.

An Ambiguous Legacy

Voiture's ambivalent relationship with the galant ideal is part and parcel of the ambivalent relationship with women highlighted by his nephew Pinchesne. If Voiture adopts the pretense of submitting to women's tastes and expectations, Pinchesne claims nonetheless that his uncle's model was one women themselves sought to imitate. He occupied at one and the same time a position of subservience and authority vis-à-vis women, and his ambivalence toward the galant homme ideal is linked to this ambivalence toward women. To distance himself from the submission to women required in galant masculinity, Voiture necessarily distances himself from the galant ideal, but without rejecting it out of hand.

This, however, was a tenuous and ambiguous position, and one easily misconstrued. Where Pinchesne, following his uncle's lead, perceived ambiguity—both difference and resemblance—commentators less favorably disposed toward the writer saw little or none. For these critics, the distance between Voiture and the women he entertained was difficult to ascertain, because he resembled them only too closely. Such at least is the conclusion that can be drawn from numerous texts that appeared during and especially after his lifetime. Voiture was at the center of numerous poetic and linguistic quarrels such as those of the *Suppositi* and the *muscadin* before his death, and afterward the *querelle* between the Uranistes and the Jobelins, and the particularly nasty war of words between Girac, a protégé of Balzac, and Costar, a defender and friend of Voiture.[23] But another controversy erupted, one that did not have the neat contours of a "quarrel" as such and consisted instead of often subtle insinuations of effeminacy. In a range of texts that appeared mostly in the 1650s (in the wake of Voiture's death in 1648), the devotion to women that Pinchesne celebrated becomes less than praiseworthy. Somaize's entry on Valère (that is, Voiture) in his *Grand dictionnaire historique des Précieuses* (1660) is as equivocal as the entire work. Crowned "the grand councillor of the *précieuses* and the founder of their empire,"[24] Voiture becomes an authority figure for Somaize's ironic enterprise: "I find in him an example that proves everything I have said about the witty women given the name 'précieuses' and that serves as an authority for what I've written about the men, and especially those who take pride in their galanterie, in a book that seems to have been written for the women" [527]). If he *is* such an authority, claims Somaize, it is because "he was no less the star of the salons *(ruelles)* than the most beautiful of the women he frequented" (528).

Other writers give a more explicitly satirical portrait of Voiture that has all the signs of a prototypically effeminate salon-goer, at least as this figure was represented in a number of texts from the middle of the century. He was frivolous and lazy,[25] he was physically frail,[26] and, above all, he was obsessed with his clothing and appearance, as many writers made clear. In his "Pompe funèbre de Voiture" (Voiture's Funeral Procession), Sarasin parodies one of his poems and describes a cortège of thirty cupids processing with the deceased's *bigotère* (cloth for curling a moustache), his mirror, tweezers, combs, powder boxes, skin creams, perfumes, oils, soaps, "and all the rest of the weapons that had served the conquests of the great Voiture."[27] The female "conquests" point to yet another sign of his effeminacy for, like the stereotypical salon denizen, he possessed an irresistible urge to regale women with "galanteries." Tallemant des Réaux, for whom he was "the most *coquet* of humans," claims that once, when deprived of the company of adult women, he began to court a seven-year-old girl, so irresistible was his desire to frequent the female sex.[28] And, although less caustic, Madeleine de Scudéry, in her *à clef* portrait of Callicrate (in *Artamène ou le Grand Cyrus,* part 6, book 1), purports that "he flaunted his galanterie, which was a universal galanterie, since it is true that one can say he loved all sorts of women."[29] Voiture himself indicates, as his later critics reiterate, that his "galanterie" was not to be confused with authentic passion. For his satirical portraitists, however, this pose becomes hyperbolic and self-conscious theatricality. Of Callicrate, Scudéry writes: "He was not as concerned with being loved as he was with having people think that he was loved."[30] Even Pellisson's otherwise laudatory entry in his *Histoire de l'Académie Française* indicates that "he was very contented at the thought that people believed he was favored by all his different mistresses."[31] Implied here and made explicit elsewhere is the notion that Voiture is an imposter and a hypocrite, as many an effete salon man was held to be. All appearances to the contrary, his self-conscious posturing feeds his own egotism and leads to homosocial bonding with other men, rather than homage to women, as Sarasin suggests metonymically through his description of the thirty cupids in Voiture's funeral procession: "They pretended to be much more grieved than their companions. But people suspected their great sadness was but hypocrisy, for these thirty were all coquettish cupids who are real actors and who never feel the passions they display. The deceased had never had dearer friends nor whom he would have more eagerly employed for his business."[32] With friends like these, Voiture showed his true colors. Putting women on a pedestal was hardly his foremost concern, or so Sarasin would have us believe.

Still, whatever Voiture's true intentions, he devoted much of his oeuvre to women, a fact that Sarasin and other critics acknowledge and make light of. Once again, they exploited a feature of the satirical portrait of men in the *ruelles*, who, as Sorel puts it, had to have their "pockets full of sonnets, epigrams, madigrals, elegies, and other poems either satirical or on the subject of love."[33] Preoccupied with entertaining his female addressees, these critics suggest, Voiture's writing had little value beyond its function as a status symbol. Hence, Somaize describes a "précieuse" by the name of Hésionide (Mlle Hardy) who read only Chapelain and Voiture—and even then rarely—because she devoted so much time to sociable pursuits.[34] The implication of frivolity, apparent in Somaize's allusion, became a leitmotiv for the critical reception of Voiture's work. Even when giving him credit as the inventor of galanterie, some observers denied him status as a serious writer. In the words of Tallemant des Réaux, "He is the one who showed others how to say things in a galant manner. He is the father of ingenious silliness *(l'ingénieuse badinerie)*. But that's all one should seek to find, for his serious tone is not worth much, and his letters, except for the parts that are so natural, are on the whole poorly written."[35]

As the critical discourse on Voiture developed throughout the century, commentators found in his writings many of the traits exposed in his satirical portrait as effeminate salon-goer. Shifting their attention from his life to his works, they nonetheless perpetuated a link between the two, if only unwittingly. Given the parallels between them, it becomes possible to read into their critiques of his writing the charges of effeminacy they leveled at Voiture the person. Just as Voiture was lazy, his style was negligent; just as he was physically weak, his writing lacked the strength of high rhetorical style; and just as he was obsessed with his clothing and appearance, his rhetoric betrayed an excessive penchant for ornamentation (in the form of hyperbole, especially). It was Méré who formulated the most sustained and elaborate critique of Voiture's style, principally in his *Discours de la justesse* (1669). In it, the Chevalier enumerates a long list of "faults," complete with quotations to support his case. Noting (what he perceives to be) grammatical errors, semantic confusion, and equivocal constructions, Méré characterizes Voiture's principal weakness as that of "affectation."[36] Whether in moral or aesthetic discourse, affectation was regularly coded as "feminine" in the early modern period, and Méré explicitly makes the connection between affectation in language and femininity elsewhere.[37] But affectation was also a characteristic frequently associated with the effeminate salon man and specifically with his use of language. For Méré, though, Voiture's affectation reveals an even deeper weakness: a lack of "good sense" *(bon sens)* and "solid reason" *(droite raison)*, the two constituent elements of *justesse*, or the ability to perceive "the true relation that one thing should have with another."[38] Here again, Méré's characterization ultimately renders Voiture implicitly "feminine." Women, according to a long-standing misogynist cliché, were lacking in "good sense" and "reason," "masculine" qualities par excellence.

A more explicit effeminization of Voiture's literary legacy came in the form of a contrast with Guez de Balzac that became a commonplace shortly after his death and remains so to this day. At the heart of the many semantic and rhetorical oppositions used to distinguish these two *épistoliers* (conversation versus oratory, circumstantial versus monumental, personal versus universal, relational versus autonomous, etc.) is the pair "feminine" versus "masculine." This gendered opposition becomes explicit when Costar, in his quarrel with Girac, admits that Voiture "does not speak Balzac": "Those striking figures that . . . enrapture minds, transport them, move them, grab them with surprise and astonishment are not to be found in his own." Voiture's works do not have "that virile and vigorous beauty of diction, that choice and arrangement of words, that very exacting cadence, those very harmonious and measured sounds" that typify those of Balzac.[39] Instead, Costar argues:

[Voiture] for his part believed it was sufficient to engage with and win over hearts and minds by a gentler, more exquisite, more refined and subtler means. He wanted to be liked, he wanted to captivate, and he found the secret for doing so. Above all else, he sought that sort of nonchalance that suits beautiful women so well, making the advantages of their birth shine forth and, after enchanting eyes, leaving to the imagination the pleasure of dreaming about what the graces of art would have added to those of nature. (15–16)

In this contrast, Costar emphasizes the very different—and explicitly gendered—effects sought by Balzac and Voiture. As Michèle Longino has put it: "In seeking 'to please,' Voiture aligned himself with the masculine prescription of a feminine ethos, whereas Balzac, in seeking admiration, upheld the masculine ethos."[40] To be sure, as a defender of Voiture, Costar's intent was not to portray his style as "effeminate." But by accentuating the "feminine" means his writing supposedly employs ("a gentler, more exquisite, more refined and subtler means") and the "feminine" effect it aims to produce ("that sort of nonchalance that suits beautiful women so well"), Costar simply puts a positive spin on what others at least implicitly perceived to be an effeminizing risk within Voiture's brand of galanterie.

As this aesthetic gained widespread and often enthusiastic approval in *mondain* circles and the *mondain* literary field, and as it became increasingly associated with women's writing, male writers came to terms with this risk in various but subtle ways. In his *Discours sur les Œuvres de Monsieur Sarasin*, Pellisson insists that his friend's galanterie cannot be confused with Voiture's. While offering praise for Voiture, Pellisson affirms that Sarasin was adept at both serious and ludic genres and that he was able to appeal to a broad spectrum of people: women, writers, courtiers, the most enlightened and the less so, those occupied with "serious matters" *(les affaires)* and those seeking "leisure" *(divertissement)*.[41] By implication, then, Voiture's galanterie is more limited, being solely ludic in nature, and unable to bridge the gap between *mondanité* and the serious world of business and politics. Whereas Voiture's writing was successful only in the feminocentric spaces of the salon, Pellisson suggests, Sarasin's addressed both these latter and the (almost) exclusively masculine worlds of erudition and public affairs. In sum, his galanterie is both "feminine" *and* "masculine."

Dominique Bouhours makes a similar attempt to develop an aesthetic that encompasses both genders. Throughout *Les Entretiens d'Ariste et d'Eugène* (1671) and *La Manière de bien penser dans les ouvrages d'esprit* (1687),

Bouhours expresses consistent praise for Voiture. Above all, his works—and his letters in particular—are exemplary for "a naturalness and refinement that are found absolutely nowhere else," as Eugène says.[42] But no matter how solid, Bouhours's admiration has its limits, for Voiture's writing is "pretty" *(joli)* and not "beautiful" *(beau)*. The distinction that Bouhours draws between these two categories is explained by way of a gendered analogy from Aristotle, which Ariste cites in *Les Entretiens:*

> The beauty of the mind is not unlike that of the body: short men, no matter how attractive, are not beautiful in Aristotle's opinion. At most, they are pretty because the benefit of stature is an essential part of beauty. Thus, small geniuses who are limited to a single thing, writers of pretty verse who can do nothing else, no matter how enticing and polished they may be, are not beautiful minds, in spite of what people may say. They are only pretty minds, to be exact, and they shouldn't be considered of any more worth in society. (246)

It is probably not irrelevant that Voiture was known to be small in stature. But what made him one of the "pretty little geniuses" for Bouhours was not his body as much as his mind. After discussing the exact same analogy from Aristotle, Philanthe and Eudoxe (in *La Manière de bien penser*) agree that Voiture's "thoughts" *(pensées)* are "jolies" and not "belles" because their "enticement" *(agrément)* derives from the intrinsic appeal of the things described, and not from their "nobility" or "majesty."[43] Compared to Voiture, "no one has been better at bringing to life all that is delectable and most joyous about nature," they concur. And after reading a passage from one of his letters, Philanthe exclaims: "One cannot imagine anything more ornate or suave."[44] The terms used to characterize Voiture's "thoughts" here ("delectable" [*délicieux*], "joyous" [*riant*], "ornate" [*fleuri*], and "suave" [*doux*]), while laudatory, are distinct from what is properly *beau*. They are tied to nature, and they lack the "greatness that always enchants the mind" the sine qua non of the *beau* (131). Hence, there is a gender opposition at work in the distinction between the *joli* and the *beau* applied to Voiture. He possesses all the traits of the "feminine" and is thus only a "pretty" man; he does not rise to the stature of the "beautiful" man.

When Bouhours defines his own aesthetic ideal, he once again employs gendered analogies. But instead of rejecting the *joli* as one might expect, he performs something of a synthesis to arrive at a cross-gendered ideal. Part of his ideal is explicitly "masculine" and opposed to effeminate softness: "The beauty of the mind is a virile and noble beauty that has nothing soft or effeminate about it," as Eugène indicates.[45] However, the vigor and nobility of this beauty does not preclude qualities associated with Voiture:

> But do not think that a clever mind, because it has more strength, is less refined. It resembles Homer's Achilles and Tasso's Rinaldo, who had extremely strong muscles and sinews under a white and delicate skin. Their solidity and incisiveness do not prevent them from conceiving things exquisitely and giving a refined turn to everything they think. The images through which they express their ideas are like those paintings that have all the finesse of art combined with an inexpressible tender and gracious air that enchants connoisseurs.[46]

By conjoining an interior force with an exterior refinement—strong muscles covered with delicate and beautiful skin—Eudoxe (the mouthpiece for Bouhours) finds a way to retain the "tender and gracious air" he admires in Voiture, rendering it unequivocally "masculine." That Bouhours appears to have fabricated the description of Achilles and Renaud as simultaneously muscular and fine skinned indicates all the more clearly how determined he is to find a gendered analogy that transcends a rigid binary.[47] In another striking passage from *Les Entretiens*, he again develops the analogy of a cross-gendered ideal, but this time using women (presumably Amazons) as his example and referring to the superiority of the French language:

> What is suave and refined about the French language is upheld by what is strong and virile about it. Thus it has neither the harshness of the German language nor the softness *(mollesse)* of the Italian language, and it can be compared to those ancient heroines who had all the sweetness *(douceur)* of their sex and all the strength of ours and who, moreover, were just as chaste as they were valiant.[48]

For Bouhours, the French language combines male strength with feminine *douceur* and refinement, thereby avoiding the extremes represented by German—brute force, that is, unrefined virility—on the one hand and Italian—mollitude, that is, effeminacy—on the other. Blending the "sweet" and the "refined" with the "strong" and the "virile," French represents something altogether different than either one of those extremes taken individually. It is as if Bouhours wants to have things both ways—as if, not wanting to reject Voiture, he recasts him according to his own criteria, making him more "virile," giving him the stature he lacks, filling his soft and *joli* exterior with an interior both firm and *beau*. It is as if he perceives a need to infuse the galant masculinity of the salons with a firm virility that would ward off any suggestion of effeminacy.[49]

At the end of the seventeenth century, Jean de La Bruyère's commentary on Voiture constitutes a new and insidious means of avoiding the risk of effeminacy. While expressing (muted) praise for him, La Bruyère is far more concerned with noting how passé this example has become. "If Voiture . . . for turn of phrase, wit and naturalness is not modern and in no way resembles our writers, it is because it was easier for them to neglect him than to imitate him and because the small number of those who chase after him cannot reach him" (*Des ouvrages de l'esprit*, 45 [V]).[50] The blame for this situation, La Bruyère strongly suggests in another *caractère*, is to be placed at the feet of women:

> Voiture and Sarasin were born for their century, and they appeared at a time that seemed to be waiting for them. If they had been less eager to come, they would have arrived too late; and I dare to doubt that they would have been today what they were then. Light conversations, salons, exquisite jokes, lighthearted and familiar letters, the small circles into which one was admitted only with wit, all that has disappeared. And don't say that they would bring it all back. What I will concede to their genius is that they would perhaps excel in another genre; but women these days are sanctimonious or coquettish or gamblers or ambitious, and a few all of these at the same time; the taste for favor, gambling, galants, spiritual directors have taken center stage and defend it against persons of wit *(gens d'esprit)*. (*De la mode*, 10 [IV], 401)

Recalling with nostalgia what he portrays as the heyday of salon life (a time he was too young to have known personally, it should be noted), La Bruyère asserts that Voiture and Sarasin were products much more than masters of their age. The reason, he implies with asyndeton (grammatical ellipsis), is that women and men are different than they were earlier in the century. Yet, the fact that women are named first strongly suggests that they are the ones responsible for allowing the enemies of "persons of wit" to take over. Among these enemies are "galants" and "spiritual directors," the masculine counterparts of the "coquettes" and the "pious women" who purportedly reign over *mondain* society along with the gambling women and the ambitious women. The truncated grammatical construction of the last sentence (the substitution of semicolons for conjunctions) neatly translates La Bruyère's desire to create a boundary between the women and the men of the *monde* and the inimitable "persons of wit" of yesteryear, Voiture and Sarasin. These two are safe from any implication of effeminacy because that vice and others have been assumed by the pejorative figures of the galants and the confessors. And we are left to infer that their authority is derived from the sorts of pernicious women who hold sway over polite society and who are the antithesis of the exclusive *esprit* of yore.

By confining Voiture to an inaccessible and inimitable past, La Bruyère effectively shields him from any association with women. Even when he admits this connection, as he does in the famous *caractère* about women's letters, he begins by framing the question to Voiture's advantage: "I do not know if anyone could ever put more wit, polish, enticement, or style into letters than what is seen in those by Balzac and Voiture. They are devoid of the sentiments that have only reigned after their time and that owe their birth to women" (*Des ouvrages de l'esprit*, 37 [IV], 79).[51] Although the rest of this *caractère* praises the "natural" elegance of women's letters, which men can only reproduce with painful effort, La Bruyère ends by criticizing women's unspecified "faults": "If women were always correct, I would dare say that the letters of a few of them would perhaps be what is the best writing in our language" (*Des ouvrages de l'esprit*, 37 [IV], 80). This final remark is predictable given the very first sentence, quoted above, which makes Balzac and Voiture the paragons of epistolary art. They may be indebted to women, he admits, but they have perfected an elegance that comes "naturally" to women, who are thus exposed to mistakes only (masculine) artistry can avoid. Placing Voiture on the side of art and women on the side of nature, La Bruyère makes distinctions that galanterie attempted to blur—the distinction between art and nature and perhaps most of all between galant men and women. The risks of effeminacy that earlier generations perceived no longer exist, so it seems, because true galanterie is a thing of the past.

From Pinchesne's deliberate celebration of his uncle's ties with women to La Bruyère's attempts to break those ties, we have come full circle. But at issue throughout the century is the place of galant masculinity in relation to femininity. How should the galant homme "imitate" women? And how should he do so in a way that paradoxically accentuates his difference and his distance from the other sex? In the aftermath of the virtuosic performances at the Hôtel de Rambouillet, Voiture the person and Voiture the body of writing illustrated the cultural authority of women and its impact on men in seventeenth-century France. For men desirous of success in the salons or the *mondain* literary field, Voiture's legacy was highly ambivalent, and increasingly so as the century progressed. It was a model to follow, to be sure, but also one to add nuance to and even transcend. The story of Voiture's reception demonstrates once again how normative masculinity continually adapts itself to keep the edge over both women and subordinate men. But Voiture's was not the only model for salon masculinity, as we will see in the next chapter. Starting from Voiture's example but deviating from it in important ways, Madeleine de Scudéry develops a variant of galanterie in which effeminacy is not a threat and the sweetness and softness of *douceur* are actually accentuated.

FOUR
~~~

Madeleine de Scudéry's
Tender Masculinity

ALONG WITH THE MARQUISE DE RAMBOUILLET, Madeleine de Scudéry stands
as the ultimate salon hostess of seventeenth-century France. Just as Rambouillet's name was associated with her *Chambre bleue,* Scudéry became famous for her *Samedis,* the name given her salon meetings, which took place
on Saturdays.[1] Like the *Chambre bleue,* the *Samedis* was a locus of considerable influence on literary and cultural life of the period. But unlike Rambouillet, Scudéry was a celebrated writer. Through her novels, novellas, poetry, and, later, collected conversations, Scudéry became a leading advocate
for sociable ideals, with both literary and social repercussions, and these
ideals illustrated the creative roles of salons within the literary field of the
day. Not only did much of her work emanate from her own *ruelle* (through
collaboration with others and the activities of its members), she also privileged the conversational aesthetic that was developed and practiced in the salons. As both product and representation of these circles, Scudéry's novels,
especially *Artamène ou le Grand Cyrus* (1649–54) and *Clélie, histoire romaine*
(1654–60), and the *Chroniques du Samedi* (the manuscript collection of letters
and poems from the first two years of Scudéry's salon, 1653–54) offer a theory and praxis of salon sociability.[2]

With their emphasis on social interaction and group harmony, Scudéry's
writings and those of her salon attach particular importance to relations between men and women. Given the genres in which she writes and the heterosocial nature of the salon more generally, this is hardly surprising. But
Scudéry's interest in sexual difference goes beyond an obvious reliance on
social and literary convention. Recent criticism has stressed how Scudéry
reconceptualizes femininity by advocating women's right to choose their
partners if not to resist marriage altogether, celebrating women's creative
endeavors, and exploring women's affective lives.[3] This latter feature, central to her work, has attracted particular scrutiny. In a now-classic study,

Joan DeJean coined the topographical metaphor *tender geography* to describe the preoccupation of Scudéry (and other seventeenth-century French women writers) with female interiority and more precisely female desire.[4] Linked to this feature, as critics have also shown, is the signal importance her work gives to *mondain* relationality, especially as it is enacted through mixed-gender conversation.[5] Indeed, Scudéry almost always situates her portrayal of women's affective and social lives within heterosocial settings, not unlike those of the salons. While scholars have noted the sustained reflection on the nature of male-female relations in her oeuvre, left unexplored is the revision of masculinity required by her revamping of femininity. In fact, masculine affectivity and subjectivity are just as important to her as their feminine counterparts. On the level of characterization, to take but this example, men are no less prominent than women and just as much the object of narrative commentary.[6]

Concentrating on *Le Grand Cyrus, Clélie,* and the *Chroniques,*[7] this chapter argues that Scudéry's model of masculinity, at first glance similar to the honnête homme and the galant homme, departs from them in important ways. For, whereas honnêteté and galanterie urge men to imitate women, Scudéry's ideal foregrounds female agency. Specifically, she calls upon women to regulate men's behavior so as to cultivate two key qualities, an extreme form of empathy she terms *tendresse* (tenderness) and an idiosyncratic version of melancholy. Unlike Méré and Voiture, then, Scudéry takes the injunction of the "female principle" at face value and does not look for ways to circumvent it. Ultimately, I contend, she offers a radical vision of gender in which the boundaries between masculinity and femininity are blurred.

GENDER AND THE *air galant*

In contrast to what we saw in the previous chapter, effeminacy is not an overriding concern for Scudéry. Rather than an excess of refinement so often derided as effeminate in this period, Scudéry sees its lack as a far more pressing problem.[8] Thus, in her conversation "De l'air galant" (On the Galant Air), the salonlike gathering around Sapho enumerates the "bad galants" who fall short of the elegant *air galant,* the "secret charm, . . . [t]his certain something that pervades the entire person who professes it—mind, actions, even dress . . . and makes people refined and cultured" (*Story,* 100; *De l'air,* 53)—those who believe that galanterie is nothing more than following the latest fashions, being persistent and brash, talking incessantly, running from salon to salon, or spouting sweet nothings and those who are "sweet talkers who are eternally languishing," "rude and proud lovers," "jovial galants who never speak of love except in jest," "the real philanderers who carry on ten or twelve intrigues at once but love no one," "those obstinate lovers who are always moping around" (*Story*, 101–2; *De l'air*, 54–55). At the end of the conversation, Sapho is asked to shift the focus from men to women: "It isn't right only to consider lovers—it would be better to talk about galanterie in general so that we may also speak a little more particularly about women" (*Story*, 102; *De l'air*, 55). To speak of "galanterie" is not only a matter for galants, but also for their "mistresses." Scudéry's concern with defining and defending "galanterie in general" helps to explain why she is less preoccupied than other writers with the risk of effeminacy. Although she claims that men and women have different means of achieving the *air galant* she so prizes, that quality is not gender specific. At its core, it is a profoundly social trait to which both men and women should aspire. Produced by individuals, the *air galant* creates the affective bond that holds the group together since it is "what makes people refined and cultured—and what makes them amiable and loved" (*Story*, 100; *De l'air*, 53).

Throughout her oeuvre, Scudéry's objective is to conceive a relational space where men and women might share a bond that is at once aesthetic and affective. As she presents it, her vision of galant relationality is something new, but it also builds on numerous traditions, such as medieval courtly love, Neoplatonism, and the pastoral novel.[9] Crafting the *air galant* through a synthesis of these and other preexisting literary and cultural discourses, Scudéry revises the gendered positions she inherits. She retains the outward appearance of these positions all the while revamping their inner motivations and goals. Thus, whereas Voiture consistently and explicitly distances himself from the neo-Petrarchan topoi he uses, Scudéry performs a far more intricate recasting that, on occasion, was willfully misconstrued as an accentuation of these topoi. Both Molière (in *Les Précieuses ridicules*) and Boileau (in "Dialogue des héros de roman"), for instance, decry what they present as the ridiculous passivity and softness of Scudéry's heroes. Molière and Boileau notwithstanding, the male characters in *Le Grand Cyrus* and *Clélie* are anything but passive. But in addition to these traditional displays of virile heroics, it is true that Scudéry devotes considerable space to her heroes' "softer" side, namely, to their affective lives with women and the other men who surround them. To be clear, there is nothing particularly unusual or untraditional about the fact that her heroes possess these two dimensions. Still, Scudéry departs from tradition in the contours she gives to her heroes' affectivity, and it was precisely this departure that seemed to provoke the ire of Molière and Boileau, among others, and that caused them to discount the wholly conventional male heroics in Scudéry's novels. For instead of distancing herself from the topoi of male submission, suffering, and sensitivity, as Voiture and his subsequent defenders and detractors did, Scudéry reinvigorated and remotivated them.

By espousing and recasting these topoi, Scudéry created what I will be calling a "tender masculinity." This ideal is "tender" insofar as it valorizes the sweetness and softness of *la douceur* and specifically the affective notion of *la tendresse*. But by prizing masculine softness and tenderness, Scudéry highlights men's connection to and dependence upon women. Sapho makes this clear when she reiterates the early modern commonplace about women's refining influence over men. To acquire the *air galant*, she argues, men must have a natural predisposition for it, but they must also experience "social exchange at its best" *(le grand commerce du monde)*, and especially interaction with women: "conversation with women gives it to men. For I maintain that there has never been a man with the galant air who flees interaction with persons of my sex. If I dare say all I think, I would say what's more that a man must have had at least once in his life some inclination to love if he is to acquire perfectly the galant air" (*Story*, 99–100; *De l'air*, 51–52). When asked whether women too must experience love in order to possess this quality, Sapho rejects any one-to-one correspondence between the masculine and feminine civilizing process: "At the same time that I maintain that for a man to have this air about him his heart must have been a little engaged, I maintain that for a woman to have this very same air, it suffices for her to have been favorably disposed to it by Nature, to have seen the world and known refined people, and to aim to captivate generally, without loving anyone in particular" (*Story*, 100; *De l'air*, 52). This passage considers how women can be not only the instruments but also the recipients of the civilizing process; and at the same time it establishes an asymmetry between men's and women's sociable refinement. As Sapho conceives things, men are more dependent on women for the *air galant* than women are on men. Men must experience love, whereas women need only have the desire to "captivate generally." To be truly galant means to be blessed by nature, whether a man or a woman; and yet women would seem to be more blessed than men.

The difference Sapho observes between the "nature" of women and men is one found throughout Scudéry's oeuvre. In the male-female couple, women occupy a position of ostensible authority over their male suitors. When Sapho describes the obligation women have to assert their power over their suitors, she evokes an asymmetrical power dynamic that is wholly congruent with this long tradition: "each in his rightful place, if mistresses *(maîtresses)* were mistresses and slaves *(esclaves)*, slaves, every pleasure would come thronging back into the world" (*Story*, 103; *De l'air*, 57). The primary heroines in Scudéry's novels assume without fail their roles as *maîtresses*, holding sway over their male suitors, their *esclaves*, but also over their male and female friends. One of the most famous examples of this authority is found in the *Carte de Tendre*, the allegorical map of friendship and love conceived by the eponymous heroine of *Clélie*. "[T]he visual record of Clélie's authority," as Jeffrey Peters aptly puts it, the *Carte de Tendre* figures the material and immaterial means of gaining Clélie's affections (her *tendresse*) as three different—and difficult—paths from "Nouvelle Amitié" (New Friendship) to "Tendre-sur-Reconnaissance" (Tender upon Gratitude), "Tendre sur Inclination" (Tender upon Inclination) or "Tendre-sur-Estime" (Tender upon Esteem), respectively.[10] Ultimately, as Peters demonstrates, the map is about neither landscape nor seduction, but about Clélie's (and potentially other women's) power, deriving from her assertion of the right to choose her friends and suitors and to withhold from these latter the "Terres Inconnues" (Unknown Lands).[11]

But the *Carte de Tendre* points to an extratextual female authority, as well. As the *Chroniques du Samedi* reveal, Scudéry and members of her salon used the *Carte* as a parlor game by which they charted out a hierarchy among themselves in relation to her unquestionable authority.[12] Yet, Scudéry's control over her salon and its members was anything but an ephemeral game. To participate in the Samedis was to pay homage to the hostess by submitting to her will in all matters deemed to concern her circle. Moreover, Scudéry is regularly cast as the Queen of Tendre *(la reine de Tendre)*, that is, the ruler of the affective realm constituted by her inner circle. Myriam Maître has shown how these references incorporate an understanding of sovereignty that resembles absolutist political theory, with the important exception that Scudéry is granted powers denied to actual queens at the time.[13] Founding her authority on human reason and will, she creates and bestows privileges and derogations for those "subjects" of her choosing. While these "subjects" include both women and men, the power she exerts over men is qualitatively different from the power she has over women. In Scudéry's salon as in her writings, there is an ambiguity between friendship and love, with friendship taking on the forms of a courtship ritual that puts men in an inherently subordinate position to the woman who presides over an informal circle of friends. And for those men who perform the courtship ritual out of authentic passion, the subordinate stance goes without saying. By contrast, the other women in the circle, although also hierarchically subordinate to her, are not required to make an emphatic display of their "lower" status. Instead, they can potentially reproduce, albeit on a hierarchically lesser level, the asymmetrical power dynamic with male suitors of their own. In Scudéry's vision of masculinity, then, men are to submit willingly to women, to hand over to women the power that is wielded over them.

On the surface, this asymmetry between women and men appears wholly conventional; but what is different is the explicit theorization she gives as justification, notably in *Le Grand Cyrus* and *Clélie*. Feminine supremacy serves first and foremost as a mechanism of self-preservation and self-determination against the backdrop of a patriarchal world where women are often victimized. Of all Scudéry's heroines, Sapho (in *Le Grand Cyrus*) and Plotine (in *Clélie*) articulate this reasoning in the most explicit (if not the most radical) terms. Insisting on unending fidelity among partners, women's freedom to choose their partners, and the right to refuse marriage altogether, Sapho and Plotine share the conviction that men's desire is fundamentally unstable and therefore untrustworthy. As Plotine explains to her suitor Mutius: "I am resolved to protect my heart my whole life long and, further, never to wed, for marrying someone without loving that person is, in my opinion, the craziest and cruelest thing in the world. And convincing oneself of someone's affections is the most reckless thing there ever was. Thus, freedom is the surest choice" (*Clélie-C*, 5:375; *Clélie-F*, 329–30). In her own rejection of marriage, Sapho notes the real or potentially tyrannical power that husbands hold over wives. "I consider it as unending slavery. . . . [T]he moment I consider them as husbands, I consider them as masters, masters apt to become tyrants, and at that moment, it is impossible not to hate them" (*Story*, 19–20; *Artamène-S*, 10:343–44). When pressed by a male friend as to whether she would change her mind if she were to fall in love, Sapho balks at having to relinquish her freedom: "I don't know if my feelings will change . . . but I know that unless I lose my reason in love, I will never lose my liberty, and I am resolved never to let my slave become my tyrant" (*Story*, 20; *Artamène-S*, 10:344–45).

Beyond her attachment to "liberty," Sapho also defends the principle of female supremacy for reasons of broader social interest. In "De l'air galant," she argues that if women were to assert their authority over men, "civility would rule, true *galanterie* would shine its brightest, and we wouldn't see what we see daily, men who speak of women in general with such obvious contempt or who boast publicly of the favors they have received. Nor would we see so many women abandon that exacting modesty so necessary to them and that is the very soul of love" (*Story*, 103; *De l'air*, 57). Assuming their rightful roles, Sapho argues, women would effect a transformation in men's behavior, a point Scudéry develops elsewhere. But for women to accomplish this, they must first of all demonstrate a measure of self-control in the form of "exacting modesty." What becomes apparent, both here and elsewhere in Scudéry's oeuvre, is that "modesty" *(pudeur)* is in fact a form of empowerment for women. When women enforce it in an "exacting" way among themselves and impose it upon their suitors, both they and men are the beneficiaries: men remain the "slaves" they should be, modifying their behavior toward women accordingly and reaping the benefits in the form of women's favor, and women are more respectful among themselves.[14] Granted, Sapho is referring here to the heterosocial dynamics of restricted sociable circles, and not to society as a whole. But within these spaces, women hold the key to social harmony, becoming the superego that men presumably lack, and consequently protecting women from the potential harm of men and other women.

The power of women's modesty manifests itself most prominently in control over men's speech. Since Scudéry's fiction gives signal importance to conversations, it thus confirms a central tenet of speech-act theory, namely that speech is action. Not surprisingly, then, women's power exerts itself in the form of the spoken word and aims to master the speech of others. This is especially the case within the male-female couple, where the *maîtresse* closely regulates what her *esclave* may and may not say about their feelings for each other. Here again, Scudéry follows, to a point, a long tradition of courtship ritual, which enjoined the male suitor to restrain his desire to declare his love and to do so only with the express consent of his beloved. But while appropriating this otherwise fairly common convention of courtship, she makes woman's modesty a means of asserting control over men's (and sometimes even her own) passions. When, in part 3 of *Clélie*, Herminius violates this code and declares his love to Valérie without her prior approval, she responds, predictably: "To prevent me from forbidding you to love me . . . you should never have told me that you loved me. But now that you've told me so, I can do nothing for you without doing something against myself" (*Clélie-C*, 3:97–98). Placing self-interest above her suitor's, she then issues an order: "I implore you in all seriousness please to order your feelings and your words" (*Clélie-C*, 3:98). Herminius objects to the strictures imposed by Valérie, but confirms her suggestion that "feelings" and "words" are one and the same. Referring to the word *amour* (love), which he may not utter, he cries: "Ah,

Madame . . . do not forbid me to use the sweetest and most pleasing word in the world for those whose heart possesses the passion it expresses." Terms such as *affection* and *tenderness* do not convey the same intensity, do not move the speaker or the recipient in the same way, and do not have the same semiotic immediacy, Herminius argues (*Clélie-C*, 3:98). Valérie, however, remains unmoved. Finally, she allows him to use the word *friendship* to signify "love," in part so as to conceal Herminius's love from the public, but also, we might surmise, so as to deny him the immediate pleasure of the word, whose power could cause him to put her reputation at risk, even if only unintentionally. As Valérie explains to Herminius, "It is not permissible for an absolutely virtuous woman to give love and even less to receive it" (*Clélie-C*, 3:98). Women's control over men's speech, then, is an attempt to use men as proxies for their own modesty, all the while "ordering" the passions men feel. That this control has its limits is foreordained by the narrative's movement toward resolution or the disruption of its equilibrium: with time, the constraints on the male suitor's speech ease and he is allowed free expression of his love, or else the heroine's efforts to control the knowledge about her love fail. In spite of these limits, though, the restrictions on men's speech are still significant insofar as they become a means of putting their fidelity to the test, and of ensuring that they are worthy defenders of their beloved's modesty.

Along with speech, women simultaneously mediate the tensions among their male suitors. Out of respect for their *maîtresses,* these men refrain themselves from the outward manifestations of hostility to which their rivalry might otherwise lead. Thus, it is to Sapho herself that the narrator of her story attributes this restraint:

> I was surprised hundreds of times at the power Sapho had over her slaves since there wasn't a one who didn't know that she loved Phaon, and Phaon alone. Nevertheless, not one gave up hope even though she gave no hope to anyone, and although they all hated Phaon, they dared not, nor could they, offend him. Since they could only be jealous of Phaon, they got along well enough and came to have a sort of trust in one another. Thus Sapho, the lovers and her chosen lover and the ill-treated rivals were always together without any disagreement to trouble their society. (*Story*, 92; *Artamène-S*, 10:507)

Sapho's seductive power is what assembles the male suitors around her, inspires their rivalry, and yet keeps the peace among them all at the same time. The end result, as the narrator indicates, is a modicum of harmony for the "society" around Sapho. Her appeasing powers are hardly exceptional, though. Clélie likewise keeps the rivalry between Aronce and Horace from boiling over, and in the *Chroniques du Samedi,* Scudéry herself tempers the rival ambitions of several male salon members.[15] It is quite probable that this mediating and pacifying function is a forerunner of the role that Dena Goodman attributes to eighteenth-century *salonnières* amongst competing philosophes.[16] But whatever the case, for Scudéry, women are once again a regulating superego for men, supplying a self-mastery they seem unable to muster when confronted with amorous rivalry. The external supplement for a missing or deficient inner force, women "civilize" men, consistent with the period's commonplace prescriptions. Policing male homosociality as they do, women turn out to be an integral component of masculine subjectivity itself.

But in order to be worthy of women's refining influence, men must display several crucial, and purportedly innate, qualities. In Scudéry's vision of ideal masculinity, men must already be blessed with an exceptional refinement before women can refine them yet further. Of course, Scudéry is by no means alone in promoting what amounts to an essentialist conception of civility, both masculine and feminine.[17] But, what distinguishes her from many of her contemporaries is the often detailed attention she gives to a wide array of personality traits. Throughout her oeuvre, Scudéry fine-tunes an elaborate typology, acknowledging a diversity of human personalities and exploring the means to bridge these differences through and for sociable interaction. More often than not, her typological acumen is trained on the many obstacles to social harmony found in personality defects, as the discussion of unrefined lovers by Sapho's circle of friends makes clear. When characters in Scudéry's fiction are presented as praiseworthy (or "ideal"), they are invariably also presented as individuals, with highly specific, usually inborn traits. It is difficult then to identify any single feminine or masculine ideal in Scudéry's writings. Furthermore, the perspectives from which prescriptive judgments are made are as diverse as the many character types portrayed, complicating any attempt to arrive at something that would represent "Scudéry's" point of view. Still, there are recurring themes and plot situations, and there are prominent heroes and heroines, all of which make it possible to speak of the basic elements of gendered ideals that are espoused at different moments in her work. Two of these, tenderness and melancholy, while applicable to both men and women, have special importance for men and masculinity. For, with these traits, Scudéry creates a fluid boundary between the two genders, reasserting feminine agency while valorizing a soft masculinity.

La tendresse

In a letter to Samuel Isarn (Thrasile), Scudéry (Sapho) creates both a filiation and a difference between the writings of her salon and those of the illustrious Voiture. Thanking Isarn for a poem he had sent her, she asserts:

Les vers que vous m'avez donnés
Sont si galants, si bien tournés,
Qu'ils sont tous faits, je vous le jure,
Comme s'ils étaient de Voiture.
Encore ne sais-je pas bien
Si je ne leur dérobe rien:
Car si je les sais bien entendre,
Ils ont quelque chose de tendre
Que ceux de Voiture n'ont pas,
Qui leur donne certains appas.[18]

[The verses you gave me / Are so galant, so well turned, / That they are all written, I swear it, / As if they were by Voiture. / Even then I am not sure / If I do not deny them something, / For if I understand them correctly, / They have something tender about them / That those of Voiture do not have, / Which gives them a certain enticement.]

If Isarn's verses are "galant" and worthy of Voiture, they also display a quality even the *alcôviste* of the Hôtel de Rambouillet lacked—"something tender." Formulated in this way, tenderness is fully compatible with galanterie, and yet it is also something different that distinguishes the ethos of Scudéry's salon from its illustrious predecessor. As the pseudonymous Sapho uses the term here, tenderness is a poetic effect, produced by writing, but at its core, it is an almost ineffable quality issuing from the heart of those fortunate enough to possess it. Clélie, the primary exponent of *la tendresse*, explains that it is "a certain sensitivity *(sensibilité)* of the heart that is almost never found fully except in people who have a noble heart, virtuous inclinations, and a well-turned frame of mind" (*Clélie-C*, 1:118; *Clélie-F*, 74). Tenderness denotes emotional sensitivity, the capacity to understand and even to experience the feelings of others.[19] The province of an elite few (those with a "noble heart, virtuous inclinations, and a well-turned frame of mind"), it provides a solid intersubjective bond. Persons who are endowed with *la tendresse* enjoy a friendship that is "sincere and passionate" and they "feel all the sorrows and all the joys of those they love so vividly that they do not feel their own nearly as much" (*Clélie-C*, 1:118; *Clélie-F*, 74). According to this definition, tenderness is an extreme form of empathy, shared among friends, that leads them each to a dispossession of the individual self and an opening onto the feelings of others. In the process, however, *la tendresse* cultivates the *enjouement* inherent in galanterie: "tenderness also has the particularity of giving [friendship] a certain sort of galanterie that renders it more entertaining; it inspires civility and punctiliousness *(exactitude)* in those who are capable of it" (*Clélie-C*, 1:117; *Clélie-F*, 74). Tenderness, then, is the underlying cause of the *air galant*, itself the pinnacle of sociable refinement for men *and* women.

In Clélie's definition, *la tendresse* applies above all to friendship, no matter what the gender of the friends involved. In the conversation during which she defines it, tenderness is a heuristic device for distinguishing "ordinary friendship" from "tender friendship." Where tender friendship is marked by sincerity, fidelity, empathy, galanterie, strong attachment ("violence"), and absolute devotion, ordinary friendship, on the contrary, reveals all that tenderness is not: it is tranquil; without sweet pleasures *(douceurs)*, worry, or melancholy; self-centered; emotionally lethargic; and easily disrupted.[20] As manifested in friendship, tenderness is anything but the languid and peaceful quality the term evokes today; indeed, those very traits characterize precisely what it is *not*, according to Scudéry. Tenderness is also not the nearly exclusive domain of femininity, as it would again seem to be today, at least in some quarters.[21] Instead, as Clélie insists, *la tendresse* is just as necessary for men as it is for women. "I'll let you judge . . . if I'm right only to want men and women friends who have a tender heart in the way I understand it" (*Clélie-C*, 1:117; *Clélie-F*, 73). Later, when Clélie is asked to sketch out the *Carte de Tendre*, it is in response to a request that she put into allegorical and cartographic form the typological hierarchy among her friends and the means of progressing toward the pinnacle of that hierarchy, her "tender friends."[22] From the context of the earlier conversation about *la tendresse*, it is clear that these friends include both women and men and that the *Carte* is a road map to Clélie's hierarchy. This is also true in the *Chroniques du Samedi*, where references to the *Carte* include both men and women navigating their way toward the inner circle of Scudéry's salon.[23] At first glance, then, it might appear difficult to make a clear distinction between tender masculinity and tender femininity. At its core, *la tendresse* applies to men and women equally, and its requirements are seemingly gender neutral.[24]

But a closer look brings the gendered contours of *la tendresse* into sharper focus. For, even if tenderness is the sine qua non for the women who aspire to be the closest friends of Clélie—or Scudéry herself for that matter—on the whole the discussions of this quality in both *Clélie* and the *Chroniques du Samedi* privilege a masculine perspective. That is, men's experience of their own and their quest for their beloved's tenderness occupy center stage of these texts, as if the stakes of tender femininity were somehow less pressing than those of tender masculinity. This becomes evident in Aronce's definition of tender love, which, instead of the gender-inclusive language and examples in Clélie's explanation of tender friendship, concentrates solely on the experience of men (the "suitors" [*amants*] with and without *la tendresse*), and forgoes any corresponding commentary on the experience of women (the *maîtresses*). This perspective is confirmed even further by Clélie's refusal to contribute to Aronce's explanation, claiming that the topic is not relevant to her.[25] When he expounds on the interconnections between tenderness and love, then, Aronce shifts the focus of the conversation from collective (and particularly heterosocial) friendship to masculine heterosexual love. However, his concern is not necessarily or immediately to protect phallic privilege, but rather to critique those *amants* lacking in tenderness so as to show how essential it is in (men's) love. He argues that the lover without *tendresse*, like his counterpart in friendship, is self-absorbed and incapable of empathy. "[He] wants everything that entices him without limits, and he even wants it in such a curt and impolite way that he asks for the greatest favors as if they were owed him as a tribute" (*Clélie-C*, 1:119; *Clélie-F*, 76–77). Lovers of this sort are "uncivil, full of vanity, easy to anger, difficult to appease, indiscreet when favored, and intolerable them mistreated." It is hardly surprising, then, that they are unable to create or grasp the more intricate pleasures of love, "those little things that provide such great and deep pleasure to those who have a tender soul." Illustrating all that tender love is *not*, these *amants* are, in Aronce's words, "enemies of tenderness and who speak ill of it" (*Clélie-C*, 1:119–20; *Clélie-F*, 77).

With this accusation, Aronce draws a clear battle line in the shifting cultural attitudes about love in mid-seventeenth-century France.[26] Casting aspersions on the "libertine" strain of galanterie, Aronce defends a conception of masculine love whose keyword is softness. By means of counterexamples, he indicates that it is refined and restrained; it considers the beloved before the self; it transforms the slightest into the greatest of pleasures; it makes the pain of love enjoyable—all this besides being faithful, sincere, modest, and discreet. In sum, tenderness in men serves to moderate, or soften, their desire. In this sense, it is even more necessary for love than for friendship, Aronce asserts, because it has a regulating effect similar to that of reason in friendship.

"As for love . . . which is almost always incompatible with reason and which at the very least can never be subjected to it, love absolutely needs tenderness to keep from being brutish, uncouth, and foolish" (*Clélie-C*, 1:119; *Clélie-F*, 76). Ultimately *la tendresse* has a refining influence homologous to that of women in the acquisition of the *air galant*. Unlike that process, however, tenderness is not external to the self and, especially, "This precious and rare quality that must be cherished even has the advantage of being something that is not acquired and that is truly a present from the gods, who are never generous with it" (*Clélie-C*, 1:120; *Clélie-F*, 78). In this doctrine of amorous predestination, a man is born with tenderness and thus is born a tender lover, or else he is condemned to the "brutish, uncouth, and foolish" existence caused by love's irrationality.

When, shortly after Aronce's exposé on tender love, Clélie produces her *Carte de Tendre*, the focus returns to friendship, and yet an inherently masculine perspective predominates the discussion and the very design of the map. If women too may travel toward any of the three Tendres (Tendre-sur-Reconnaissance, Tendre-sur-Inclination, and Tendre-sur-Estime), as we have already seen, it is for men that the *Carte* has the greatest didactic relevance. The four figures in the bottom right corner of the map stage in allegorical form this gendered reading of the map: two women, facing forward, greet two men, one of whom has reached the summit of the hill where the women are standing and the other who is still climbing and about to join them. That the men are the travelers is suggested by the walking sticks they both hold, and that the women are the guides or destinations is indicated by the outstretched arm of the first woman, either pointing toward the land of Tendre yet to be explored or welcoming the first man as he arrives. These four figures create an interpretive *mise-en-abyme* of the gendered positions inscribed in the main body of the *Carte*. The paths toward Tendre-sur-Reconnaissance and Tendre-sur-Estime, on either side of the river Inclination, pass through small cities and towns that signify qualities, actions, or attitudes reminiscent of the rituals of male courtly love. These small towns and cities are so many allegorical figurations of the "thousand good qualities" (*Clélie-C*, 1:184; *Clélie-F*, 95) a man must have in order to win Clélie's friendship, and presumably any woman's, as the presence of the second woman on the hill overlooking Tendre would seem to suggest. The three desirable destinations on the *Carte*, the three cities of Tendre, represent as many variants of the tenderness Clélie will potentially share with those men who successfully navigate one of the routes to her heart and avoid going off course toward either the Lake of Indifference or the Sea of Enmity.

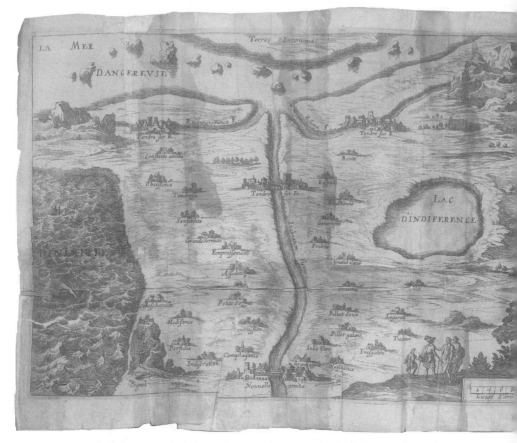

FIGURE 1. "Carte de Tendre," in Madeleine de Scudéry, *Clélie, histoire romaine* (Paris: Augustin Courbé, 1656), vol. 1. Reproduced by permission of the John Hay Library, Brown University.

And yet, the *Carte de Tendre* makes clear that the practice of tenderness by men aiming to win over women and thus their *tendresse* is anything but straightforward. Except in the case of "inclination," where Clélie and her new friend are immediately drawn to each other, tenderness involves an elaborate ritual, the contours of which fluctuate unpredictably, and even indefinitely. "One can stray from any of the paths," says Célère while explaining the *Carte* to Clélie's friends (*Clélie-C*, 1:184; *Clélie-F*, 94). One cannot travel through Tendre as one would through real space because it is cloaked in obscurity, as is the *Carte* that ostensibly charts its territory.[27] Indeed, several features make it impossible to use as any ordinary road map.

The fact that there is a town called "Tendresse" on the path from Nouvelle Amitié to Tendre-sur-Reconnaissance but on neither of the other two is puzzling. (Why is there no equivalent town on the path toward Tendre-sur-Estime, assuming that Inclination presupposes *la tendresse*? Is this town the same sort of tenderness defined by Clélie and Aronce or something different, which they do not articulate? Is tenderness really innate, or is it a quality that can be attained by effort, as the metaphors of the path and the journey would suggest?)[28] Furthermore, if the four figures in the bottom right-hand corner are indeed taken as a *mise en abyme* of the map's interpretation, then that process is polysemous if not obscure. For, as I indicated above, it is unclear whether those four figures stage a scene of departure or arrival—whether the women are guides or destinations and whether the men are about to begin or have already completed their journey. This undecidability, captured as it is in the meta-allegorical scene of the bottom right corner, is yet another reminder that Tendre and its map have anything but transparent meaning for men.

But the most significant impediment for any attempt to "read" the *Carte* is surely that only Clélie herself can determine where exactly the travelers are—how far they have come and how far they have yet to go before reaching their destination (or more precisely, one of the three possible destinations, assuming they do not veer off course toward the Lake of Indifference or the Sea of Enmity).[29] Men cannot rely on their own hermeneutic skills and are instead dependent upon women in order to (hope to) receive Clélie's (or another woman's) tenderness. But even the object of their quest, *la tendresse*—the realization of their own and the attainment of women's tenderness—remains elusive since, as Peters has noted, Tendre, as a place and a goal, is not "whole, complete, and uninterrupted."[30] For the male traveler/friend, this elusiveness requires that he accept what turns out to be an open-ended voyage unlike any other. According to literary and romantic convention, a male lover's quest ends with possession of the female beloved, body and soul. But the *Carte de Tendre* tells a very different story. If, as has been suggested, the *Carte* is an allegorical figuration of Woman (as both the female body and feminine tenderness), then she cannot be possessed or conquered, she is never completely knowable to men.[31] This unknowability resists the patriarchal regimes of knowledge to which women are subjected and from which men most often benefit. It also prevents masculine tenderness from achieving the plenitude of empathy on which it is predicated. For, without full knowledge of Woman, a man cannot hope to adopt a woman's feelings as his own. We might expect, then, that the men traveling through Tendre would balk at such a constraint. But in fact it is an experience that they freely, even gladly accept, in both *Clélie* and Scudéry's salon. They hope to make themselves worthy of Clélie's and Sapho's tenderness, with no assurance of ever being so; and yet they desire and find pleasure in this intransitive state of suspension.

In yet a further sign of the nebulous nature of *la tendresse*, Clélie and Scudéry herself insist that the trip through different levels of friendship have all the hallmarks of love. Granted, the ambiguity between friendship and love is a topic of recurring interest in Scudéry's work, and one that often pits men against women, with men pleading for love and women insisting on friendship.[32] While friendship occasionally resolves into love, the ideal of a friendship that resembles—but never becomes—love is a constant throughout *Le Grand Cyrus*, *Clélie*, and the *Chroniques du Samedi*. But although a commonplace of salon heterosociality, Scudéry's variant is predicated on a sentiment that it is itself ambiguous. The male friends of Clélie take on the outward trappings of a suitor (e.g., their language and attitude), but, more significantly, they also admit to feelings that are stronger than those of ordinary friendship. No matter how consistent with Clélie's ideal of tender friendship, the external signs of these feelings are easily confused with love. Such is the case of Herminius, the impetus behind the *Carte de Tendre*, who is said to have a "passionate friendship" *(violente amitié)* with Clélie. "We would almost have thought that he was in love with Clélie," Célère says of him, "since he praised her in a sort of exaggerated way that is typical of love, sought her out with great care, was filled with joy whenever in her presence, was bored when he wasn't with her, and desired her friendship so deeply that Aronce and Horace hardly desired her love any less passionately" (*Clélie-C*, 1:176; *Clélie-F*, 88). As Célère also explains, though, Herminius is *not* in love with Clélie since he has a "passionate love" *(violente amour)* for a woman elsewhere. The effect of Herminius's devotion to Clélie is unequivocal: "All those who saw him with Clélie had great affection for him, and Clélie had infinite esteem for him" (*Clélie-C*, 1:176; *Clélie-F*, 88). Why tenderness in friendship would be so powerful is revealed later in the novel when Herminius argues that friendship is a necessary element in love:

> As for me . . . I believe that it is not impossible to unite these two sorts of pleasures, and I even contend that for love to be long lasting a woman must be the friend and the mistress of her lover. I'd even go so far as to say that every time friendship precedes love in the heart of a lover his passion will be stronger, longer lasting, more respectful, and even more ardent for it. (*Clélie-C*, 3:125)

In Herminius's logic, friendship (and we can assume he means *tender* friendship) has all the qualities ordinarily associated with love; in fact, it would seem to be the very essence of what is ordinarily taken to be love. But of more immediate interest to Herminius are the benefits women derive when men blend (tender) friendship with love. Unsurprisingly, these are consistent with the objectives laid out by several heroines, including Sapho and Plotine: if a man's love is built on friendship, it is strong, long-lasting, respectful, and passionate all at once. Implicit here, and made explicit in Clélie's definition of *la tendresse*, as we have seen, is the notion that true (i.e., tender) friendship enables the male suitor to resist his "natural" propensity toward infidelity, a fault of men often castigated in Scudéry's oeuvre.[33] More surprising, perhaps, is the fact that it is Herminius who articulates a logic more readily espoused by women. Capable of identifying with a woman's perspective and making her benefits his own, Herminius is close to being a tender friend-lover par excellence. He prizes friendship as much as if not more than love and renounces the telos of the traditional romantic hero, thus becoming the *esclave* who promotes the interests of his *maîtresse* as his own.

By observing the gendered polarity between mistress and slave, tenderness paradoxically aims to blur any distinction between the affective life of the female beloved and her male suitor. In this utopian version of amical and amorous relations, *la tendresse* points toward an affective life beyond gender. Still, this gender-neutral ideal presupposes a masculine self-dispossession that blends into feminine self-interest. Although critics have asserted that this form of empathy at the heart of tenderness works both ways (men adopting women's self-interest and vice versa), this point is at best implicit in Scudéry's writings.[34] The process she describes more prominently involves men adopting women's feelings as their own. Whether or not it is the starting point for a sort of mutual self-sacrifice between men *and* women, men's affective being must fuse with—must become—women's to the point of being indistinguishable from it. In this fully realized form, there are neither men nor women, neither masculine nor feminine. But since *la tendresse* can never be fully realized, this state of gender neutrality is itself elusive. Masculine tenderness is a constant state of becoming, a striving for an ideal that is always just beyond its reach. It has at its core a lack that propels it toward a goal as nebulous as it is desirable. Moving toward but never reaching an affective state beyond gender, *la tendresse* would seem to be one mechanism for regulating a dynamic that is *not* within its bounds. For, in spite of all their apparent idealism, Scudéry's writings evince an unabashed realism about the asymmetrical division of social power between men and women, confirmed

for instance by Sapho's and Plotine's resistance to the institution of marriage.[35] In the face of a world where masculinity assumes a role of dominance
that passes itself off as stable, natural, and atemporal, tender masculinity is
defined by instability, contingency, and temporality. Within the restricted
arena of interpersonal and affective relations, *la tendresse*, precisely *because* it
is elusive, creates a space where an egalitarian heterosociality can begin to be
envisioned, if not lived out, in Scudéry's novels and her salon.[36]

Une certaine mélancolie douce

When Aronce describes the various qualities that are missing in male suitors
bereft of *la tendresse*, he emphasizes one in particular that is crucial for Scudéry's vision of love. Without tenderness, he claims, "they are lovers whose
hearts experience not the slightest fluttering when they see their mistresses,
who know neither how to dream nor how to sigh pleasantly, who are unfamiliar with a certain sweet melancholy that is born from the tenderness of a
heart in love and that provides it sometimes more sweet pleasure than joy
could ever do" (*Clélie-C*, 1:120; *Clélie-F*, 77). By way of counterexample,
Aronce highlights melancholy as both a sign and an affect of tender love.
Given the importance of *la tendresse* as an affective ideal in Scudéry's fiction,
it is hardly surprising that melancholy is likewise a recurrent feature of her
representation of love. Not only do many central characters, such as Aronce
and Clélie, possess melancholic temperaments, but melancholy itself is a
prized quality. On occasion, it may even be worn as a badge of honor, as is it
in the "Histoire des amants infortunés" (Story of the Unfortunate Lovers, in
Le Grand Cyrus), which features four suitors each of whom, in a sort of
melancholic parlor game, attempts to convince a group of assembled friends
that he is the most unlucky in love and, thus, the most worthy of pity.[37] Of
course, the melancholy caused by love has a long tradition to which Scudéry
owes much. Besides the Petrarchan topoi we have already seen, the long-
winded anguish of pastoral heroes such as Céladon (in d'Urfé's *L'Astrée*),
separated by a series of events from his beloved Astrée, provided a ready-
made model as popular as it was conventional. This literary tradition is part
of a broader topos famously termed "poetic melancholy" by Kiblansky,
Panofsky, and Saxl because it designates a temporary state arising from a
known circumstance (such as unrequited love) and not a temperament or
physiological state depicted in medical texts, for instance.[38] However, Scudéry's understanding of melancholy complicates this distinction in more than

one way. Most significant is the fact that she does not restrict melancholy to men, as do most strains of "poetic melancholy." Instead, as Noémi Hepp has shown, she is perhaps the first writer to depict a feminine melancholy equivalent in most ways to that of male genius, an association first made by the Pseudo-Aristotle.[39] Clélie, as Hepp argues, illustrates many traits associated with this "noble" melancholy: premonitions, innate wisdom, audacity, and composure, among others.[40] At the same time, however, Scudéry places great importance on the "poetic melancholy" of the hero of prose romance, the melancholic "mood" provoked by an unrequited or otherwise impossible love, all the while refashioning it. Occupying a central place in Scudéry's vision of ideal manhood, melancholy has meanings and functions that serve her conception of both the masculine subject and the heterosocial dynamic.

Those hostile to Scudéry's work, such as Boileau, were quick to highlight the prominence of melancholy for her male characters. In his "Dialogue des héros de roman," he singles out Artamène, the hero of *Le Grand Cyrus*, whom Scudéry transforms from "the greatest conqueror ever seen" to "one crazier than all the Céladons and Sylvandres, whose only concern is his Mandane [his beloved] and who does nothing else all day long than lament, moan, and cajole his mistress."[41] No matter how inaccurate Boileau's claims about Artamène's lack of heroics may be, his focus on the hero's "lamenting" and "moaning" contains more than a grain of truth. Love causes Artamène, like so many other male characters in *Le Grand Cyrus* and *Clélie,* to suffer seemingly endless emotional torment, noted at (sometimes excruciating) length by the characters themselves and the narrator. But this melancholy has a meaning and a function that seem to escape the satirist.[42]

Indeed, Scudéry develops a detailed theory of melancholy. In his defense of tender love, for instance, Aronce uses the ambiguous qualifiers *certain* and *sweet*, thereby signaling a desire to redefine and remotivate the concept, or at least to indicate a subgroup within the larger category called "melancholy." Later in the novel, Célère confirms this desire by fleshing out a theory of the connections between melancholy and love. In a conversation about which of three sorts of women is most worthy of love, "a proud and capricious beauty," "a lighthearted beauty," or "a melancholic beauty," Célère defends the last, and what begins as a description of the female melancholic character-type quickly becomes an explanation of the benefits both women *and* men derive from a melancholic love. The melancholy that Célère advocates (and that Scudéry valorizes elsewhere in her oeuvre) is not what is usually understood as such, particularly that diagnosed by humoral medicine. "One mustn't imagine that I mean those women who are of a somber, grieving, disagreeable and brutish humor," he says. Instead, the melancholy and the character type he defends are not only pleasing but inclined toward sociability. "I'm thinking of a sweet and charming melancholy that is not the enemy of pleasures and that is not incompatible with all galant and reasonable diversions" (*Clélie-C*, 1:430; *Clélie-F*, 123). What at first glance might appear to be counterintuitive or even contradictory is in fact a paradox that pushes the aestheticization of the topos of melancholy in love to an extreme. This paradox is itself founded on another concerning the commensurability of melancholy and happiness in love. "All the great and deep joys that truly belong to love are characterized by languor rather than lightheartedness *(enjouement)*, and . . . melancholy is so particular to this passion that its very pleasures sometimes have something melancholic about them, and yet we are still happy" (*Clélie-C*, 1:430; *Clélie-F*, 124]). If melancholy is sometimes pleasurable, it can at other times be a genuine suffering, but a suffering that leads to greater pleasure. "To be familiar with all the pleasures of love, one must be familiar with all its suffering and . . . whoever is incapable of making a great sadness out of a very small thing will not find a great pleasure in a great favor" (*Clélie-C*, 1:433; *Clélie-F*, 128). What might also appear to be a softening of melancholy is actually a redeployment of its intensity. As Célère puts it, "I mean a melancholy that puts languor and passion in one's gaze, that makes the heart great, noble, tender and sensitive *(grand, généreux, tendre, et sensible)*, and that gives it a certain disposition that is so well suited to loving ardently that whoever is unfamiliar with the love of a melancholic heart is unfamiliar with love" (*Clélie-C*, 1:430; *Clélie-F*, 123). Paradoxically rendering one both noble and sensitive, melancholy ensures that one's love will have the "ardor" without which love is not truly love, according to Célère. With this *ardeur*, melancholic lovers are more persistent and deliberate than those who are lighthearted. A *maîtresse* who is melancholic will proceed slowly and cautiously, parceling out only small and occasional "favors" to her suitor. As a result, though, "discovering new graces every day, you have new pleasures every day," whereas a *maîtresse* who is "lighthearted" is profligate, sharing all she has from the beginning, and ultimately "will only give you mediocre pleasures" (*Clélie-C*, 1:431; *Clélie-F*, 125). Compared to *enjouement*, melancholy guarantees a love that is deeper and more solid. "It is only charming melancholy that inspires a passion that is ardent, long lasting, and entertaining all at once. . . . Melancholy is the vestal virgin who guards the flame of love in the heart of a person who loves" (*Clélie-C*, 1:433–34; *Clélie-F*, 128–29).

For all the idiosyncrasy of Célère's (and Scudéry's) understanding of melancholy, one aspect is at first glance more traditional. For, although melancholic love is characterized by its exteriority, that is, its preoccupation with the loved one, it also produces that most classic of symptoms, the turn to interiority. When prescribing the recipe for happiness in love, Célère describes an inner life of melancholy:

> To be happy in love . . . one must have a heart so sensitive that the mere sight of the place where the loved one lives gives joy, and a joy that troubles the heart. The inadvertent mention of her name must make you blush. You must wish that she were with you wherever you are or that you were wherever she is. Your heart must be completely filled with her. You must think of nothing else, and you must think of her at times with joy and at other times with sorrow. (*Clélie-C*, 1:433; *Clélie-F*, 128)

In this passage, Célère evokes the familiar image of the male lover obsessed with the thought of his beloved nearly to the point of madness, seeing her where she is not, shifting back and forth between ecstasy and despair. Another aspect of Célère's description, however, recalls more recent discussions of melancholy, which in turn elucidate the gendered meanings of Scudéry's adaptation. Inherent in the interiority of melancholic love, according to Célère, is a preoccupation with absence and loss that is reminiscent of the Freudian theory of melancholy as the incorporation of a lost object, a process that, for Freud, occurs in the unconscious.[43]

Without offering a rigorous psychoanalytic reading, I would nonetheless suggest that elements of Freud's theory provide a means of identifying the gendered consequences of Scudéry's reworking of melancholy. Speaking of the (universal male) melancholiac, Freud asserts that he may know "whom he has lost but not *what* it is he has lost in them."[44] Applied to Célère's description of the interiority created by melancholic love, this insight would suggest that the lover—male *or* female—has lost something other than the person her- or himself who is loved and whose loss is recognized and mourned. One way of understanding this "something"—or unconscious "object"—would be to turn to some of the recurring scenarios in Scudéry's novels that pit *maîtresse* against *amant*. Two of these in particular involve loss, one for the male suitor and the other for the female beloved.

Following a topos of the prose romance tradition, many of Scudéry's heroes lament their beloveds' refusal to acknowledge that they are actually loved. A wholly conventional part of the courtship ritual, this topos is given an extreme form in the portrayals of several heroes, who are refused not only the assurance of being loved but the very possibility of obtaining the status of *amant*. Such is the case of the men whom Clélie at least initially requires to be nothing more than friends, Aronce, Célère, and Horace among them. Such is the case of Herminius, whom Valérie forbids to pronounce the word "love" when speaking of their relationship, and who pines to become her *amant* nevertheless.[45] And such is even more dramatically the case of Phaon, who aspires to become what Sapho has warned is a nonexistent ideal. "I seek so many different things in the person by whom I wish to be loved," she says, "that it will be difficult to find them in one person alone. . . . If I were to wish for a lover, I would wish for one over whom neither time nor absence had any power. The lover I wish for is not to be found in this world" (*Story*, 67; *Artamène-S*, 10:452; *Artamène-GF*, 525). In this sense, longing to be the lover who quite literally does not exist, Phaon incorporates an "object" that is always already lost, at least from Sapho's perspective. Even after Sapho acknowledges her feelings for Phaon, she continues to insist, as she will to the very end, that marriage is impossible. "If he wishes me to love him: he must content himself with the hope of being loved without expecting anything more" (*Story*, 68; *Artamène-S*, 10:454; *Artamène-GF*, 527). Forced to settle for hope instead of love and obliged to abandon the possibility of physical possession, Phaon must reckon with the loss of the traditional telos of the romantic hero. It is significant, then, that he falls into a melancholic crisis of sorts when he is unable to recognize that *he* is the dedicatee of a love poem by Sapho (the letters of his name having been replaced by asterisks).[46] Assuming that he has a (nonexistent) rival, Phaon has incorporated the lost ideal to the point of becoming his own rival. His inability to furnish the "proper" reading of Sapho's poem—his willingness to see and especially mourn what *is not* and what *cannot be*—encapsulates an extreme form of the melancholic dilemma that Scudéry repeatedly stages for her romantic heroes.

For her heroines, the unacknowledged lost "object" of melancholic love is often the ideal of the *amant* to which they hold their suitors. With the exception of characters such as Aronce, who are melancholic by temperament, many of Scudéry's *amants* fall short of their beloveds' expectations about melancholy, creating the necessary diegetic conflict but also putting the focus squarely on masculinity. Phaon and Herminius, for instance, provoke anguish in Sapho and Valérie, respectively, when, separated from their *maîtresses*, they fail to display the sadness deemed appropriate for the circumstances.[47] Although Phaon and Herminius are each described as being "naturally" inclined toward *enjouement*, their failure to conform to the melancholic ideal unleashes melancholy in their beloveds. For Sapho and

Valérie, the suffering caused by absence is the necessary proof that a man's love is authentic. "[T]he most moving and certain sign of a tender affection is sorrow in absence," as Sapho says (*Story*, 107; *Artamène-S*, 10:544). Reiterating the "joy = melancholy" formula, she also tells Phaon: "There are moments when I think that seeing me gives you no joy because my absence causes you no melancholy" (*Story*, 114; *Artamène-S*, 10:559). Sapho and Valérie experience the *lack* of "the pain of absence" as an "object" that they necessarily incorporate. For each of them, loving a man incapable of melancholy provides the very basis for their melancholy. Concentrating on her heroines' suffering in this way, Scudéry departs from the preponderant tendency in western European literature to glorify male melancholy and to make women its lost "object." In these instances, it is the ideal of the melancolic *man* that is the "object" lost to *women*.

What I am arguing, then, is that for both men and women in this scheme, melancholic love involves the loss of "objects" that are ideals about masculinity, albeit two very different ones. For men, the "object" lost is the telos of the traditional hero, and for women, it is male melancholy itself. In its ideal—melancholic—form, the love valorized by Scudéry's fiction focuses attention on male desire, making it the problem that melancholy attempts to resolve. To think of melancholy as problem solving is once again to refer to Freud, who famously conceived it as "countless single conflicts in which love and hate wrestle together are fought for the object; the one seeks to detach the libido from the object, the other to uphold this libido-position against assault."[48] Seen in this light, Scudéry's ideal love is at its core a conflict between the desires for attachment to and detachment from the "object," be it either the traditionally conceived or the melancholic *amant*.

For Freud, the resolution of the conflict at the heart of melancholy (when it occurs) remains mysterious;[49] but Scudéry seems to envision a clear resolution to the conflict within melancholic love, albeit a temporary one. In a conversation in *Clélie*, Herminius explicitly recognizes the conflictual nature of the amorous relationship while arguing that "glory" *(la gloire)*, traditionally part of the noble warrior's ethos, extends as much if not more to love, among other domains. He tells Mutius, who contends that *la gloire* is relevant for military triumph alone: "I think that glory comes from love as well as from war and that this is so because of a similarity in the combats, victories, and triumphs" (*Clélie-C*, 2:174; *Clélie-F*, 229.). Even in Herminius's revised definition, however, *la gloire* still signifies by homology with its semantic origins in the feelings aroused by military victory. Within the realm of love, as he explains, glory is the feeling of triumph one experiences upon realizing that one is loved by the person one loves. It is being able to take pleasure in saying to oneself: "I finally triumph over the heart of a person I admire and whom I love more than myself " (*Clélie-C*, 2:179; *Clélie-F*, 235.). While making *la gloire* the triumph experienced in a wide range of "combats" ("glory's power extends everywhere," Herminius says [*Clélie-C*, 2:177; *Clélie-F*, 233]), it is clear from the conversation that women as well as men may feel glory in love.[50] By broadening both its reference (beyond warfare) and its possessors (women *and* men), Scudéry performs a significant revision of a highly valued cultural construct in this period, as many critics have noted.[51] Speaking from his own experience, however, Herminius privileges the benefits that men might gain from the revised version of *la gloire*. Besides the fact that men would seem to acquire more glory in love than women ("it is more glorious to be loved by an honnête woman than it is for her to be loved by a perfect honnête homme" [*Clélie-C*, 2:174; *Clélie-F*, 228]), men are at least implicitly able to retain the prestige of *la gloire* as a component of the noble warrior ethos away from the battlefield. Yet, unlike its counterpart in military victory, the prestige of amorous glory cannot be shared openly, according to Herminius, first of all because *la gloire* is self-sufficient and not the result of social mediation, but also because "it is secrecy that creates a lover's glory" (*Clélie-C*, 2:180; *Clélie-F*, 237). Without secrecy there can be no glory in love: "Whoever knows how to love knows how to remain silent, and secrecy is a thing so sweet in love that without it all the favors one might receive are almost neither sweet nor glorious" (*Clélie-C*, 2:180; *Clélie-F*, 236). Consequently, the male suitor must eschew the fame prized by military heroes: "Mars absolutely needs fame at various moments, but as for love, the god of silence must be his only friend" (*Clélie-C*, 2:180; *Clélie-F*, 236). He keeps secret the combat and the victory he wins in love because the struggle and its resolution take place within himself. When it comes to *la gloire*, "One must be one's own spectator," Herminius asserts (*Clélie-C*, 2:176; *Clélie-F*, 232). If glory in love is, accordingly, only ever a spectacle on the inner stage, we might conjecture that it is so because it serves a purpose that is not and cannot be fully acknowledged. For women but especially for men, it would seem, *la gloire* marks the sort of triumph over melancholy that Freud deemed impossible.[52] It is an end to the inner conflict surrounding the lost "object" of melancholic love, a triumph of self over self that affords pleasure. With *la gloire*, Scudéry further distances herself from early modern traditions of melancholy, especially those deriving from Petrarch, for whom love of an other produces hatred of the self.[53] Rather than self-hatred and the psychic and symbolic disruption of the masculine self that Juliana Schiesari and Lynne Enterline have analyzed, Scudéry conceives a means of transcending the self's conflict and of giving a measure of stability to the masculine subject.[54]

But this transcendence and this stability are only temporary as the inevitable back-and-forth movement of the pleasure and suffering of love resumes. *La gloire* is itself lacking, incomplete, and unstable as ever more obstacles are strewn in the paths of the many couples in Scudéry's novels. Ultimately, the major objective of melancholic love is to prolong courtship as long as possible, to extend the pinings of unfulfilled desire until the exigencies of narrative closure supervene. If the courtships of *Le Grand Cyrus* and *Clélie* are so protracted and if they are replete with impediments of various sorts, it is to ensure that men will remain faithful and that women will retain a measure of self-determination. When Scudéry's star-crossed lovers are finally united in the end, their bliss is anticlimatic and comes almost as an afterthought.[55] In fact, these definitive final reunions appear to be beyond representation, as if only melancholic love falls within the bounds of discourse. This unrepresentability takes on quite literal form at the end of "Histoire de Sapho" when Phaon accompanies Sapho to the Pays des Nouveaux Sauromates, a utopian land, inaccessible to all but the privileged few, where fidelity is enforced by law.[56] Phaon offers to move there so as to remain under Sapho's watchful eye, never again to risk being separated from her and, thus, being insufficiently melancholic.[57] When they leave for the Pays des Nouveaux Sauromates, though, they intentionally shroud their departure in mystery, and Sapho deliberately lets her compatriots believe that she has died. Démocède, the narrator of Sapho's story, is forced to rely on secondhand testimony to assert that a long-lasting passion exists between the two. Without melancholic love, happiness can only be preserved in an inaccessible utopia where an external regulating power enforces (male) fidelity. When Phaon asks the judges in his new homeland to force Sapho to marry him, they side with her against him: "[T]he judges ordered Phaon not to press her further and declared that only she might grant such a favor. In the meantime, he should consider himself the happiest and most glorious lover on earth to be loved by the most perfect person in the world, a person who refused him her hand only because she wished always to possess his heart" (*Story*, 136; *Artamène-S*, 10:607; *Artamène-F*, 586). Relaying the secondhand knowledge he possesses, Démocède assures us that Phaon and Sapho "enjoy all the sweet pleasures a galant, delicate, and tender love can inspire in the hearts of those who possess it" (*Story*, 136; *Artamène-S*, 10:607; *Artamène-F*, 586). But only in the Pays des Nouveaux Sauromates, a land the narrator cannot visit or know, can such perfect love, devoid of melancholy, exist. Only in such a utopian land, beyond direct representation, can nonmelancholic masculinity produce amorous bliss. In the here and now, only melancholic masculinity ensures at least the prospect of comparable happiness.

A Fly in Tendre

Freed from the exigencies of narrative convention, tender masculinity would at first glance seem to be more easily realized in the real spaces of the Samedis than in the fictive worlds of Scudéry's novels. Unburdened by the *dépits amoureux* and, especially, the closure that prose fiction requires, the men of Scudéry's circle can aspire almost indefinitely to *la tendresse* and that "certain sweet melancholy" which accompanies it. But these aspirations are intermittent at best. The Samedis, after all, met only once a week, even if the aura of those meetings were extended through the writings, such as the *Chroniques*, that were the basis for the potlatch among its members. When they set aside their responsibilities in the outside world to enter the enclosed literal *and* discursive space of Scudéry's salon, men shed much of their public personas in order to adopt deliberately staged roles, which they would in turn cast off once outside again. Suspending the movement of desire in a never-ending quest for Tendre might indeed be easier to accomplish if such a quest were the intermittent leisure activity of like-minded friends rather than the all-consuming task of Aronce or Herminius. It is not insignificant that *Clélie* was written after the Samedis were first organized (in 1653). For, with this novel, Scudéry was able to create a more enduring form of the relational ideals that could only ever be enacted sporadically and that could only ever be ephemeral in her salon. Ironically, though, with the form of the novel came constraints that gave a different cast to those same ideals, rendering them even more difficult to realize in fiction than in the salon.

Still, the ideals in question—tenderness and sweet melancholy especially—are not altogether the same when represented in the novel as they were when lived in the salon. At least as far as the *Chroniques du Samedi* allow us to see, such ideals were staged by members of Scudéry's circle with a self-conscious theatricality that aimed at *enjouement*. Such is certainly evident when Acante (Pellisson) writes to Sapho of his desire to become a fly so as to reach Tendre more quickly. "This metempsychosis would be easy for me provided that I could travel, quietly and without drawing attention to myself, from the region of Particular to that of Tender, where I've desired to be for so long" (*Chroniques*, 127). Acante/Pellisson's musings on his imagined transformation into a fly provide a particularly apt illustration of the sorts of metamorphoses women and men underwent in order to participate in the Samedis. They did so first of all by donning pseudonyms taken from various literary sources, including pastoral romances and imitations of "Greek" novels. Among the many functions of these names (most prominently, obscuring real social distinctions and conferring an aesthetic aura on individuals and the group as a whole) is the fact that they highlighted salon interchange as role-playing based on the character types of prose romance.[58] Such pseudonyms gave members of Scudéry's salon license to play their parts in the novel they were collectively improvising, and to do so as self-consciously and emphatically as Acante/Pellisson desired to become a fly. Just how theatrical this role-playing could become is illustrated by several letters in the *Chroniques* that are practical jokes within transparent pastiches of letters by other members and even nonmembers of the salon.[59]

Of course, a crucial part of this pseudonymous role-playing was the hyperbolic enactment of preestablished gender positions. In what might be thought of as an allegorical metamorphosis, men would play the parts of male suitors courting their beloved (Sapho in the first instance, but other women of the Samedis as well), in hopes of gaining no more—and no less— than her (their) friendship. At the same time as using the tropes of courtly and pastoral romance, members of the Samedis deployed many of the same affective constructs Scudéry was simultaneously integrating into her fiction—but with a difference. For while the members of her salon *play* the roles of *maîtresses* and *esclaves* and *stage* this role-playing in their writings, the characters in her novels *are* those roles. The point for the women and men of the Samedis is thus to use these roles to emphasize, with virtuosity and lightheartedness, their respective gendered positions within the salon. Once again, Acante/Pellisson's fantastical desire to become a fly can serve as an example. After describing the "parallels" *(rapports)* he has with this insect (he is quiet, he importunes but is harmless, he loves "sweet things," and he is easy to "catch"), he uses the allegory of the fly traveling through Tendre in order to accentuate his subservience to Sapho. "But, Mademoiselle, when I am transformed thus by metamorphosis and metempsychosis, of which I do not despair, how do I not lose my way? Do you want a poor fly to travel the world over without knowing where it is going? . . . Pray, Mademoiselle, show him the route he should take, the places he should pass, which dangers he should fear, and tell him the secret for bringing his quest to an end" (*Chroniques*,

127–28). Desiring to become a lowly fly is a means of reiterating—and exaggerating—his dependence upon Sapho, who alone determines where her male "suitors" stand in relation to Tendre. In reply to Pellisson's allegorically inflected subservience, Scudéry in turn plays the role of the cautious and resistant beloved, telling him that he is more like a wasp or a bee than a fly and that, in any event, flying in whatever form is not safer or faster than walking, so long is the road from Particulier to Tendre. And in a final rebuff as the haughty *maîtresse* she claims to be, she tells Acante not to become a fly, "For I am so accustomed to shooing them away with my fan, when I have it, or even with my sleeve when I find flies in the winter, that you could be exposed to the same fate if you approached me" (*Chroniques*, 130). As comical as all this posturing is, it still does not undermine the gendered polarity of masculine submission and feminine authority that exists between Acante/Pellisson and Sapho/Scudéry. On the contrary, it shows that these positions are at once arbitrary, because freely created and adopted, and fundamental, because the very basis for interaction within the Samedis.

With their self-consciously ludic role-playing, the women and men of Scudéry's salon create a distance between themselves and the fictionlike gender roles they enact so as to fashion these in accordance with Sapho's wishes and to use them in celebration of the group assembled around her. It is against this backdrop that the ritual protestations of tenderness and melancholy made by the men in the *Chroniques du Samedi* should be read. When, in a poem offered to Sapho, Thrasile (Isarn) describes his *tendresse*, he compares it to love, but insists on its difference:

> Ce qu'on sent pour une maîtresse
> N'approche point de la tendresse
> Que je sens pour vous chaque jour.
> Ne craignez pourtant pas mes désirs ni ma flamme,
> Sapho, ce que je porte en l'âme,
> A plus de raison que l'amour.
>
> (*Chroniques*, 133)

[What one feels for a mistress / Does not even approach the tenderness / That I feel for you each day. / But do not fear my desires or my flame, / Sapho, what I carry in my soul, / Is more reasonable than love.]

More reasonable but also more intense than love, his paradoxical *tendresse* for Sapho fulfills to the letter the requirements for a friend qua amant in the Samedis. He must be in perfect control of his passions (and love, by defini-tion, was a loss of reason, and thus control), and yet he must also demonstrate an unquestionable, deep devotion to Sapho. Since it is reasonable, the tenderness Thrasile feels for Sapho is part of the role he plays, enthusiastically but also self-consciously. But since his *tendresse* incorporates all the literary trappings of love, he must also necessarily feel the lover's torment:

> Je vous ouvre mon cœur, je me plains, je soupire . . .
>   Pourtant une flamme discrète,
>   Pleine de respect et secrète,
>   Mériterait quelque pitié.
>   (*Chroniques*, 133)

[I open my heart to you, I complain, I sigh . . . / Yet a discreet flame, / Full of respect and secret, / Deserves some pity.]

All in all, though, Thrasile's quasi-amorous laments pale by comparison to the emphatic displays of his ardent *tendresse*. Likewise, throughout the *Chroniques*, expressions of melancholy by men are formulaic and invoked with little of the anguish of the heroes in Scudéry's novels, if indeed it is melancholy at all.[60] Granted, playing her role as Queen of Tendre, Sapho expects a measure of self-abjection on the part of her "suitors": "Whoever is unafraid of losing my friendship does not deserve to possess it" (*Chroniques*, 120–21). But in an unusual letter responding to Pellisson's fears of having displeased her, she admits that her verbal authority is based in part on convention: "Just as I don't believe absolutely literally all the flatteries I'm told, you shouldn't always give to my words, when they're harsh, all the force they seem to have" (*Chroniques*, 255). Her expectations for melancholic abjection in the men of the Samedis are, then, partially conventional, an aspect of the gendered role-playing in which women and men both participate.

If melancholy is less crucial in the *Chroniques* than in either *Le Grand Cyrus* or *Clélie*, it is because the masculinity practiced in Scudéry's salon (or at least the writings that emanated from it) has structural means of suspending the progression of (male) desire that are unavailable to the male characters in the novels. The intermittent and ephemeral performances of gender in the Samedis are not only carefully staged by highly self-aware actors, but also frozen in time and place through the meticulous compilation of the

Chroniques.[61] As snapshots of the salon, the *Chroniques* potentially *become* the gendered role-playing of the salon; they are a *lieu de mémoire* that compensates for the messy contingency of desire and imposes the difficult stasis required of Scudéry's friends. So doing, of course, this record of the Samedis also enshrines *la tendresse* and the gendered positions stipulated by it. The men of the *Chroniques* submit to the authority of women and above all of Scudéry herself, aiming to prove that these women's affective priorities are their own, that no affective boundaries separate women from men. Perhaps, then, it is this objective that gives us one of the reasons why Acante/Pellisson desires a metamorphosis in the first place: it would make his male body disappear, leaving only his affective being for Sapho. It is essentially just such a decorporealizing metamorphosis that Acante envisions when, as he tells her, "I've wished to be a wren and a fly, but as I write you I would like to be a letter, and, unable to be as happy as it is, I'm doing everything I can to put the best part of myself into it. This best part of myself, if you don't understand, Mademoiselle, is my heart. For my body is worth nothing, and my mind even less" (*Chroniques,* 144). By transforming himself into a wren, a fly, or even a letter, Pellisson hopes that Scudéry would look beyond his body and his mind so as to concentrate on the gift of that "best part" of himself, his heart. But in whatever form, it is the affective union with Sapho that is most important to him. Leaving aside his corporeality, he would be unencumbered by the reality of gender and would instead be nothing more and nothing less than the "best part" of himself—his affective being.

Within the exchange of *billets* and poems that make up the *Chroniques,* another sort of gender blurring occurs as well. For, if it is true, as Luce Irigaray has concluded from linguistic experiments, that women's discourse is more dialogic in structure and more affective in content than men's, which privileges their relationship to objects and the world as they conceive it,[62] and if this distinction holds true for the early modern period, then the *Chroniques* would suggest that the men of the Samedis actually adopt women's discourse rather than imposing their own. Their writings, which dominate the *Chroniques,* spin a dialogic web among the men and women of Scudéry's salon, and they foreground the affective dimension of their collective existence. But even leaving this hypothesis aside, it is still true that the ideal masculinity imagined by Scudéry in her fiction and staged in her salon is predicated on a rapprochement with women and femininity and, further, on the notion that men needed to become more like women than the reverse. Rather than paying mere lip service to the principle of women's refining influence all the better to reassert phallic privilege, as Méré's honnête homme and Voiture the galant homme do, the masculinity Scudéry envisions gestures toward a state beyond gender but under the auspices of femininity. Although it is never (able to be) fully realized, tender masculinity is the quest for a heterosocial relationality that takes the prescriptions about women's civilizing authority at face value and does so in spite of the risks of effeminacy.

PART TWO   ☙   Sexuality and the Body at the Margins

FIVE

Writing Sodomy:
Satire, Secrets, and the "Self"

In our own time and our own culture, it is by and large a given that normative masculinity is defined in opposition to homosexuality. Even if cultural attitudes are slowly shifting (but not without often virulent backlash), there is a widely held and mostly unquestioned belief that homosexuality is incompatible with the sort of iconic masculinity displayed by athletes and military heroes, for instance. Just as widely held and unquestioned is the assumption that men—whether they aspire to iconic masculine status or not—will eschew any signs of sexual ambiguity, especially in their interactions with other men. Countless jokes, television advertisements, and sit-com episodes remind us that "real" men are supposed to know when and how to display admiration for other men, express their enjoyment of other men's company, and so on. Although much less widely understood or questioned, in popular culture at least, these cultural expectations about the "necessary" distinction between homosexuality and masculinity require arduous and incessant surveillance, both on a collective and on an individual level. In fact, one of the primary functions of all the jokes, advertisements, sit-com episodes, and so on, that make light of men who unwittingly transgress or simply do not respect the taboo on homoerotic ambiguity is to enforce and uphold the distinction between homosexuality and (normative) masculinity. That this distinction is the object of so much cultural work is telling in at least two respects. The need/desire to reiterate this distinction suggests that the supposed gulf between homosexuality and masculinity is not nearly as self-evident as our culture would have us believe. Consequently, this need/desire also hints at a deep-rooted anxiety that requires both a cultural and an individual response. To conform to the dictates of the cultural code of a masculinity that is (seemingly) unambiguously distinct from homosexuality, individual men must police themselves for any signs of homoerotic ambiguity. At the same time, of course, they can perhaps best prove their adherence to the dominant cultural code by policing similar signs of ambiguity in other men. This, at least, is one of the most familiar ways that masculinity affirms itself in our present world.

But this was not necessarily the case in seventeenth-century France, as a poem about Louis II de Bourbon, the "Grand Condé" (1621–86), one of the most famous military heroes of the seventeenth century, demonstrates. In it, the chevalier de Lignières, a member of Condé's entourage, recognizes the Prince's much-vaunted battlefield exploits while making light of his equally widely known (if less openly discussed) sexual inclinations.

> Prince, en parlant de vos exploits,
> Soit dans la paix, soit dans la guerre,
> On vous compare quelquefois
> A celui qui donna des lois
> Aux maîtres de la terre.
> De votre honneur je suis jaloux:
> Ce parallèle me fait peine;
> César, à le dire entre nous,
> Fut bien aussi bougre que vous,
> Mais jamais si grand capitaine.[1]

[Prince, when speaking of your exploits, / Either in peace or at war, / People compare you sometimes / To the one who gave laws / To the masters of the earth. / Of your honor I am jealous: / This parallel pains me; / Caesar, just between us, / Was every bit the bugger you are, / But never as great a captain.]

With not a little irony, Lignières implies that the comparisons of Condé to Caesar are warranted, but not for the reasons that are commonly evoked. Still, while poking fun at the Prince's sexuality, Lignières does not question that he can be both a "capitaine" and a "bougre." Indeed, the Grand Condé was in many ways an icon of noble masculinity: the victor of the battles of Rocroi, Philippsbourg, Nördlingen, Lens, and Sennef (among others), a "prince of the blood," widely admired at court, whom Louis XIV called "the greatest man in my kingdom," and a patron of many of the most important artists and writers of the day. That he was a "bugger" was also known at the time, but this fact did not tarnish his image. If it had, Lignières would most certainly have refrained from joking about it with the Prince. Instead, the poet uses it to equate him with Caesar.[2]

In seventeenth-century France, and more broadly in the early modern past, the radical distinction between masculinity and what we now call homosexuality did not enjoy the status of an unassailable cultural assumption. This is not to say that this distinction, so familiar to us today, did not exist at the time—it did, as this chapter will demonstrate. But it was not applied consistently, and it was not yet a dominant paradigm of masculinity. Of course, in no way does this mean that homosexuality—or to use the more historically accurate (albeit far less neutral) term, sodomy—was in any way considered innocuous. Sodomitical acts continued to be punishable by death (specifically, by burning at the stake), as the well-publicized convictions and executions of Jacques Chausson and Jacques Paulmy (1661) and that of Philippe Bouvet de La Contamine (1677) amply demonstrate.[3] But throughout the seventeenth century, enforcement of existing laws against sodomy was highly erratic and always took into account the social station of the accused sodomite. Those from the upper echelons of society, such as Philippe d'Orléans and the Grand Condé (among numerous others), were granted considerably more leeway to express and act upon sodomitical desires than those without powerful connections at court, in the Parlement, or in the church.[4] As was often the case in early modern French society, one could say in a twist on the biblical injunction that to whom much had been given, much was allowed.[5] Even then, however, with the reputation of "sodomite" always came risk, if not to one's life then to one's career and social standing, especially for those whose social status was lesser than someone like the Grand Condé's (the quasi-totality of the population, that is).[6] As I will show with the example of the Abbé de Boisrobert, the charge of sodomy could be—and frequently was—used as an opportunistic weapon by one's rivals and enemies. But at issue in such cases was something other than the masculine identity of the target "sodomite." In other words, the point of such attacks was not to highlight and denounce the incompatibility of masculinity and sodomy, but rather to indicate something potentially more damning. In early modern Europe, sodomy was an "utterly confused category" (as Foucault famously called it) that signified a crime against the divine cosmological order in addition to a range of sexual acts over and beyond sex between men.[7] To accuse a man of sodomy was tantamount to accusing him of utter moral depravity and worse, heresy. Used as an insult or an attack, the accusation of sodomy carried with it a weighty religious subtext, even if its precise terms were more often implicit than explicit. But it is one of the internal contradictions of seventeenth-century French society that the charge of sodomy as a crime against divine law was deployed in anything but a predictable and uniform fashion throughout the century, even though the period has a deserved reputation for religious fervor. And, as the century progressed, such religiously inspired accusations (or accusations with religious undertones) seem to have become less frequent, although they did not disappear entirely.[8]

In sum, sodomy and the sodomite occupied uncertain places in the collective imagination and judicial practices of seventeenth-century France, and no more certain were their relation to masculinity. In spite of the risk such a reputation entailed, being a sodomite was not necessarily incompatible with iconic masculinity. Yet, at the same time, over the course of the seventeenth century the "sodomite" became an increasingly specific masculine type. Even as this broad definition of sodomy continued to be evoked, the seventeenth century marked a transition in the understandings and the treatment of sodomy, and one of the consequences of this transition, I argue, is that sodomy's relation to masculinity likewise changed.

Michel Foucault was among the first to identify the seventeenth century as a pivotal moment in the history of (homo)sexuality. In volume 1 of *The History of Sexuality*, he famously traces the "incitation to discourse," the obligation to speak the "truth" of one's sexuality, to the Tridentine theory and practice of confession.[9] Generally overshadowed by his oft-repeated statement (in that same volume) that the homosexual was "invented" in the nineteenth century is the rather different chronology he provides in *History of Madness*.[10] In this earlier study, Foucault argues that the movement to exclude and intern "madmen" during the seventeenth century (the "Great Confinement") gave consistency to the "homosexual" as such, a consistency that nineteenth-century medicine and psychiatry would then further reinforce with its "gaze." In *History of Madness*, he also contends that the repression of "homosexuality" was dramatically transformed during the seventeenth century: from judicial and corporeal punishment it shifted to "moral condemnation and the air of scandal."[11] This new type of repression was the beginning of a "morality" that desacralized the religious condemnation of sodomy while extending it to cover "the amorous ambiguities of homosexuality" and thus inciting "modern forms of guilt."[12] In other words, Foucault argues that during the seventeenth century, the "homosexual" (sodomite) becomes a readily identifiable social type who is viewed differently than he had been up to this point and who consequently views himself differently ("modern forms of guilt").

It is certainly possible to question whether the transitions that Foucault situates in the seventeenth century were as straightforward and as dramatic as he claims (some evidence suggests that they may have begun even earlier and continued through the eighteenth century);[13] however, the symptoms he identifies are at least useful starting points for considering the relation of sodomy to masculinity in this period. As I will show in the first part of this chapter, there is indeed evidence that by midcentury the sodomite was a social type defined in secular and not in religious terms and that he was much more an object of scandal or at least pithy rumors than of judicial repression. What Foucault does not show but what his comments help us to see is that the sodomite's change of status during the seventeenth century (and perhaps over a broader period) was concomitant with a tendency to define sodomy and normative masculinity in opposition to each other. Increasingly, the repression of sodomy was being grounded not on religious condemnation but rather on its perceived incompatibility with masculinity per se. Under the pressure of secular trends in political and *mondain* culture, gender came to fill a void being created by the waning of the religious argument against sodomy. And yet, this transition was anything but complete in the seventeenth century, as this chapter will also show. The traditional religious condemnation coexisted with the secular, as did the assumptions of the compatibility and incompatibility of sodomy and masculinity. Further complicating the understanding of sodomy at the time was the widespread assumption that sexual object choice was fundamentally fluid: a man or a woman could just as easily be attracted to a member of his or her own gender as to someone of the other gender.[14] Until sexual object choice came to be seen as relatively stable—until it lost its fluidity—it is difficult to see how sodomy and masculinity could be solidly opposed to one another. If sodomitical desire was considered a latent potential within any man, how could sodomy be defined as "unmasculine"? Before the "invention" of heterosexuality as a stable construct, in other words, sodomy (homosexuality) could not be radically contrasted with masculinity as a normative heterosexual construct.

This chapter focuses on three moments from the myriad of discourses that define sodomy in seventeenth-century France. Doing so, I do not set out to provide a comprehensive or synthetic overview of the history of male same-sex relations or their representations in this period.[15] Rather, I want to highlight the range of discursive problems that confronted those who wrote about sodomy and its relation to masculinity at the time. Concentrating on literary (as distinguished from judicial or religious) examples, this chapter will consider both texts that attack sodomy and "sodomites" and those that defend against or even counter such attacks. My aim is not to recover the lives of "sodomites" in any direct way, but much more to expose what Jonathan Goldberg has called "sodometries," "relational structures precariously available to prevailing discourses, . . . what the category [of sodomy] enabled and disenabled, . . . the complex terrains, the mutual implications of prohibition and production."[16] This chapter will investigate some of the ways that sodomy intersected with notions of celebrity, authorship, and friendship in particular and what those intersections reveal about what masculinity was and was not, could and could not be. Above all, I argue that sodomy continued to be spoken and spoken about in seventeenth-century France. Unlike those who claim with Foucault that "homosexuality, to which the Renaissance had accorded a liberty of expression, now passed into silence,"[17] I will show to the contrary that sodomy was audible and very much so, but that the loci from which it was spoken (about) have mostly been marginalized by the ideological forces of literary history. To hear it, we must listen to the voices of manuscript poems and songs confined to the archives, the life and works of purportedly minor authors or purposefully overlooked moments in the writings of better-known authors.

Of course, what these very different, often marginal sources tell us varies considerably depending on the motivation of the speakers. The three sections of this chapter correspond to three different motivations and thus three different discourses of sodomy in seventeenth-century France. The first section concerns a group of texts that satirize "sodomites," the second section concentrates on accusations made against the Abbé de Boisrobert and his responses to them, and the third part explores Théophile de Viau's strategic but also ambiguous expression of what I call a sodomitical "self," or persona. Moving from satire to secrecy and finally to the question of the "self," this chapter follows the movement from subjection to self-reinvention that constitutes the emergence of gay or lesbian (or any other minoritized) subjectivity. This organization is inspired by Didier Eribon's illuminating reflection on how insult and violence form the gay/lesbian sense of self and how the gay/lesbian subject might theatrically "reinvent" him- or herself. According to Eribon, insult and violence bifurcate the self, which desires to speak but is obligated to be silent. As a result, a gay/lesbian must first unlearn the "false self" imposed by normative sexual subjectivity before "playing" a homosexual self by reference to visible models but without hope of any lasting stability or authenticity. To be sure, it would clearly be anachronistic to "apply" Eribon's model directly and uncritically to the discourses of sodomy in seventeenth-century France. To do so would also imply a collective consciousness or discursive evolution, neither of which I aim to show. Rather, I follow Eribon's model of subjective movement in order to reflect on the multiple and contradictory discourses of sodomy in this period. As is the case in so many periods, the discourses of repression coexist with the discourses of secrecy and of self-expression. Interconnected, they enabled each other in various ways that are both predictable and unpredictable.

In addition to considering discourses of sodomy in a progression from subjection to self-reinvention, this chapter proceeds in reverse chronological order: the satires I discuss in the first section are from the second half of the century, the scandals surrounding the Abbé de Boisrobert occur in the 1640s, and the trial of Théophile de Viau takes us to the 1620s. I do not contest the important changes that occur in the discourses of sodomy over the course of the century—in fact, some of these very changes are the object of the first part of this chapter. Rather, I use the reverse chronological order that ensues from the thematic organization of this chapter to complicate a reductive narrative about the "emergence" of a recognizably "modern" conception of homosexuality, the "homosexual," or a subculture in this period. Moving backward through the century from the satires to Théophile—from subjection to self-reinvention—I want to suggest that the undeniable changes in the discourses of male same-sex desire over time should not overshadow those moments that defy a linear trajectory. At the beginning of the century, Théophile created a sexual persona that already anticipates many features of sexual subjectivity associated with much later periods. And the satires from the end of the century retain aspects of a distinctly early modern conception of sexuality, among others that are more familiar to us as "modern." In sum, the thematic and chronological organization of this chapter aims to show that there are multiple discourses, multiple trends, and multiple chronologies of sodomy in seventeenth-century France.

MASCULINITY AND SATIRES OF
"SODOMITES," 1660–1715

Throughout ancien régime France, charges of sodomy were a recurrent feature in satires of public figures. In the larger scheme of things, to be sure, such charges were far outnumbered by allusions to the heterosexual transgressions of cultural, ecclesiastical, and political personages during the same period. And yet, accusations of sodomy gained particular prominence in two of the most turbulent moments of the ancien régime. At the end of the Wars of Religion, Henri III was the object of virulent pamphlets, many of which put sodomy high on the list of his "crimes."[18] Later, during the Fronde, charges of sodomy surfaced in a number of the *mazarinades* that targeted Anne of Austria's Italian minister, Jules Mazarin.[19] Given that the satires of Henri III and Mazarin appeared at times of severe political turmoil, it is hardly surprising that they invoked the widespread early modern understanding of sodomy as a symptom of cosmic or cultural disorder.[20] That is, the term *sodomy*, which during this period *denoted* a wide range of sex acts over and beyond sex between men, *connoted* charges of heresy, tyranny, graft, and gluttony, and even responsibility for natural disasters such as earthquakes, storms, and the like.[21] For satirists of Henri III and Mazarin, then, the charge that their victims engaged in sodomy with other men was shorthand for expounding upon their (perceived) threat to the divinely ordered body politic.

In satires from the second half of the seventeenth century, by contrast, accusations of sodomy assumed different meanings. The volumes of the manuscript *Chansonnier Maurepas* for the period 1660 to 1715 contain several hundred texts that connect prominent men to sodomitical acts or inclinations.[22] Ranging from drinking songs and parodies of operatic libretti to epigrams and other poems not set to music, these manuscript texts are considerably lighter in tone than the pamphlets published during the Wars of Religion and the Fronde. Even more significant, they, unlike the political pamphlets that preceded them, make little or no effort to conflate sodomy with cosmic or cultural disorder. In this respect, they employ the type of satirical discourse that was probably a ubiquitous feature of early modern court gossip. Late sixteenth- and early seventeenth-century manuscript satires of sodomy in such sources as the *Registres-Journaux* of Pierre de l'Estoile and the *Historiettes* of Tallemant des Réaux do bear resemblance to those of the *Chansonnier Maurepas*, although they are far less numerous.[23] But even if they continued a long-standing tradition, the manuscript satires composed between 1660 and 1715 constituted the dominant satirical discourse for this period. During Louis XIV's reign, then, there were not two, parallel types of satire about sodomy—as there had been in the late sixteenth and early seventeenth centuries—but one.

At first glance, it might be tempting to concur with the critics of generations past that these texts are useful for little more than anecdotal biographies of members of the high nobility and royal family, military officers, cultural personalities, judges, and church officials. To adopt such a dismissive attitude, though, would be a mistake. Like all satires, these poems and songs reveal the phantasmatic fears of at least a certain section of the public of their time. Using satirical humor, they are also an imaginary response to these fears. From this perspective, satires reveal less about the satirized than they do about the satirists and their public. In what follows, I will work from the presupposition that what is being satirized becomes a means of identifying some of the cultural anxieties of a particular period. The satires of "sodomites"[24] discussed in the following pages reveal not only anxieties about sodomy during the second half of the seventeenth century, but also anxieties about masculinity in general. For, not only did these poems and songs appear during a period of intense "gender trouble" (as evidenced, among other things, by the recurrence of the centuries-old *querelle des femmes*), they were also contemporaneous with a burgeoning discourse on sexuality that took the form of pornographic novels and medical treatises. As we will see, the satires of "sodomites" in the pages of the *Chansonnier Maurepas* suggest that late seventeenth-century France was preoccupied not only with femininity and heterosexual desire, but also with masculinity and male same-sex desire.

A Crisis of Representations

It is extremely difficult to reconstruct in any detail the historical contexts of production and reception of the late seventeenth-century satires of "sodomites." Most of them remain anonymous, and it is hard to ascertain either the extent or the nature of their circulation. This said, we can glean a few clues from the collections in which they are found—the multivolume *Chansonnier Maurepas* at the Bibliothèque Nationale de France. Collected, organized chronologically, carefully annotated, and bound in volumes by Pierre Clairambault (1651–1740),[25] these songs and poems were then recopied in elegant script and supplemented with later (eighteenth-century) texts under the supervision of Jean-Frédéric Phélypeaux, comte de Maurepas (1701–1781). From all indications, this *Chansonnier*, one of many compiled in the eighteenth century, was created to satisfy its owners' historical and anecdotal interests rather than to serve as a genuine songbook.[26] About the composition and reception of the songs themselves, we have less precise information. We do know that these *Chansonniers* include texts penned by members of court (even by two of Louis XIV's illegitimate daughters, the Princess of Conti and the Duchess of Bourbon) and that some of them circulated there as well. But we also know that these collections contain poems by the famous Pont-Neuf bards known as the Savoyard and the Cocher de M. de Verthamont; that satirical songs are said to have been written and sung in cabarets of the *quartier du Temple* by the likes of Boileau, La Fontaine, and Racine;[27] and further, that the lieutenants general of police, La Reynie and d'Argenson, made note of potentially subversive songs sung in the streets of Paris in their *gazetins*, from which Clairambault is said to have taken many texts.[28] All of this seems to indicate that these satires were composed and circulated both at court and in the city. It is possible, then, that satires of "sodomites" circulated in both venues as well.

In the absence of more precise information about their composition and reception, we are forced to turn our focus to the songs and poems themselves. Fortunately, the historical events and persons satirized in most of the texts included in the *Chansonniers* have been identified (often amply so) by Clairambault, although their authors remain for the most part anonymous.[29] Accordingly, the allusions and plays on words in these manuscript texts are often far less mysterious for us than many of those in the earlier printed political pamphlets. Even without the benefit of Clairambault's erudition, the manuscript satires, beyond the reach of censorship, eschew the types of intentionally enigmatic turns of phrase employed—of necessity—by the pamphlets.

Beyond this, the manuscript satires also differ from the earlier printed ones in terms of motivation, content, and humor. While the *libelles* against Henri III and Mazarin emanated from readily identifiable political factions, such was not nearly as often the case for songs and poems about late seventeenth-century "sodomites." In these latter satires, as I have already mentioned, sodomy is not implicated either in cosmic and cultural disorder or in political instability. Of course, one explanation of this fact would be that the second half of the seventeenth century was a period of relative cultural and political stability, corresponding as it did to the reign of Louis XIV. Satirists lacked the explicit political motivation to invoke sodomy as part of any particular crisis. In comparison with the printed pamphlets from the Wars of Religion and the Fronde, these songs and poems seem to present satire for satire's sake. More precisely, their satire is akin to the perennial gossip about public figures during the ancien régime. This is not to say that these satires were without political meaning or ramifications. Like the secret histories of (mostly fictional) sexual liaisons at court published in the Netherlands beginning in the 1680s and smuggled into France, the songs and poems about "sodomites" were part of an emerging "literary underground" (to use Robert Darnton's phrase) that, in the eighteenth century, would play such an important role in undermining the philosophical foundations of the ancien régime. To be sure, these brief satires are hardly the extended sexual/political biographies of members of Louis XIV's court found in historical novellas *(nouvelles historiques)* and manuscript newspapers *(nouvelles à la main)*. And yet, like them, they provide the elite political class with the opportunity to laugh at itself—or its favorite victims from within its own ranks.[30] Occupying an intermediary position between the attack on individual reputation that characterized the Renaissance style of politics and attacks on the regime that appeared during the Enlightenment, the satires of "sodomites" contribute in their own way to the faultlines in the representational system of Louis Quatorzean absolutism. That is, they are part of what Peter Burke has termed a "crisis of representations."[31]

One of the most salient aspects of this "crisis" during the reign of Louis XIV is a preference for empiricism over mysticism and literalism over metaphor and analogy, features that are illustrated in the poems and songs about "sodomites."[32] On the whole, explicit descriptions of male same-sex desire and sex acts are preferred to euphemisms and vague allusions. There are nonetheless important differences among these texts. On the basis of rhetoric and thematics, they can be sorted into five different categories. By far the most common are texts that make an accusation of sodomy in a third-person voice and that refer to historical events. Thus, one satire, which takes the form of an extended parody of a popular song, mockingly recounts the aftermath of the Louis XIV's discovery of the so-called Confraternity of "sodomites" at court in 1682 and specifically names seven individuals implicated in this scandal.[33] However, the vast majority of these satires concern incidents involving just one individual. For instance, to mark the death of Philippe d'Orléans, brother of Louis XIV, in 1701, one poem purports to rectify the official account and to reveal a "secret" truth that goes against accepted wisdom:

> Philippe est mort la bouteille à la main;
> Le Proverbe est fort incertain
> Qui dit, que l'homme meurt comme il vit d'ordinaire;
> Il nous montre bien le contraire;
> Car, s'il fut mort comme il avoit vescu,
> Il seroit mort le v[it] au c[ul].[34]

[Philippe died with a bottle in his hand; / The Proverb is far from certain / Which says that man dies in the manner that he lives; / He shows us quite the contrary; / For, if he'd died as he had lived, / He would have died with his cock up an ass.]

Besides Philippe (who was a favorite target of the satirists), Jean-Baptiste Lully, the famous seventeenth-century composer and superintendent of the king's music, was satirized almost as frequently for "offenses" ranging from his responsibility for a botched fireworks display to his relationship with a musician at court. Other personalities mentioned include Jacques Chausson, Achilles de Harlay, Auguste Servien, Charles-Belgique-Hollande de la Trimouille, Henri de Turenne, Louis-Joseph de Vendôme, and Louis de Vermandois.[35]

A smaller number of satires employ rhetorical and thematic strategies other than the third-person accusation. These include the following:

a. Link between anal intercourse and venereal disease. A piece entitled "Vers pour mettre sous le portrait du duc de Vendosme" (Verses to put under the portrait of the Duke of Vendôme), for instance, equates his siege of Barcelona with his syphilis:

> Ce héros que tu vois icy représenté,
> Favori de Vénus, favori de Bellone,
> Pris la vérole et Barcelone,[36]
> Toutes deux du mauvais costé.[37]

[This hero whom you see represented here, / Favorite of Venus, favorite of Bellona, / Got syphilis and Barcelona / Both from the wrong side.]

b. Phantasmatic punishment for sodomy. One frequently quoted song (dated 1674) suggests that people make up for their disappointment at Lully's failed fireworks by watching him burn at the stake alongside Chausson, who was indeed executed for sodomy in 1661 and whose case gained notoriety at the time:

> Excusés Messieurs[38] si Batiste[39]
> Vous a fait un feu si lugubre, et si triste,
> Et vous a mal servis pour vos demis Louis,[40]
> Le procés des Chausson[41] se poursuit,[42] s'il s'acheve
> Il vous en fera voir bientost un autre en greve,[43]
> Dont vous serez plus rejouis.[44]

[Apologies, Sirs, if Baptiste / Prepared so lugubrious, so sad a fire for you, / And served you so ill for your *demis louis* [paid to watch fireworks],

/ Chausson's trial continues; if it ends / It will soon show you another [fire] on the *grève* [site of executions], / About which you will be even happier.]

c. Mock confession or request in the first person. In one song, Chausson, at the stake, cries out for Tarnaut (who was tried and punished with him):

Chausson s'écria tout haut:
    Où est Tarnaut?
Ah! Monsieur le lieutenant,
    Avant que l'on me brûle,
    Souffrez que je l'encule
    Et je mourrai content.[45]

[Chausson cried out: / Where is Tarnaut? / Ah! Lieutenant Sir, / Before you burn me, / Permit me to fuck him in the ass / And I will die happy.]

d. Mock imperative. In this group, the poet invites readers or the target(s) to engage in anal intercourse. One song, dated 1668, enjoins

Amis, imitons ces grands personnages,
    La gloire de leurs aages,
    Qui preferent au con
    Le cul d'un beau garçon.[46]

[Friends, let us imitate those great personages, / The glory of their ages, / Who preferred to the cunt / The ass of a beautiful boy.]

The poem then lists "sodomites" from ancient Greece and Rome and six-teenth- and early seventeenth-century France before mentioning contemporaries from the entourage of Philippe d'Orléans.

No matter which rhetorical or thematic strategy they employ, the songs and poems about "sodomites" in the *Chansonnier Maurepas* highlight a fundamental ambiguity. According to its classic definition, satire constitutes a form of aggression, and its target is made responsible for corrupting an ideal order. By depicting this corruption, satire is said to enact a symbolic punishment and to express the desire for return to the lost ideal, and such a definition can be applied to the satires of "sodomites" from the reign of Louis XIV. Nearly all of these satires display a hostility toward the "sodomite(s)" they portray; yet this hostility is made explicit to widely varying degrees. On one end of the spectrum is a small subset of satires in which hostility is not only explicit, but takes the form of phantasmatic violence. Thus, one song (dated 1661) laments the unequal treatment given to two "sodomites" of different social backgrounds (Chausson, a bourgeois, and Guitaut de Comminges, an aristocrat) and implies that both deserved to die at the stake:

Grands dieux! quelle est votre justice?
Chausson,[47] va périr par le feu,
Et Guitaut[48] par le même vice,
A mérité le cordon bleu![49]

[Good gods! Where is your justice? / Chausson is going to die at the stake, / And Guitaut with the same vice, / Earned the *cordon bleu*!]

In many other satires, though, hostility is made explicit through insults, as in the following song about the playwright Campistron (dated 1686) that plays on the word *bardache* (the pejorative term frequently used until the end of the eighteenth century to designate the passive partner in anal sex):

Qui croiroit que Ca[m]pistron[50]
En cul, comme un infâme,
Fout la plus laide femme
Comme le plus beau garçon?
Sans craindre poil, ni moustaches,
Maquereaux, ni putains,
Sauvez-vous, petits bardaches,
Du plus bardache des humains.[51]

[Who would believe that Campistron / In the ass, like an infamous one / Fucks the ugliest woman / As much as the handsomest boy? / Without fearing hair nor moustaches, / Pimps nor whores, / Keep clear, little bardashes, / Of him the most bardash of humans.]

At the other end of the spectrum are satires in which hostility is implicit, if indeed it can be detected at all. Perhaps the most extreme example is a song (dated 1677) in which La Trimouille, a peer of France, admits his pleasure at the thought of oral sex:

Ah! que le nez[52] me chatouille!
Disoit le bon la Trimouille;
Quel plaisir quand il me mouille
    Et quand il me fait cela!
J'aime le jus de la couille,
Et souvent je m'en barbouille;
Un vit ne sort point bredouille,
Quand on me le fiche là là là là là
    Un vit bandant
    Est bien charmant,
Et quiconque dit autrement
    Ment, ment, ment, ment, ment[53]

[Ah! how the nose tickles me! / Said the good La Trimouille; / What pleasure when it / wets me / And when it does that to me! / I love the juice from the balls / And often I cover myself with it / A cock never comes out unsatisfied / When it's put there, there, there, there, there / A hard cock / Is so charming / And whoever says otherwise / Lies, lies, lies, lies, lies.]

To be sure, this song is not quite devoid of satire. La Trimouille admits to being the passive partner, a role routinely stigmatized in this period and, moreover, deemed all the more unworthy for those of elevated social status.[54] Ridicule is also apparent in the two monosyllabic series "là là là là là" and "Ment, ment, ment, ment, ment," which are elements of the song that is parodied. Beyond this, though, the text does not allude to any form of punishment, nor does it explicitly insult La Trimouille. And ultimately, a homoerotic reading is entirely conceivable.

Whether they are more or less explicitly hostile, the satires of "sodomites" as a whole display a humor that is considerably lighter in tone than what is found in the pamphlets about Henri III and Mazarin, and this lighter tone generally softens allusions to sodomy. In the pamphlets from the Wars of Religion and the Fronde, humor serves above all to underscore the disorder purportedly created by the "sodomite" who becomes "abject," that is, the embodiment of an alterity that both defines and threatens order.[55] In Paul Scarron's "La Mazarinade," for instance, the repetition of the word *bougre* (bugger) in one passage stretches semantic reference far beyond ordinary usage. With a flourish typical of the mid-seventeenth-century burlesque aesthetic, Scarron uses *bougre* to refer to sex acts (bestiality, pederasty, masturbation, anal intercourse) but also—and especially—to tyranny. Mazarin is portrayed as a "Bougre sodomisant l'Estat" (Bugger sodomizing the State).[56] In the end, the relentless repetition of the word *bougre* and the multiple referents applied to it make Mazarin abject, as it does the synecdochic category of sodomy itself, which covers a wide range of vices and crimes.

As a whole, the satires produced during the reign of Louis XIV also render "sodomites" and sodomy abject. And yet over and beyond the comparatively lighthearted humor, at least three features of these songs and poems combine to alter the nature of the disgust that the satirical "sodomite" is supposed to inspire. First, in the satires from the period 1660 to 1715, the referents for sodomy are considerably fewer than in the pamphlets about Henri III and Mazarin. Indeed, sodomical acts among men are in and of themselves the primary focus, and such descriptions are not nearly as frequently linked to political, social, and religious disorder. Second, these satires not infrequently employ ironic approval of sodomy, a stance that is only rarely found in the earlier pamphlets. Third, and related to this irony, the songs and poems from the *Chansonnier Maurepas* occasionally express mock admiration for their very targets. Thus, the marquis de Créquy is addressed as "Beau Créquy" (Handsome Créquy),[57] and, in one distinctly ambivalent song, Vendôme is called the "meilleur bougre du monde" (best bugger in the world).[58] The combined effect of these features is to humanize, in a relative sense, the "sodomites" targeted by the manuscript satires. This is obviously not to say that satirists from the second half of the seventeenth century express anything approaching sympathy for their victims, but rather that the "sodomites" ridiculed are less frightening and less caricatural than the subjects of the earlier pamphlets.

This different satirical approach makes it possible to understand these songs and poems as an example of what Peter Stallybrass and Allon White have termed "phobic enchantment." In this type of fantasy, "repugnance and fascination are the twin poles of [a] process in which a *political* imperative to reject and eliminate the debasing 'low' conflicts powerfully and unpredictably with a desire for this Other."[59] I do not mean to imply that the notion of "phobic enchantment" could not be applied to the attacks on Henri III and Mazarin. Yet, precisely because their tone is lighter and their satire less dehumanizing, the satires from the *Chansonnier Maurepas* are better illustration of this notion, or at the very least of a "phobic enchantment" in which fascination with the debased Other is expressed more openly and explicitly. Of course, it is not only the Others—the "sodomites"—who are the object of fascination, but sodomy itself. This is all the more significant since sodomy is not primarily functional, not first and foremost a means to the end of attacking the actions, beliefs, or policies of the men who are satirized. Allusions to their actions, beliefs, and policies do appear in these songs and poems; however, it is questionable whether many of them would have been targeted by satirists at all had it not been for their reputations as "sodomites."[60] Singling out the sexual proclivities and acts of their targets in this way, these satires would seem to confirm Foucault's assessment that the seventeenth century gave a new specificity to the "homosexual" (his term).[61] In any event, sodomitical reputations and, especially, sodomitical acts are the central focus of the songs and poems from the *Chansonnier Maurepas*. This centrality thus raises the question of how we are to understand satirists' predilection for the motif of sodomy during the years 1660–1715.

Defining Masculine Desires

Maurice Lever has described the second half of the seventeenth century in France as "homophobic," in contrast with what he considers to be the decidedly more "homophilic" first half.[62] Part of Lever's argument is based on literary sources: during the first half of the century, as he shows, several poets incorporated homoerotic themes into their verse, whereas the second half of the century witnessed the flourishing of the satires I have been discussing here. Beyond the properly historical problems with Lever's thesis,[63] the literary sources he cites cannot be so easily reduced to the homophilic-homophobic opposition he tries to establish. In particular, as we have already seen, the satires constitute more than a verbal repression or an expression of hostility toward sodomy. Rather, they might be seen as an example of "phobic enchantment," in which repugnance and fascination are conjoined. Reading them in this way would encourage us to reevaluate the complexity of attitudes toward sodomy during the reign of Louis XIV. This is hardly to deny that this period was marked by persecution of sodomites. On the contrary, the executions of Jacques Chausson, Claude Le Petit, Jacques Paulmy, and Philippe Bouvet de La Contamine and the disbanding of the infamous "Confraternity" at court in 1682, to cite but a few examples, demonstrate its very real consequences. At the same time, this repression contributes in many cases to a fascination with the "sodomite" and sodomy, a fascination that is amply expressed in the songs and poems of the *Chansonnier Maurepas*.

It is crucial to recognize the complexity and, specifically, the ambivalence of attitudes toward sodomy during the reign of Louis XIV. Indeed, the fascination-cum-repression that characterizes the production of satires about "sodomites" is part of a broader fascination with sexualities and gender differences in this period. It is now well known that the second half of the seventeenth century was a period of intense "gender trouble" during which the discourses of sexual difference addressed the roles of women in society. From the proto-feminist treatises of François Poullain de la Barre (*De l'égalité des deux sexes* [*On the Equality of the Two Sexes*, 1673]) and (*De l'éducation des dames* [*On the Education of Ladies*, 1679]) to the latter-day *querelle des femmes* between Nicolas Boileau ("Satire X: Contre les femmes" ["Satire X: Against Women," 1694]) and Charles Perrault ("L'Apologie des femmes" ["In Defense of Wives," 1694], written in response to Boileau's satire) and including the substantial writing—both fiction and nonfiction—by women, the reign of Louis XIV was marked by fierce debates about the place of women in society. During the same period, as is increasingly well known, discourses of sexuality in the form of pornographic novels and marriage treatises were also flourishing. As Jean Mainil in particular has shown, novels such as *L'Escole des filles* (*The School of Girls* [1655]), *Le Rut ou la pudeur éteinte* (*Lust or Modesty Undone* [1676]), *Vénus dans le cloître* (*Venus in the Cloister* [1672]), *L'Académie des dames* (*The Academy of Ladies* [1660]) and treatises such as Nicolas Venette's *Tableau de l'amour considéré dans l'Estat du mariage* (*Portrait of Love Considered in the State of Marriage* [1687]) were part of a broad epistemological attempt to define women as radically "other," fundamentally different from men. Although they give detailed descriptions of the sexualized female body, texts such as these nonetheless never quite accord women a complete ontological autonomy, nor do they articulate their submission to patriarchal dominance. What they ultimately serve to do, according to Mainil, is to define that which is *not* male, that which gives consistency to the male and the masculine.[64] At first glance, the satires of "sodomites" that circulated during the second half of the seventeenth century would also seem to define that which is *not* male all the better to reaffirm, by contrast, what normative masculinity *should* be. In this way, sodomites would seem to fulfill a role similar to that of women in the pornographic novels and the medical treatises. They are one of the means by which a heterosexual masculine norm can be defined. In this sense, they resemble the "mollies" of early eighteenth-century London studied by Randolph Trumbach.[65]

This, however, is only part of the story, because women are not entirely absent from this corpus. A number of the satirical songs and poems from the *Chansonnier Maurepas* juxtapose male-female and male-male sex acts and desires. The king and his brother offered satirists obvious material for such a juxtaposition. One poet declares:

L'Amour de diverses façons
Brûla deux freres de ses flames.
L'un a soupiré pour les Dames;
L'autre n'aima que les garçons.[66]

[Love in different ways / Ignited two brothers with its flames. / One sighed for the Ladies; / The other loved only boys.]

Usually, however, the juxtapositions of heterosexual and sodomitical acts concern the same person. For instance, one of several songs devoted to Lully's leaving Mlle Certain for the musician Brunet has the composer confess, in the first person:

La vieille Certain se fasche
Que Brunet soit mon mignon
Elle est vieille vache
Il est un joly bardache
Elle a le C[on] large et profond
Il a le C[ul] petit et rond.[67]

[The old Certain is angry / That Brunet is my minion / She is an old sow / He is a pretty bardash / Her cunt is wide and deep / His asshole is small and round.]

Satires such as these exploit the motif of the grotesque female body prevalent in sixteenth- and early seventeenth-century libertine poetry. Still, the reappearance of this motif later in the century, at a time when women's social and sexual roles were of central interest, demonstrates a recognition that sexualities and gender differences are inextricably intertwined. Moreover, by satirizing sodomy, these songs and poems not only delineate the contours of heterosexual masculinity, they also sketch out a hierarchy of relations among sexual and gendered identities that aims to reestablish a sense of order and propriety, the ultimate goals of all satire.

But precisely what sort of hierarchy do these particular songs and poems endorse? Most obvious and most central is the fact that sodomitical desire is usually portrayed as subordinate and inferior to different-sex desire. In a song about Louis XIV and Philippe d'Orléans, the *derrière* is rejected by the king and is hierarchically inferior to the object of his own pleasure:

> Quand Louis prit le devant,
> Il laissa le derrière;
> Il abandonna ce lieu
> Pour apanage à Monsieur
> Son frère, son frère, son frère.[68]

[When Louis took the front, / He left the backside; / He abandoned that part / As the prerogative of Monsieur / His brother, his brother, his brother.]

It is worth noting that sodomy, however subordinate and inferior, is not made overtly abject by the comparison with different-sex desire or sex acts. Nor is it in any of the satires that juxtapose male-female and male-male inclinations or acts. Indeed, in some of the texts heterosexual and sodomitical inclinations are seemingly interchangeable. One song, for instance, declares that the marquis de Breauté "ne sçait que choisir, / Ou de Venus, ou bien de Ganimede"[69] (does not know which one to choose, / Between Venus and Ganimede). More important, though, is the fluidity and instability of the male-female and male-male desires that are portrayed by this subgroup of satires about sodomy. In one song, Lully states that the beauty of the duchesse de la Ferté enchanted him so much that "Moy qui suis Florentin, j'ai changé de côté"[70] (I who am Forentine, I've changed sides). Like Lully, the "sodomites" targeted by late seventeenth-century satirists may have a predisposition for same-sex desire;[71] but such a predisposition does not signify an immutable and unidirectional "sexual orientation." Rather they suggest that different-sex and sodomitical desires and acts are fluid. More generally, in many of these satires, sodomy is not—and seemingly cannot be—cordoned off from different-sex desires and acts.

By relegating sodomy to the subordinate position, then, these satires (attempt to) counteract the fluidity between hetero- and homoerotic desire. Many of them do so by linking sodomy and misogyny. In extreme cases, "sodomites" are accused of rejecting women altogether. Thus, one song devoted to the "Confraternity" of 1682 depicts its members as "anticonistes" (anticuntists) who leave the women at court disconsolate.[72] More often, however, women appear as the less desirable of two erotic objects available to the "sodomite." Such is certainly the case of another song (dated 1681) about Lully's rejection of Mlle Certain for Brunet that recalls depictions of the grotesque female body common in early seventeenth-century libertine poetry:

> Laisse là ta Certain, ragraffe ton pourpoint;
> Croy moy, mon cher Lully, passe plus outre;
> Voy sa vieille maman,[73] là bas de dans un coin,
> Qui gratte un con où tiendroit une poutre!
> Laisse là tous ces cons qui ne te foutent point:
> Prens le vit de Brunet[74] qui te va foutre.[75]

[Leave your Certain there, button up your doublet; / Believe me, my dear Lully, go on to other things; / See her old ma, over there in a corner, / Who stratches her cunt where a beam would fit! / Leave all those cunts that don't fuck you: / Take the cock of Brunet who is going to fuck you.]

Through its ironic imperatives, this song of course targets the "sodomites" Lully and Brunet. Yet it establishes a causal link between the ironic endorsement of sodomy and the degrading portrait of Mlle Certain's mother. The final imperative, because it mockingly approves Lully's passivity as a "bardash," is obviously ironic, a fact made all the more blatant by the reference to what is an anatomical impossibility ("tous ces cons qui ne te foutent point") but also an assimilation of Lully and the "vieille maman." Even as Lully is enjoined to reject the two female erotic objects, he resembles them, paradoxically, because he is a *bardache* and thus, womanlike, if not effeminate. By degrading the "vieille maman," then, this satire simultaneously degrades the "sodomite" Lully all the more forcefully. And ultimately, Lully is the "feminized" sodomite, but he is also, by association, a misogynist. In the seventeenth century, mocking women was an outright rejection of the good taste and refined manners of which they were the supreme arbiters. As a "sodomite" and a misogynist, according to this song, Lully is presumed to be a double social outcast.

Of course, in a twist of the very irony directed at Lully, this satire reveals that it is actually the songster who is responsible for misogyny. This (seemingly unintentional) admission is hardly insignificant, and this for two reasons. First of all, it is indicative of a broader strategy on the part of the satirists whose songs are preserved in the *Chansonnier Maurepas*. Throughout this collection, misogyny is rampant, not only in satires of "sodomites" but also in the (far more numerous) poems about the heterosexual liaisons of various well-known figures. If all of these satires—sodomitical and hetero-sexual—are considered as a whole, the implicit causality between "sodomites" and misogyny may offer a means for songsters, poets, and lis-teners to defend themselves against charges of hostility toward women and to preserve sociable respectability. Misogyny, they might claim, is ultimately the fault of the "sodomites" they deride in so many of their songs and poems.[76]

More generally, though, the unwitting admission by the songster in the poem about Lully reveals just how central—and how linked—the epistemo-logical problems of femininity and sodomy become in this period. At this specific moment in the never-ending, always morphing process of giving consistency to normative masculinity, it was imperative to establish concep-tual boundaries against which this norm could be defined. By intervening so directly in the song about Lully, the songster reveals the sleight of hand that is at work in *all* of the satires I have been discussing here. In an important sense, the "sodomites" in the *Chansonnier Maurepas* are indeed creations, both *by* and *for* satirical songsters during the reign of Louis XIV. These "sodomites" are proof of just how concerted the efforts were to give solid-ity—through (satirical) subjection—to a heterosexual masculine norm.[77]

But the fundamental principle of these satires is not a thing of the past. At their core there is always an insult that, as Didier Eribon has suggested, is a historically transcendent feature of homophobic discourse. In the late seven-teenth-century satires as in those of our own time, insult functions in similar ways. It targets a specific person but, at the same time, creates a class of indi-viduals ("homosexuals" or "sodomites"). On the whole, though, insult "globalizes more than it singularizes. It works by attributing to a category (treated as a whole or treated through the example of one individual) a group of characteristics that are conceived of as derogatory and that are considered applicable to each and every member of that category."[78] As such, insult is al-ways a form of symbolic violence. According to Eribon, the homophobic in-sult has the added particularity of being anchored in masculine domination, that is, "the domination of a 'masculine principle' over a 'feminine principle,' and thus of a heterosexual man (which is to say, a man!) over a homosexual one (who is not considered to be a man)" (79–80). If satirical images of "sodomites" before 1660 do not necessarily bear out this observation, as I have argued, those that appear after that date do, at least on the whole. Just as important, though, is the "citationality" of insults, which always recycle ma-terial that is available from a stock of insults (which does not preclude the possibility of transforming them, of course).[79] Consequently, any insult "has been shaped by its history, and its present-day possibilities are the fruit of that history."[80] Seventeenth-century satires of sodomites are part of the history of modern-day homophobic discourse and in particular of the discourse that opposes heterosexual to homosexual masculinity. This historical genealogy reveals that the general social structures and patterns of thought that make the homophobic insults "work" in late seventeenth-century France make similar insults "work" in our own day.

One of the most important effects of such insults in both the seventeenth century and today is to impose the obligation of keeping nonnormative sexual desires and acts secret. The next section of this chapter explores the contours of the sodomitical secret. As we will see, it could become material for insult, but it could also escape insult altogether and even become an "open secret." It is this ambiguity that constitutes the uncertain space of what might be called the seventeenth-century closet.

Boisrobert's Cabinet and the Seventeenth-Century Closet

The word *cabinet* had a multitude of meanings in seventeenth-century France. Beyond designating a piece of furniture (a sort of buffet), a literary anthology, a musical instrument (a portative organ), and occasionally the W.C. (equivalent of the "garderobe"), the word was especially associated with a semiprivate space within a house—"the most remote space *(lieu retiré)* in the most beautiful apartment of palaces, great houses" or "a small remote space in ordinary houses," as Furetière says.[81] The uses of the "remote space" of the cabinet recall its connection to what we would today call "privacy." Seventeenth-century dictionaries and usage both suggest that the cabinet, a small room often adjoining a bedroom, was a place where one could retire from *le monde* to read, write, or simply seek solitude. At the same time, dictionaries and usage indicate that the word was also associated with intimate conversations, and in particular those that tended toward the satirical and the heterodox.[82] The cabinet, then, was a place of *greater* and *lesser* privacy: it could serve as a study for an individual or a meeting place for small groups. In this sense, it offered a link between the solitary and the intimate, a link that fostered the expression or discussion of the self, including (if not especially) the unconventional or subjected self.[83] It was a space where one could *be* oneself, where one could give voice to feelings and emotions not easily represented—or, even, not permissible—on the fully public stage.

The link between the individual and the intimate group is also apparent in metaphorical uses of the word. Furetière, for instance, states that the cabinet "means figuratively that which happens, that which is said in a cabinet, either to the princes about the council that takes place there or for the study that individuals conduct there." He also indicates that "it is said that a man holds his cabinet to mean that he receives in his home the *honnêtes gens* who want to assemble there for scholarly and pleasing conversation."[84] In these meanings, the activities of the cabinet are transactions of and among *particuliers*— transactions where the *particulier* is privileged over the collective, transactions where the *particulier* is privileged *tout court*.[85] Given this emphasis, it is not surprising that the cabinet was also associated with secrecy.[86] From outside its seclusion, the cabinet was perceived, metonymically, as a locus where knowledge was created and circulated even as it was concealed.

In this section, I will not concentrate on these seventeenth-century meanings as such. Rather, I would like to suggest that they evoke both parallels and differences between the cabinet and a spatial metaphor from contemporary American culture—the closet. Living in and coming out of the closet are metaphors for the secrecy and disclosure, respectively, of a nonheterosexual identity. More generally, as Eve Kosofsky Sedgwick has argued, since at least the late 1960s, the "closet" has been the privileged trope in North America for describing the ways that the known and the unknown construct, contrast, and regulate both heterosexuality and homosexuality.[87] I will argue here that, to the extent a "closet" could be said to have existed in seventeenth-century France (a question to which I will return in just a moment), a more appropriate metaphor would be the cabinet. Its semantic associations with greater and lesser privacy, with the *particulier,* with the intimate group, and with secrecy all point to ways the cabinet does and does *not* intersect with the closet. Like the literal cabinet, the seventeenth-century version of the closet was not a hermetically sealed space, but instead one situated at the unstable border of the private (or, more precisely, the *particulier*) and the public, secrecy and disclosure.[88] The "closet" and the cabinet are heuristic metaphors that I will be using to consider not only this unstable border, but also the polemical uses of knowledge about transgressive sexuality in seventeenth-century France.

Of course, to speak of a seventeenth-century closet is to raise the specter of anachronism. Is it possible to posit the existence of a "closet" long before the appearance of the "homosexual" (an invention of nineteenth-century medical discourse) and even longer before the historical conditions that allowed "coming out" of the closet? I would submit that these difficulties can be addressed by considering the historical specificity of homosexuality in seventeenth-century France. First, although there are important differences between the contemporary "homosexual" and the early modern "sodomite," the latter was nonetheless seen to occupy a distinct social position, as does the modern "homosexual." Thus, while the sodomite's social visibility was not comparable to that of contemporary gays and lesbians, he still had to negotiate the boundaries between secrecy and disclosure. Yet these boundaries were not like those of our own day. Although the practice of sodomy was fairly widely tolerated among elites at court, in the church, in the army, and elsewhere, accusations of sodomy continued to result in a variety of punishments—the *galères,* the *hôpital,* and occasionally, burning at the stake—especially for those from the lower echelons of society. There was, then, a profound ambivalence toward sodomy and sodomites in seventeenth-century France. Recently, the question of how to interpret this ambivalence has divided scholars into two camps, those who accentuate tolerance and those who emphasize repression.[89] To negotiate between these two positions, I would propose that the terms of the debate could be fruitfully reframed in terms of secrecy and disclosure of sodomitical reputations. Doing so would allow us to measure the nuances of tolerance (or even acceptance) while recognizing the undeniable role of repression. Certain elites built reputations as sodomites with relative openness, but within definite limits.[90] What was known and knowable about the elite sodomite in seventeenth-century France was kept in constant tension with—and defined by—what had to remain secret or at least unmentioned.

To explore the parameters of these tensions, I turn to the case of François Le Métel de Boisrobert (1589–1662). Remembered by literary history as a poet, a playwright, a novelist, a ubiquitous salon denizen, and above all the member of Richelieu's entourage perhaps most instrumental in founding the Académie Française, the Abbé de Boisrobert was a familiar presence at court and in the emerging literary field of his time.[91] If he was known for his literary ambitions, the Abbé was also widely reputed to have a penchant for pages and lackeys. Several writers, and especially Tallemant des Réaux, allude to this reputation.[92] Considered together, their accounts suggest how knowledge of Boisrobert's sodomy was circulated, and the consequences it entailed. In reconstructing these accounts, my concern is less with their veracity as records of events and much more with their representation of the dynamics surrounding the disclosure of Boisrobert's reputation. What I will be analyzing, then, is above all a textual dynamic, but a textual dynamic of seventeenth-century France and, as such, linked (in perhaps unknowable ways) to its lived experience.

By all accounts, Boisrobert's reputation as a sodomite was something of an open secret during his lifetime. In a satire about the Académie Française composed circa 1638, Charles de Saint-Evremond has Nicolas Faret recount the reasons for Boisrobert's success both as a courtier and a writer before adding an allusion to the Abbé's penchant for "Greek love":

Boisrobert est plaisant autant qu'on sauroit l'être:
Il s'est assez bien mis dans l'esprit de son Maître [Richelieu]:
A tous ses Madrigaux il donne un joli tour,
Et feroit des leçons aux Grecs de leur amour.[93]

[Boisrobert is as pleasing as one could ever be: / He's gotten into his Master's good graces. / To all his Madrigals he gives a pretty turn of phrase / And could give lessons to the Greeks about their love.]

Much less lighthearted is an allusion to Boisrobert's "greatest crime" in a vituperative manuscript satire that attacks the Abbé's success among women. Working from the assumption that a sodomite is a misogynist, the narrator tells the women whom Boisrobert frequents that the Abbé is deceiving them and using them solely to build his reputation:

You are too kind to be aware of something that is disagreeable to your sex. Let it suffice for me to say that although he is almost always among you, he doesn't really like you all in a general sense; but because he knows from experience that the reputation of a man depends entirely on those of your sex, he cajoles you and pretends to adore you when in his heart he composes satires against you. . . . If all women were to discover what I prefer not to mention, I believe that his fate would be no more favorable than Orpheus's.[94]

Without the overtly vicious intent of the anonymous satirist, Tallemant nonetheless goes even further in discussing Boisrobert's open secret by claiming he himself circulated it. "He hid few of his little habits,"[95] claims Tallemant, and his *historiette* provides us with numerous examples to substantiate this claim. Boisrobert purportedly boasted on several occasions about "knowing" all of the pages of Marie de Médicis (1:392). He told of complaining to Ninon de Lenclos about a "pretty young lad" who refused to leave his service (to which she was alleged to have replied: "It's because no one anywhere does for him what you do for him" [1:407]). He loudly proclaimed Ninon had written him from a convent, to which she had been confined, "I think I'll imitate you and begin to love my own sex" (1:413). He recounted his trysts with both a brother and a sister to "young men whom he didn't trust at all" (1:414). He bragged about being sodomized by "one of the most beautiful boys" in the service of Mme de Piémont (1:414). And, when he protested at seeing one of his own lackeys being kicked in the rear end, the onlookers mockingly agreed with him, responding: "He's right. . . . That's the noblest part of those Messieurs" (1:414).

Taken at face value, these anecdotes lead us to believe that Boisrobert himself actively promoted his reputation as a sodomite. However, what they do not indicate is how widely Boisrobert made his reputation known. Consistent with his portrait of a gregarious, even fool-hardy Abbé, Tallemant claims that Boisrobert discussed the intimate details of his sex life with people beyond his immediate circle of acquaintances (such as telling about his trysts to "young men whom he didn't trust at all"). And yet, exactly *who* knew of his reputation as a sodomite *did* matter to Boisrobert, a fact that even Tallemant acknowledges. On two occasions, he was publicly and explicitly denounced as a sodomite. And both times, he defended himself. *How* Boisrobert was denounced in each case, and *how* he responded to the charges reveal the different sorts of tensions between secrecy and disclosure that constituted what I am calling the seventeenth-century closet, the metaphorical cabinet.[96]

The first scandal occurred in 1641, when a certain Palevoisin, a *capitaine des gardes*, told courtiers assembled in the king's antechamber that Boisrobert had "abused" *(vituperé)* the son of another *capitaine des gardes*, Saint-Georges (1:403). Tallemant explains Palevoisin's slanderous gossip as a desire for revenge on behalf of his cohort. Previously, it seems, Boisrobert had discovered that Saint-Georges was imposing illegal tariffs and embezzling the money, and Boisrobert had reported his findings to Richelieu, who then relieved Saint-Georges of his duties. When Boisrobert learned of Palevoisin's accusations, he immediately enlisted the help of the Maréchal de Grammont and had Saint-Georges *fils* (a page in Richelieu's service) appear in the antechamber to issue a categorical denial. The effect was so convincing, says Tallemant, that Palevoisin was forced to contradict his earlier claims: "[He said] to the full *garde-robe* that those who said he had said such and such thing about M. de Boisrobert were lying" (1:404). In the end, then, Palevoisin's accusations came full circle. The accuser became the accused, and the attempt to discredit him was discredited, but not without first coming to the attention of the king. Tallemant claims that this incident caused Louis XIII to conclude that Boisrobert had dishonored Richelieu, which in turn forced the minister to temporarily banish him from court.[97]

The second scandal involving the Abbé's reputation as a sodomite was, in one way, less serious. It did not involve an act for which the Abbé could theoretically have been prosecuted (and executed), but rather a reference to his sexual desires. Still, it evoked a more lasting response from the Abbé, this time in writing. In 1646, "Le Parnasse alarmé" (The Parnassus Alarmed), a manuscript satire about the Académie Française by Gilles Ménage began to circulate in Paris.[98] In it, Ménage accuses several academicians of attempting to "effeminize" the French language by inflecting masculine nouns as feminine. Singling out the Abbé, Ménage further claims that they would have succeeded:

> Sans que l'abbé de Bois robert
> Nommé grand Chansonnier de France,
> Fauory de son Eminence,
> Cét admirable patelin,
> Ayman le genre masculin,
> S'oppose de tout son courage
> A cét effeminé langage.[99]

[Except that the Abbé de Boisrobert / Appointed great Songster of France, / Favorite of his Eminence [Richelieu], That admirable jester, / Loving the masculine gender, / Opposes with all his might / That effeminate language.]

To avenge himself of the offending clause "Loving the masculine gender," Boisrobert is said to have paid his nephews to rough up Ménage. Shortly thereafter, however, the two were reconciled, and Boisrobert included some of his former adversary's Latin verses among the liminary poems that preface his first volume of *Epistres en vers* (Epistles in Verse, 1647). Then, two years later, Ménage could not resist the temptation to publish his satire, which drew a swift and sharp response from Boisrobert. In his own pamphlet, "Response au Parnasse alarmé par l'Académie Française" (Response to the Parnassus Alarmed by the Académie Française [1649]), the Abbé does not directly answer the charge made by Ménage. Instead, he depicts him as an incompetent pedant who attacked the Academy out of spite at its success. In the final verses, Boisrobert goes even further and questions Ménage's poetic and seductive graces:

Entre ta Muse & les neuf Soeurs
Nous verrons un triste ménage;
Aussi ne t'appartient-il pas
Ny de te plaire à leurs appas,
Ny de connoistre leurs Mysteres.[100]

[Between your Muse and the nine Sisters / We will see a sad *ménage;* / And it is not your fate / Either to find their beauties pleasing, / Or to know their Secrets.]

By alluding to his adversary's "sad ménage," Boisrobert obviously attempts to redirect attention away from himself and onto Ménage, as if to imply that his adversary had projected his own sexuality onto *him*. (Tallemant asserts that Boisrobert employed an even more explicit version of this same strategy in a now-lost manuscript satire in which he purportedly accused Ménage "of using Giraut [his servant] for all sorts of things" [2:322].) When Boisrobert's sodomitical reputation was recorded and circulated in writing, he was reduced to responding in kind.

Through their similarities as well as their differences, these two scandals highlight key features of the metaphorical cabinet. In both instances, the open secret of Boisrobert's sodomitical reputation only became problematic when it was formulated as an accusation or a critique. It was at that point that the closet, as such, was constituted. In other words, although *who* possessed knowledge of the secret was undoubtedly crucial, equally so was *how* and for what *purpose* that knowledge was communicated. When Boisrobert's public reputation was at stake, his open secret required responses that might be taken to be retreats into relatively greater secrecy. Beyond this similarity, the two scandals diverge when we consider the specific nature and form of the accusations that caused them. In the first, the accusation by Palevoisin arose from the exigencies of court intrigue. It was useful as such because it involved a criminal act that could have potentially led to Boisrobert's ultimate demise. Still, knowledge of the Abbé's open secret only became useful when political circumstances warranted. In the second scandal, however, Ménage's attack appeared unmotivated (Tallemant, for instance, states that it was all the more surprising because it was made "even though [Boisrobert] had never done anything to him").[101] In and of itself, Boisrobert's reputation was grounds for the barb, which invoked not criminal activity but sexual desires. A less serious charge than Palevoisin's accusation, Ménage's allusion took on serious proportions because it was formulated in print, which put Boisrobert's reputation at risk on a broader public stage.

The differences between these two scandals reveal different formulations of the link between knowledge and sexuality. In the first, the knowledge of Boisrobert's open secret was used to supplement the desire for retribution. In the second, however, that knowledge was sufficient in and of itself. Thus, Ménage's allusion invokes knowledge as primarily sexual knowledge, a link that Foucault attributes to the modern construction of sexuality.[102] By the different ways they deploy knowledge, these two scandals suggest yet again that the seventeenth century was an important moment in the emergence of modern sexuality.[103] Boisrobert's enemies used knowledge of his sodomy as a means to an end, but also as an end in and of itself. They both did and did *not* connect it to broader (personal, political, and social) imperatives.

Ultimately, Boisrobert's scandals suggest that the seventeenth-century closet, like the cabinet and unlike the contemporary closet, was an unstable and intermediary space. Not only did it occupy an uncertain place on the continuum from public to private, it was at the center of ongoing historical shifts in the links among sexuality, knowledge, and power. For Boisrobert, who valorized his own cabinet as a space of inspiration for his writing (much of which was intended for an intimate circle of acquaintances),[104] discussion of his sodomy was seemingly acceptable so long as it was contained within somewhat protected discursive spaces. However, once this discussion, in the form of writing, print, or public accusations, threatened to jeopardize his more fully public reputation, it became threatening and required a response. Within circumscribed gatherings, the open secret was (daring) boastfulness or gossip; beyond these spaces it could easily become slander, libel, or accusation. In Boisrobert's case, the cabinet became a locus of protective secrecy and self-misrepresentation—the closet in the contemporary sense—precisely at the point when knowledge or the open secret circulated beyond the bounds of intimate conversation and with the intent to do him harm.

To be sure, Boisrobert's was doubtless an exceptional limit-case. If we are to believe Tallemant's *historiette*, he was unusually open, even recklessly so, about his sodomy. But even then, it would be historically and culturally inaccurate to claim that he was "out of the closet" as we would understand that phrase in contemporary parlance. Rather, Boisrobert exploited the full potential of the literal and figurative cabinet. He created and projected an idiosyncratic persona for a relatively circumscribed group, but with risks, to which on occasion he fell victim. Even then, however, he was always able to recover from these mishaps. On the border of secrecy and disclosure, the known and the unknown, the *particulier* and the public, Boisrobert's cabinet was an ambivalent and fluid space. But thanks to that ambivalence and that fluidity, it allowed him to adopt a social persona whose equivalent, in terms of openness, would remain rare until our own time.

All told, though, we know nothing of Boisrobert's own views of his sexual persona. As is so often the case of this period, we must rely on the (usually hostile) reports of his contemporaries. In the next section, I turn to Théophile de Viau, who, unlike Boisrobert and before him, dares to speak of sodomy, and he makes it possible for us to consider the question of a "sodomitical" subjectivity.

THÉOPHILE AND THE TRIALS OF THE SODOMITICAL "SELF"

Much work on the history of sexuality has stressed the differences that separate us from the past, and particularly from the pre-nineteenth-century past. Among the most prominent of these divides is characterized in Foucault's famous statement that before the nineteenth-century invention of the category "homosexuality," acts were pursued and punished, and not persons or subjects.[105] According to this account, it was only with the development of psychiatry and sexology in the nineteenth century that sexuality—and homosexuality in particular—was conceived as constituting an identity per se. Only then were sexual acts understood to be the manifestation of a psychosexual being, which mechanisms of power could then seek to control. In contrast to this view, several scholars have recently attempted to give nuance to the Foucauldian opposition between acts and identities (and the sudden appearance of the latter during the mid-nineteenth century) by arguing for a more gradual emergence of sexual identity or even for a limited, transhistorical continuity. Among others, Didier Eribon and David Halperin have proposed models that are sensitive to historical specificity but nonetheless provide a way of understanding what is familiar to us in the past and, thus, of recognizing our political investment in the history of (homo)sexuality.[106] To understand and shape our present, we necessarily project ourselves into the past. We imagine our preoccupations (of the present) within contexts that are not those of our present. But to do so requires that spark of recognition provided by what is familiar to us in our present.

What follows is a reflection on the delicate balance that is to be struck when examining what is familiar and unfamiliar in past sexualities. In this vein, I will reopen the case of Théophile de Viau (1590–1626), a poet whose work has appealed to scholars *both* because of its modernity *and* because of its historical specificity—its embeddedness within a context that is unlike our own. While scholars interested in the history of ideas and in literary and poetic form have emphasized the poet's injunction that "we must write as the moderns do" *(il faut écrire à la moderne),*[107] those working on his place in the history of sexuality have generally done so to demonstrate the difference of the early seventeenth-century context from our own.[108] While reexamining some of Théophile's writings from the last three years of his life (particularly from his two-year-long imprisonment [1623–25]) and what they might tell us about the sexual persona the poet creates, I would like to keep in play both contextual specificity and transhistorical continuity. So doing, and unlike previous scholars, I will confront head-on the question of what might be called the sodomitical "self" in Théophile's oeuvre.[109] At a time when the voices of those accused of sodomy are virtually inaudible, Théophile speaks. But the answers he gives are anything but simple and straightforward. I will argue that the complexity of his response to accusations of sodomy and the sodomitical "self" he constructs elude any clear-cut distinction between the past and the present.

No doubt the most (in)famous moment in Théophile's short life and career was his imprisonment and trial for free-thinking and sodomy.[110] Arrested on 17 September 1623 (after being ordered into exile in 1619 and, then, after a short return to favor, being condemned to have his effigy burned at the stake in August 1623), Théophile languished for over two years in a dark and damp cell of the Conciergerie that had once housed Henri IV's assassin, François Ravaillac. During his trial prosecutors repeatedly confronted the poet with specific passages from his writings[111] as well as witnesses to his purported blasphemy and debauchery. But the prosecution based many of its indictments not on an independent investigation but rather on the work of a Jesuit priest, François Garasse, who had written a vitriolic and rambling diatribe against "libertines" in which Théophile figures prominently (*La Doctrine curieuse des beaux esprits de ce temps* [The Curious Doctrine of the Fashionable Minds of Our Time, 1623]). Like Garasse, the prosecution and its witnesses based their charges principally on Théophile's writings (although many of the witnesses had only hearsay knowledge of them). Among the most frequently examined of his writings during the trial was the (in)famous "sodomite sonnet," which was published on the first page of the *Parnasse des poètes satyriques* (Parnassus of the Satirical Poets, 1622), probably without Théophile's consent, and which he refused to acknowledge in any event. The opening piece of this collection of "libertine" verse, the sonnet depicts a poetic "I" who is suffering the effects of syphilis, which he blames on Phylis. The final tercet is an act of mock penance: the poet declares that if God spares him he will vow to engage only in anal intercourse:

Mon Dieu je me repans d'auoir si mal vescu
Et si vostre courroux à ce coup ne me tuë,
Je fais veu desormais de ne . . . tre qu'en cu![112]

[My God, I repent for having lived so wickedly / And if your wrath at this moment does not kill me, / I vow from now on only to . . ck in the ass!]

Only once, toward the very end of his trial was Théophile questioned directly about whether he had engaged in sodomy, but even then the questioner extrapolated the charge from his writings: "Reminded that he is also accused of sodomy, which is seen in his verses he has published everywhere. [Asked] if he did not write the first letter, which he [the court reporter] read to him."[113]

Armed with several different strategies, Théophile time and again deftly eluded the traps set for him: he claimed he did not know a number of the witnesses, he showed that many were not credible, he denied authorship of numerous works attributed to him, and he contested the interpretations imputed to the writings he acknowledged. Beyond the walls of his prison cell and the courtroom, Théophile appealed directly to the reading public in a series of texts that refute the charges brought against him, but that also (at least ostensibly) present an image of the poet as a pious Catholic and a faithful royal subject. In September 1625, lacking clear evidence of guilt and pressured by high-placed acquaintances of the poet, the Parlement de Paris did not condemn Théophile to be executed (as would have been expected given the charges), but rather banished him from the kingdom. Just a year later (25 September 1626), he died in hiding while attempting to orchestrate a pardon from Louis XIII.[114]

The importance of Théophile's trial for literary history has not been lost on critics, who have seen in it both literary modernity and early modern specificity, both a sign of things to come and a sign of the time, so to speak. If his trial evokes the famous literary trials of the nineteenth and twentieth centuries by recognizing the cultural capital of an author (the trials of Baudelaire, Flaubert, and Wilde come to mind), it differs from them in one crucial way. As Joan DeJean has observed, the prosecution did not distinguish between Théophile's works and his life. Rather, by projecting a fiction derived from his oeuvre onto his life, it sought to suppress not the works as much as the man.[115] More recently, DeJean has demonstrated how Théophile's trial marked the beginning of organized state censorship of "obscenity" in France and, concurrently, the end of a literary tradition of homoerotic representation in print.[116] In an altogether different vein, Christian Jouhaud has suggested that the legal proceedings were actually a success for Théophile inasmuch as he was able to make his imprisonment a public scandal and to transform himself into a hero of popular literature with the texts he published while in prison.[117] But the relatively light sentence Théophile received at the conclusion of his trial was the benefit of having followed the highly traditional path of a court poet, a path from which many seventeenth-century writers were distancing themselves at the time, and increasingly so thereafter.[118] Depending on the vantage point adopted, then, Théophile's trial can mean very different, even contradictory things.

But my interest here is less the ambivalent significance of the trial itself and more the ambiguities of Théophile's self-defense in the face of the charges of sodomy. At various moments in these verse and prose pieces, the poet alludes to the accusations that had been made against him.[119] But he does so in a way that eschews coherence and embraces contradiction. Ambiguously denying and affirming a nonnormative sexual persona, he both does and does *not* acquiesce to the demands of church and state. Théophile's self-defense is unusual when we consider that, at a time when ecclesiastical and juridical condemnation dominated the discourse on sodomy, he writes as one who has been charged with this so-called crime against nature. His is the voice of the accused in a period when the voices of the accusers very nearly drowned out all others. And Théophile's self-defense is even more unusual if we remember that his trial marked the beginning of a long-standing taboo on the representation of homoeroticism in print, a taboo that has only partially eased almost four centuries later.[120] Against this backdrop, the ambiguity of Théophile's self-defense is certainly understandable, but we should not lose sight of its audacity. To be ambiguous in the face of an unambiguous threat is always a risky enterprise, and Théophile's ambiguity constitutes an attempt to find a means of expressing a nonnormative sexual persona precisely at the time when it was becoming increasingly difficult to do so. But my intent is not to reconstruct the sex life or sexual desires of Théophile de Viau the historical person, unlike Frédéric Lachèvre, Antoine Adam, Maurice Lever, and Didier Godard, all of whom end up putting the poet back on trial. Instead, I will consider how Théophile's discursive "I" responds to the accusations of sodomy.

Théophile, or the Paradoxical Self

The possibility of a nonnormative sexual persona in Théophile's prison writings necessarily raises the methodological problem of studying pre-nineteenth-century sexualites. If Foucault famously equated sodomy with acts and not what we would call an identity before the mid-nineteenth-century invention of the homosexual and homosexuality, recent scholars have been less categorical. Among them, David Halperin has proposed a distinction between sexual subjectivities and sexual identities. The latter construct (sexual identity) conforms to our contemporary understanding of the connections between sexual acts or desires and a psychology, a style of gender presentation, mannerisms, among other things. The former (sexual subjectivity), while not implying such connections, still constitutes "a defining feature of [one's] life as a sexual subject, as well as a distinctive feature of [one's] life as a social and ethical subject."[121] According to Halperin, the early modern notion of sodomy is a sexual *subjectivity* in the sense that it is considered to be a deviant erotic desire, whereas the modern construct of homosexuality implies a sexual *identity* since it evokes, in addition to a deviant desire, a deviant personal style (42). No matter how important the differences between sexual subjectivity and sexual identity, though, they both involve "links between sexual acts, on the one hand, and sexual tastes, styles, dispositions, characters, gender presentations, and forms of subjectivity, on the other" (43–44). And, while the nature of these links varies according to historical and cultural context, the fact that they exist is an important factor of continuity.

Alongside the connections between sex and identities, the condemnation of same-sex desires and acts directed at Théophile also crosses historical periods and cultural differences. Granted, the expression and severity of that condemnation can vary considerably, but all in all homophobic discourses have proved to be remarkably consistent and resilient. Working from this recognition, Didier Eribon has given a highly suggestive account of how heterosexist domination and, more specifically, homophobic insult shape the gay or lesbian sense of self. Adapting Irving Goffman's work on stigma, Eribon explores both the symbolic violence and the productive potential of homophobic insults. The self-censure required to avoid the stigma attached to homosexuality produces what Eribon (following Goffman) calls an "intolerable tension" that, in turn, must be resolved either by escape into a false sense of self (a "pretense") or by "self-reinvention."[122] In the latter case, self-censure unleashes a creative potential that is in many ways theatrical. In Eribon's words, "it is because a gay man must for so long *play at being what he is not* that he can later only *be what he is* by playing at it" (106). Ultimately, as Eribon's use of the threatrical metaphor suggests, homosexual identity is "unrealizable" in a vaguely Sartrean sense: it entails an unresolvable tension between coincidence and noncoincidence with the self. "The notion of being 'unrealizable' refers both to the fact that one can never coincide with oneself and that one must nevertheless pursue this very goal of self-coincidence" (116). While this tension can have destructive effects, especially on the psychic level, it can also be productive, Eribon suggests. "[T]his same inadequation, this same division within the self, provides the possibility for a kind of existential and cultural richness. . . . [I]f you are inadequate to your own identity, then you are inadequate as well to all the shackles that accompany various ways of stabilizing an identity" (116–17). Of course, Eribon's analysis of homophobic insults and their consequences is derived from—and most directly applicable to—contemporary Western societies, in which gays and lesbians are able to maintain a more and more visible social presence. Still, much of Eribon's discussion of insults and stigma can illuminate premodern contexts, especially if we follow David Halperin's distinction between sexual identity and sexual subjectivity. By examining specific moments of Théophile's self-defense, I will argue that Eribon's work on the formative effects of insults and stigma—and specifically the tension they produce between "selves"—can indeed be useful for exploring not only contemporary sexual *identities*, but also premodern sexual *subjectivities*.

In his prison writings Théophile presents a complex, multifaceted self. As several critics have noted, he does not construct a single, authentic, prediscursive self, but rather invites readers to imagine multiple interpretations of his writings and of his very being. This is perhaps nowhere more obvious than in his use of the quasi-pseudonymous "Théophile." Joan DeJean and Hélène Merlin have suggested that by signing his works "du sieur

Théophile"[123]—that is, appropriating the honorific title *sieur* while suppress-
ing his family name (de Viau)—the poet refuses the referential specificity of
a proper surname, but asserts nonetheless a sense of public recognition. Dis-
avowing or at least omitting his patronymic, he attempts to become "evasive"
(insaisissable), as DeJean says, almost anonymous, indistinguishable from a
host of historical and contemporary "Théophiles."[124] But his pseudonym is
not *completely* anonymous (Théophile is his real given name, after all), and it
even bespeaks a desire for a singularizing respectability through the title *sieur*.
As a *quasi*-pseudonym, "le sieur Théophile" ambiguously reiterates and
negates the meaning of the Greek *pseudonumos,* which Maurice Laugaa has
proposed to translate as "one who lies about his name."[125] With his pseudonym, Théophile does and does not present himself as a liar, one might say.
But, with his choice of pseudonym, he demonstrates something else as well.
"Le sieur Théophile" contitutes a refusal of his full given name as a source of
enunciative authority. In the place of Théophile de Viau, it is "le sieur
Théophile," the discursive creation of the poet, who lays claim to the texts in
his collections. (Re)naming himself, he asserts a control over his being and
his work that rebels against the meanings that higher powers attempt to impose. Hélène Merlin has argued that the authority Théophile assumes
through his quasi-pseudonym is an instance of a broader and highly paradoxical mechanism. Repeatedly throughout his works, he actually expresses
the desire to be banished, the desire for the status of a *banni*. But, so doing, he
assumes the sovereign authority necessary to banish himself and, thereby, to
allow the public to do with him what it will even as he reveals the arbitrary
nature of sovereign power. For instance, in a poem dated 1620 ("Au Roi sur
son exile" [To the King on his Exile]), during his first exile, he declares:

Aussitôt que je fus banni
Je souhaitai d'être coupable
Pour être justement puni.[126]

[As soon as I was banished / I wished to be guilty / So as to be justly punished.]

And, in an undated letter to a "sot ami" written after either his first or second
banishment, he justifies this curious desire thus: "You rebuke me . . . for having banished myself. I owed this obedience to the king's anger, and could not
complain of my disgrace without making myself worthy of it nor appeal my
banishment without deserving death."[127] As Merlin puts it, "[T]he strange

Théophilian subject is a Subject abandoned by the king in sovereign fashion."[128] What interests me in this paradoxical strategy is that Théophile assumes two personae simultaneously: that of sovereign authority and that of *banni*. Both accuser and accused, both sovereign and banished subject, Théophile takes an overtly theatrical stance that recalls Eribon's description of the creative "self-reinvention" of the stigmatized subject. In hyperbolic fashion, by assuming an authority not unlike that of the king he is *not*, Théophile *plays* the role of the *banni* he *is*. Ambiguously, he maintains both a distance from and a proximity to the banished self.

A similar ambiguity is visible at those moments of Théophile's prison writings when he specifically addresses the charges of sodomy. While distancing himself from these accusations, the poet nonetheless leaves them curiously unanswered and, even further, I would argue, invites readers to consider a conclusion very different from his ostensible argument. For he paradoxically maintains a proximity to the sodomitical desires from which he seemingly distances himself. Over and beyond its use in Théophile's prison writings, to which I will turn shortly, this paradoxical stance is apparent in the defense he used during the court proceedings. Leonard Hinds has demonstrated how he repeatedly turned the tables on his accusers by employing a line of argumentation that I would call "it takes one to know one." He effectively seized upon an "epistemological trap" that Garasse and witnesses for the prosecution set for themselves by claiming to have firsthand knowledge of the accused's sodomitical intentions or acts.[129] This was precisely the line of counterattack Théophile used against his perhaps most damning witness, Louis Forest Sageot, who had become acquainted with the poet in Saumur and who accused him of having composed the "sodomite sonnet," of trying to seduce him by reciting a poem with the refrain "Et tu me branleras la pique" (And you will jerk my rod) and, finally, of admitting to having had "the carnal enjoyment of boys."[130] Faced with these accusations, Théophile not only denied having written the poems in question, but also accused Sageot of seeking revenge on him for having found Sageot in a compromising position similar to that evoked in the refrain "Et tu me branleras la pique" ("The said accused [Théophile] stated that, as concerned the refrain about jerking the rod of which the witness speaks, [it] was to get revenge for the fact that he the accused found him in that act ten or twelve years ago, for which he mocked him . . . and never composed those verses or the refrain").[131] As Hinds observes, Théophile's counteraccusation eventually helps to entrap Sageot, who seven months later (May 1625) retracted his deposition on fears that his spiritual confession, in which he purportedly confessed to sodomy, had been given to the court.[132] To this astute observation, I would add that Théophile's counteraccusation effectively draws attention *away* from the accusation of sodomitical acts leveled at him by Sageot. While the poet is careful to deny the authorship of the incriminating poems, he does not respond to the allegation that he had confessed to having "the carnal enjoyment of boys." Perhaps rattled by Théophile's counteraccusation, Sageot failed to point out this omission. And faced with a discredited witness, the prosecution perhaps decided to cut its losses and to abandon further investigation of the accusation. Whatever the case, Théophile's defense using the logic that "it takes one to know one" leaves him vulnerable to a counter-counterattack on the same grounds. After all, how does one know that "it takes one to know one" without *being* one? Théophile's discovery of Sageot in the compromising position he relates to the court had the potential to raise further questions about Théophile himself. But the poet preempts any such line of questioning by keeping the focus on Sageot: he asks if the witness can recite any of the poem he attributes to Théophile and when he cannot concludes that "since the witness does not know what the accused wrote and what he said, [he] does not know what he says nor what he deposed."[133]

A Natural Pleasure . . . Permitted or Punished?

An ambiguity similar to that of Théophile's "confrontation" with Sageot appears in the textual dialogue between the poet and Garasse about a passage in "La Plainte de Théophile à son ami Tircis" (The Lament of Théophile to His Friend Tircis). In this instance, however, the ambiguity of Théophile's response is more pronounced, more deliberately staged, one might even say. Less wide ranging, compared to Sageot's accusations, Garasse's gloss of this passage provoked a complex response from the poet, first in the Latin appeal "Theophilus in carcere" (Théophile in Prison) and then in his "Apologie de Théophile" (Apology of Théophile), both written and published early in 1624.[134]

"La Plainte de Théophile à son ami Tircis" is an elegy discovered among the poet's writings at the time of his arrest in Le Catelet (Picardy), where he was hiding, on 17 September 1623. Unfinished, the poem was entered into evidence during his trial, but it was also published late in 1623, without Théophile's consent.[135] In it, the poet rebukes his friend "Tircis" for abandoning him at the moment his effigy was about to be burned (August 1623), loudly proclaims his innocence on all charges brought against him, imagines his life and his friendship with "Tircis" had he avoided the limelight of Paris and stayed close to his native Gascony, and expresses confidence in his eventual re-habilitation.[136] The passage of this poem that caught the eye of Garasse—verses 75–84—has a tangled "genetic" history of its own. In the version published in 1625 and most likely authorized by the poet, these verses describe an innocent "natural pleasure" that his detractors pursue nonetheless:

> Un plaisir naturel, où mes esprits enclins
> Ne laissent point de place à mes désirs malins;
> Un divertissement qu'on doit permettre à l'homme,
> Ce que Sa Sainteté ne punit pas à Rome;
> Car la nécessité que la police suit
> [Permettant/En souffrant][137] ce péché ne fait pas peu de fruit.
>
> Ce n'est pas une tache à son divin Empire
> Car toujours de deux maux faut éviter le pire.
> Encore ai-je un défaut contre qui leur abois
> Eclate hautement: c'est, Tircis, que je bois.[138]

[A natural pleasure, to which my spirit so inclined / Leaves no room for my malicious desires / A diversion that must be permitted to man, / Which His Holiness does not punish in Rome; / For, the City has needs such that / Allowing this sin does not yield just a little fruit. // It is not a stain on his divine authority / For always of two evils the worst must be avoided. / Yet I do have a fault about which their shrieking / Cries out loudly: it is, Tircis, that I drink.]

This entire passage creates suspense about the exact nature of the "natural pleasure," suspense that the poet ends with the comic answer "it is, Tircis, that I drink." At first, he insinuates that the "natural pleasure," the "diversion that should be permitted to man" is something other than drinking. But what, exactly? Modern critics have suggested that Théophile recycled a traditional joke about revenue the papal see derived from bordellos it tolerated within Vatican walls: for the needs of the city, tolerating this "sin" is indeed fruit-ful.[139] However, this interpretation was never mentioned in the controversy that ensued from Garasse's commentary, mostly because the earliest printed versions of the poem include a curious variant. In verse 77, "permet" (per-mits) replaces "punit" (punished); and in verse 80, "Punissant" (Punishing) is substituted for "Permettant / En souffrant" (Permitting/Tolerating).[140] Instead of what His Holiness leaves unpunished ("Ce que Sa Sainteté ne punit pas à Rome"), the verses of the original edition point out what he actually prohibits ("Ce que Sa Sainteté ne permet pas à Rome"). For Garasse, the meaning of this prohibition is clear: Théophile is endorsing sodomy. Citing the verses in question, Garasse declares:

> He confesses, he recognizes, he recounts with laughter all of his debaucheries, and what I cannot utter without horror, he admits of brutality and Sodomy, not in the quality of a penitent, but accusing the Pope of not permitting it in the city of Rome. . . . I ask Théophile Viau for a clarification of these six verses [vv. 77–82], let him explain to me frankly what he means by these words, that the debaucheries of his youth are a diversion that must be permitted to man and that His Holiness does not permit in Rome. It cannot be simple fornication, so what does Viau insinuate by this vice that he says is not permitted in Rome if it is not that unnatural vice that is rigorously punished and is tolerated nowhere in the world?[141]

The reasoning Garasse uses to conclude that Théophile was endorsing sodomy is strange, to say the least. Although the allusion to Rome in Théophile's verses could perhaps evoke the "Italian vice" (as sodomy was often called in France at the time), it is still difficult to rule out the possibility that the passage could be referring to what the Jesuit polemicist calls "fornication simple," or heterosexual sex outside of the bonds of wedlock. It is the polysemous ambiguity of the "natural pleasure" that Garasse refuses to acknowledge. As we will see in a moment, the narrow interpretation on which Garasse insists in turn exposes him to accusations of libel and blasphemy against the pope, something that Théophile was quick to recognize.

But the more immediate question is how this passage from the "Plainte de Théophile" might have been read at the time. In a gesture that reproduces Garasse's single-minded reading of the "natural pleasure," albeit toward a wholly different conclusion, modern critics have insisted that Théophile was in no way referring to sodomy and have strongly implied that the passage in question is more or less commonplace.[142] However, several clues about reception at the time might lead us to a rather different conclusion. Based on the trial proceedings and later seventeenth-century editions, Mario Roques established that Théophile indeed intended "ne punit pas" (does not punish) rather than "ne permet pas" (does not permit), which means that the first printed versions of the poem were altered mistakenly (by the printer) or deliberately (by an enemy of the poet). If the latter was true, then the intent was obviously to harm Théophile through scandalous insinuations by the passage in question. Whatever the case (and it seems impossible to determine the intent behind this alteration), this entire section of the "Plainte" (verses 75–84) was omitted from a subsequent printing undertaken by Théophile's friends in 1624.[143] Since this edition of the poem appeared after Garasse's attack, it is likely that Théophile's friends attempted to circumvent the hermeneutic difficulties created by these verses. In other words, it is quite possible that they themselves found the passage troublesome. Further proof that these verses were not necessarily perceived as innocuous is found in an anonymous response to the "Plainte" by a writer who purports to be Tircis.[144] Referring to the passage about the "natural pleasure," the author distances himself from Théophile and tells him: "I owe the good of having left you to God alone, who deigned to have me spurn the company of the evil ones or suspected as such, without being accomplice to your filthy diversion *(ton vilain divertissement)*, of which you accuse yourself as blatantly as you unjustly accuse Rome of permitting it."[145] While the referent of "your filthy diversion" is unclear (though an argument for a reference to sodomy could certainly be made), it is anything but innocuous, according to the author. In fact, Théophile's "diversion" is "vilain" (filthy, indecent, licentious) even though the author seems to be reading the intended "ne punit pas" (does not punish) rather than "ne permet pas" (does not permit).[146]

Théophile's own responses to Garasse's critique of the "Plainte de Théophile" do nothing to resolve the polysemicity of verses 75–84. Instead, the poet revels in ambiguity and contradiction. In a brief allusion to the poem in his "Theophilus in carcere," he neither acknowledges nor denies authorship and yet accuses Garasse of replacing "punit" (punishes) with "permet" (permits) in order to "reproach the most innocent of Muses with the most shameful of crimes."[147] Théophile plays a cat-and-mouse game with Garasse's attribution ("the *Elegy to Tircis* that you attribute to me even though you have no way of knowing" [56]; "that poet [whoever that poet may be, in any event]" [57]), but indirectly he indeed acknowledges the poem: how can he allege that Garasse had altered it if Théophile had not written it? The poet claims authority over the poem even as he refuses to call it his own. He adopts an overtly theatrical stance that allows him both to own and disown the incriminated verses in the "Plainte à Tircis." But to the extent that he acknowledges the poem, he does so in order to use the logic that "it takes one to know one" against Garasse. Théophile contends that his accuser disguises his own "crimes" as Théophile's by attributing to him verses that Garasse himself has written: "you omit entire lines, you substitute your own, exposing thus in public your own crimes under my name" (56). Just as in the confrontation with Sageot, however, Théophile leaves himself curiously vulnerable to countercharges. By pointing out "the most shameful of crimes" that is implied by Garasse's (putative) changes, Théophile contradicts his vow not to counter or even mention tendentious accusations made against him. In the preface to the second part of his works ("Au Lecteur," 1623), he alludes to "some crimes to which common sense cannot consent":

> I would speak more clearly for my defense, but my reverence for the public and my own discretion require me to squelch these insults and to hide from the curiosity of weak minds the confusion of a few accusers for fear that it would be an instruction in crime for everyone. The wrong that people do by condemning an unknown sin is that they actually teach it.[148]

If we follow the reasoning here, we might conclude that, ironically, by highlighting Garasse's reference to "the most shameful of crimes," Théophile actually "teaches" it. Of course, even his vow *not* to mention "the crime" or "the wrong" in the "Au Lecteur" ends up provoking curiosity about it and underscoring it all the more. The rhetorical figure the poet uses here is preterition (whereby the refusal to mention something mentions that very thing), and it is this same figure that frames the self-defense in "Theophilus in carcere." In both texts, the paradoxical nature of preterition allows Théophile to (appear to) remain silent about the charge of sodomy at the same time as he mentions it. In "Theophilus in carcere," though, he claims the authority to deny the accusation made against him and then to level the same accusation against Garasse. But he also uses this authority to commit the same "error" as his accuser. He exposes to public view and, thus, teaches what should remain hidden—"the most shameful of crimes." And, if we follow the logic Théophile uses against Garasse ("it takes one to know one"), the poet in turn implicates himself in sodomy. With a gesture analogous to the souvereign/*banni* paradox, then, Théophile occupies both the position of accuser and of accused, both that of moral judge and of sodomite sinner.

In the "Apologie de Théophile," published only a few months after "Theophilus in carcere," the poet returns to Garasse's indictment of verses 75–84 in the "Plainte de Théophile," rehearsing many of the same arguments he had used previously. However, the "Apologie" relies even more heavily on preterition, not only because it is composed in French and not in Latin (with thus a far wider audience), but also because its counterattack on Garasse is far more detailed than that of "Theophilus in carcere." Once again, Théophile contradicts his pledge not to give "an instruction in crime for everyone" by putting allegations of sodomy front and center. In response to the claim that Théophile was an "unnatural mind" *(esprit dénaturé),*[149] the poet suggests the multiple ways that Garasse is himself "unnatural." Among other things, he is suspiciously interested in cabarets, bordellos, and other "places of debauchery" where he sends spies "to discover the extent and the ways that God is offended there" (66). The Jesuit priest also goes against the "nature" of his vocation by seeking out and publicizing verses about sodomy: "After taking the vow of chastity and assuming the sacred title of Jesuit, you surely go against the nature of your calling with the care you devote to contriving verses of sodomy and publicly teaching such an enormous vice under the guise of correcting it" (63). And allusions to young male students in his writings suggest feelings unsuited to a man of the cloth: "He calls young men fresh from his school 'tender young things, fresh sprouts, and kindling' *(jeunes tendrons, germes et bourrées),* and ornaments his words for boys with a kindness that is more than priestlike" (64). A priest who follows with interest places of ill repute, who is obsessed with denouncing homoerotic poetry, and who writes passionately about young men, Garasse is what he accuses Théophile of being, so the apologist contends—an "unnatural" mind. To discern the "crime against nature" is to be "dénaturé" onself, to be consumed with "unnatural" desires. But where does that leave Théophile?

Once again, the answer is far from clear. In fact, it is even more ambiguous than in "Theophilus in carcere." In his reply to Garasse's reading of the "Plainte de Théophile," the poet gives anything but a straightforward response. He begins, as before, by distancing himself from the poem: "In a certain *Elegy to Tircis,* uncertain as you are about the author, you insult him under my name" (68). Then, as before, he insinuates that he might indeed be the author, claiming that the "rimeur" did not want to publish the poem ("the rhymer, less indiscreet than you, did not want to publish" [68]). This time, though, he concedes that the verses are a "bad example," but only after he has accused Garasse of contorting them to mean "fornication," "to the bewilderment of this poor rhymer." As in "Theophilus in carcere," whether or not Théophile is the "poor rhymer" remains an open question.

The poet-defendant then reformulates his central charge against Garasse: unable to make the verses imply sodomy, as he wished, Garasse substituted "permet" (permits) for "punit" (punishes). With this alteration, he transformed a "poetic license" into a "public lesson in sodomy" (68). But instead of questioning whether the line "And that His Holiness does not permit in Rome" in fact denotes sodomy, Théophile points out the libelous, if not blasphemous consequences of Garasse's reasoning. "You say that the vice that His Holiness does not permit should be understood as sodomy, as if His Holiness permitted all the others. O profane one! Carrying your filth all the way to the Holy See! May God keep me from thinking that His Holiness would permit any sort of vice at all!" (68). By altering the poem to suggest that the pope does not tolerate sodomy, Garasse has inadvertently implied that His Holiness tolerates all other "vices," says Théophile. And yet, this argument, no matter how clever, begs the question even as it directs attention away from the "Plainte de Théophile." The poet performs a sleight of hand by focusing on Garasse and not the signification of the incriminated verses.[150] But just when the spotlight has been squared on his accuser, Théophile moves back to the (anonymous?) poet's frame of mind, for which he gives a curious defense:

> Even if some filthy idea *(sale conception)* had passed through the mind of this poet, even if he had written it, the Jesuit Vasquez teaches us that the most devout people can have abominable thoughts *(pensées abominables)* that are not faults so long as we do not persist in them. *But you, reader, whoever you are, you are mistaken if you judge our conduct by simple words. These words, certainly, haunt bad conduct but glide by the good.* For casuists, words are words and are nothing more, in case of an offense, than simple thoughts. Composing verses about sodomy does not make a man guilty of the act. Poet and pederast are two different things. (68–69)

Théophile's defense of the "poète" is dizzyingly complex. Couched in doubly hypothetical speculation ("Even if . . . even if . . ."), it is composed of multiple layers of irony. Even if the poet had composed "Et que Sa Sainteté ne *permet* pas à Rome" (instead of "Et que Sa Sainteté ne *punit* pas à Rome") and even if he had had "filthy thoughts" when writing, Théophile declares, an eminent theologian contends that evil thoughts and the words they inspire are not necessarily sins in and of themselves.[151] Citing the authority of Gabriel Vasquez (1549?–1604), whose name was synonymous with Jesuit casuistry at the time, is itself most likely ironic and meant to discredit the order to which Garasse belongs. But the examples Théophile cites to illustrate the quote from Vasquez is casuistry to the second degree. They make assumptions that the master of Jesuit casuistry would most surely have rejected. Granted, speaking of the sweetness of revenge is not the same thing as killing one's enemy. But are we thus to assume that speaking of the sweetness of revenge is acceptable?

Tongue firmly in cheek, Théophile then makes analogous distinctions between writing about and committing sodomy and between being a poet and being a pederast. Ironically, if these distinctions were not ironic, then they would undermine Théophile's earlier insinuation that Garasse's words about his male students indicated untoward desires on his part. But if we read the distinctions between words and deeds and between poet and pederast as ironic, then ironically, Théophile exposes himself to the assertion that "it takes one to know one." Since he does not rule out the possibility that the verses in the "Plainte de Théophile" can suggest sodomy and since the distinction between writing about and committing sodomy cannot be made, it follows that the "poète" (whom he might be) is himself a pederast.

Both "Theophilus in carcere" and the "Apologie de Théophile" intensify the paradoxical effects of preterition. By denouncing Garasse for writing about sodomy and thus unwittingly "teaching" it, Théophile necessarily (and ironically) also writes about and "teaches" it. It might be argued that preterition always implies a smug or even slightly perverse narcissistic pleasure on the part of the writer who employs it because the reader's attention is so clearly drawn to the act of enunciation and by extension to the enunciator, the writer. Relying as he does on preterition, the poet-defendant clearly draws attention to himself and to the pleasure he derives from drawing attention to himself. But just as he invites readers to focus on him, he attempts to slip away from his readers' view. Théophile refuses to recognize the "Plainte" as his own, but he suggests, indirectly, that it is. He deflects Garasse's accusation only to raise the question of sodomy all the more insistently. Thus, Théophile plays the roles of both accuser and accused, both judge and sodomite. He assumes the persona of accuser not only to denounce Garasse but also to allow readers to see him in the role of the accused. While this tactic clearly discredits Garasse, it grants Théophile the authority to judge himself and to put himself in the position of the sodomite. Granted, this oblique self-indictment is an iteration of the desire to be a *banni* that both DeJean and Merlin have analyzed. But I would argue that it is also part of the complex sexual persona Théophile creates, particularly in his prison writings. To illustrate this point, I turn to yet another text from his prison writings.

Friendship on Trial

In his confrontation with Sageot and his responses to Garasse's reading of the "Plainte," Théophile's ambiguous proximity to sodomy is expressed by default, couched in preterition. But at another moment in his prison writings he addresses the charge more directly, although no less ambiguously. "La Maison de Sylvie" (The Hamlet of Sylvie [1624]), dedicated to Marie-Félice des Ursins, the wife of his protector, the duc de Montmorency, contains a moving hymn to friendship between men that expands on themes from earlier poems by Théophile.[152] In Ode IV of this poem, the poet explicitly refutes the insinuations made by his accusers ("certain curious critics")—but never made explicitly in the course of his trial—that his relationship with a man who was probably Jacques Vallée Des Barreaux (and who appears under the name "Tircis" in this poem) was more than platonic.[153] Before countering this accusation, Théophile uses the myth of Phaethon and Cygnus to illustrate ideal friendship. According to this myth, when Phaethon, son of Helios, was cast into the sea by Zeus after losing control of his father's chariot, Cygnus, inconsolable at his friend's (Phaethon's) death, provoked the pity of the gods, who then transformed him into a swan. What interests Théophile is the fate of Cygnus, to whom he implicitly compares his friend Tircis.[154] The ode opens with the poet expressing his pity and admiration for Cygnus, the "chaste bird." The epithet "chaste," the very first word of the ode, becomes a leitmotif throughout ("chaste" [v. 29, v. 64]; "chasteté" [v. 35]). But it is also a curious word. It calls attention to the absence of homoerotic interpretations of this myth (and unlike those of other male friendships of Greek mythology, between Achilles and Patroclus, Hercules and Hylas, Zeus and Ganymede, for instance), but also to the ambiguous description of Cygnus in the previous ode where Théophile calls him:

[C]e pauvre amant langoureux,
Dont le feu toujours se rallume,
Et de qui les soins amoureux
Ont fait ainsi blanchir la plume,
Ce beau cygne à qui Phaéton
Laissa ce lamentable ton
Témoin d'une amitié si sainte.
(vv. 81–87)

[[T]his poor languorous lover / Whose flame kindles still, / And whose amorous cares / Thus whitened his plumage, / This beautiful swan to whom Phaethon / Left this lamentable chord / Witness to such a sacred friendship.]

Following this description almost immediately as it does, the adjective "chaste" (in "Chaste oiseau") at the beginning of Ode IV is a surprising counterpoint. Ostensibly, of course, it defuses the homoerotic ambiguity of the previous description. But it also calls attention to this ambiguity. "Chaste" becomes an overdetermined signifier.

Rather than dissipate this ambiguity, the rest of the ode only compounds it. The poet exhorts Cygnus to defy those who might condemn his love for Phaethon:

> Pour avoir aimé ce garçon
> Encore après la sépulture,
> Ne crains pas le mauvais soupçon
> Qui peut blâmer ton aventure.
> (vv. 21–24)

[For having loved this boy / Beyond the sepulture still, / Do not fear the malicious suspicion / That might indict your adventure.]

To defend his position, Théophile intones a vaguely Neoplatonic vein (the love of all beauty by the "virtuous," those with "virile" qualities, in the etymological sense), and he cites his own description of Cygnus's love:

> Les courages des vertueux
> Peuvent d'un vœu respectueux
> Aimer toutes beautés sans crime,
> Comme, donnant à tes amours
> Ce chaste et ce commun discours,
> Mon cœur n'a point passé la rime.
> (vv. 25–30)

[The courage of the virtuous / Can with a respectful vow / Love all beauties without crime, / Just as, giving to your love / This chaste and this ordinary utterance, / My heart has not exceeded poetic bounds.]

Although Théophile claims that his depiction of Cygnus's love is indeed a "chaste and ordinary utterance" and that "[his] heart has not exceeded poetic bounds"—that it is well within the limits of "chaste" poetic convention—he immediately recognizes that not everyone agrees. In the next strophe, he rails against those (the "docteurs") who imagine "crimes" where there are none and who, thereby, reveal their own sodomitical desires.

Certains critiques curieux
En trouvent les mœurs offensées,
Mais leurs soupçons injurieux
Sont les crimes de leurs pensées.
Le dessein de la chasteté
Prend une honnête liberté
Et franchit les sottes limites
Que prescrivent les imposteurs
Qui, sous des robes de docteurs,
Ont des âmes de sodomites.

(vv. 31–40)

[Certain curious critics / Find morals offended by it / But their injurious suspicions / Are crimes of their thoughts. / The intention of chastity / Assumes an honorable liberty / And exceeds the foolish limits / That are prescribed by impostors / Who, in robes of doctors, / Have souls of sodomites.]

Beyond denouncing the hypocrisy of the critics who imagine what their "souls of sodomites" desire, Théophile contests the constraints they place on male friendship, if not chastity itself. But, so doing, he inverts the logic of conventional moral discourse. He equates "chastity" not with strictures but with freedom, not with the observation of rules but with the rejection of limits. And, retrospectively, he casts doubt on the extent to which his own depiction of Cygnus's love really is conventional, an "ordinary utterance."

As Théophile goes on to describe his ideal of friendship, it becomes even clearer that it is both conventional and *un*conventional, both familiar and *un*familiar. Invoking once again Neoplatonic concepts, he cites the divine source of all beauty: "Le Ciel nous donne la beauté / Pour une marque de sa grâce" (The Heavens give us beauty / As a sign of their grace [vv. 41–42]). Thus, physical beauty actually *requires* love: "Tous les objets les mieux formés / Doivent être les mieux aimés" (All the best-formed objects / Must be the best loved [vv. 43–44]). But this love is not "the blind desire" of the "the debased soul" (vv. 51–52); instead, it is the "mouvement réglé / Dont le cœur vertueux soupire!" (just temperament / That moves the virtuous heart [vv. 52–53]). It is the moderate passion of the "virile" heart. Against the backdrop of this seemingly familiar ethical binary ("brutal" [debased] versus "vertueux" [virtuous]), the poet gives voice to what is strange and unfamiliar:

> Que ce feu que nature a mis
> Dans le cœur de deux vrais amis
> A des ravissements étranges!
>
> (vv. 55–57)

[This flame that nature has placed / In the hearts of two true friends / Has extraordinary joys!]

The love ("feu" [flame]) between two true friends is inspired by nature, and yet it provokes "extraordinary joys." Such love is both natural and extraordinary or strange. Or, put another way, nature itself is strange, and the love between two friends has unexpected pleasures that are nonetheless grounded in nature.

What these "extraordinary joys" entail is made clear in the next strophe when the poet describes his friendship with Tircis (Des Barreaux):

> Ainsi malgré ces tristes bruits
> Et leur imposture cruelle,
> Tircis et moi goûtons les fruits
> D'une amitié chaste et fidèle.
> Rien ne sépare nos désirs,
> Ni nos ennuis, ni nos plaisirs:
> Nos influences enlacées
> S'étreignent d'un même lien,
> Et mes sentiments ne sont rien
> Que le miroir de ses pensées.
>
> (vv. 61–70)

[Thus in spite of these pathetic rumors / And their cruel imposture / Tircis and I taste the fruits / Of a chaste and faithful friendship. / Nothing separates our desires, / Neither our troubles nor our pleasures: / Our intertwined destinies / Embrace each other in a single bond / And my feelings are nothing / But the mirror of his thoughts.]

The "extraordinary joys" that are the fruit of a chaste and faithful friendship would seem to be summed up by the commonplaces about the perfect union of friends. But in the midst of this conventional invocation, the strangeness of friendship's joys emerge in the peculiarly corporeal figurative language depicting the effect of cosmological forces upon Tircis and the poet. The past participle "enlacées" (intertwined [v. 67]) and the verb "s'étreignent" (embrace each other [v. 68]), suggesting as they do physical passion (especially in the French), are all the more striking because they defy the poet's overt insistence on a "platonic" friendship. Chaste friendship, or at least Théophile's understanding of it, becomes strange itself.

In the end, Théophile seeks to heighten rather than lessen the ambiguity in the signs of male friendship, and this at a time when, as Alan Bray has argued for early modern England, such signs were less clear than they had likely been before.[155] Defending his friendship with Tircis as "chaste," Théophile contests the limits that "chastity" entails in the eyes of his censors. He seemingly submits to the demands of dominant authority, only to claim a voice of his own by redefining ideal male friendship beyond the bounds imposed by "certain curious critics." This paradoxical stance highlights the theatricality of the poetic voice in this ode. But it also makes it impossible to distinguish between actor and character. The "I" who affirms the ideal of "chaste" friendship and the "I" who renders it ambiguous are at odds with each other. In this sense, Eribon's notion of theatrical "self-reinvention" applies to Théophile's poetic "I."

But this rapprochement has its limits as well. If Théophile depicts the tensions and contradictions of an "unrealizable" identity, it is not in the contemporary sense, outlined by Eribon, that presumes a stable self projected onto a social role. Rather, it is in the sense of a perpetual noncoincidence with theatrical roles that are themselves social roles. Not unlike Montaigne's stance in his famous essay "De l'amitié" (I, xxviii), "chaste" male friendship and same-sex desire are held in tension, contradicting each other.[156] Put another way, Théophile refuses the stability of a coherent, nonnormative sexual self not only because it was not an option at the time, but also because he eschews a subject position that is somehow outside of language. At moments, it might even be possible to see in Théophile's refusal something analogous to the rejection of stable sexual identities by contemporary theorists of sexuality and gender.[157] More obvious, though, is the creative potential he harnesses by depicting these unresolved tensions. Théophile is not reduced to silence, as were most of those accused of sodomy. He dares to write about same-sex desire and a sodomitical self, as fleeting and amorphous as they might be in his work. Though clearly strategic, the ambiguities he introduces into his polemical and poetic discourse at the same time disrupt our attempts to impose stable subject positions on him. For Théophile, the sodomitical self can only be expressed to the extent that it embraces ambiguity and contradiction and puts itself into question. In this sense, we might conclude that he lives up to his famous credo: "We must write as the moderns do." But the preoccupation with the sodomitical self that I have been describing up to now comes in a larger defense meant for the public sphere. In the rare glimpses we are afforded into the private writings of Théophile, a different preoccupation and a different set of questions come to the fore. He again appears ambiguously modern, but in different ways.

"Theophilus Vallaeo suo"

During the last year of his life, Théophile, out of prison but in hiding, once again wrote about male friendship. This time, however, he did so not with a polemical intent and most likely not with a view to a larger public audience. In a series of Latin letters addressed mostly to a small group of male friends and published fifteen years after his death, he was freed from the imperative of defending himself and concentrated instead on interpersonal ties. Instead of the tensions within the self, he describes the tensions and especially the joys that connect him with some of his closest friends at the end of his life. But there are other sorts of tensions that are produced by these letters—those within and among readers. Since the seventeenth century, readers have been startled, even unsettled by the rhetoric Théophile employs to describe male friendship throughout the Latin letters. This reaction centers specifically on the characterization of Théophile's relationship with Jacques Vallée Des Barreaux, which has been variously described as "a truly exclusive and unique feeling"[158] and "bonds going beyond a deep friendship."[159] Of all the friendships evoked in the Latin correspondence, the one with Des Barreaux is clearly central. He is the most frequent recipient, and he is mentioned in several letters to Théophile's other friends.[160]

Most important, though, are what one might call the topoi of friendship in the letters to (and from) Des Barreaux. On the level of epistolary rhetoric, Théophile seems to delight in varying the opening, finding different superlatives to express affection: "Theophilus Vallaeo suo" (Théophile to his dear Vallée [Letter II]), "Vallaeo suo amatissimo" (To his most beloved Vallée [Letter VII]), "Ad carissimum Vallaeum" (To my very dear Vallée [Letter

XII]), "Ad Vallaeum suum dilectissimum" (To his Vallée, dearest of all [Letter XXI]). In the body of the letters, numerous motifs evoke the intensity of the bond between the two friends. Each is another self for the other: "Non quo me in animum revocem tuum, mi Theophile, (quis enim unquam oblitus sui), sed ut ad me rescribas tibi scribo" (It is not that I want to remind you of me, my Théophile—who has ever forgotten himself?—but I write you so that you will answer me [Epistola I]).[161] Absence is a source of pain: "Ingratum est tamen quod in remotioribus haeres locis; et ultra triginta leucas distare adhuc. Vallaeum meum aegere ferrem aut incusarem, ni excusaret secessus tui causa" (It pains me however that you are still held back so far away; and I would not tolerate it if my dear Vallée were separated from me by more than thirty leagues. I would scold him if the reason for his absence weren't excusable [Epistola VII, 4:155]). Only the friend can provide happiness: "Si me amas salvus sum" (If you love me, I am saved! [Epistola II, 4:152]). Thus, the fear of losing the friend's love is ever present: "Verendum mihi semper quia tantopere amaris ne minus ames" (I must always fear that because you are so loved you will love less [Epistola XVII, 4:224]). The act of writing seeks the assurance of the friend's love: "Amas me equidem, et plane constat, sed amari te nimium secure intelligis" (Of course you love me, it's very clear, but you are too certain of being loved [Epistola II, 4:151]). But the act of writing is also, in and of itself, the performance of friendship and an act of love: "Nihil habeo quod ad te scribam, at scribo tamen; tu quoque licet nullam habeas amandi mei causam, ama me tamen" (I have nothing to write you, and I write you anyway. You, as well, even if you don't have reason to love me, love me anyway [Epistola XVI, 4:172]).

Evoking as they do intense feelings comparable to erotic love, the topoi of friendship used by Théophile are difficult to interpret and are made even more opaque by the idiosyncratic nature of the letters themselves. Guido Saba has suggested that the use of Latin by Théophile and his friends was "a sort of initiatory or exclusive language to distinguish themselves from those who are not intimate friends and, also, to recognize themselves as devotees under the sign of an exclusive friendship."[162] Saba has also noted that the tone and content of Théophile's Latin letters are highly unconventional, even "authentic" (as Saba puts it), but that their language and form are necessarily conventional, being imitations of classical Latin texts (4:lv). Unlike his French letters, which respect "social conventions and differences of rank or category in their formulaic language," the Latin epistles give voice to "deep sentiments, without any restraint, without any barrier" (4:lv). Unlike Saba, I would prefer to speak of "authenticity" and "deep feelings" as textual effects;

still, the paradoxical enterprise of Théophile's Latin correspondence, noted by Saba, has parallels with divergent readings of male friendship in the letters to Des Barreaux.

Both conventional (in form) and unconventional (in content), the letters have provoked opposing interpretations. On the one hand are those who insist on the conventional nature of the Théophile–Des Barreaux correspondence, most notably Adam and Lachèvre, albeit in cursory fashion. Adam points out that the opening "Theophilus Vallaeo suo" is formulaic and on this basis alone concludes that "the Latin letters of Théophile to Des Barreaux do not authorize any suspicion."[163] Lachèvre, while expressing surprise at the intense passions, dismisses any possibility of homoeroticism because both men refer to female love interests in their letters.[164] For Lachèvre, who—not surprisingly—does not consider the possibility of polyvalent male erotic desire, the Latin letters are simply "exercises in sentimental rhetoric and nothing more." On the other hand are the historians Godard and Lever, both of whom take the letters as proof that Théophile and Des Barreaux were lovers.[165] In this, they follow (at least partially) the lead of seventeenth-century readers, some of whom saw the correspondence as a sign of a sodomitical relationship. In the *historiette* he devotes to Des Barreaux, for instance, Tallemant des Réaux references the Latin letters to make just such an insinuation. "It is to him [Des Barreaux] that Théophile writes in his Latin letters, where there is in the opening *Theophilus Vallaeo suo*. People did not hesitate to say in those days that Théophile was in love with him, and all the rest."[166] It is also worth noting that during the course of Théophile's trial, allusions to a correspondence between the two friends that predated the published Latin letters raised the suspicions of prosecutors (suspicions that not were not pursued, according to the trial proceedings).[167] Thus, it is possible that the Latin letters are the continuation of a correspondence that was read by at least some as evidence of an "unchaste" friendship.

How then are *we* to read this correspondence? Is it unquestionably conventional or brazenly unconventional? Does it prove or even suggest that Théophile and Des Barreaux were lovers or not? In the end, it is impossible to come down definitively on one side or the other. Granted, one might extrapolate from the work of Alan Bray on friendship in early modern England to show that Théophile and Des Barreaux indeed conformed to an ideal of friendship that was subsequently lost. Their correspondence certainly evinces the intensity of affective bonds that (according to Bray) stem from the status of friendship as a sort of voluntary kinship on a par with marriage.[168] The correspondents also express the desire for each other's physical presence—indeed, each other's bodies—in ways that we would find sexually ambiguous today, but were not necessarily so among male friends at the time.[169] For all these indications of conventionality, however, the fact remains that at least some seventeenth-century readers found Théophile's letters to be anything but conventional. Yet, should we attribute their reaction to the letters themselves or rather to these readers' changing expectations about ideal male friendship, which (again according to Bray) over the course of the seventeenth century gradually lost the emphases on voluntary kinship and desire for the friend's body?

With all these unresolved questions, we might be tempted to conclude that these letters are signs of our distance from the past. They remind of us that the signs of intimate friendship among men at the time are excruciatingly difficult to interpret and, further, that the signs of the sodomitical "self" are even more so.[170] Unlike the prison writings, though, the tension we perceive between the signs of a "chaste" and "unchaste" friendship is not produced by Théophile, but rather by his readers and their regimes of reading. That recognition we seek in the past is incomplete, and necessarily so. And yet we still identify with at least some of Théophile's seventeenth-century readers. We, like them, are left puzzled and may be tempted to decide that Théophile and Des Barreaux were indeed "in love, and all the rest," as Tallemant put it so indecorously. We, like them, are not quite sure what to make of their relationship. But this shared uncertainty says as much about our respective understandings of male friendship as it does about Théophile and Des Barreaux. The pleasures these correspondents evoke seem as alien to us as they did to the seventeenth-century observers who gossiped about them.

Perhaps we would do well to part company with those earlier readers and instead see in the Théophile–Des Barreaux correspondence something akin to Foucault's call for "friendship as a way of life." In a 1981 interview, Foucault urged gay readers to move beyond the question of identity to the problem of relationality. "The problem is not to discover within oneself the truth of one's sex, but rather, from now on, to use one's sexuality so as to produce a multitude of relations."[171] When we shift the focus from self-recognition to intersubjective realization, a new set of questions present themselves: "What does it mean to be among men, 'stripped down' outside of relationships in institutions, families, professions, or obligatory comradery? It's a desire, an anxiety, a desire-anxiety that exists in a lot of people" (164). We, too, might gain from reframing the questions we pose about the Théophile–Des Barreaux correspondence. Instead of "Were they lovers or not?" we should ask, "What sorts of affective ties did they share?" It is clear that they were bound by something other than what might have been dictated by institutions, family structure, professional relations, or obligatory comradery. It is clear that their friendship provoked in each of them both desire and worry, desire for each other and worry about each other for a host of reasons. But it is also clear that their relationship—or rather its traces in the correspondence—caused anxiety in outside observers at the time. To understand this reaction, we might once again take our cue from Foucault when he explains: "I think that [what] makes homosexuality 'troubling' is the homosexual way of life more than the sexual act itself " (164). When we put aside the undecidable question of the precise physical relationship between Théophile and Des Barreaux, the fact remains that it was their "way of life" that troubled contemporaries. It exceeded the limits of conventional friendship among men in this period.

In our present moment, though, the correspondence between Théophile and Des Barreaux reminds us that we are not alone in searching for what Foucault calls the "affective and relational possibilities" of friendship (166). In the utopian pursuit of "a relation still without form that is friendship, which is to say the sum of all the things by which we can give pleasure to each other" (164), we should remember that we are not the first to conceive of this goal. The past, in spite of its distance and its difference, can occasionally shed light on ways of life yet to be lived.

SIX

Border Crossings:
For a Transgendered Choisy

OF ALL THE SURPRISING FIGURES who complicate the traditional image of a "Grand Siècle" typified by binaristic order, François-Timoléon de Choisy (1644–1724) is certainly at the top of the list. Some facets of Choisy's public persona made him a mainstream and fairly illustrious figure for the period: he was an ordained priest (or more precisely an abbot), a published author of historical and religious works, a member of the Académie Française, and an ambassador of the king of France. But the side of Choisy's life and works that has garnered the most attention is unquestionably his interest in cross-dressing. Choisy authored either alone or collaboratively a novella about two transvestites who fall in love and are married ("Histoire de la marquise-marquis de Banneville" [The Story of the Marquise-Marquis de Banneville, 1695–96]). And, many years later, Choisy recounted several episodes of his own cross-dressing in autobiographical fragments collected by subsequent editors under the title *Mémoires de l'abbé de Choisy habillé en femme* (Memoirs of the Abbot of Choisy Dressed as a Woman).[1] Since virtually none of his contemporaries mention his cross-dressing, we have no means of verifying the authenticity of Choisy's claims.[2] And, as a result, we have no option but to focus our attention on the discursive "Choisy," the narrative creation that may and/or may not have corresponded with the "real" historical figure named the Abbé de Choisy.[3] For my purposes, whether or not Choisy cross-dressed in exactly the ways he asserts in his *Mémoires* (indeed, whether or not he even cross-dressed at all) is beside the point; for, whatever the case, the fact remains that the writings I will consider in this chapter (the *Mémoires de l'abbé de Choisy habillé en femme* and the "Histoire de la Marquise-Marquis de Banneville"), by depicting men cross-dressing as women, invite us to reflect on the meanings of men traversing gender boundaries. How do we make sense of the (attempted) passages from masculinity to femininity that Choisy depicts? And what are the political implications of the various interpretive options available, for Choisy in late seventeenth- and early eighteenth-century France and for readers in the twenty-first century? These are the questions I will keep in mind as I explore the ways that Choisy attempts to marginalize his own masculinity.

Assuming that Choisy's accounts of his cross-dressing are accurate, the fact that none of his contemporaries left independent accounts might suggest that it was not perceived as shocking or unusual. But that conclusion would be erroneous, no matter how one interprets this silence.[4] Recent work by Joseph Harris, Julia Prest, and Sylvie Steinberg allows us to speculate that although cross-dressing was not really unusual in literary and theatrical representations during the seventeenth century, Choisy's depictions would have been perceived as unusual (if not worse) at the time, and this for several reasons. During the second half of the century, for instance, the performance of gender ambiguity in theatrical and musical settings were more and more restricted: cross-cast roles became increasingly rare and hostility toward the castrato hardened.[5] Additionally, although cross-dressed characters were a stock feature of prose fiction throughout the period, Harris argues that they were most often anything but "subversive" of norms of gender and sexuality.[6] Instead, cross-dressing provided a means to an end, which rarely put into question one's gender identity or behavior. In these fictional guises, cross-dressing is almost never motivated by what resembles personal pleasure alone, as it appears to be in Choisy's writings,[7] but rather by other imperatives. Outside the realm of fiction, cross-dressing by men was condemned by ecclesiastical observers as a sign of an inherent femininity or effeminacy,[8] and the period's general presumption about the perfection of the male body rendered the donning of female clothing by men an incomprehensible rejection of their "natural" superiority.[9] Against the backdrop of these literary and social discourses, Choisy's case (and by this I mean his representation of cross-dressing in his autobiographical and fictional writings) was indeed unusual and transgressive in the sense that it contravened social attitudes, literary conventions, and moralist prescriptions. During a period that was resistant to gender ambiguity on stage, Choisy performs the spectacle of the male transvestite. Where literary convention dictated that cross-dressing be subordinated to diegetic necessity, Choisy seems to make it an end in and of itself. And at a time when male cross-dressing was widely viewed as a perversion of the "perfect" and "natural" order, Choisy took the risk of being viewed as "imperfect" and "unnatural."

All of these reasons help to explain why Choisy has attracted the interest of critics, particularly over the past two decades. At a time when our own sex/gender system has been subjected to profound critique and sustained theorization, Choisy's narratives of transvestism offer an obvious window onto the ideological structures of gender and sexuality and the possibilities of reflecting and acting upon those structures during a period when the state is seen as repressing "deviance" of many sorts, including that from the gendered and sexual orders.[10] A formulation by Mitchell Greenberg might serve as a statement of critical consensus about Choisy's transgressive stance: "He is the motley, the 'both/and' (both man and woman, both inside and outside, both aristocrat and bourgeois), the hybrid 'monstrosity' that is anathema to Absolutism's compulsion for the 'either/or.'"[11] Beyond the broad critical agreement about Choisy's transgressiveness, two major emphases characterize scholarship on his depictions of cross-dressing. On the one hand is a reliance on moralizing and pathologizing discourses that cast Choisy's transgression as a departure from prescribed social or psychosexual norms. If this is hardly unexpected in early work on the Abbé (Georges Mongrédien, writing in 1966, views the transvestite memoir as "equivocal and sick," for instance),[12] even more recent and theoretically sophisticated scholarship perpetuates an analytical framework dependent upon a logic of deviance and illness, giving center stage to constructs such as exhibitionism, fetishism, narcissism, and the castration complex, for instance.[13]

The other major emphasis in critical work on Choisy has been on what might be termed the "performative" nature of the cross-dressing he portrays. If not explicitly inspired by Judith Butler's famous exposé of the performativity of gender, this critical leitmotiv is at least consistent with it. Implicitly or explicitly equating transvestism with drag (which Butler uses to illustrate the imitative and parodic nature of gender),[14] this critical tendency assumes a theatrical intentionality on the part of Choisy's cross-dressers. Typical of this emphasis is Frédéric Charbonneau's statement that "transvestism alone is a theatricalization of sex; the theater and sex are in a circular relationship for Choisy, one leading to the other in a vertiginous sort of way"[15] or Dominique Bertrand's assertion that "the games of dressing as a woman proceed from an attentive and deliberate imitation of the appearances of femininity: the patient construction of feminine characters, consciously executed, derives from a concerted and controlled performance."[16] Privileging as they do the supposed voluntarism of Choisy's (depictions of) cross-dressing, such readings point toward or lead to constructivist understandings of the body. According to Elizabeth Guild, for instance, Choisy's transvestite writings invite us to ask: "Is the body, then, not to be immediately and assuredly identified with nature—being, rather, already something of a construction, and a site of being to which unmediated access is not possible?"[17]

My own reading of the *Mémoires de l'abbé de Choisy habillé en femme* and the "Histoire de la marquise-marquis de Banneville," while not rejecting these critical perspectives outright, nonetheless develops a different stance. For at the center of my understanding of these two texts is the conviction that what is increasingly recognized as "transgender" experience is of fundamental relevance to Choisy's representations of cross-dressing. By "transgender" I am referring to a broad range of experiences resulting from the conviction that the inner sense of one's gender conflicts with the external perception of one's sex (and thus of one's gender). In this definition, the label *transgender* can be applied to "discomfort with role expectations, being queer, occasional or more frequent cross-dressing, permanent cross-dressing and cross-gender living, through to accessing major health interventions." Hence, a transgendered person is anyone "who has a gender identity at odds with the labels 'man' or 'woman' credited to them by formal authorities."[18] The political consciousness that has accompanied the emergence of transgender as a category forcefully rejects the moralizing and pathologizing discourses that have traditionally cast aspersions on the transvestite and the transsexual and instead advocates their inclusion in the symbolic and material regimes that inherently exclude these individuals and their experiences. At the same time, the work that has begun to appear in the new field of transgender studies has called into question many of the prevailing theoretical assumptions about gender and the body. Resisting the poststructuralist accounts that see them solely as cultural constructions, this field returns to the materiality of embodiment, a question often elided, and intentionally so, in contemporary gender and queer studies. For transgendered persons, as this new scholarship shows, the theoretical erasure of the material body does not take account of the stigma and oppression to which they are often subjected, precisely because they give a bodily form to their inner sense of gender. Furthermore, the common theoretical understanding of gender as performative, equivalent to drag, collides with "the self-understanding of many transgender people, who consider their sense of gendered self *not* to be subject to their instrumental will, not divestible, not a form of play. Rather they see their gendered sense of self as ontologically inescapable and inalienable."[19] Thus, by adopting the prism of transgender in this sense to read Choisy's narratives, I will consciously put aside or at least suspend several of the presuppositions that have dominated critical perspectives to date. I will argue that being attentive to the political and theoretical questions raised by transgender experience should make us wary of the moralizing and pathologizing bent that has often typified discussions of Choisy's cross-dressing just as it should provoke us to think further about the often facile comparisons with the performativity of gender.

Reading Choisy in this way comes with an obvious risk of anachronism. Even if we consider Choisy's case as a forerunner of the construct "transgender," the word itself being of very recent facture, other historical problems come to the fore.[20] Perhaps most fundamentally, this construct, which relies heavily on a binary relationship between biological sex and social gender, would seem to be inconceivable during the early modern period, when, according to Thomas Laqueur at least, a "one-sex" model dominated thinking about the male and female body well into the eighteenth century.[21] But such a conclusion needs to be qualified by several other considerations. First, even if the one-sex model had the dominance Laqueur claims in this period (and some evidence suggests it may not have),[22] he and other scholars acknowledge the emergence of both a two-sex model and the sex-gender binary during the second half of the seventeenth century.[23] And, as will become clear, Choisy's cross-dressing narratives explicitly rely on this distinction. Next, whereas Laqueur contends that during this period "gender as a social category was made to correspond to the sign of sex without reference to personhood,"[24] Choisy's writings again lead to a very different conclusion, at least about the late seventeenth century. Gender is very much a part of the "personhood" that Choisy imagines, and the tension between sex and gender is central to the cross-dressing dramas he narrates.[25]

Anachronism is also at issue in several facets of contemporary transgender experience that would arguably have been inconceivable before the advent of the concept itself. Thus, for instance, the notion of "transitioning" from one gender to the other (with or without surgical intervention), which has become a central focus for many transgendered persons today, was of course an unimaginable concept before the mid-twentieth century, even if cross-dressing might itself be seen as a partial gesture toward it. If it would be anachronistic to seek clear parallels with "transitioning" in earlier periods, more ambiguous is the disparity between the inner sense of gender identity and outwardly recognized embodied sex, the expression and consciousness of which is crucial to contemporary transgender experience. Whether or not this disparity would be readily perceived and articulated as such before transsexualism (a subcategory of transgenderism) was defined in the late nineteenth century is an open question. This is not to say that such a disparity would not have been felt by individuals before this period, but rather that the medicalization of this feeling as a "disorder" (specifically, "gender dysphoria") facilitated its recognition and expression. Hence, to claim that certain pre-nineteenth-century transvestites were not transsexuals because they did not articulate this feeling of disparity is itself anachronistic.[26] My point here is simply that the absence of an expressed disparity between one's (inner) gender and one's (outward) sex is not sufficient evidence to conclude that a pre-nineteenth-century individual was *not* transsexual or transgendered.

In spite of the risks of anachronism, I propose to approach Choisy's cross-dressing from the perspective of transgendered experience, putting the past in dialogue with the present so as to (re)consider the Abbé's understanding of gendered embodiment as well as the purported subversiveness of his narratives. In so doing, I wish to explore the extent to which Choisy's transvestite narratives portray what might be considered forerunners of transgendered existence. While there are many aspects of Choisy's case that elude one-to-one correspondence with the contemporary understanding of this notion, I contend that there are enough points of convergence to make this exercise worthwhile. Those points of convergence are likewise indications of the political benefit to be derived from seeking precursors for a group that remains very much on the margins of contemporary society. Just as gay and lesbian studies have profited from recovering the long neglected story of same-sex desire in the past, thereby demonstrating its persistence and varieties over cultural and historical divides, so too transgender studies could reap equivalent benefits, Choisy's case being one piece of this largely yet-to-be-realized project.[27]

Several critics have gestured toward the reading I will be developing here, but, ultimately, fall back on the pathologizing and performative approaches already mentioned.[28] Dirk van der Cruysse refers to the Abbé as a "transsexual" and at one point even claims that he would have taken hormone treatments had they been available in the seventeenth century;[29] but as his biography unfolds, van der Cruysse opts for the terms *transvestite* and *androgyne* to describe his subject. If he never defines with precision what he means by any of these terms, the latter two coincide with an analysis that highlights the performative aspects of Choisy's cross-dressing. More precise is the discussion by Geneviève Reynes, even if she uses definitions that are now contested. Reynes claims that Choisy is more of a "transsexual" than a "transvestite" since cross-dressing has more than fetishistic value for him, but that he is nevertheless not a "transsexual" in the fullest sense of the word since he questions neither the fact that he is a man nor his intention to remain so.[30] Besides the pathologizing framework that Reynes reproduces by way of the psycho-analytic models she adopts, her contention that Choisy does not question his gender identity ("he never puts into question his conviction that he is a man" [59]) goes to the very heart of the problem that I consider in this chapter.

As should be clear by now, I will be arguing something quite different. It is precisely because Choisy invites readers to question his self-identity as a masculine subject, if only temporarily and if only in his writings, that his case falls into the category of transgendered experience. The term *transgender* is also useful because, as Reynes's analysis confirms, Choisy does not fit neatly into any of the available categories that preceded it. Neither a "transvestite," usually defined as a person who engages in episodic cross-dressing, nor a "transsexual," generally understood today as someone who undergoes med-ical intervention to change biological sex, the Abbé is difficult to classify other than through the intentionally broad definition of "transgender," a per-son who "has a gender identity at odds with the labels 'man' or 'woman' cred-ited to them by formal authorities."[31]

As the prefix *trans* indicates, "transgender" experience is premised on crossing, above all of gender boundaries. Choisy's narratives put on display this sort of crossing—from masculine to feminine and from feminine to mas-culine identities—and this crossing is evident even in the unstable linguistic gender of the first-person narrator in the *Mémoires,* an instability I will try to reproduce by alternating masculine and feminine pronouns and possessive adjectives to refer to the Abbé.[32] But these narratives effect other crossings as well. Choisy's cross-dressing traverses many of the subcategories encom-passed by the umbrella term *transgender:* it resists being fully explained by any one and engages with several of them. The Abbé's narratives entail a crossing of temporal boundaries as well, in his own lifetime, of course, since his *Mémoires* were written at the end of his life and recount episodes from his youth, but also in our time since, by evoking a category from our own pres-ent, we seek to revisit the past. As I turn to Choisy's autobiographical ac-count of cross-dressing, I have all of these crossings in mind.

"Un plaisir si bizarre": *Memoirs of the Abbé de Choisy Dressed as a Woman*

When, at the end of his life, Choisy penned his memoirs about cross-dress-ing, he did so in a fragmentary manner. The text that we now know as the *Mémoires de l'abbé de Choisy habillé en femme* was published piecemeal, based on manuscript papers preserved by the marquis d'Argenson. The *Mémoires* are composed of two major sections (the episodes "Madame de Sancy" and "La Comtesse des Barres"), with one other very brief fragment ("Les Intrigues de l'abbé avec les petites actrices Monfleury and Mondory"). "La Comtesse des Barres," the second half of the text in modern editions, was published first, in 1735, eleven years after the Abbé's death. "Madame de Sancy" was not published until 1839, and then, in 1862, these two sections were finally published together, along with the fragment about the actresses Monfleury and Mondory.[33] If I mention these bibliographic details, it is first because the publication history of this text echoes Choisy's own fragmentary and piecemeal approach to his cross-dressing. Rather than a coherent whole, he leaves two major episodes whose interconnections are unclear at best.[34] The second half of the *Mémoires*, "La Comtesse des Barres," probably occurred first chronologically (1670–71, according to Van der Cruysse)[35] and recounts the Abbé's decision to leave Paris for Bourges, after receiving his inheritance from his mother's estate so as to assume the cross-dressed identity as the "comtesse des Barres." There, the comtesse is the center of attention and, on her estate, receives numerous guests, including two teenage girls, La Grise and Roselie, each of whom is seduced by her/him. After Roselie becomes pregnant, the comtesse/Abbé returns to Paris and, after providing for the child and marrying off Roselie, is forced by her/his family to abandon his cross-dressed "personnage,"[36] whereupon he travels and falls victim to his weakness for gambling. The first half of the *Mémoires*, "Madame de Sancy," probably transpired a couple of years after the "Comtesse des Barres" episode (1673–74),[37] and relates the Abbé's decision to set up a household in the Faubourg Saint-Marceau of Paris, a bourgeois neighborhood where he hoped to live as "Madame de Sancy" without undue scrutiny or interference. In this episode, Choisy is recognized by almost everyone as a cross-dressed man, unlike his time in Bourges. As was the case with the comtesse des Barres, though, Madame de Sancy receives guests, puts herself on display, and forms close friendships with two girls, but this time without seducing them, we are told. After returning to court and amassing gambling debts, the Abbé no longer has the means to "to dress up as a woman" (*faire la belle* [469]), as he puts it, so he sells his house in the Faubourg Saint-Marceau and travels "to hide his misery and [his] shame" (470).

As even these highly cursory summaries suggest, there are striking similarities between the two major episodes in the *Mémoires:* among other things, the decision to set up a household as a cross-dressed persona, the reception of guests, the friendships with two girls in succession, the final decision to abandon women's clothing, and his penchant for gambling. Granted, there are also significant differences between these two narratives, some of which have led scholars to speculate that "La Comtesse des Barres" might be more fantasy or fiction than the seemingly "authentic" "Madame de Sancy."[38] For the moment, however, I am less concerned here with the questions of historical authenticity they may raise (in any event, a largely fruitless task given the lack of other evidence) than with noting the similarities between the two episodes and the repetition they reveal. Twice, Choisy returns to his past and narrates the transition from a masculine to a feminine identity; and twice, Choisy explains his move back to a masculine persona.[39]

Alongside the other repetitions, these in particular bear at least some resemblance with autobiographical accounts by transgendered persons. Jay Prosser has shown that transsexual autobiographies are premised on a retrospective return to a point in the subject's history before transition, before s/he was able to "pass" as the gender s/he has become. By invoking and preserving the history of the subject's transition, this return invites us to "read" the earlier difference between her/his inner sense of gender and outward sex, thereby contradicting her/his desire to "pass."[40] Prosser argues, however, that this apparent contradiction not only constitutes the transgendered person's status as a subject, and thus with a history, but that it also sustains her/his capacity to write. There is thus a paradox in this sort of autobiography, a paradox "between passing as nontranssexual and writing as an autobiographer who wants to be read as transsexual" (131). Of course, Prosser's observations about transsexual autobiographies apply only partially to the *Mémoires de l'abbé de Choisy habillé en femme*. Neither the comtesse des Barres nor Madame de Sancy qualify as "transsexuals," and the Abbé is unable to "transition" in anything approaching a permanent or complete way. And yet, a paradox applies to Choisy nonetheless. Like the transsexual autobiographers, Choisy desires to preserve the memory of her transitional moments, making the difference between her inner sense of gender and her outward sex readable as such. But unlike them, she writes not because this difference has disappeared but rather because it has become or risks becoming invisible. Just as transsexual autobiographers inscribe transsexuality as a subjectivity in their narratives, we might say that the Abbé inscribes her subjectivity as a transgendered person within her *Mémoires*. In both cases, the autobiographical gesture makes possible a process of "becoming through returning," as Prosser puts it (117). The fact that Choisy returns to her crossdressing past three separate times (once in "La Comtesse des Barres," once in "Madame de Sancy," and another time in the Bordeaux episode), in narratives that mirror each other in several ways, might even be interpreted as showing just the intensity of her desire to preserve the memory of her "becoming" and indeed the very possibility of that "becoming." But to preserve this memory—if not this possibility—requires that Choisy take advantage of the splitting of the subject inherent in the genre of autobiography. Predicated on a distinction between the self who is reflected upon and the self who reflects, autobiography is, in this way, not unlike transgendered experience. As Prosser has noted, "autobiography, like transsexuality [and I would say transgendered experience generally], instantiates (or reveals) a difference in the subject" (102). The difference between the autobiographical past and present is all the more accentuated in the case of transgendered persons because they narrate the process of moving from the past to the present and from a state of lesser to greater coherence between inner and outward gender identity. If Choisy's narratives mark a rupture between the past and the present that is no less pronounced, it is not because of an irreversible, one-way process of becoming, but rather because of its irresolution and its fluidity. Choisy does not become once and for all either the comtesse des Barres or Madame de Sancy. She becomes each in succession only to revert to a nominal masculine state and, then, at the end of her life, through autobiographical fragments, to return to each of these feminine personas. She maintains a link with these past moments even as she asserts their difference from the present.

When it comes to making sense of his past cross-dressing, though, Choisy often bridges the gulf between past and present. At the beginning of "Madame de Sancy," he explains that it was his mother who instilled in him a taste for women's clothing: "A childhood habit is a strange thing, impossible to rid oneself of. My mother, almost from my birth, accustomed me to women's clothes. I continued to use them into my youth" (432). If this quasi-etiological reflection at least implicitly places blame on the mother and absolves the "I" of responsibility, it also (and especially) emphasizes the insurmountable force of the "childhood habit," a habit so ingrained and so enduring, we are lead to believe, that it surely remains with him as he writes. A few pages later, in an often glossed passage, Choisy sets aside any cause for blame or guilt and instead explains his penchant for cross-dressing as a universal truth:

> I've tried to discover why I enjoy such a bizarre pleasure, and here is the reason: it belongs to God to be loved, adored; man, as much as his weakness permits it, strives for the same thing; thus, since beauty pro-

duces love and is ordinarily women's destiny, when it happens that men have or believe they have a few beautiful features that can make them be loved, they try to enhance them with women's attire, which is very flattering. They then feel the inexpressible pleasure of being loved. (435)

Critics have often—and justifiably—emphasized the apology for narcissism evident in this passage. Here and indeed throughout the *Mémoires,* Choisy insists on the pleasure to be derived from being admired and loved (the two go together for him), and specifically from being admired and loved as a woman. Without denying that the recurring descriptions of this sort of pleasure throughout the text correspond strikingly to classic definitions of narcissism and without entirely discounting the interpretations of Choisy's cross-dressing that equate it with narcissism, I would nonetheless propose another way of reading the "pleasure" he mentions. What begins as an explanation of a singular pleasure quickly becomes an explanation with a universal pretense. The desire to be loved, which men have in common with God, Choisy asserts, quite "naturally" pushes *all* men endowed with beauty to augment their physical advantages with women's "attire" since women hold a monopoly on beauty. This is not simply a matter of "appropriating" the feminine, I would argue, nor is it solely an invocation of the commonplace early modern equation of beauty with women.[41] Something more fundamental, more deeply rooted is suggested by the universalizing logic at work here, so universalizing, indeed, that the "I" seems to have lost sight of the fact that he had called it "a bizarre pleasure." By asserting that all beautiful men feel the need to don women's attire, Choisy in effect normalizes (or attempts to normalize) a claim that is based on his own experience alone, as if the pleasure he feels in cross-dressing is so much a part of himself that he cannot imagine that it would *not* be a universal experience. Thus, in his illustration of the "inexpressible pleasure of being loved," Choisy returns to the first person:

I have felt more than once what I say through sweet experience, and when I have found myself at a ball or the theater, with beautiful dresses, diamonds and *mouches,* and have heard people around me say quietly: "There's a beautiful woman," I've savored within myself a pleasure so great that it can be compared to nothing else. Ambition, riches, love itself do not equal it because we always love ourselves more than we love others. (435)

The link between his own and universal experience is suggested here through the shift from the first-person singular to the first-person plural in the last, maxim-like sentence. The truth he expresses, at once personal and universal, has all the trappings of narcissism, to be sure. But this truth is not simply about the pleasure of being loved. It is also about the pleasure that results from being recognized as a beautiful woman and being loved as a beautiful woman would be, at least according to Choisy. It is the pleasure of overhearing other people saying "There's a beautiful woman," of knowing they see him as a beautiful woman. The truth that he expounds, then, concerns not only the universality of narcissism, but even more fundamentally the pleasure of feminine being and being feminine.

But it is not pleasure alone that explains Choisy's decision to cross-dress, at least as the Abbé tells the story. In a brief anecdote at the beginning of the "Comtesse des Barres" episode, she attributes her decision to dress as a woman after her mother's death to Madame de Lafayette, who had been a friend of Madame de Choisy: "Madame de Lafayette, whom I saw frequently, saw that I was always decked out with earrings and *mouches* and told me in a friendly way that this was not the fashion for men and that I'd be better off dressing as a woman" (476). When, later, Choisy visits her in full feminine attire, Lafayette reacts enthusiastically: "Ah! What a beautiful woman! So you followed my advice, and you were right to do so" (476). Choisy admits that Lafayette may have advised her to dress as a woman "perhaps a bit insincerely" *(peut-être un peu légèrement);* still, the advice that may have been a "a bit" tongue-in-cheek allows the Abbé to justify her cross-dressing. Beautiful men wearing women's adornments (earrings and *mouches*) are better off becoming women than running the risk of appearing effeminate, it would appear. The link between beauty and women is so strong, it is implied, that beautiful men should *become* women rather than attempting to *resemble* them. And so the universal truth that Choisy originally tries to establish from her own experience here finds its validation in the advice and approval of another, no matter how sincere or insincere.

Body/Image

The justifications Choisy provides for his cross-dressing emphasize its inevitability, be it through the habit instilled by maternal influence, through his desire to be loved and the link between his beauty and women, or through the advice of others. But what these justifications do not illuminate in any detailed way is his relation to his male-sexed body. Throughout the *Mémoires,* however, Choisy stresses the ease with which his body crosses from masculinity to femininity, as if it were foreordained to "pass" as female. (The only obstacle to doing so comes in the form of social disapproval; but even this obstacle is muted, if indeed it can be considered to be an obstacle at all.)[42] Choisy's male body is in no way an impediment to his identities as the comtesse des Barres and Madame de Sancy, and this fact is an important difference with transgendered experience as it is currently defined. Unlike Choisy, contemporary transgendered persons commonly express a feeling of deep conflict between their pretransition bodies and their sense of gender identity, between their outward appearance and their inner sense of gendered being. But the absence of such a conflict in Choisy's narratives does not invalidate the reading I am proposing here. For besides the fact that the historical conditions making the expression of this conflict between the inner gender and outward body had not yet been produced (as I have previously explained) and the fact that transgendered persons may feel such a conflict to varying degrees,[43] there are other ways in which Choisy's accounts do indeed parallel transgendered experiences of the body.

Central to these experiences is the distinction between the material body and what Freud called the "bodily ego," the sense of reality for the imaginary body. For transgendered and particularly transsexual persons, this distinction explains their expressed ability to experience their bodies as differently sexed from physical corporeality, an experience that puts into question poststructuralist dogma about the imaginariness of the material body.[44] Their inner sense of gender identity, with a corresponding "bodily ego" or body image, contradicts the physical appearance of their sexed bodies. And thus, the reality of their experience of themselves as gendered beings is that of their body image and not their actual physical bodies. That Choisy writes of an equivalent experience has been intimated by Mitchell Greenberg, who, in reference to the numerous elaborate descriptions of women's clothing, writes that "the enormous *jouissance* the abbé experiences is not in the reality of the body— its *Kreaturlichkeit*—but in its displacement, in the symbolic exchanges of the sexed body into and as the material construction of a body image."[45] For Greenberg, however, the body image is linked to a fetish "whose role is to both hide and reveal castration" (140). Rather than equating Choisy's body image with a fetish or reducing it to Choisy's preoccupation with clothing alone, I want to argue that there are other ways of understanding the notion of "body image" that are more affirmative of transgendered experience even as they take a more literal and sympathetic look at Choisy's narratives.

Theorists of transsexualism have noted that the term *body image,* evoking as it does the visual, is misleading insofar as the transsexual experience of this notion actually privileges the sentient (the sense of touch and internal perception) over the visual.[46] While it is difficult to assert that Choisy actually *privileges* the sentient (her descriptions of herself are eminently visual), it is still true that the sense of touch and internal perception play a fundamental role in her body image (or bodily ego) as a woman. Thus, describing the layers of clothing she was wearing one day early in the "Madame de Sancy" episode ("a white damask dress . . . a silver moiré bodice . . . a black velours skirt . . . two white petticoats underneath"), Choisy explains that "from the time I'd been wearing skirts, I didn't put on *haut-de-chausses* [breeches] anymore; I believed I really was a woman" (436). What is significant in this description is that a *haut-de-chausses*, a piece of masculine attire, had she continued to wear one, would not have been visible under the layers of dresses and skirts she was wearing. The absence of the *haut-de-chausses* would of course have been noticed by Choisy herself, but only because the bodily sensation produced by wearing the dresses and skirts would itself be different. Yet most important here is the reason Choisy decides to abandon the *haut-de-chausses:* "I believed I really was a woman." Convinced that she is a woman—*as* a woman—she is compelled to dispense with an article of men's clothing that made no change in her outward appearance. The inner conviction of being a woman combines with the sensation of not wearing a *haut-de-chausses* to create Choisy's sentient body image, a reality that was felt even more than it was seen.[47] This, however, is only one of many references by Choisy to "feeling like"—having an inner perception of being—a woman. Throughout the *Mémoires*, Choisy describes her propensity for cross-dressing as a "penchant" (476), a "goût" (477), an "inclination" (477), all terms that, while particularizing and at least implicitly moralizing, evince a deeply ingrained preference, a perception of the self as driven and defined by uncontrollable feelings.

Far and away the most important means by which Choisy realizes his female body image is through cross-dressing, and numerous are the elaborate descriptions of the exquisite skirts, dresses, scarves, trains, and so forth in his wardrobe. But Choisy's body image also leads him to transformations of his body, albeit minor ones compared to the sorts of surgical procedures sought out by many contemporary transgendered persons. In spite of these obvious differences, though, it is through these manipulations of his own material body that he strives for a coherence of body image and material body, a goal he shares with transgendered persons in our own time. One such transformation is of his chest, which he claims was as ample as an adolescent girl's.

While describing his attire for his first visit to Bourges, he explains: "my corset was very high and stuffed in front to give the impression that there was cleavage, and I actually *(effectivement)* had as much as a fifteen-year-old girl" (485–86).[48] That his cleavage was not a mere illusion created by stuffing his corset is already suggested by the somewhat incongruous adverb "actually," but Choisy goes on to explain that his "cleavage" was the consequence of careful attention since childhood: "From childhood I'd been given corsets to wear that squeezed me greatly and pushed up my flesh, which was thick and plentiful" (486). Also transformed was his skin, particularly on his upper torso: "I had also taken great care of my neckline which I rubbed every evening with calf water and a cream of sheep's feet, which makes skin smooth and white" (486).[49] Elsewhere he explains that yet another practice, learned from childhood, gave his facial skin a female appearance: "I didn't have a beard; from the age of five or six I'd been rubbed every day with a type of water that kills the roots of the hair provided that one begins early enough" (475). Saint-Simon provides further details still about Choisy's preoccupation with his skin, asserting: "He was a tall man, very handsome, of an unusual paleness that he maintained by means of bleedings, which he called his little treat. He slept with his arms tied so as to have more beautiful hands."[50] Subjecting himself to bleedings, binding his hands, and using a variety of lotions and creams, Choisy seeks to acquire the soft, white skin prized by women of his day. But what is particularly striking is that Choisy's preoccupation with his skin parallels that found in autobiographical accounts by transgendered persons, for whom the skin quite literally embodies their discomfort with their material bodies before transition.[51] If Choisy does not explicitly express discomfort with his untransformed (male) skin, the fact that he delights in his transformed (female) skin would seem to imply by negation at least that he prefers it over his "natural" skin, that he finds in his soft, white skin a different, more authentic body. No matter how limited by today's standards, then, the transformations of Choisy's chest and skin can indeed be seen as part of his quest for greater correspondence between his body image and his material body.

Recognition

The ultimate proof that this correspondence has been achieved depends upon the gaze of others, for, to "pass," transgendered persons must rely on the recognition of their sexed body. Only then is the coherence between body image and material body fully realized. Understanding in this way the recognition of the sexed body sheds different light on the passages where Choisy notes, with obvious relish, that she has a woman's body, and a *beautiful* woman's body at that. Rather than see these passages only as manifestations of narcissism, as most critics have done, I would argue that it is more important to see in them moments of recognition, moments that produce obvious pleasure, but moments that are crucial for the constitution of Choisy's body as an integrated whole. One such occurs the very first time she goes out in public in Bourges. After describing her jewelry, coiffure, mask, gloves, and fan, she concludes: "One would never have guessed that I wasn't a woman" (486). Proof of this supposition comes in the form of comments she overhears while leaving mass: "After mass, we passed between two hedges to go to our carriage, and I heard several voices in the crowd say: 'There's a beautiful woman,' which hardly failed to please me" (487). The comtesse feels pleasure at knowing that she has indeed "passed," that she has been recognized as a woman, that her body image, bolstered by her attire, is reflected in the observations of others. In another scene later in this same episode ("La Comtesse des Barres"), a moment of recognition highlights the beauty and the femaleness of Choisy's very body. The adolescent Mademoiselle de La Grise, who stays with the comtesse ostensibly to learn hairstyling, is surprised when her benefactor gives her many of her jewels to wear, and exclaims: "'And you, Madame,' said Mademoiselle de La Grise, 'You won't have anything left. But it's true that you're beautiful, you don't need to be dressed up'" (507).[52] At the same time it recognizes the comtesse's beauty, the reaction by La Grise underscores its bodily incarnation. The comtesse is beautiful not because of her dresses, jewels and hairstyles, but because of her body, which requires no adornment. She is, quite simply, a beautiful woman.

When reactions similar to those by La Grise are recorded in the "Madame de Sancy" episode, the fact that Madame de Sancy is known to be a biological man heightens the focus on her body. While collecting money during mass at her Parisian parish church, Choisy explains, "Two or three times I heard in different parts of the church people say: 'But is it really true that's a man there? He's absolutely right to want to pass for a woman'" (440). The churchgoers do far more than express approval of Madame de Sancy's crossdressing; at least implicitly grounding their judgment on the materiality of her body, they recognize its femaleness and its inaptness for masculine attire. Even those who disapprove of Choisy's cross-dressing are forced to admit their admiration of his beauty. One of his uncles arrives to reprimand his nephew as he is dressing for mass, but after witnessing the scene, exclaims: "'From what I see,' he told me, 'I should call you my niece. You really are very pretty *(bien jolie)*'" (437–38). If it is Choisy the autobiographer who is careful to add the feminine "e" on the adjective "jolie," this feminizing linguistic gesture is consistent with his uncle's purported recognition of his nephew's transformation into a niece. Another detractor proves to be far more intractable, even though he admits that Madame de Sancy is beautiful. In an exchange at the opera, Monsieur de Montausier avers: "I admit, Madame, or Mademoiselle (I don't know what I'm supposed to call you), I admit that you are beautiful, but how can you not be ashamed to wear such clothing and act like a woman?" (478). Because it is laced with sarcasm and counterbalanced by a reprimand, Montausier's admission is all the more telling, demonstrating as it does that even those hostile to Choisy's cross-dressing recognize his feminine beauty. It is as if his body has a quasi-magical effect on all those who view it by forcing them to recognize the innateness of its superlative femaleness.

Staging Femininity

But the seductive appeal of Choisy's body is the direct consequence of her deliberately theatrical self-display, and in both diegesis and narration, the *Mémoires* emphasize literal and figural theatricality. Choisy makes numerous references to the theater: one fragment alludes to a brief stint with a troupe in Bordeaux where Choisy lived as an actress (471–74); the comtesse des Barres coaches her two adolescent *protégées* in acting, rehearsing and performing scenes from Corneille's *Polyeucte* with them (499–500, 510–11); and one of these girls, Roselie, is an actress whose success on stage is assured by the theatrical training offered by the comtesse (513, 520). At several points, Choisy explicitly characterizes herself as an actress. After her impromptu performance as Pauline in *Polyeucte*, the Intendant compares the comtesse to a famous actress: " 'I've seen Duparc,' he said, 'she doesn't come close to Madame la Comtesse.' 'Well, Monsieur l'Intendant,' I told him, 'It's my true vocation'" (499).

The importance the *Mémoires* give to Choisy's connections to the theater puts into relief her use of figural theatricality. While she frames her autobiographical narratives as theatrical (at the beginning of "Madame de Sancy" she tells the marquise de Lambert, "I'll write a few acts from my play" [431], for instance) and while the repetitions between the two main episodes recall techniques of theatrical improvisation,[53] she also incorporates a sort of play acting into her everyday existence, including, as I will discuss below, the mock weddings with two of the girls she befriends and seduces, complete with wedding bed scenes in front of visitors. But more relevant to my discussion here is the self-display that Choisy so insistently *redisplays* in her *Mémoires*. Whether in public or private, she revels in giving repeated, in-depth descriptions of her jewelry, clothing, and hairstyles, descriptions that might lead us to conclude with several critics that her theatrical self-display amounts to a performative construction of the body whose meaning is derived from the outward performance of gender rather than from its materiality. According to this interpretation, Choisy's theatrical self-display would be tantamount to drag in that it ties her femininity not to her material body but rather to its performance, which thereby exposes the arbitrary construction of all gender identities. As we have already seen, however, Choisy insistently grounds her femininity in her body and its feminine beauty. What she seeks through her theatricality, I would contend, is not a performance of the disjunction between sex and gender but quite the opposite. Her deliberate, and at times narcissistic, self-display is wholly aimed at making a seamless connection between the two—between her body and her femininity—even when everyone knows she is a man.

That Choisy's penchant for theatricality has little in common with our contemporary understanding of drag is made evident in a series of descriptions at the beginning of his existence as Madame de Sancy when he gradually transitions from wearing his priestly garb (a long black soutane) to full-fledged women's clothing. At each stage of his transition, in this reverse striptease, he visits more and more people, testing their reactions at every step. Wearing what he calls a "robe de chambre" (which critics have identified as a cassock),[54] a train held by a lackey, a wig, and earrings, he visits the parish priest, "who gave me many compliments on my dress, telling me that it was much more graceful than all those little abbots, who didn't command any respect with their waistcoats and their little vests" (432). Bolstered by this success, he sports his androgynous fashion as he visits prominent women in his neighborhood, attends mass, meets with his confessor, and distributes alms to the poor. After a month, he undoes the upper buttons of his cassock to reveal a "silver moiré bodice" underneath and wears new diamond earrings, a longer wig carefully styled to accentuate his earrings, and several small *mouches* around his mouth and forehead. Once again, he carefully gauges his effect on his public: "For a month I stayed as I was without dressing up any further so that everyone would slowly grow accustomed to it and would think they'd always seen me that way, which is what happened" (433). Seeing that his experiment was succeeding, he then undoes the bottom of his cassock to reveal a "stippled black satin dress" and a "white damask petticoat," dispenses with his *haut-de-chausses,* and dons a "muslin *cravate*" to accentuate his neck and upper chest. Attired thus, his "transition" is in the end explicitly acknowledged by neighbor women and the parish priest. One of these women, Madame d'Usson declares: "From now on . . . I'll call you *madame*" and even the priest admits that he is a "beautiful lady" *(belle dame)* (434). But when this same priest points out that this "beautiful lady" is "in disguise" *(en masque),* Choisy makes clear that his new attire is neither a passing nor an unseemly fancy: " 'No, monsieur,' I told him. 'In the future, I won't dress any other way. I only wear black dresses with a white lining, or white dresses with a black lining. No one can accuse me of anything. As you see, these ladies recommend this outfit for me and assure me that it suits me quite well' " (434). Choisy's newfound appearance is not some carnivalesque disguise, he claims, but instead a permanent fixture in keeping with the norms of propriety. Restricting himself to black and white dresses, he observes the modesty required of pious women. But perhaps most significant in this impromptu self-defense is the fact that he seeks counsel from other women. By approving his "outfit" they not only attest to its modesty but also, at least implicitly, to Choisy's place within their ranks. So convincing is Choisy that the priest relents and recognizes both his femininity and his propriety: "I have to admit, Madame, that you are perfect as you are" (434). With this approval, Choisy abandons his remaining scruples about his feminized cassock and, in the end, "Everyone became accustomed to it" (435). Eager to be one of (or even, first among) the "ladies" of his neighborhood, to receive his priest's blessing, and to accustom others to his new persona, Choisy seeks to blend in as Madame de Sancy and not to stand apart as a man in women's attire. The performance he gives is not motivated by a desire to show a disparity between (male) body and (feminine) gender; it is not the parodic theatricality of drag. Instead, his is a performance that seeks in the adulation of others the confirmation of his desire to pass as a woman. His is a theatrical spectacle, to be sure, but a spectacle whose objective is to make spectators conclude that the actor Choisy is uniquely suited for the role of Madame de Sancy and is fully deserving of the title *madame,* whatever else they might know about him to the contrary.

When Choisy makes a spectacle of herself, she endeavors to embody (quite literally) a femininity that is anything but unconventional. Indeed, her penchant for the theater and social theatricality serves to underscore all the more forcefully the wholly traditional quality of her embodiment of femininity. If Madame de Sancy is able to accustom her neighbors to her appearance—in fact, her very being—through her deliberate self-display, it is surely because she conforms so closely to their expectations for femininity. And if she meets these expectations, as Choisy would have us believe, then it is hardly surprising that she illustrates certain of the misogynist clichés of her time. In the seventeenth century as in our own, the prevailing cultural expectations for women were/are invariably determined by the patriarchal forces that seek to dominate women. And Choisy, attempting as she does to incarnate the feminine—to blend into the world of women even as she stands out as an exemplary woman—cannot help but reiterate patriarchal expectations.

One particularly telling instance occurs early in the "Madame de Sancy" episode when the heroine volunteers to collect money at her parish church.

> I was teased about having been a bit coquettish when, passing among the chairs, I occasionally stopped while the parish clerk made room for me and playfully looked at myself in a mirror to adjust my earrings or my *stinquerque*. But I only did that in the evening, during the "Hail Mary," and few people noticed. I worked a lot all day long, but I'd been so delighted to see everyone acclaim me that I only felt tired once I was in bed. (440)

Now the obsession with one's appearance is a trait frequently attributed to the coquette throughout this period.[55] Choisy reproduces the teasing criticisms she received about conforming to this image only to negate them halfheartedly at best. For Madame de Sancy there is an obvious pleasure at being identified as a coquette, a pleasure that she justifies, indirectly, by the fact that "never was so much money collected at Saint-Médard [her parish church]" (440). It is difficult not to see in this episode something akin to the narcissism of a Célimène in Molière's *Le Misanthrope*. But what interests me here is Choisy's / Madame de Sancy's relation to femininity. For, if we take seriously the transgender hypothesis I have been developing, then it is not at all obvious that Choisy, either as Madame de Sancy or as the narrator of his *Mémoires*, is perpetuating misogyny from a masculine (or masculinist) position. Instead, we might conclude that she illustrates once again the all-too-frequent phenomenon of women imposing upon themselves the misogynist expectations of a patriarchal culture. It may well be that Choisy, here and elsewhere, "mirrors the production of femininity as cultural fetish" and illustrates the Lacanian notion of "feminine masquerade," as Greenberg has argued.[56] But a reading of this episode that privileges transgendered experience would resist an explanation that presupposes Choisy is, at bottom, a man who appropriates femininity so as to reinforce a masculine subject position.[57]

If we accept that Choisy's subjectivity is transitional, that it is in the process of crossing from the masculine to the feminine, then it is difficult to accept such a clear-cut conclusion. In the end, the theatricality Choisy strives for, but never fully achieves, is one in which the personas she stages reiterate the (largely patriarchal) femininity to which she aspires.

Spectacles of Sexuality

Now, by far the most daring theatrical displays by Choisy occur during his relationships with the four adolescent girls he claims to have befriended (Mademoiselle de La Grise and Roselie in "La Comtesse des Barres" and Charlotte and Babet in "Madame de Sancy"). In these moments of the *Mémoires*, however, it is not Choisy's person that is the spectacle but rather his "friendship" with each of them. From friendship to friendship, however, there are repetitions that suggest a deliberate and quasi-theatrical staging on the level of narration.[58] Whether or not this discursive mise-en-scène proves that at least some parts of these two episodes are fictional, Choisy's desire to showcase these four relationships is unambiguous. Moreover, the very fact that readers find the symmetry between the two sets of friendships suspect proves if nothing else that they occupy a peculiarly central place within the economy of the *Mémoires* to which readers' attention is drawn by the narrative design of the text.

What we are initially drawn to, so to speak, is the spectacle of Choisy's role as mentor to each of the girls as they cross the threshold into adult femininity.[59] The comtesse des Barres invites Mademoiselle de La Grise to stay with her first to teach her hairstyling and then acting; she takes Roselie under her wing to perfect the latter's skills as an aspiring actress; and, in addition to the clothes and gifts she lavishes on both Charlotte and Babet, Madame de Sancy also initiates each into either physical sexuality or at least the affective domain of love. With each girl, then, Choisy (as the comtesse des Barres and as Madame de Sancy) serves as a female mentor, using her person/persona as a goal to which each girl can aspire, either explicitly or implicitly, and what she says of Roselie—"I saw her as my piece of work *(mon ouvrage)*" (512)— applies to all four of them. At the same time, Choisy succeeds in demonstrating her own femininity, even when she is known to be a biological man. When Charlotte assures Madame de Sancy of her love, for instance, the young girl attributes to her both a masculinity and a femininity: "'I was not on my guard . . . as I would have been with a man. I only saw a beautiful lady, and why stop myself from loving her? What benefits women's clothes give you! You have a man's heart that has its influence over us, and yet the charms of the beautiful sex enchant us in a moment and prevent us from taking precautions'" (442). That Charlotte admits to being disarmed by Madame de Sancy's charms is yet another indication of how compellingly feminine they are. And that Charlotte is able to recognize and articulate the difference between Madame de Sancy's purportedly "masculine" heart and "feminine" charms is itself proof that she is stepping over the threshold from girlhood into womanhood. In addition to Charlotte, all of the other girls Choisy befriends or seduces are at precisely the same liminal stage. Once they effect that passage (by marriage or childbirth, for instance), they are no longer of interest to her, by Choisy's own admission.[60] Although there is doubtless an erotic component to this proclivity for adolescent girls, of more immediate interest to me is its serial nature. If we read Choisy as a transgendered subject, attempting to effect her own passage into femininity, then her interest in these four girls might be read as offering her something of a vicarious experience. As Choisy the narrator relives her youth through the *Mémoires*, the stories of Charlotte, Babet, Mademoiselle de La Grise, and Roselie provide her with "proof" of her own womanhood, to be sure, but also with material for reliving, both at a distance and in multiple variants, the experience of crossing over into the realm of femininity.

But the overtly erotic component in each of the friendships Choisy reminisces about and restages in his *Mémoires* is still significant because the theatrical spectacle he makes of each of these friendships offers him the occasion to stage his own sexuality. For theatricality and sexuality are closely linked for Choisy, as several critics have noted. "His sexual life is theatrical," Greenberg observes, "it is performed for an audience, an audience that gazes on the spectacle produced by Choisy for the confusion of their eyes and the delectation of his own."[61] It is in front of others that he caresses and kisses Mademoiselle de La Grise, Roselie, Charlotte, and Babet; it is in front of others that he and the girls engage in conjugal role playing (adopting the title of "petite femme" or "petit mari" [449, 465–66, 505, 517]); it is in front of others that he cross-dresses Roselie and Charlotte (446–50, 517); and, especially, it is in front of others that, while in bed, he kisses and fondles Charlotte and goes even further with La Grise (449, 492–94, 502–5). There can be no doubt, then, that exhibitionism is an integral part of his sexuality and that the gaze of an audience heightens the pleasure he derives from his encounters with these girls, whether or not his public fully understands what is transpiring in front of their eyes (and, in at least one instance, Choisy claims they do not).[62] If Choisy's exhibitionism is quite obvious, less so are the meanings that can be derived from it, especially if we consider Choisy as a transgendered subject. Several critics have proposed that the spectacle of Choisy's escapades with the four girls severs the normative bond between sex and gender and undermines the institutions, notably heterosexual marriage, that are founded upon this bond.[63] What such a reading presupposes, of course, is that Choisy is a man who *performs* femininity and, from this posture, goes on to *stage* mock marriages with his adolescent girl lovers. In other words, this interpretation posits that Choisy and his lovers stage a disjunction between sex and gender whereby the sexed body remains a stable referent. If, however, we consider Choisy to be a subject crossing from masculine into feminine embodiment, both at the moment of his friendships and at the moment of writing his *Mémoires*, then the theatrical mise-en-scène of his erotically charged relationships with the girls would lead to rather different conclusions.

To begin with, the conjugal role-playing by Choisy and his lovers would seem to be something more than mere carnivalesque play. Granted, the mock wedding ceremony that Madame de Sancy organizes for Charlotte occurs during Carnival and, more generally, the friends who observe this role-playing (both with Charlotte and the other girls) react with amusement, suggesting that for them it is little more than a game (446–47). For Choisy, however, there are indications that its significance goes deeper. After explaining how Charlotte decides, of her own accord, to cross-dress for Choisy (she declares: "I notice that you like me better in a waistcoat. If only I could always wear one!" [445]), Choisy concludes: "Thus I had the pleasure of having her often as a boy, and since I was a woman *(comme j'étais femme)*, that made for a true marriage" (446). In this statement, Choisy claims a correspondence between the truth and the appearance of marriage that is made possible by her own womanhood ("since I was a woman"). Her relationship with Charlotte (whom she later dubs "Monsieur de Maulny") is thus an extension and a reaffirmation of her femininity. But it is the neighbors of Madame de Sancy who first propose the idea of a mock wedding. "'What a good-looking couple. They should be married; they'd truly love each other.' My neighbors laughed as they said that and didn't realize how right they were" (446). The phrase "they didn't realize how right they were" here is perplexing given, first, that the neighbors know Madame de Sancy to be a biological man and, second, that Choisy elsewhere insists that this was a "mariage de conscience" (447) and that even during the wedding bed ritual they never exceeded "the limits of virtue" (449). Thus, rather than referring to a duplicitous sexual arrangement, the phrase "they didn't realize how right they were" would seem to indicate an affective bond whose veracity is known and experienced by Choisy because she has accepted herself as a woman and wife just as Charlotte has become a "boy" *(garçon)* and a "dear husband" *(cher mari)* (449).[64] Rather than disrupting heterosexual marriage through a parodic reenactment, then, Madame de Sancy and Charlotte to the contrary live out (or seek to live out) an existence they both see as authentic.

For at least some outside observers, however, the union of Madame de Sancy and Monsieur de Maulny was anything but authentic and all too subversive. In a letter Choisy claims to have kept and that he reproduces in the *Mémoires*, an anonymous moralist condones (to a point) his cross-dressing but condemns his relationship with "a young maiden of our neighborhood whom you dress as a man the better to whet your appetite for her." "No one criticizes your dressing as a woman," this letter concludes, "that doesn't harm anyone. Go ahead and be a coquette; but don't sleep with a person you haven't married. That goes against the rules of propriety, and even if it weren't an offense against God, it would still be one against men" (457). For those such as this anonymous critic, the "marriage" with Charlotte / M. de Maulny might indeed be parodic; but if so, it is because it subverts the "rules of propriety" and not because it disrupts the correlation between sex and gender. The realms of gender and sexuality are distinct for this critic, who makes a point of praising Choisy's feminine beauty (even as s/he censures the relationship with Charlotte). At the beginning of the letter, the author tells Choisy, who is addressed as a woman: "I admit that you are beautiful and I'm not surprised that you like women's attire, which suits you very well," and then, in closing, confides: "Moreover, beautiful lady, do not ascribe my protest to a sour mood but to pure friendship for you. One cannot see you without loving you" (457). It is neither the couple's cross-dressing nor Choisy's purportedly feminine body that motivates the attack on his mock marriage. If it is subversive for Madame de Sancy's neighbors, Choisy would have us believe, it is because it flouts the "rules of propriety." It is not so much the parody of a heterosexual marriage that bothers the anonymous moralist as it is the possibility that this marriage is a cover for authentic sexual license. Finally, then, it is not the theatrical illusion, but rather the underlying reality that is bothersome.

Fluid Desires

In the conjugal role-playing that Choisy and her girl lovers exhibit for their friends and neighbors, there is a symmetricality that at first glance reaffirms the heterosexual order. Thus, for instance, the couple Choisy forms with each girl respects the husband / wife binary, with each party choosing to be either the "little husband" *(petit mari)* or the "little wife" *(petite femme)*. But as critics have often noted, what appears to be conformity to heterosexual convention, especially in Choisy's relationships with the four girls, coexists with occasional hints of homoeroticism throughout the *Mémoires*. We find, for instance, allusions to Choisy attracting *amants* while living as an actress,[65] a song (perhaps composed by the Abbé) about Madame de Sancy with the refrain "He will soon have lovers [*amants*],"[66] a description of Choisy hesitating between the love of an actress and that of a marquis,[67] another about the Abbé attracting *amants* at a ball given by Monsieur (Philippe d'Orléans),[68] and the flirtation of the comtesse des Barres with the Chevalier d'Hanecourt.[69] But, of course, these moments in the *Mémoires* are only homoerotic if we assume that Choisy is a man. If, however, we take the transgender hypothesis seriously, then our understanding of not only these instances but of all the other depictions of her sexuality necessarily change. Thus, contrary to what is often claimed, the attraction to her various *amants* instead would be more akin to heterosexual desire,[70] and the relationships with Mlle de La Grise and Babet (Mlle Dany) would instead be examples of same-sex female eroticism. But when we consider the Abbé's friendships with Roselie and Charlotte, each of whom she cross-dresses as a *garçon* and takes to be her *petit mari*, we arrive at the crux of matter. Moving back and forth between the *petites femmes* and the *petits maris*, between handsome men and adolescent girls, Choisy's desire is polymorphous and fluid. Of course, even if the Abbé is not seen as a transgendered subject but instead as a man masquerading as a woman, her sexuality still exceeds the bounds of heterosexual object choice. What changes if we take Choisy to be a transgendered woman is that her sexuality appears even more profoundly polymorphous and fluid. The theatrical mises-en-scène of the seduction of her four girl lovers, so central to the *Mémoires*, then display the spectacles of female same-sex desire (Mlle de La Grise and Babet) and female same-sex desire disguised in the trappings of heterosexual conjugality (Charlotte / M. de Maulny and Roselie / M. Comtin).[71]

No matter how unacceptable the representation of Choisy's libidinal fluidity would have been in this period (at least in an officially sanctioned form), it is still difficult to conclude that it "contests" the heterosexual order. For at a time before the binary construction of heterosexuality and homosexuality, a time before the "invention" of heterosexuality, the Abbé's polymorphous sexual object choice, although hardly condoned by authorities at the time, would still be understood as part of the natural (albeit "sinful") order of things. Choisy would be seen as running the gamut of what was generally considered to be the continuum of sexual desire. But then, as she tells the story at least, the public for the most part was unaware of her same-sex desires. It is only through the confessional posture of the *Mémoires* that readers glimpse the inner drama of Choisy's cross-dressed life. What they see is not the *disembodiment* of gender and, thereby, the subversion of heterosexuality, but rather the fluidity of *embodied* gender and desire. If we are justified in concluding that Choisy's transvestite memoirs expose a "category crisis," it is not because her life story demonstrates the arbitrariness of the links between sex and gender and between gender and sexuality. The "crisis" at the heart of the *Mémoires de l'abbé de Choisy habillé en femme* involves a life lived in the no-wo/man's-land *between* the boundaries of sex, gender, and sexuality.

Corriger la nature: "The Story of the Marquise-Marquis de Banneville"

The three fragments that compose the *Mémoires de l'abbé de Choisy habillé en femme* all end in the same way: the Abbé is forced to give up cross-dressing and, while trying to compensate for this lost pleasure, falls victim to his penchant for gambling.[72] In each of these endings, Choisy evinces a mix of self-reproach and nostalgia. He is quick to condemn the negative consequences of his gambling (which he calls his "rage" [470]); and he casts slight aspersions on his cross-dressing, referring to it as one of his "childish ways" (473) and a "silly game" (522). Even so, he remains nostalgic about his cross-dressed existence, which he puts in stark contrast with his gambling: "The mania for gambling possessed me and turned my life upside down. How happy I'd have been if I'd always played the beautiful woman, even if I were ugly! Ridicule is preferable to poverty" (522). No matter how lighthearted the narrator manages to be while recounting the adventures of the comtesse des Barres and Madame de Sancy, the overall message of these narratives is a dystopic one. In these closures, Choisy is forced to acknowledge the end of a period during which he knew "a pleasure so great it can be compared to nothing" (435).

Far more euphoric is the novella "Histoire de la Marquise-Marquis de Banneville" Choisy authored many years before she penned her *Mémoires*. Perhaps coauthored with Charles Perrault and Marie-Jeanne Lhéritier de Villandon, this short story was first published in 1695 in the *Mercure galant* and then republished in expanded form a year later. Whether or not Perrault or Lhéritier collaborated with Choisy (and I am skeptical that they did),[73] this tale had particular resonance for Choisy. Besides the presence of no fewer than three cross-dressed characters (two in addition to the eponymous hero/ine), Choisy alludes to it in the *Mémoires* where, writing presumably to the marquise de Lambert, the Abbé sees both parallels and contrasts with her own life: "I have no doubt, madame, that the story of the Marquise de Banneville pleased you. I was delighted to see my own conduct authorized by the example of such a delightful person. However, I have to admit that we cannot conclude too much from her example. The little marquise could do many things that were forbidden of me since her prodigious beauty protected her from everything" (471).[74] Without explicitly claiming authorship of the tale, Choisy jokingly refers to the hero/ine's providing an example she both could and could not follow. This passing allusion thus invites not only the Marquise de Lambert but all of us to read Choisy's life into the novella—but only to a point. The power Choisy attributes to the hero/ine's "prodigious beauty" is quasi-supernatural, so it seems, freeing the marquise-marquis de Banneville from the real social constraints that dogged the Abbé. The unreality of the hero/ine's beauty is also that of her adventures since, while Choisy was forced to abandon her cross-dressing, the hero/ine of the novella is able to continue to do so indefinitely and in tandem with a husband who turns out to be a cross-dressed woman. Of course, the double cross-dressing that concludes the novella bears striking resemblance to the double cross-dressing scenes in the *Mémoires*, with the important difference that the (explicitly) fictional version escapes the temporal and societal constraints both the comtesse des Barres and Madame de Sancy experienced. In this instance as in others, Choisy reconceives her own existence, writing beyond the ending and outside the limits of her own experience. At the same time, as we will see, she goes beyond identifying with a single character, the remarks about the Petite Marquise's example notwithstanding. In sum, it would not be an exaggeration to see in the "Histoire de la Marquise-Marquis de Banneville" an experimental text in which Choisy explores both familiar and unfamiliar means of realizing a body image in conflict with biological sex, both within and beyond the limits of the "real" or the plausible.

What is at stake here, I will argue, is the extent to which "nature" (a word that recurs frequently in the text) can be molded and transformed. Is one's birth sex necessarily and inevitably one's "nature"? Can another "nature" supplant one's biological sex? If "nature" is fluid and malleable—if not only gender but also sex can be refashioned/reembodied—what of sexuality? Is it, too, unstable and unfixed? These are but a few of the questions this story invites us to ask. However, as experimental as this novella may be, it still does not dispense with all of the literary and social conventions of the day. As we will see, no less than Choisy himself, this novella comes up against socially sanctioned conceptions of the fixity of nature even as it questions the boundaries of sex, gender, and sexuality.

The notion that nature is a driving force in one's gender identity is brought to the fore in the Preface of the 1695 edition of the novella.[75] In it, the author (who claims to be a woman) presents her story as a act of *hommage* to her fellow women writers, but also as evidence for the specificity of women's writing generally:

> Since women dabble in writing *(se mêlent d'écrire)* and are proud of their wit, I do not want to remain the last to show my zeal for my sex, and I will not be the cause of people thinking that we are not important individuals, in spite of all the little mannerisms *(les petites façons)* we cannot rid ourselves of. Indeed, however staid we may be in our works, the woman comes through everywhere, and the most extreme, violent, and sublime passions cannot hide from the eyes of the attentive reader a certain softness *(mollesse)*, a certain weakness *(un certain faible)* that is natural for us and that we can never get away from.[76]

Behind the difference between women's and men's writing, the author claims, is an essential difference between women and men. And no matter how hard women try to disguise their difference, it will always, in the end, show through. Precisely what shows through—what comprises the specificity of women's writing/being—is an array of traits found in misogynist satire in this period: "little mannerisms," "softness," "a certain weakness." But rather than read the authorial stance here as ironic (Choisy, as a man, impersonating a woman writer and using his disguised masculine gender to denigrate women), I would instead propose to take this passage at face value.[77] Assuming for herself the misogynist clichés of her time, the "I" here asserts that she is a woman and thus can only write *as* a woman, even if she tries to reproduce the grandiloquence of men. Nature, it seems, is an irrepressible force; but it is uncertain whether or not it is necessarily an *inborn* force. Referring to the effect of women's upbringing on their writing, the author cautions: "To believe that a rather pretty young girl, raised among ribbons, would be capable of writing like M. Pellisson strains belief. She will have the passion of her age, new turns of phrase, lively expressions, a cheerful imagination."[78] Is it the fact of being raised among ribbons that explains a woman's inability to write like Pellisson or, instead, the state of being "rather pretty" and having "the passion of her age"? Or do both her upbringing *and* her physical existence account for this difference? Or is it perhaps even that her upbringing shapes her physicality? The answer is unclear in this passage, but these are the very questions the author takes up in a story whose veracity she swears by ("I saw everything, knew of everything, and heard everything; I'm an eyewitness to all this"), no matter how unusual it may appear ("Some circumstances will appear rather unusual to you; but that's exactly what made me want to put them down on paper").[79]

Literary Travesties

As its title indicates, the "Histoire de la Marquise-Marquis de Banneville" tells the adventures of a young marquis who was raised from birth as a girl by his mother. Fearing that her son would know the same fate as his father, a military officer killed on the battlefield while his son was still in the womb, Madame de Banneville raises the newborn marquis as a girl. As a result, Mariane (the name given to the Petit Marquis become Petite Marquise) has no inkling that she is anything other than a girl until the very end of the story. From an early age, she (or "he," but the narrator uses only feminine pronouns) has the appearance and behavior of an elegant and beautiful young girl who invariably attracts everyone's admiration. One day, she catches the eye of the marquis de Bercour, who, in spite of his earrings, is himself an exemplary young man, handsome and adept at arms. Quickly the two fall in love and, just as quickly, they encounter the requisite obstacles to their happiness. For reasons that remain mysterious until the very end, Bercour repeatedly rejects Mariane's suggestions that they wed. Predictably, Mariane's mother also does everything in her power to keep the two from marrying. Finally, faced with her daughter's intransigence, Madame de Banneville is forced to tell her that she is in fact a man, something Mariane has difficulty believing. After her mother dies, Mariane continues to cross-dress and continues to see Bercour. When the public is scandalized to see the two spend more time together than is deemed acceptable, Mariane proposes that they marry, and Bercour agrees, on condition that they live together "as brother and sister."[80] But on their wedding night, in bed, they discover with surprise and joy that their platonic prenuptial agreement is unnecessary: when Bercour tells his wife that he is actually a woman, Mariane reveals (and finally accepts) that she is a man. But, once the marriage has been consummated, the couple decides to continue their doubly cross-dressed existence and to retire to the countryside where, the narrator assures us, "a lovely boy" (63 [61]) will be born to them.

As this brief synopsis will suggest, Choisy's novella follows to a point the well-worn path of many a love story. In fact, critics have noted its points of resemblance with one of the most famous in seventeenth-century France, *La Princesse de Clèves.*[81] But the hero/ine's extraordinary beauty, the obstacles to love, the final union and promise of indefinite happiness are so familiar as to be quasi-universal and fairy-tale-like. More striking and ultimately more relevant to my discussion are the differences from literary convention, especially in the uses of the cross-dressing motif. Of course, cross-dressing was frequent in dramatic and prose fiction of seventeenth-century France and, as Joseph Harris has shown, was only occasionally subversive of gender and sexual norms.[82] It is not the appearance of cross-dressing that is unusual in this text, then, but instead the departure from the period's conventional treatment of this motif. From the very beginning, the narrative breaks new ground. First, the very choice of a cross-dressed man as the lead character is significant since women in male disguise appear much more often in cross-dressing plots of the period. Even more significant is the fact that Mariane is unaware of her cross-dressed state for most of the story, a situation virtually without parallel in seventeenth-century fictions of cross-dressing, which feature characters who consciously and strategically choose their disguise. Also unconventional is the case of the secondary character Prince Sionad / princesse de Garden, who decides to cross-dress because of personal preference and not strategic benefit. Finally, and most unusual of all, one might venture, is the decision by Mariane and Bercour to continue their cross-dressed identities at the end of the plot when conventionally they would reassume, with great fanfare, the gender dictated by their biological sex.

Nature and Nurture

If the motif of cross-dressing in the seventeenth century most often reasserts the "natural" correspondence between sex and gender (in addition to other purportedly "natural" hierarchies),[83] the departures from literary convention in Choisy's novella open a space for exploring how this link is forged in the first place. In contrast to characters who must deliberately learn how to assume their new gender identity, and not without the occasional faux pas,[84] Mariane's initiation into femininity is seamlessly woven into her childhood. Early on, her mother does everything possible to assure that no one—not even Mariane—will discover the biological sex of her child. Even before giving birth, the narrator tells us, "she determined to correct nature" (4 [4]). The word "nature" here should be understood in the broadest sense. It comprises in the first instance the formal instruction Madame de Banneville gives her child, both "everything a young noblewoman should know—dancing, music, the harpsichord" in addition to the subjects usually reserved for boys, "foreign languages, history, and even philosophy" (4 [4]). But the "nature" the mother is determined to correct is also, of course, corporeal. Beyond the clothing given to the young Mariane, she, similar to the young Choisy, was given "iron stays to increase her hips and uplift her bosom" (5 [5]). But this intellectual and bodily training is only partially responsible for what appears to be the Petite Marquise's feminine "nature." When the narrator tells us that, at twelve years of age, "all this had succeeded, and her face . . . was already perfect in its beauty" (5 [5])—a beauty described as being the highly conventional feminine blond, blue eyes, white complexion, and coral red lips[85]—it is clear that Mariane's body—her "nature"—is predisposed to the life as a young woman her mother chose for her. Like Choisy, then, Mariane "corrects" nature but she also lives out the "nature" she seems destined to embody.[86] Madame de Banneville recognizes as much when she tells Mariane the truth about her sex: "[Your] sweetness, [your] inclinations, [your] beauty, all contributed to my plan. . . . Habit has created another nature in you" (55 [53]). A feminine nature made even more so by habit leaves Mariane with little doubt that she is a woman. However, when we are told that "such a fine mind seemed to be housed in the body of an angel" (4 [4])—a description that echoes the exclamation by Mlle de La Grise about the comtesse des Barres: "You are as beautiful as an angel"[87]—we might venture a doubt about the sex of Mariane's "nature." Angels, after all, are neither male nor female. But however we read the comparison to an angel here, the fact remains that Mariane's beauty is incomparably superlative, even otherworldly in its femaleness.

Whether by upbringing or by instinct, Mariane is inclined toward the "feminine" vice of coquettishness, we learn. When she tells her mother how she wants to "captivate everyone" without committing to any one man, Madame de Banneville warns her, "take care, my child, that you do not sound like a coquette" (5 [5]). In truth, though, the mother is delighted to see her child display such a "feminine" attitude since it makes it even less likely that Mariane's biological sex will be discovered. Hence, it is not so surprising when, upon moving to Paris, the mother entrusts her daughter to a most un-usual tutor, the comtesse d'Aletref, who had separated from her husband so as to indulge her proclivity for gambling and attract male suitors. "[Madame de Banneville] was well aware of the countess's reputation, which was some-what questionable, and she would never have entrusted a real daughter to her. But in addition to the fact that Mariane had been brought up to have moral feelings, her mother wanted, for her own amusement, to trust Mariane a lit-tle" (10 [10]). What would have been a grave failing in the case of a "real" daughter becomes acceptable in this circumstance not only for the mother's amusement but also, we surmise, for her plan to "correct nature."

It soon becomes apparent that her plan has succeeded. Following the ex-ample of the comtesse, Mariane becomes enchanted with her own beauty and revels in the adulation of an admiring public. She would always go to the the-ater early, the narrator informs us, "in order to receive the applause of the whole company" (27 [26]), and at one performance spectators actually stop the action on stage to acclaim Mariane as the "Goddess of Youth" when this character's arrival is announced.[88] If the public's recognition of the hero/ine's beauty here and elsewhere do not provide Mariane with the same sort of pleasure the comtesse des Barres and Madame de Sancy experience when they overhear praise for their beauty, this recognition nonetheless so-lidifies Mariane's (unconscious and unquestioned) understanding of herself as a woman.

Of course, what distinguishes Mariane's narcissism from the comtesse des Barres's and Madame de Sancy's is that Choisy's fictional hero/ine is un-aware she is anything other than a beautiful young woman. Just how "nat-ural" her feminine persona is to her is made clear by her reaction to the story about the Prince Sionad told by the comtesse d'Aletref. A Nordic prince, "handsome" Sionad (whose name is an anagram of *Adonis*) was cross-dressed and coached in feminine manners by the comtesse for a play at his *col-lège*. As a result of this experience, he took a liking to his feminine existence and, later, decided to spend the summer on the battlefield as Prince Sionad and the winter in Paris as the princesse de Garden. It is in the latter guise that the unwitting Mariane meets him/her, and when she learns that the princess is none other than the prince, she exclaims: "I do not believe I should want to dress up as a girl if I were a boy" (15 [15]). To this ironic confession, the mother responds: "Don't swear any oaths. . . . Be content, my child, to do your duty, and never criticize what others do" (15 [15]). In her response, Madame de Banneville blurs the difference Mariane establishes between her own gendered existence and that of Prince Sionad / the princesse de Garden, and the conclusion of the story proves the mother right, to be sure. Through her warning not to "swear any oaths," then, Madame de Banneville inadvertantly frames the story of Prince Sionad (told to Mariane by the comtesse d'Aletref) as an exemplum for the hero/ine herself. For, in spite of the obvious differences between the two, the conclusion reveals their similarities. Like Mariane, Prince Sionad receives accolades for his "feminine" beauty; and like Mariane's, his body is subjected to a feminizing transformation.[89] What Sionad's example shows and what the hero/ine's will confirm is that one's body image does not necessarily correspond to one's anatomical sex. One's gendered "nature" is not always as easily determined as Mariane might think.

Anagnorisis

Madame de Banneville's advice to "never criticize what others do" implies that the reasons for enacting a gender identity cannot be easily grasped. And in the cases of Mariane, Prince Sionad, and Bercour, this plea for tolerance is only too relevant. All three of these characters contravene the literary conventions of the day, which stipulated that cross-dressing be motivated by reasons of familial, political, or amorous necessity that disappear at the end of the plot. Instead, like the Abbé de Choisy, their impulse to cross-dress and, more fundamentally, to live out a body image at odds with their assigned sex is part of and is inseparable from their very being. However, it is not an impulse that serves an instrumental function.

But by far the most significant departure from the literary conventions of cross-dressing in this story occurs at the end when the suspense of the narrative (the mutual misunderstanding between Mariane and Bercour) is resolved. In most seventeenth-century literary depictions of cross-dressing, there is a dénouement, judiciously called anagnorisis by Harris, in which the true sex of the cross-dressed character is revealed.[90] Usually, this is also the moment at which this character abandons her/his disguise in front of a public that expresses its astonishment and admiration at the illusion it has witnessed. In the "Histoire de la Marquise-Marquis de Banneville," however, the conventional scene of anagnorisis is significantly altered. First, there are two such scenes, and not one (Madame de Banneville explains the "truth" to Mariane, then Mariane and Bercour reveal their mutual secrets to each other). Neither of these scenes occurs in front of a public, and as a result these dénouements do not include the social recognition of cross-dressing that was conventional in literary portrayals. Mariane and Bercour nonetheless inspire astonishment and admiration in their public; but these expressions occur *before* the moment of anagnorisis and not in response to the end of their double disguise. It is not cross-dressing that attracts the public's attention but rather the bodily appearance of the two, and especially of Mariane.[91] What amounts to a displacement and reformulation of the conventional reactions by the public implicitly prepares the way for the couple's final decision to keep their cross-dressed identities, which is without question the most dramatic alteration of the anagnorisis scene. On their wedding night, having overcome the surprise at their mutual revelations, they promise "an eternal fidelity" not only to each other, but also to their accustomed gender identities (which are also their body images):

> "As for me," the little marquise said, "I am too used to being a girl; I want to be a woman all my life. How could I learn to wear a hat?"
>
> "And as for me," the marquis said, "I've drawn my sword more than once without its making me feel ill at ease, and I shall tell you my story someday. Let us remain, then, as we are. Enjoy, beautiful marquise, all the pleasures of my sex, and I shall enjoy all the freedom of yours." (62–63 [60])

Now according to the logic of anagnorisis, the end of the suspense created by the cross-dressed disguise corresponds to a reestablishment of order, that of the "natural" link between sex and gender, of course, but by extension that of political, familial, and economic power as well. But the order that is established by the wedding bed revelation between Mariane and Bercour is less clear-cut. On the one hand, they recognize that they each "have" a sex that is being lived ("enjoyed" as the marquis would say) by the other partner. In this sense, they each acknowledge the principle of sexual difference grounded in biological reality. But on the other, they each also assert their desire to assume the gender that corresponds not to the sex they "have" but to the sex of the other partner, because of habit and experience and not (I would argue) because of a willfully performative act.[92] There are thus two coexisting orders, two coexisting natures at work here, the order of sex and that of gender/body image, but there is not a correspondence between the two, at least for Mariane and Bercour. For the public, of course, these two coexisting yet independent orders would be the height of *dis*order. But no one other than the doubly cross-dressed couple has any way of knowing that they are flouting the correspondence between the orders of being and appearances.[93] From the outside, it seems as if they are upholding the order of correspondence between sex and gender when, in fact, they are not.

Nature Is Wise

And yet, in another sense, the disorder they secretly create does not preclude an order of a different sort. Throughout the courtship of Mariane and Bercour, as in many texts about cross-dressing, the possibility and the appearance of a homoerotic relationship contributes to the suspense that the final scene of anagnorisis must resolve.[94] For each of these characters, such appearances provoke a deep crisis. For Bercour, it is only retrospectively, during the wedding bed scene, that we understand his hesitancy to wed Mariane: believing that she was a woman, Bercour refuses almost to the end to accept her proposals of marriage, and even when he does he breaks into tears on the wedding bed. "You see," he tells the Petite Marquise, "I can do nothing for you, because I am a woman just as you are" (62 [60]). Mariane's version of homosexual panic is even more agonizing for her. When she learns that she is a man and, believing Bercours to be a man as well, she sees in her passion a desire that cannot be named: "What have you done," she asks herself, "and what name can you give to the favors you've granted the marquis?" She then blames "nature" for leading her into a passion that has all the hallmarks of transgression: "Blush," she exclaims, "you unfortunate child, blush, blind nature, who did not teach me my duty. Alas! I acted in good faith, but now that I understand, I shall have to act quite differently in the future, and despite my love I must do what I should" (56 [54]). Afflicted with self-doubt, she is distrustful of the very force, nature, that is vaunted by her mother, the public, and the entire text . . . until she sees Bercour once again. In that instant, she cannot keep herself from reaching a conclusion that goes against all appearances: "No, no . . . no, that is not so, and if it were, I should not feel what I feel. Nature is wise, and her impulses are reasonable" (57 [55]). Of course, in the final analysis, the text proves Mariane's instincts to be right: nature is indeed "wise," if by this it is meant that her desire for Bercour is heterosexual.[95] Mariane refuses to believe that she is a man until Bercour "[takes] her hand . . . and [puts] it on the most beautiful bosom in the world," at which point the narrator asks: "Who could describe the little marquise's surprise and joy? At that moment she no longer doubted that she was a man" (62 [60]). In a *chassé-croisé* the stakes of which escape both Mariane and Bercour until the final wedding bed revelation, heterosexual desire is stronger than appearances and, in the end, allows the couple to avoid the "trap" of homo-eroticism.

It is at this point that the significance of the distinction between Mariane's and Bercour's two coexisting natures comes into sharper focus. If one is malleable and allows each to continue to live as the gender she and he are accustomed to, the other is fixed and ensures that heterosexual desire alone will prevail. Both Mariane and Bercour have a sexed "nature" that allows them to form a legitimate heterosexual couple; but they both also have a "nature" that, in its gendered manifestations, contradicts their sexed body. Thus, unlike Choisy, for whom the fluidity of the sexed body is accompanied by a fluidity of sexual desire, the protagonists in this novella experience only the fluidity of sex and not that of sexuality.

Effeminate Manners

But the complexity of the novella does not end there. Where we might expect to find a perfectly symmetrical arrangement among the coexisting "natures" of the newlyweds (Mariane living as both a woman and a heterosexual man; Bercour as a man and a heterosexual woman), the text introduces a curious twist that takes us back to a fundamental principle in Choisy's *Mémoires*. For although Mariane strives to be the embodiment of feminine beauty, Bercour deviates from accepted masculine appearance. When Mariane first sets her eyes on him she notices in his ears "sparkling diamond earrings . . . and three or four beauty spots on his face" (29 [28]). Later (in a dialogue with Mariane that appears in the 1723 edition of the text), he admits that he likes "women's attire," by which he means earrings and *mouches* (65 [63]). And after agreeing with Mariane to continue his existence as a man, he offers to correct "the somewhat effeminate manners I have not been able completely to abandon." Mariane, however, refuses: "Ah, Marquis, don't abandon them. Is there anything more delightful than knowing how to combine the valor of Mars with the charms of Venus?" (63 [61]). Bercour, we can assume, will continue to sport his earrings and *mouches* and, so doing, give the lie to those who claim that Mars and Venus cannot be reconciled. In urging her groom to persist in his "effeminate" ways, Mariane accedes to the logic that Bercour had himself used to justify his proclivity for female attire: "What in fact is more innocent than the desire to please? And since women are made to please, isn't it natural for men to make use of this kind of masquerade to win hearts?" (64 [62]).[96] The logic here, of course, is the same that Choisy uses to justify his own cross-dressing, namely that beauty, being fundamentally feminine, drives men to become women. To the extent that Bercour is a man, and a handsome man at that, it is only "natural" that he should attempt to imitate women, so the logic of the novella would have us conclude.

In spite of this logic and the hero/ine's endorsement of it, the text makes a point of noting that not everyone is so favorably disposed to "effeminate manners," which are often equated with same-sex desire. For instance, when Mariane expresses concern about Prince Sionad's request to visit her, the comtesse d'Aletref reassures her that she has nothing to fear and quips: "These handsome fellows love themselves [each other] and only themselves [each other]" *(Ces beaux garçons s'aiment et n'aiment qu'eux)* (26 [25]). The phrase the comtesse uses is highly ambiguous, indicating either narcissism (the "beaux garçons" love themselves) or homoeroticism (the "beaux garçons" love each other). However, I would contend that the ambiguity is deliberate in that it echoes the link between male narcissism and same-sex desire that is occasionally made in satires of salon effeminacy. A few pages later, the comtesse expresses her disapproval of Bercour's appearance as a "beau garçon": "He's making himself pretty, and that's not fitting for a young man. Why doesn't he dress as a girl?" (29 [28]). It is difficult to know whether she, like Madame de Lafayette in Choisy's *Mémoires,* is being ironic when she asks why he doesn't cross-dress. But given her gibe about Prince Sionad shortly before, it would be logical to conclude that her disapproval is motivated by antipathy for homoeroticism, which is clearly on display in a scene (added in the 1723 version of the novella) where Mariane decides to dress Bercour as a woman, thinking he would not be recognized. Not only does he not "pass" but he also attracts homophobic remarks: "A few young people were so rude as to tell them publicly that such ladies would keep the world from continuing on" (66, translation modified [64]). If this unsuccessful attempt at cross-dressing demonstrates once again how much of a man Bercour really is, it is also another signal by the text that adorning masculine beauty with the trappings of femininity can be interpreted as a sign of same-sex desire. Of course, as the final anagnorisis scene confirms, the novella explicitly rejects such an interpretation for Bercour. Perhaps, then, by evoking and acknowledging this interpretation, the text seeks to preempt it even as it defends Choisy's equation of beauty with femininity?

In an otherwise fairy-tale-like, even utopian narrative about the possibilities of crossing gender boundaries, the specter of effeminacy and its supposed corollary, same-sex desire, introduces a hint of dystopic reality. The assurances of "happily ever after" notwithstanding, the world that Mariane and Bercour inhabit is not an idyllic paradise. How else can we explain their decision to lead a more discreet life in the countryside? And how else are we to understand Bercour's anxiety about his "effeminate manners" at the very end of the tale? Like Bercour, the novella as a whole evinces a nervousness about the perception of same-sex eroticism, and this nervousness contrasts all too clearly with the depiction of sexual fluidity in Choisy's *Mémoires.* We can only speculate about the reasons for this difference. Perhaps, conscious of the exigencies of publication, Choisy had no choice but to make the story conform to the conventions of the cross-dressing plot. Even so, by specifically delineating the possibility of homoeroticism, the novella paradoxically draws attention to it and, arguably, makes it an option at the same time as it forecloses that option for Mariane and Bercour. Perhaps, through a sort of Freudian denial, Choisy's tale acknowledges and savors sexual fluidity after all?

However difficult it may be to reconcile the depiction of sexuality in the novella with that in the *Mémoires de l'abbé de Choisy habillé en femme,* there are clear parallels between the Abbé (as he tells his story at least) on the one hand and Prince Sionad, Bercour, and Mariane on the other. Like Prince Sionad, Choisy used theatrical spectacle as a pretext for his own cross-dressing and, like the prince, he crossed from masculinity to femininity and back again on multiple occasions. Like Bercour, he incurred accusations of effeminacy when he added earrings to his ordinary masculine attire. And like Mariane, he was raised as a girl from childhood. Similar to all three of these characters, Choisy sought to embody a gender that is ostensibly at odds with his biological sex, but which he is "naturally" destined for as well. He, like Sionad, Bercour, and Mariane, "corrects" nature, but the cross-dressed existences they lead come from a nature that *is* their very being.

Unlike the fictional characters in the novella, however, Choisy was unable to continue cross-dressing indefinitely or with impunity. The "Histoire de la Marquise-Marquis de Banneville" tells a story whose conclusion Choisy was unable to experience for herself. At the end of both "La Comtesse des Barres" and "Madame de Sancy" episodes, she crosses back into masculinity, filled with nostalgia for the pleasures of being loved as a woman. Still, after abandoning women's clothing, Choisy did not leave femininity entirely behind. Through her writing, she returned, on multiple occasions, to cross-dressing and experienced anew life as a woman. As the comtesse des Barres and Madame de Sancy, as Prince Sionad, Bercour, and Mariane, she crosses from masculinity to femininity in not just one but many ways—with and without the public's knowledge, consciously and unconsciously, episodically and continually, by partial and complete sartorial transformation. That she envisions so many different ways of making this transition suggests a quest to find a resolution that eludes her, a quest to resolve an enduring tension. From the "Histoire de la Marquise-Marquis de Banneville" to the later *Mémoires de l'abbé de Choisy habillé en femme,* we move from a text with a happy ending to one with a far more dystopic closure. When Choisy turned from fiction to her own life, then, the euphoric tone fades, especially when reflecting on the end of her adventures in Bourges and Paris. She remains unsettled and unsatisfied, and this tension manifests itself perhaps most poignantly in the ambivalent linguistic gender of the narrative voice throughout the *Mémoires.* At times feminine and at other times masculine, the "I," even many years later, finds her/himself in between genders, striving toward womanhood yet tied to manhood. It is this unresolved tension that compels Choisy to write, searching for an elusive closure by (re)writing an unending transition.

Afterimage

IN A 1629 FASHION ENGRAVING by Abraham Bosse, an elegantly dressed young man strides down the aisle of a church in a pose that is strikingly similar to that of a twenty-first-century male model on a runway.[1] One leg forward, hips swayed, arms gently bent, his face confident and serene, he seems intent on displaying his youth, his social position, and of course his sense of refinement. With his hair fashionably coiffed and his moustache and goatee perfectly trimmed, he sports a *fraise* around his neck, a cape draped on one shoulder and wrapped around his waist, an *haut-de-chausse* on his legs, and *bottes à entonnoir* on his feet, in his left hand a *feutre à pleureuse*, and, not insignificantly, an *épée* at his waist, all indispensable accessories for the fashionable nobleman of the 1620s and 1630s. As he moves toward us, he seems unconcerned by what is happening behind him in the distance: two no less elegant men entering on his right and, on his left, what appears to be a man in armor, his hands reverently clasped in prayer. But no matter what his apparent poise might lead us to think, the performance of the fashionable young man cannot be divorced from these other spectacles. From the way that Bosse depicts him, the young nobleman seems to have come to church to be recognized as part of the fashionable *monde* of his day. To secure his place in that elite group, he must necessarily be seen by other men, such as those in the background. And given the heterosocial dynamics of the *mondain* society of the time, he must also be noticed by women who, although absent from the image, were known to rendezvous with male suitors in the relative safety of churches.

Like many of the masculine figures we have seen in this study—the honnête homme, the galant salon man, Vincent Voiture, Théophile de Viau, or the Abbé de Choisy—Bosse's elegant young nobleman performs his gender deliberately and insistently. This is not *only* to say, with Judith Butler, that his masculinity has no essence other than the socially defined role he plays for the

De S.^rIgny jnuen et excud Cum Pri Regis   Bosse jnsidit.

FIGURE 2.   Abraham Bosse (after Jean de Saint-Igny), "Un Homme marchant de face," *La Noblesse française à l'église*, c. 1629, BNF, Estampes, collection Hennin, 2243. Reproduced by permission of the Bibliothèque Nationale de France.

most part unconsciously; it is *also* to say, simply, that his masculinity is a production that he creates quite intentionally using the fashionable codes of his day.[2] But the scene of the young *gentilhomme* strolling through the church in the midst of other elegant men also reminds us that the performativity of gender is inconceivable outside of broader social ties. Based on socially defined conventions, his performance is addressed to others, both men and women, who may or may not acknowledge him as the elegant noble*man* he obviously wants to be. In sum, the performance of his masculinity (along with his social status, to be sure) is inseparable from the relational networks in which he finds himself. His air of self-confidence is by no means sufficient to ensure the masculine dominance projected by his demeanor. That status can only be conferred by his success among elite men and women. In this, Bosse's young nobleman is not unlike the honnête homme, the galant salon man, Voiture, Théophile, and Choisy, all of whom must negotiate risks that, although very different in each case, are nonetheless established by and for dominant masculinity. Méré's honnête homme must simultaneously imitate and distance himself from a host of masculine and feminine prototypes, but for aesthetic and social dominance he must ultimately rely on the ineffable *je ne sais quoi*, a quality ratified not by himself but by an elite few. For the galant salon man, observing the commonplace injunction to seek out women's refining influence ran the risk of blurring the border between the masculine and the feminine and, thus, of being perceived as effeminate. It was precisely this risk that Voiture attempted to counter by balancing the imperative to follow women's tastes with the desire to affirm a virile difference, but with mixed results. Rather than struggling with the paradoxes of women's "civilizing" influence, Théophile de Viau was preoccupied with defending himself against accusations of sodomy, which he did by ambiguously resisting and consenting to a heterosexual masculine norm. For Choisy, the challenge was to find a way to renounce masculinity altogether, something made impossible by the privileges and obligations of his own masculinity.

In Bosse's engraving, however, tensions such as these—tensions that underlay and give form to masculinity—are more than a little difficult to detect. So too is any trace of the marginal masculine positions studied in this book. Embodying the noble masculine elite of his day, the dapper young man moves self-assuredly through the church, surrounded by men of similar status. Still, it would be a mistake to assume that Bosse's engraving succeeds in keeping all signs of marginality on the other side of the open doors in the far background. For some seventeenth-century observers, the fashionable young gentleman would have been the very incarnation of the effeminacy often associated with men deemed to be overly preoccupied with their appearance. And the two young men conversing among themselves behind the gentilhomme obliquely recall the accusations of homoeroticism that could be leveled at elegant men who were seen as privileging homosocial over heterosocial bonds. But there is an even more fundamental way in which Bosse's engraving evokes marginality. In order for the sartorial, behavioral, and social elegance of the young nobleman to be perceived as such, the engraving relies on all that elegance is *not*. In other words, the elite masculinity showcased by Bosse depends upon the nonelite, marginal masculinities that are banished from the image. The presumed appeal of this fashion plate is that it instills in those male viewers who have not crossed the threshold of the church—who have not yet attained the status of the debonair young man—a desire to conform to this noble's manliness. And for female viewers, at stake is not the desire to become like the man in the church but rather to uphold the ideal of masculine refinement portrayed by the engraving.

In this image, then, marginalized masculinities are present in spite of their ostensible absence. Even so, at first glance, it would seem difficult to ascertain anything of those positions that resist the predictable dynamics of masculine domination. Scudéry's tender masculinity, Théophile's search for a new way of life through male friendship, and Choisy's attempt to realize an inner sense of gender at odds with his outwardly recognized sex, all these and many other efforts to reshape the period's predominant sex/gender system are nowhere to be found, or so it would seem. And yet perhaps it would be possible to take the confident self-assertion of Bosse's model as an emblem for the unorthodox stances adopted by Scudéry, Théophile, and Choisy. For, through their writing, each of them in very different ways and with varying degrees of success dared to contest the prevailing structure of masculine domination that, as Bourdieu noted, dominates not only women but also men.[3] In each case, marginal positions are presented forcefully, through notable acts of writing that issue from unconventional acts of living.

Finally, we might reflect a bit further on the fact that Bosse's stylish gentleman is coming toward us with a pose nearly identical to that of a model for a men's collection at a New York, Paris, or Milan fashion show. We can almost imagine him walking out of the seventeenth-century church and onto a twenty-first century runway. It is as if he is striding toward us in our here and now to capture our attention with a fashion statement circa 1629. If he *were* somehow magically to appear before us, we might be overwhelmed by the antiquarian oddity of his 370-year-old outfit, and we would doubtless be inclined to notice all that makes him different from us. Those differences are as important as they are obvious, and they should not be glossed over. But we should also keep in mind the very twenty-first-century-like stance he adopts with his arms and legs, moving like a model for Jean-Paul Gaultier or Calvin Klein. There is something distinctly familiar about him that reminds us of our own culture and own our time, and we should not be too quick to assume that between him and ourselves there are only discontinuities, differences, otherness. Taking Bosse's *gentilhomme* as an allegory for gender constructions from the past allows us to seize the importance of adopting a bivalent perspective that considers both distance and proximity. On the one hand, there is much to be said for Judith Butler's statement that "the recurrence [of terms such as *masculine* and *feminine*] does not index a sameness, but rather the way in which the social articulation of the term depends upon its repetition, which constitutes one dimension of the performative structure of gender."[4] On the other hand, I would argue, with Bourdieu, that there are also important continuities across time and place—important factors of sameness—that we should recognize and reflect upon.[5] By this, I mean not only that the social structure of masculine domination, in its broadest outline, is a constant across most all cultures, but also that past efforts to resist the oppressive strictures of the patriarchal sex/gender system can still be relevant to us today, conceptually and perhaps even pragmatically. To be sure, it is the first rather than the second sense of continuity that is most readily apparent in Bosse's seventeenth-century male model. But if we take him to represent past masculinities, from seventeenth-century France and other periods before and after, in their diversity and complexity, then we will surely see in him familiar problems and struggles amid all that is strange about him.

Notes

INTRODUCTION

1. Molière [Jean-Baptiste Poquelin], *Oeuvres complètes*, ed. Robert Jouanny, Classiques Garnier (Paris: Garnier frères, 1962), 1:645, 2 vols.

2. For an overview of the now vast literature across the wide spectrum of disciplines that constitute masculinity studies, see among others R. W. Connell, *Masculinities* (Berkeley and Los Angeles: University of California Press, 1995); Stephen M. Whitehead and Frank J. Barrett, eds., *The Masculinities Reader* (Malden, MA: Blackwell, 2001); Rachel Adams and David Savran, eds., *The Masculinity Studies Reader*, Keyworks in Cultural Studies (Malden, MA: Blackwell, 2002); Judith Kegan Gardiner, ed., *Masculinity Studies and Feminist Theory: New Directions* (New York: Columbia University Press, 2002).

3. On this debate, see Fidelma Ashe, *The New Politics of Masculinity: Men, Power, and Resistance*, Routledge Innovations in Political Theory (New York: Routledge, 2007); Tom Digby, ed., *Men Doing Feminism* (New York: Routledge, 1998); Tania Modleski, *Feminism without Women: Culture and Criticism in a Postfeminist Age* (New York: Routledge, 1991); Alice Jardine and Paul Smith, eds., *Men in Feminism* (New York: Methuen, 1987).

4. To date, there has been more work on masculinities in sixteenth-century than in seventeenth-century France. See the collections Philip Ford and Paul White, eds., *Masculinities in Sixteenth-Century France* (Cambridge: Cambridge French Colloquia, 2006), and Kathleen P. Long, ed., *High Anxiety: Masculinity in Crisis in Early Modern France*, Sixteenth Century Essays and Studies (Kirksville, MO: Truman State University Press, 2002) and the books by Todd W. Reeser, *Moderating Masculinity in Early Modern Culture*, North Carolina Studies in the Romance Languages and Literatures, 283 (Chapel Hill: UNC Department of Romance Languages, 2006) and David LaGuardia, *Intertextual Masculinities in French Renaissance Literature: Rabelais, Brantôme, and the Cent Nouvelles Nouvelles* (Burlington, VT: Ashgate, 2008). Studies at least partially devoted to seventeenth-century masculinities include Katherine Crawford, "The Politics of Promiscuity: Masculinity and Heroic Representation at the Court of Henry IV," *French Historical Studies* 26, no. 2 (2003): 225–52; Katherine Crawford, *Perilous Performances: Gender and Regency in Early Modern France*, Harvard Historical Studies (Cambridge: Harvard University Press, 2004); Gary Ferguson, "Masculinity, Confession, Modernity: François de Sales and the Penitent Gentleman," *L'Esprit Créateur* 43, no. 3 (2003): 16–25; Orest Ranum, "Judicial Virtue and Masculinity: The Image of the Judge in the 1660s," in *Curiosité: Etudes d'histoire de l'art en l'honneur d'Antoine Schnapper*, ed. Antoine Schnap-

per et al. (Paris: Flammarion, 1998), 75–82; Hélène Merlin, "Les Troubles du masculin en France au XVIIe siècle," in *Le Masculin: Identité, Fictions, Dissémination*, ed. Horacio Amigorena and Frédéric Monneyron (Paris: L'Harmattan, 1998), 11–57; Jeffrey N. Peters, "Boileau's Nerve, or the Poetics of Masculinity," *L'Esprit Créateur* 43, no. 3 (2003): 26–36; Jeffrey N. Peters, "Is Alceste a Physiognomist? Toward a Masculinity of Reference in the Seventeenth Century," in *Entre Hommes: French and Francophone Masculinities in Culture and Theory*, ed. Todd W. Reeser and Lewis C. Seifert (Newark: University of Delaware Press, 2008), 87–114; Lewis C. Seifert, "Masculinity in *The Princess of Clèves*," in *Approaches to Teaching Lafayette's "The Princess of Clèves,"* ed. Faith Beasley, Approaches to Teaching World Literature (New York: Modern Language Association of America, 1998), 60–67; Lewis C. Seifert, "Pig or Prince? Murat, d'Aulnoy and the Limits of 'Civilized' Masculinity," in Long, *High Anxiety*, 183–210; Lewis C. Seifert, "The Male Writer and the 'Marked' Self in Seventeenth-Century France: The Case of the Abbé de Boisrobert," *EMF: Studies in Early Modern France* 9: The New Biographical Criticism (2004): 125–42; Gretchen Elizabeth Smith, *The Performance of Male Nobility in Molière's Comédies-Ballets: Staging the Courtier* (Burlington, VT: Ashgate, 2005).

5. On the one hand are those, and foremost among them Susan Bordo, who argue that the mind/body opposition inspired by Descartes and presumed by the subsequent reception of his thought has made the mind masculine and the body feminine, effectively disenfranchizing women from philosophical discourse. (See Susan Bordo, *The Flight to Objectivity: Essays on Cartesianism and Culture* [Albany: State University of New York Press, 1987] and Genevieve Lloyd, *The Man of Reason: "Male" and "Female" in Western Philosophy* [Minneapolis: University of Minnesota Press, 1984].) If this argument is largely valid for dominant interpretations of Cartesianism, recent work by scholars such as Stanley Clarke, Erec Koch, and Rebecca Wilkin points out that mind and body are actually integrated in Descartes's later work (particularly in the *Passions de l'âme* and the correspondence with Princess Elizabeth), a fact that not only refutes the presupposition of a gendered dualism but also posits a fundamental (but mostly implicit) equality between the sexes. (See Stanley Clarke, "Descartes's 'Gender,'" in *Feminist Interpretations of René Descartes*, ed. Susan Bordo [University Park: Pennsylvania State University Press, 1999], 82–104; Erec R. Koch, "Cartesian Corporeality and [Aesth]Ethics," *PMLA* 121, no. 2 [2006]: 405–20; Rebecca Wilkin, "Descartes, Individualism, and the Fetal Subject," *differences* 19, no. 1 [2008]: 96–127; Rebecca Wilkin, *Women, Imagination, and the Search for Truth in Early Modern France* [Burlington, VT: Ashgate, 2009].) The place of Cartesianism in seventeenth-century French culture is further reason to elaborate the argument concerning a gendered mind/body split. There were, for instance, the efforts by various women (termed "Cartesian women" by Erica Harth) to appropriate or engage with elements of Descartes' thought, and then there was the explicitly Cartesian protofeminism of François Poullain de la Barre, whose famous watchword was "The mind has no sex." See Erica Harth, *Cartesian Women: Versions and Subversions of Rational Discourse in the Old Regime* (Ithaca, NY: Cornell University Press, 1992). On Poullain de la Barre, see Madeleine Alcover, *Poullain de La Barre: Une aventure philosophique*, Biblio 17 (Paris: Papers on French Seventeenth Century Literature, 1981); François Poullain de La Barre, *Three Cartesian Feminist Treatises*, ed. Marcelle Maistre Welch, trans. Vivien Bosley (Chicago: University of Chicago Press, 2002); Siep Stuurman, *François Poulain de la Barre and the Invention of Modern Equality* (Cambridge: Harvard University Press, 2004). Within the context of seventeenth-century France (and leaving aside the question of the broader influence of what is taken to be Cartesian dualism), it is difficult to con-

clude that the "modern" Cartesian subject is unfailingly masculine and, even less, masculinist. From all appearances, our understanding of the masculine subject of seventeenth-century philosophical discourse needs to be reconsidered.

6. The considerable body of scholarly work on the representations of Louis includes relatively little on the king's masculinity per se. Exceptions are Mark Franko, *Dance as Text: Ideologies of the Baroque Body* (Cambridge: Cambridge University Press, 1993) and Abby Zanger, "Lim(b)inal Images: 'Betwixt and Between' Louis XIV's Martial and Marital Bodies," in *From the Royal to the Republican Body: Incorporating the Political in Seventeenth- and Eighteenth-Century France*, ed. Sara E. Melzer and Kathryn Norberg (Berkeley and Los Angeles: University of California Press, 1998), 32–63. Both of these studies touch on questions of gender representation in relation to Louis XIV without explicitly foregrounding masculinity as such. For a stimulating analysis of royal masculinity the likes of which has yet to be applied to Louis XIV, see Crawford, "The Politics of Promiscuity." Clearly the Sun King's masculinity mattered, for political and symbolic reasons of great consequence, but the question that remains to be examined is *how* his masculinity was managed, constructed, and projected and the extent to which representations of his gender did and did not serve the interests of royal power. *Manning the Margins* does not take up these questions but rather sheds light on gender dynamics Louis XIV both sidelined and rearticulated. Beyond this, I have purposefully avoided extended discussion of the Sun King so as to bring to the fore problems that might be obscured by giving him privilege of place. Seventeenth-century studies must tread carefully so as to avoid reproducing the "absolutist" claims of his propaganda machine, which is always the risk of excessive preoccupation with the king and court culture, I would submit. This concern is part of my motivation for marginalizing the role of Louis XIV in this first book-length study of seventeenth-century French masculinities.

7. In a pan-European and transhistorical context, Thomas Laqueur's seminal study, *Making Sex: Body and Gender from the Greeks to Freud* (Cambridge: Harvard University Press, 1990), proposes that a one-sex model, positing the female body as an analogous but imperfect form of the male body, dominated much of the early modern period and considered sex to be an epiphenomenon of gender. But in the seventeenth century, he contends, a two-sex model began to overtake the one-sex model, and it was "sex" that increasingly determined "gender." ("Sex before the seventeenth century . . . was still a sociological and not an ontological category," he argues [*Making Sex*, 8].) Whether or not the one-sex body theory dominated the early modern period as Laqueur contends is the subject of debate among historians of science. (See Katharine Park and Robert Nye, "Destiny Is Anatomy," *New Republic*, 18 February 1991, 53–57.) The larger point that Laqueur makes is that sex, as a cultural category, was—and is—"situational . . . explicable only within the context of battles over gender and power" (*Making Sex*, 11), such that the male body is construed as stable and unproblematic, in contrast to the female body. As a result, Laqueur claims, "[I]t is probably not possible to write a history of man's body and its pleasures because the historical record was created in a cultural tradition where no such history was necessary" (*Making Sex*, 22). It may be that this startling claim is a rhetorical overstatement meant to emphasize the unmarked status of the male body during the many centuries of scientific inquiry that he studies. Whatever the case, the fact that there were competing theories of the sexed body during the period that interests me here is itself evidence for a "history of man's body" and part of a history of masculinity. It is hard to see how the shifting and unstable understandings of the female body that seemed to have occupied the center stage of scientific discourse for such a very long time

would *not* have provoked a reevaluation of masculine embodiment, even if this reflection may have been largely "silent." But it was not entirely so, as Jeffrey Peters has shown in an illuminating study of the shifting referents of masculine selfhood in seventeenth-century French literature, civility, and medical texts (see Peters, "Is Alceste a Physiognomist?"). Peters concludes that this period was moving away from understanding the masculine self as the product of the humoral body toward a conception of the self as disembodied consciousness that instead found its meaning through social reference. But this shift was not complete, Peters argues, and the masculine self was seen as being immanent to the body at the same time that it was constituted through social exchange in *reference* to the body. However it is approached, there is indeed evidence for a "history of man's body" in the seventeenth century, and that history would appear to be one in which the status and meanings of the male body were very much in flux.

8. There is now a vast literature on this topic. For book-length studies, among many others, see Faith E. Beasley, *Salons, History, and the Creation of Seventeenth-Century France: Mastering Memory* (Burlington, VT: Ashgate, 2006); Crawford, *Perilous Performances;* John J. Conley, *The Suspicion of Virtue: Women Philosophers in Neoclassical France* (Ithaca, NY: Cornell University Press, 2002); Elizabeth Goldsmith, *Publishing Women's Life Stories in France, 1647–1720: From Voice to Print* (Burlington, VT: Ashgate, 2001); Nathalie Grande, *Stratégie de romancières: De "Clélie" à la "Princesse de Clèves" (1654–1678)* (Paris: Champion, 1999); Myriam Maître, *Les Précieuses: Naissance des femmes de lettres en France au XVIIe siècle*, Lumière Classique, 25 (Paris: Champion, 1999); Linda Timmermans, *L'Accès des femmes à la culture (1598–1715): Un débat d'idées de Saint François de Sales à la Marquise de Lambert* (Paris: Champion, 1993); Harth, *Cartesian Women;* Joan DeJean, *Tender Geographies: Women and the Origins of the Novel in France* (New York: Columbia University Press, 1991); Faith E. Beasley, *Revising Memory: Women's Fiction and Memoirs in Seventeenth-Century France* (New Brunswick, NJ: Rutgers University Press, 1990); Wendy Gibson, *Women in Seventeenth-Century France* (New York: St. Martin's Press, 1989).

9. On this question, see in particular Grande, *Stratégie de romancières;* Timmermans, *L'Accès des femmes.*

10. See Seifert, "The Male Writer" for an exploration of some of the constraints involved in male authorship in this period.

11. Pierre Bourdieu, *La Domination masculine* (Paris: Seuil, 1998), translated as *Masculine Domination* by Richard Nice (Stanford, CA: Stanford University Press, 2001). For critiques of this work, see Thierry Vincent, *L'Indifférence des sexes: Critique psychanalytique de Bourdieu et de l'idée de domination masculine* (Strasbourg: Arcanes, 2002); Marie-Victoire Louis, "Bourdieu: Défense et illustration de la domination masculine," *Les Temps modernes* 604 (May–July 1999): 325–58; Nicole-Claude Mathieu, "Bourdieu ou le pouvoir auto-hypnotique," *Les Temps modernes* 604 (May–July 1999): 286–324; Janine Mossuz-Lavau, "Dominants et dominées," *Magazine littéraire* 369 (October 1998): 58. Several English-language critics have been much more sympathetic to Bourdieu's contribution to gender studies. See Beate Krais, "The Gender Relationship in Bourdieu's Sociology," *SubStance* 93 (2000): 53–67; Marie-Pierre Le Hir, "Cultural Studies Bourdieu's Way: Women, Leadership, and Feminist Theory," in *Pierre Bourdieu: Fieldwork in Culture*, ed. Nicholas Brown and Imre Szeman (Lanham, MD: Rowman and Littlefield, 2000), 123–44; Terry Lovell, "Thinking Feminism with and against Bourdieu," *Feminist Theory* 1, no. 1 (2000): 11–32; Toril Moi, "Appropriating Bourdieu: Feminist Theory and Pierre Bourdieu's Sociology of Culture," *New Literary History* 22, no. 4 (1991): 1017–47.

For a review of these interpretations and a reading of Bourdieu's conception of masculinity, see Todd W. Reeser and Lewis C. Seifert, "Oscillating Masculinity in Bourdieu's *La Domination masculine,*" *L'Esprit Créateur* 43, no. 3 (2004): 87–97.

12. Thus, analyzing the ambivalent situation of Mr. Ramsey in Virginia Woolf's *To the Lighthouse,* he writes: "One begins to suspect that the executioner is also a victim, and that the word of the father is liable, because of its very power, to convert the probable into destiny" (*Masculine Domination,* 73). Making social expectations ("the probable") into reality ("destiny") renders Mr. Ramsey at once an "executioner" and a "victim," torturing others, to be sure, but also himself.

13. This is the case because, according to Bourdieu, the binary oppositions that structure the gender habitus (dominant versus dominated, above versus below, active versus passive, etc.) are all homologous to the "fundamental opposition" of "masculine" versus "feminine": "[T]he insertion into different fields organized according to oppositions (strong/weak, big/small, heavy/light, fat/thin, tense/relaxed, hard/soft, etc.) which always stand in a relation of homology with the fundamental distinction between male and female and the secondary alternatives in which it is expressed (dominant/dominated, above/below, active-penetrating/passive-penetrated) is accompanied by the inscription in the body of a series of sexually characterized oppositions which are homologous among themselves and also with the fundamental opposition" (*Masculine Domination,* 104–5).

14. Kaja Silverman has provided a very different model of marginal masculinity with her stimulating Lacanian readings of post–World War II film in *Male Subjectivity at the Margins* (New York: Routledge, 1992). As is clear from the foregoing discussion, her model is not one I adopt here given my desire to provide a more historically and sociologically supple account than allowed by Lacanian and psychoanalytical paradigms.

15. For a critique of the "crisis" model in American masculinity studies, see Bryce Traister, "Academic Viagra: The Rise of American Masculinity Studies," *American Quarterly* 52, no. 2 (2000): 274–304.

Mark Breitenberg has proposed a theoretically sophisticated model of masculine "anxiety" that in some ways parallels Bourdieu's theory of masculine domination. See especially Mark Breitenberg, *Anxious Masculinity in Early Modern England,* Cambridge Studies in Renaissance Literature and Culture, 10 (Cambridge: Cambridge University Press, 1996), 1–17. Breitenberg's model accounts for both social and psychic tensions within the elaboration of masculine subjectivity, as does Bourdieu's. But unlike the latter's, his model privileges the male-female binary (see *Anxious Masculinity,* 7, 10, 11) and does not explicitly make provision for tensions *among* men and differing masculine positions. And although Breitenberg acknowledges the persistence of "anxious masculinity" across cultures, he nonetheless asserts that "the early modern sex/gender system [by which he means the sex/gender system in early modern *England*] experienced an especially heightened period of agitation and unrest" (*Anxious Masculinity,* 17). I do not make an equivalent claim for early modern and specifically seventeenth-century France. To be sure, this period saw its fair share of "agitation and unrest" in the sex/gender system, but so did periods before and after. In my view, it is difficult if not arbitrary to claim that one period witnessed more anxiety about gender than another given its persistence. More useful, ultimately, is to examine the forms such "anxiety" takes in specific and across different cultures.

16. An exception to this trend is Robert A. Nye, *Masculinity and Male Codes of Honor in Modern France* (New York: Oxford University Press, 1993), which focuses on the di-

alectic of honor and shame that defined noble and increasingly bourgeois masculinity from the seventeenth century on, but with most attention to the nineteenth century. Without foregrounding masculinity as an analytical category, Robert Muchembled, *L'Invention de l'homme moderne: Sensibilités, mœurs et comportements collectifs sous l'Ancien Régime* (Paris: Fayard, 1988); Robert Muchembled, *La Société policée: Politique et politesse du XVIe au XXe siècle* (Paris: Seuil, 1998); and Jonathan Dewald, *Aristocratic Experience and the Origins of Modern Culture: France, 1570–1715* (Berkeley and Los Angeles: University of California Press, 1993) point to the ways that the "civilizing process" transformed the roles of male aristocrats and fathers in this period.

17. See the dated but classic study by Maurice Magendie, *La Politesse mondaine et les théories de l'honnêteté en France au XVIIe siècle, de 1600 à 1660*, 2 vols (Paris: Félix Alcan, 1925), 1:165–304, 2:599–836. For a more recent account that incorporates a rigorous analysis of class, see Thomas DiPiero, *Dangerous Truths and Criminal Passions: The Evolution of the French Novel, 1569–1791* (Stanford, CA: Stanford University Press, 1992).

Among the many factors that explain this phenomenon are the expanding ranks of the *noblesse de robe*, who were attracted to this literature by a desire for success at court and among the nobility at large. See, for instance Muchembled, *La Société policée*, 82, but especially Roger Chartier, "Distinction et divulgation: La civilité et ses livres," in *Lectures et lecteurs dans la France d'Ancien Régime* (Paris: Seuil, 1987), 45–86.

18. For instance, about women's increased "freedom" after the Middle Ages, he makes the dubious claim that "[t]he woman was more free from external constraints than in feudal society. But the inner constraint which she had to impose on herself in accordance with the form of integration and the code of behavior of court society, and which stemmed from the same structural feature of this society as her 'liberation,' had increased for women as for men in comparison to chivalrous society" (*The Civilizing Process*, trans. Edmund Jephcott [Oxford: Blackwell, 1994], 152).

19. "[T]he drives, the passionate affects, that can no longer directly manifest themselves in the relationships *between* people, often struggle no less violently *within* the individual against this supervising part of himself. And this semi-automatic struggle of the person with himself does not always find a happy resolution; not always does the self-transformation required by life in this society lead to a new balance between drive-satisfaction and drive-control" (*The Civilizing Process*, 453).

20. See Stuart Carroll, *Blood and Violence in Early Modern France* (Oxford; New York: Oxford University Press, 2006).

21. See Domna C. Stanton, *The Aristocrat as Art: A Study of the Honnête Homme and the Dandy in Seventeenth- and Nineteenth-Century French Literature* (New York: Columbia University Press, 1980).

22. Nicolas Faret, *L'Honnête homme ou l'art de plaire à la cour*, ed. Maurice Magendie (Geneva: Slatkine Reprints, 1970), 15–16.

23. See Benedetta Craveri, *The Age of Conversation*, trans. Teresa Waugh (New York: New York Review of Books, 2005) and Claude Habib, *Galanterie française* (Paris: Gallimard, 2006).

24. For instance, Habib states that *galanterie* "acts as a brake on male impulses" (*Galanterie française*, 221), a claim that is problematic on several counts, as I show in chapter 2.

25. Many anecdotal accounts of the salons tend to present a utopian vision. See, for instance, Dorothy Anne Liot Backer, *Precious Women* (New York: Basic Books, 1974). At the other extreme is Jolanta K. Pekacz, *Conservative Tradition in Pre-Revolutionary*

France: Parisian Salon Women, The Age of Revolution and Romanticism: Interdisciplinary Studies, 25 (New York: Peter Lang, 1999). For nuanced visions of the gendered constraints in salon interactions, see Beasley, *Salons, History;* Erica Harth, "The Salon Woman Goes Public . . . or Does She?" in *Going Public: Women and Publishing in Early Modern France*, ed. Elizabeth C. Goldsmith and Dena Goodman (Ithaca, NY: Cornell University Press, 1995), 179–93; and Harth, *Cartesian Women*.

    26. See for instance Michel Foucault, *History of Madness*, ed. Jean Khalfa, trans. Jonathan Murphy and Jean Khalfa (New York: Routledge, 2006), 35–115; and the many references in Michel Foucault, *The History of Sexuality: An Introduction*, trans. Robert Hurley (New York: Vintage Books, 1978), 3, 17–21, 115, 139–40.

    27. Foucault, *History of Madness*, 77.

    28. About the "power over life," he states: "In concrete terms, starting in the seventeenth century, this power over life evolved in two basic forms . . . an *anatomo-politics of the human body* . . . [and] an entire series of interventions and regulatory controls: *a bio-politics of the population*" (*The History of Sexuality*, 139).

    29. Foucault, *The History of Sexuality*, 20.

    30. For an overview of these debates, see especially Susan J. Hekman, ed., *Feminist Interpretations of Michel Foucault* (University Park: Pennsylvania State University Press, 1996) and Margaret A. McLaren, *Feminism, Foucault, and Embodied Subjectivity* (Albany: State University of New York Press, 2002). To date, most of the scholarship applying Foucauldian paradigms to gender has concentrated on women and femininity, but the study of men and masculinity, especially within the purview of gay studies, is also gaining ground. See for instance Steve Garlick, "The Beauty of Friendship: Foucault, Masculinity and the Work of Art," *Philosophy and Social Criticism* 28, no. 5 (2002): 558–77; Judith Surkiss, "No Fun and Games until Someone Loses an Eye: Transgression and Masculinity in Bataille and Foucault," *Diacritics* 26, no. 2 (1996): 18–30. For a Foucault-inspired morphology of masculinities, see David M. Halperin, *How to Do the History of Homosexuality* (Chicago: University of Chicago Press, 2002), 104–37. Foucault's analysis of the ancient Greek ideal of masculine moderation is a starting point for Reeser's study of sixteenth-century French masculinity. See especially Reeser, *Moderating Masculinity*, 27–31.

    31. For Bourdieu power is both "symbolic" and social reality in action. Foucault, by contrast, concentrates on the discursive manifestations of power. In spite of this difference, I would contend that these two positions are not entirely incommensurable. For a comparison of Bourdieu's and Foucault's thought, with attention to each thinker's conception of power, see Staf Callewaert, "Bourdieu, Critic of Foucault: The Case of Empirical Social Science against Double-Game-Philosophy," *Theory, Culture and Society* 23, no. 6 (2006): 73–98.

    32. In terms of theoretical approach, the two most prominent representatives of each tendency are Halperin, *How to Do* and Carla Freccero, *Queer/Early/Modern* (Durham: Duke University Press, 2006). Halperin argues for sensitivity to the variability of sexual identities over time, but Freccero takes a position diametrically opposed to Halperin's and resists what she calls "a notion of historical progression that makes modernity the culmination of identity" (*Queer/Early/Modern*, 48). Among historians of early modern sexuality, there seems to be a growing consensus for the need to occupy a middle ground between emphasizing discontinuities and continuities with the past. See Katherine Crawford, "Privilege, Possibility, and Perversion: Rethinking the Study of Early Modern Sexuality," *Journal of Modern History* 78 (2006): 413.

33. To be clear, however, I do not follow every aspect of Foucault's version of the ambiguities between past and present sexualities, not only because the category of gender is fundamental to my narrative, but also because I am attentive to local cultural details that are glossed over in a transhistorical, programmatic study like the first volume of Foucault's *History of Sexuality*.

34. See David M. Halperin, *What Do Gay Men Want? An Essay on Sex, Risk, and Subjectivity* (Ann Arbor: University of Michigan Press, 2007).

35. Halperin states that "[a]bjection . . . describes a dynamic social process constitutive of the subjectivity of gay men and other inferiorized groups" (Halperin, *What Do Gay Men Want?* 77).

36. One of the central notions in Bourdieu's analysis is that of "symbolic violence," the wide range of mechanisms that work to prevent consciousness of the illegitimacy of masculine domination. See *Masculine Domination*, 33–42.

CHAPTER 1

1. See Elias, *The Civilizing Process.* On Elias's work, see especially Jonathan Fletcher, *Violence and Civilization: An Introduction to the Work of Norbert Elias* (Cambridge: Polity Press, 1997); Stephen Mennell, *Norbert Elias: An Introduction* (Dublin: University College Dublin Press, 1998); Robert Van Krieken, *Norbert Elias* (New York: Routledge, 1998).

2. In the extensive literature on honnêteté, Magendie, *La Politesse mondaine* is a dated but still useful point of departure, but more for its descriptive rather than its interpretive aspects. The seminal study of the honnête homme and honnêteté for its comprehensive and rigorous analytical perspectives is Stanton, *The Aristocrat as Art.* With special emphasis on the Chevalier de Méré, Jean-Pierre Dens, *L'Honnête homme et la critique du goût: Esthétique et société au XVIIe siècle,* French Forum Monographs (Lexington, KY: French Forum, 1981) concentrates especially on aesthetic considerations. Taking a long-term perspective, Emmanuel Bury, *Littérature et politesse: L'invention de l'honnête homme, 1580–1750* (Paris: Presses universitaires de France, 1996) examines this notion against the changing fortunes of *paideia* and the history of ideas. Michael Moriarty, *Taste and Ideology in Seventeenth-Century France,* Cambridge Studies in French (Cambridge: Cambridge University Press, 1988), 83–105 provides a stimulating and fruitful critique of social ramifications. For sixteenth-century precursors, see the studies in *La Catégorie de l'honnête dans la culture du XVIe siècle* (Saint-Etienne: Institut d'études de la Renaissance et de l'âge classique, 1985). The changing meanings of *honnête* and *honnêteté* are examined in Rolf Reichardt, "Der Honnête homme zwischen höfischer und bürgelicher Gesellschaft. Seriell-begriffsgeschichtliche Untersuchungen von Honnêteté-Traktaten des 17. und 18. Jahrhunderts," *Archiv für Kulturgeschicte* 69 (1987): 341–70. On the posterity of the honnête homme ideal in eighteenth-century France, see Elena Russo, *La Cour et la ville de la littérature classique aux Lumières: L'invention de soi* (Paris: Presses universitaires de France, 2002) and Elena Russo, "Sociability, Cartesianism, and Nostalgia in Libertine Discourse," *Eighteenth-Century Studies* 30, no. 4 (1997): 383–400. For sociopolitical interpretations of honnêteté, see Jorge Arditi, *A Genealogy of Manners: Transformations of Social Relations in France and England from the Fourteenth to the Eighteenth Century* (Chicago: University of Chicago Press, 1998), 122–54 and Muchembled, *La Société policée,* 114–20.

3. This expression is notoriously difficult to translate, for reasons that will become clear in the following discussion, and I retain the French expression here. For a useful descriptive account of the differences between masculine and feminine honnêteté, see Jean Mesnard, "'Honnête homme' et 'honnête femme' au XVIIe siècle," in *Présences féminines: Littérature et société au XVIIe siècle français*, ed. Ian Richmond and Constant Venesoen, Biblio 17, 36 (Tübingen: Papers on French Seventeenth Century Literature, 1987), 15–46, although the corpus with which he works is quite limited given the vast number of texts devoted to the notion. On the honnête femme, see Noémi Hepp, "A la recherche du mérite des dames," in *Destins et enjeux du XVIIe siècle*, ed. Yves-Marie Bercé (Paris: Presses universitaires de France, 1985), 109–17. At moments in her study, Stanton comes close to articulating the honnête homme as a gendered figure (see *The Aristocrat as Art*, 135–39).

4. Pierre Richelet, *Dictionnaire français* (1680; reprint, Marsanne: Redon, 1999), CD-ROM.

5. Antoine Furetière, *Dictionnaire universel* (1690; reprint, Marsanne: Redon, 1999), CD-ROM.

6. Mesnard claims that during the seventeenth century "the 'honnête femme' was the object of much more discussion than the 'honnête homme'" ("Honnête Homme," 18). However, he provides little evidence to support this claim and bases his own analyses on an extremely limited corpus (Faret's *L'Honnête homme ou l'art de plaire à la cour* [1630] and Dubosc's *L'Honnête femme* [1632]). The bibliographies of conduct manuals by Alain Montandon, *Bibliographie des traités de savoir-vivre en Europe* (Clermont-Ferrand: Association des publications de la Faculté des lettres et sciences humaines de Clermont-Ferrand, 1995) reveal far more titles concerned with men than with women. The same phenomenon can be observed in the bibliographies of major studies of honnêteté. See, for instance Magendie, *La Politesse mondaine;* Stanton, *The Aristocrat as Art* and Bury, *Littérature et politesse*. Of the twenty-nine treatises studied by Reichardt, for instance, twenty-one are addressed to men, six to women, and two to both men and women. See Reichardt, "Der Honnête Homme," 347–48.

7. These contextual factors have yet to studied in a comprehensive fashion. For explanations that accentuate the sociopolitical sphere, see for instance Arditi, *A Genealogy of Manners*, 122–54. And on the religious and philosophical trends, see Bury, *Littérature et politesse*. For brief consideration of the evolving literary field, see Alain Viala, *Naissance de l'écrivain: Sociologie de la littérature à l'âge classique*, Le Sens Commun (Paris: Editions de Minuit, 1985), 147–50. See also Chartier, "Distinction et divulgation" for a broad overview of publication and reception history of conduct manuals during the early modern period.

8. Méré's principal writings on honnêteté are *Les Conversations* (1668–69), *Le Discours de la Justesse* (1671), *Le Discours des Agrémens* (1676), *Le Discours de l'Esprit* (1677), *Le Discours de la Conversation* (1677), and *Œuvres posthumes* (1700, which includes: "De la vraie Honnêteté," "De l'Eloquence et de l'entretien," "De la délicatesse dans les choses et dans l'expression," and "Le Commerce du monde"). Also important is Méré's published correspondence (*Lettres*, 1682).

9. On the *je ne sais quoi* as a "cultural quality" of the ruling class under Louis XIV, see Richard Scholar, *The Je-Ne-Sais-Quoi in Early Modern Europe: Encounters with a Certain Something* (Oxford: Oxford University Press, 2005), 182–222.

10. For a detailed account of these intertextual influences on the elaboration of honnêteté, see especially Stanton, *The Aristocrat as Art*, 14–30. See also Bury, *Littérature et politesse*.

11. Marcus Fabius Quintilian, *The Institutio Oratoria of Quintilian*, trans. Harold Edgeworth Butler, 4 vols. (Cambridge: Harvard University Press, 1976), 2:499.

12. See Marcus Tullius Cicero, *De Officiis*, trans. Walter Miller, Loeb Classical Library, 30 (Cambridge: Harvard University Press, 1997), 17, 97.

13. See Corrado Rosso, "L'Honnête homme dans la tradition italienne et française," in *Actes de New Orleans*, Biblio 17, 5 (Paris: Papers on French Seventeenth Century Literature, 1982), 105–23; Stanton, *The Aristocrat as Art*, 19–20; and Bury, *Littérature et politesse*, 68.

14. Stanton, *The Aristocrat as Art*, 25.

15. Roger de Bussy-Rabutin, *Lettres*, 2 vols (Paris: Delaulne, 1697), 1:342.

16. That several of his most definitive "Discours" were published posthumously, in 1700, demonstrates the enduring popularity of this ideal, among other competing ideals. For an overview of the semantic shifts in notion of the "honnête homme" during the later seventeenth and eighteenth centuries, see Reichardt, "Der Honnête homme." On the influence of honnêteté in the eighteenth century, see Russo, "Sociability."

17. *Lettres de Monsieur le Chevalier de Méré*, 2 vols. (Paris: Denis Thierry, 1682), 1:317–18. Subsequent references are given in the text and designated as *L*.

18. In seventeenth-century usage, the verb *plaire* evoked a magical power and is best translated as "to captivate." According to Stanton, "synonymous with *enchanter* (<*incantare*) and *charmer* (<*carmen*) in their etymological sense, the connotational semes of *plaire* suggest ideas of magical control over the other" (*The Aristocrat as Art*, 120).

19. *Oeuvres complètes du chevalier de Méré*, ed. Charles-H. Boudhors 3 vols. (Paris: F. Roches, 1930), 3:70. Subsequent references will be given in the text and designated as *OC*.

20. Russo, *La Cour et la ville*, 20.

21. See especially Russo, *La Cour et la ville*, 23–79, 117–46.

22. Stanton, *The Aristocrat as Art*, 197.

23. See *The Aristocrat as Art*, 193.

24. On Méré's understanding of *bienséance*, see Dens, *L'Honnête homme*, 110–38.

25. Méré identifies another sort of *justesse* as well: "The other *justesse* consists in the true relation that one thing has with another, either from being compared or contrasted. And this sort results from good sense and solid reason" (*OC*, 1:96). I discuss Méré's conception of *justesse* further in chapter 3.

26. Speaking of the skills necessary for elegant conversation, for instance, Méré explains that "the accuracy of feeling *(justesse du sentiment)* knows how to find between lack and excess a certain middle, which is of no less consequence for captivating than all the best things that one may say" (*OC*, 1:127). On the "mean" in early modern culture, see Joshua Scodel, *Excess and the Mean in Early Modern English Literature* (Princeton, NJ: Princeton University Press, 2002), and on the mean and masculinity in the sixteenth century, see Reeser, *Moderating Masculinity*.

27. "What I say about an honnête homme should also be understood about an honnête femme," he says while prescribing how to use the *agréments* (enticements) so as to inspire ethical conduct (*OC*, 2:31). In another text he writes: "It seems to me . . . that the Ladies desired and sought after the most have, more or less, the same feelings and thoughts [as the honnête homme]" (*OC*, 3:70).

28. This reliance on the mean continues its idealization in Renaissance discourses of masculinity. See Reeser, *Moderating Masculinity*. If the moderate mean is less central in honnêteté and other seventeenth-century discourses of masculinity, it nonetheless re-

mains a conventional but important feature. On women as immoderate in early modern discourses of masculinity, see Reeser, *Moderating Masculinity*, 14–18, 23–25.

29. See Stanton, *The Aristocrat as Art*, 19–20, 209–10.

30. *Masculine Domination*, 51.

31. Furetière, *Dictionnaire universel*.

32. Semantically related to *plaire*, both *agréable* and *agrément* connote a quasi-magical power in seventeenth-century usage. See, for instance, Richelet's definition (Richelet, *Dictionnaire français*). I translate the adjectival form as "enticing" but retain the French for the noun *agrément*.

33. This is one of the central arguments made by Moriarty: "Honnêteté operates in the first instance to preserve social stratification by requiring the subject to act out his or her place within the hierarchy through conformity to the appropriate ideological codes" (*Taste*, 88–89); "The honnête homme thus participates ideologically in a monarchical-nobiliary order; his detiny is realized at the court" (*Taste*, 91); "The discourse of honnêteté . . . postulates a subject participating in a nobiliary scheme of values under the aegis of a monarchical order" (*Taste*, 93).

34. The transition from an emphasis on merit over birth to birth over merit in definitions of aristocracy occurred in the late sixteenth and early seventeenth centuries. See Ellery Schalk, *From Valor to Pedigree: Ideas of Nobility in France in the Sixteenth and Seventeenth Centuries* (Princeton, NJ: Princeton University Press, 1986) and especially 112–15.

35. See Jean Nagle, *La Civilisation du cœur: Histoire du sentiment politique en France, du XIIe au XIXe siècle* (Paris: Fayard, 1998), especially 159–98.

36. Moriarty, *Taste*, 95.

37. Moriarty, *Taste*, 98.

38. "Among all the manners *(airs)* that are recognized the only enticing one I see is that of courts and *le grand monde*" (*OC*, 3:142).

39. At the beginning of *Les Conversations*, Méré presents the Mareschal de C. as a "galant homme who has a perfect knowledge of society. He has spent his life at court or in the army, and few people have had more than he that natural intelligence that renders one clever and enticing" (*OC*, 1:7). Having spent time at court is a sign of being a galant homme, a near-synonym of the honnête homme, as I discuss below.

40. See Magendie, *La Politesse mondaine*, 1:120–24, and Russo, *La Cour et la ville*.

41. "One must . . . instruct oneself in the manners of the court, and everyone is capable of doing so. Thus, to be good company, this is not the most important thing, and the extreme difficulty only appears in thinking of what is the best thing to say about each topic and in finding in language inexpressible nuances that depend upon recognizing what is best suited in terms of expression and knowing how to put it into practice" (*OC*, 2:104–5).

42. Moriarty, *Taste*, 90, 93.

43. See, for instance, Davis Bitton, *The French Nobility in Crisis, 1560–1640* (Stanford, CA: Stanford University Press, 1969); Schalk, *From Valor to Pedigree;* and more recently Carroll, *Blood and Violence*.

44. Stanton, *The Aristocrat as Art*, 65, 235 n. 2.

45. I discuss the implications of *galanterie* for gender and particularly masculinity further in chapter 2.

46. Stanton, *The Aristocrat as Art*, 139.

47. Eve Kosofsky Sedgwick, *Between Men: English Literature and Male Homosocial Desire*, Gender and Culture (New York: Columbia University Press, 1985), 21.

48. Méré expresses similar anxiety about male homosociality in an anecdote about Alexander being "galant" with Ephestion (*OC*, 3:75).

49. For two particularly striking examples of this phenomenon (among many others), see Letters 72 (*L*, 317–20) and 146 (*L*, 533–37).

50. Even as Méré insists on women's formative influence and the necessity of respecting and praising them, on occasion he displays a distinctly misogynistic bias. Citing the one maxim he holds to be universal, for instance, Méré equates women's erotic weakness with public displeasure at those who are "bothersome": "[O]ne needs to take great care not to become bothersome, and to be truthful I am astounded by what Tasso says: 'there is no woman so prudish nor so severe such that a lover who badgers her incessantly cannot not win her over.' For when one makes oneself bothersome in the best society, no matter how much merit one has, one always displeases" (*OC*, 3:101). Incorporating into his own maxim Tasso's adage about prudish and serious women, Méré uses their putative weakness as part of a broader counterexample for the honnête homme. He must avoid bothering those around him just as a lover must not badger his beloved. For the honnête homme, being bothersome translates into *dis*pleasure just as it means the proof of Woman's weakness—and his own triumph. Granted, this quote is replete with ambiguity. Méré distances himself from Tasso's maxim by prefacing it with "I'm astonished." More important, Méré here at least implicitly denounces the harrassing lover and his abuse of "the prudish and severe woman." But this does not change the fact that the honnête homme values above all the instrumentality of women and their purported weakness.

51. Sedgwick, *Between Men*, 22.

52. See for example *OC*, 1:22–24, 64–65. In the preface, the narrator, who presents himself as the Chevalier of the dialogues, dedicates the volume to the memory of the Mareschal (the Maréchal de Clérambault), whom he eulogizes in superlative terms.

53. Among the moments when Méré relies on male homosocial desire is a striking passage that illustrates Julius Caesar's honnêteté by his affection for Curion, one of his generals. See *OC*, 1:85–87.

54. I discuss Théophile de Viau's trial further in chapter 5.

55. "The two men of the old court whom I would have liked to meet were Saint-Surin and Théophile, who each had something excellent about them. I am aware of what was bad about Théophile" ["Divers," 1923: 526]). For other references to Théophile in the *Divers propos*, see "Divers," 1923: 79, 84, 526; "Divers," 1925: 345, 435, 444.

56. "She was more severe and more restrained than an honnête femme should be in order to live happily and make those around her happy" (*L*, 676–77).

57. Sedgwick, *Between Men*, 50.

58. This point has been made with particular acuity by Russo (*La Cour et la ville*, 129).

59. On the *je ne sais quoi* in honnêteté, see Stanton, *The Aristocrat as Art*, 207–11, and Scholar, *The Je-Ne-Sais-Quoi*, 182–222. On the *je ne sais quoi* in Méré, see Dens, *L'Honnête homme*, 52–58.

60. Scholar, *The Je-Ne-Sais-Quoi*, 184.

61. Scholar, *The Je-Ne-Sais-Quoi*, 211.

62. Peters, "Boileau's Nerve," 35.

CHAPTER 2

1. "Metrosexual," in *Merriam-Webster Online*, http://www.merriam-webster.com/dictionary/metrosexual.

2. Georges de Scudéry, "Le Pousseur de Beaux Sentiments," in *Poésies choisies de Messieurs Bensserade, Boisrobert, Bertault, de Marigny, de Lafemas, Boileau, de Montereuil, de Francheville, Testu, Petit, Loret, Le Bret, Bardou, et de plusieurs autres* (Paris: Charles de Sercy, 1665), 411.

3. See Reeser, *Moderating Masculinity* and especially the discussion of moderation in conduct literature (77–120). On the lesser importance given to moderation in the seventeenth century, see 267-68.

4. Faret, *L'Honnête homme*, 26.

5. See Ranum, "Judicial Virtue" and Wilkin, *Women, Imagination*, chap. 3.

6. Pierre Charron, *De la sagesse*, ed. Barbara de Negroni, Corpus des œuvres de philosophie de langue française (Paris: Fayard, 1986), 700. This passage is taken directly from Montaigne's "De l'institution des enfans" (1:xxvi). See Michel de Montaigne, *Les Essais de Michel de Montaigne*, ed. Pierre Villey, 3 vols. (Paris: Presses universitaires de France, 1965), 1:165.

7. Molière, *Oeuvres complètes*, 2:707.

8. Molière, *The Misanthrope and Other Plays*, trans. Donald Frame (New York: Signet Classics, 2005), 385.

9. Nicolas Pasquier, *Le Gentilhomme* (Paris: Iean Petit-Pas, 1611), 83.

10. Guillaume Colletet, *Poësies diverses* (Paris: L. Chamhoudry, 1656), 59.

11. Faret, *L'Honnête homme*, 20.

12. Abbé Morvan de Bellegarde, *Réflexions sur le ridicule, et sur les moyens de l'éviter, où sont représentez les differens Caracteres & les Mœurs des Personnes de ce Siècle* (Paris: Jean Guignard, 1698), 232–33.

13. For an eighteenth-century example of this usage, see especially Charles Gaudet, *Bibliothèque des petits-maîtres* (Paris: Chez la petite Lolo, Marchande de Galanteries, à la Frivolité, 1762). See also my discussion of the *petit-maître* at the end of this chapter.

14. Faret, *L'Honnête homme*, 93.

15. Faret may be exhibiting his bourgeois origins in this prescription, which would be taken up in earnest in what has been called the "Great Disappearance" of male fashion in the nineteenth century. Throughout the seventeenth and eighteenth centuries, male fashion, especially for aristocrats, continued to be quite extravagant, especially from the perspective of later generations. For a discussion of this question in relation to masculinity, see Margaret Waller, "The Emperor's New Clothes: Display, Cover-Up and Exposure in Modern Masculinity," in Reeser and Seifert, *Entre Hommes*, 115–42.

16. "De la mode," 14 (VI), *Les Caractères de Théophraste traduits du grec avec Les Caractères ou les Mœurs de ce siècle*, ed. Robert Garapon (Paris: Garnier Frères, 1962), 402–3. See Cédric Coignet, "Une masculinité en crise à la fin du XVIIe siècle? La critique du courtisan efféminé chez La Bruyère," *Genre & Histoire* no. 2 (Printemps, 2008) http://genre-histoire.fr/document.php?-249.

17. See Isaac de Benserade, *Iphis et Iante, Comédie*, ed. Anne Verdier, Christian Biet, and Lise Leibacher-Ouvrard (Vijon: Lamsaque, 2000). The story upon which Benserade bases his play is taken from the ninth book of Ovid's *Metamorphoses*.

18. La Bruyère, *Les Caractères*, 403.

19. Fitelieu, *La Contre-mode* (Paris: Louys de Hevqveville, 1642), 29–30.

20. Nicolas Boileau-Despréaux, *Satires, Epîtres, Art poétique,* ed. Jean-Pierre Collinet, Poésie/Gallimard (Paris: Gallimard, 1985), Satire IV, 82.

21. Félix Juvenel de Carlincas, *Le Portrait de la Coquette, ou la Lettre d'Aristandre à Timagène* (Paris: Sercy, 1659), 222.

22. Pasquier, *Le Gentilhomme,* 162.

23. In *Le Misanthrope,* see especially act 3, scene 1, and in *Les Femmes savantes,* act 3, scene 3. In each case, what begins as mutual self-congratulation descends into mutual recrimination.

24. Juvenel de Carlincas, *Le Portrait,* 95–96.

25. See especially Reeser, *Moderating Masculinity,* 235–65; Michael Wintroub, "Words, Deeds, and a Womanly King," *French Historical Studies* 28, no. 3 (2005): 387–413; Katherine Crawford, "Love, Sodomy, and Scandal: Controlling the Sexual Reputation of Henry III," *Journal of the History of Sexuality* 12, no. 4 (2003): 513–42; and Rebecca Zorach, "The Matter of Italy: Sodomy and the Scandal of Style in Sixteenth-Century France," *Journal of Medieval and Early Modern Studies* 28, no. 3 (1998): 581–609.

26. See Jeffrey Merrick, "The Cardinal and the Queen: Sexual and Political Disorders in the Mazarinades," *French Historical Studies* 18, no. 3 (1994): 667–99, and Lewis C. Seifert, "Eroticizing the Fronde: Sexual Deviance and Political Disorder in the *Mazarinades,*" *L'Esprit Créateur* 35, no. 2 (1995): 22–36.

27. Jean-François Sarasin, *Œuvres de J.-Fr. Sarasin,* ed. Paul Festugière, 2 vols. (1656; Paris: Champion, 1926), 2:180.

28. See Halperin, *How to Do,* 110–13. "For the ancient Greeks and Romans, a man who indulged his taste for sexual pleasure with women did not necessarily enhance his virility but often undermined it. To please women, such a man was likely to make an effort to appear smooth instead of rough, graceful instead of powerful, and might even compound that effeminate style by using makeup and perfumes, elaborate grooming, and prominent jewelry" (111).

Some evidence suggests that the association of effeminacy with homosexual desire and "lifestyle" becomes more frequent, at least in the English context, by the end of the seventeenth century (see Randolph Trumbach, *Heterosexuality and the Third Gender in Enlightenment London,* vol. 1 of *Sex and the Gender Revolution* [Chicago: University of Chicago Press, 1998]). And yet, based on a wide review of eighteenth-century English material, specifically around the figure of the "fop," Philip Carter concludes: "That fops were occasionally accused of sodomy does not substantiate the claim that the eighteenth century witnessed the collapse of the character into a sexually defined molly type. It was far more common for discussions of fops' sexuality to focus on their relations with female, not male, company" (*Men and the Emergence of Polite Society, Britain 1660–1800,* Women and Men in History [New York: Longman, 2001], 145).

29. Jeffrey Merrick and Bryant T. Ragan, eds., *Homosexuality in Early Modern France: A Documentary Collection* (New York: Oxford University Press, 2001), 2. The second degree of mollitude, according to Benedicti, is masturbation, and the third, passive anal sex.

30. The intersection of humoral theory and early modern gender ideologies has been explored quite extensively, and my brief account here cannot do justice to the complexities of this question. For general considerations of this topic, especially with reference to literary culture, see Gail Kern Paster, *The Body Embarrassed: Drama and the Disciplines of Shame in Early Modern England* (Ithaca, NY: Cornell University Press, 1993)

and Gail Kern Paster, *Humoring the Body: Emotions and the Shakespearean Stage* (Chicago: University of Chicago Press, 2004). For useful discussions of humoral masculinity, see Peters, "Is Alceste a Physiognomist?" and Breitenberg, *Anxious Masculinity*, 35–68.

31. Jacques Ferrand, *Traité de l'essence et guérison de l'amour ou De la mélancolie érotique (1610)*, ed. Gérard Jacquin and Eric Foulon (Paris: Anthropos, 2001), 69, 73.

32. Ferrand, *Traité*, 19.

33. Ian Moulton, *Before Pornography: Erotic Writing in Early Modern England*, Studies in the History of Sexuality (New York: Oxford University Press, 2000), 16.

34. Moulton, *Before Pornography*, 16.

35. Breitenberg, *Anxious Masculinity*, 50.

36. This quote is from the *Lettre à d'Alembert:* "[T]his weaker sex, unable to adopt our way of living that is too difficult for it, forces us to adopt its own that is too soft for us, and refusing to tolerate a separation, unable to make themselves men, women make us women" (*Lettre à d'Alembert sur son article Genève*, ed. Marc Launay [Paris: Garnier-Flammarion, 1967], 195–96).

37. Fitelieu, *La Contre-Mode*, 290–91.

38. Juvenel de Carlincas, *Le Portrait*, 24.

39. *Nouvelles œuvres, suivies du Dialogue de l'Amour et de la raison*, ed. Albert de Bersaucourt, Collection des chefs-d'œuvre méconnus (Paris: Editions Bossard, 1925), 171. Le Pays's *Nouvelles œuvres* was first published in 1672. It should be noted that Le Pays's dialogue ends with the triumph of Amour over Raison. The perspective here is thus antithetical to that of Fitelieu and Juvenel.

40. For discussions that demonstrate, albeit indirectly, a preoccupation with effeminacy in the musical culture of this period, see Georgia Cowart, "Of Women, Sex, and Folly: Opera under the Old Regime," *Cambridge Opera Journal* 6, no. 3 (1994): 205–20, and Catherine E. Gordon-Seifert, "Strong Men—Weak Women: Gender Representation and the Influence of Lully's 'Operatic Style' on French *Airs Sérieux* (1650–1700)," in *Musical Voices of Early Modern Women: Many-Headed Melodies*, ed. Thomasin Lamay, Women and Gender in the Early Modern World (Burlington, VT: Ashgate, 2005), 135–67.

41. Nicolas Boileau-Despréaux, "Dialogue des héros de roman," in *Œuvres complètes de Boileau: Dialogues, Réflexions critiques, Œuvres diverses*, ed. Charles-H. Boudhors (Paris: Société Les Belles Lettres, 1960), 17.

42. Boileau-Despréaux, "Dialogue," 36.

43. This said, it is well known that Boileau delayed publishing this dialogue until after the novelist's death because of his particularly nasty personal attack on her. On the meaning of this work within the context of seventeeth-century French women's writing, see DeJean, *Tender Geographies*, 165–69.

44. Granted, Boileau also lays blame on the purportedly bourgeois origins of the novel. At the end of the dialogue, it is revealed that the "heroes" whom Pluto had assembled are in fact bourgeois impostors and that the authentic heroes are waiting in the wings to come to the rescue of Hades. With this final twist, Boileau indicts not only the gendered but also the social origins of the novel, and he suggests that effeminacy is an inherently bourgeois phenomenon, an affected parody of an inimitable noble ethos.

45. *Muguet* was commonly used in the sixteenth century, but archaic by the mid-seventeenth century. *Marquis* is a title of nobility, but it was also used derisively to refer to a man whose refinement is affected and often implicitly effeminate (e.g., Molière). The

term *galant* when used as a noun was by no means always pejorative. As I discuss later, *précieux* to designate a man (adjective or noun) was rare, especially when compared to use of *précieuse*.

46. See John of Salisbury, *Frivolities of Courtiers and Footprints of Philosophers*, http://www.constitution.org/salisbury/policrat123.htm. My thanks to Michel-André Bossy for this reference.

47. Baldassarre Castiglione, *The Courtier*, trans. George Anthony Bull, Penguin Classics (New York: Penguin, 1976), 61.

48. On the ambiguities but also frequent misunderstanding surrouding Ottaviano's call for temperance in book 4 of *The Book of the Courtier*, see Jennifer Richards, "'A Wanton Trade of Living?' Rhetoric, Effeminacy, and the Early Modern Courtier," *Criticism* 42, no. 2 (2000): 185–206. And on the reception of Castiglione in a pan-European perspective, see Peter Burke, *The Fortunes of the Courtier: The European Reception of Castiglione's Cortegiano* (University Park: Pennsylvania State University Press, 1996).

49. See Wintroub, "Words, Deeds."

50. On the sixteenth-century reception of Castiglione in France, see Pauline Smith, *The Anti-courtier Trend in Sixteenth-Century French Literature* (Geneva: Droz, 1966), 26–29, and Burke, *Fortunes of the Courtier*, 35–36, 63–64, 67–68, 75–76, 93–94, 112–13, 125–28.

51. Quoted in Pauline Smith, *Anti-courtier Trend*, 87.

52. Philibert de Vienne, *Le Philosophe de Court*, ed. Pauline M. Smith, Textes Littéraires Français (Geneva: Droz, 1990), 143.

53. Wintroub, "Words, Deeds," 405.

54. On this trend, see Muchembled, *La Société policée*, 77–122.

55. See especially *L'Honnête homme*, 95–101.

56. Muchembled, *La Société policée*, 99–101.

57. See Carroll, *Blood and Violence* and the numerous examples of misbehavior by young aristocrats in Mark Motley, *Becoming a French Aristocrat: The Education of the Court Nobility, 1580–1715* (Princeton, NJ: Princeton University Press, 1990), 169–208.

58. Muchembled notes the more rounded poses struck by males in court portraiture as evidence for this toning down of aggression (*La Société policée*, 160).

59. See Schalk, *From Valor to Pedigree*, who argues that the decade of 1590s witnessed this shift (92).

60. Dewald, *Aristocratic Experience*, 58.

61. Muchembled, *La Société policée*, 117.

62. See Dewald, *Aristocratic Experience*.

63. See Jean-François Solnon, *La Cour de France* (Paris: Fayard, 1987), 419–20.

64. See Muchembled, *L'Invention*, 341, 362; Habib, *Galanterie française*, 311–19; Alain Viala, *La France galante: Essai historique sur une catégorie culturelle, de ses origines jusqu'à la Révolution*, Les Litteraires (Paris: Presses universitaires de France, 2008), 84–112.

65. Wintroub, "Words, Deeds," 390; see also Nicolas Le Roux, *La Faveur du roi: Mignons et courtisans au temps des derniers Valois*, Epoques (Seyssel: Champ Vallon, 2001).

66. See Muchembled, *La Société policée*, 132–38.

67. François-Timoléon de Choisy, *Mémoires de l'abbé de Choisy: Mémoires pour servir à l'histoire de Louis XIV. Mémoires de l'abbe de Choisy habillé en femme*, ed. Georges Mongrédien (Paris: Mercure de France, 2000), 332.

68. Choisy frames his anecdote with "dit-on," indicating a certain hesitancy to give full credence to this story. And immediately after the passage cited he insists on Philippe's martial (and thus virile) qualities (Choisy, *Mémoires*, 332). Biographers of Philippe generally discount the story about Mazarin's desire to "effeminize" him. See Nancy Nichols Barker, *Brother to the Sun King—Philippe, Duke of Orléans* (Baltimore: Johns Hopkins University Press, 1989), 58.

69. On the efforts to differentiate between Louis and Philippe in iconography from the beginning of the reign, see Zanger, "Lim(b)Inal Images."

70. This discussion is found in book 4 of *The Book of the Courtier*. See Richards, "A Wanton Trade."

71. François du Soucy de Gerzan, *La Conduite du courtisan: Dedié à Mr de Bassompierre* (Paris: Iean Bessin, 1646), 44–45.

72. Other writers also recognize the strategic role of women for currying favor at court. See, for instance, Faret, *L'Honnête homme*, 88–90.

73. Gerzan, *La Conduite*, 43.

74. The term *salon* is anachronistic when applied to the seventeenth century. On the appearance of this word in criticism of salon culture of the ancien régime, see Antoine Lilti, *Le Monde des salons: Sociabilité et mondanité à Paris au XVIIIe siècle* (Paris: Fayard, 2005), 10–11. However, following critical convention, I will use it alongside the terms employed during the period (principally, *assemblée, alcôve, cercle, réduit*, and *ruelle*).

75. *Traitté de la fortune des gens de qualité, et gentilhommes particuliers. Divisé en deux parties* (Paris: Louis Chamhoudry, 1658), 125–26.

76. Caillières, *Traitté*, 126, 383.

77. There is an extensive bibliography of scholarship on the salons of the ancien régime. For studies that concentrate in a general way on the role of women within the salons of the seventeenth century, see especially Carolyn C. Lougee, *Le Paradis des femmes: Women, Salons, and Social Stratification in Seventeenth-Century France* (Princeton, NJ: Princeton University Press, 1976); Renate Baader, *Dames de lettres: Autorinnen des preziösen, hocharistokratischen und "modernen" Salons (1649–1698): Mlle de Scudéry, Mlle de Montpensier, Mme d'Aulnoy*, Romanistische Abhandlungen (Stuttgart: J. B. Metzlersche Verlagsbuchh., 1986); DeJean, *Tender Geographies;* Harth, *Cartesian Women;* Harth, "Salon Woman Goes Public"; Timmermans, *L'Accès des femmes*, 63–236; Maître, *Les Précieuses;* Anne-Madeleine Goulet, *Poésie, musique et sociabilité au XVIIe siècle: Les Livres d'airs de différents auteurs publiés chez Ballard de 1658 à 1694* (Paris: H. Champion, 2004); Craveri, *The Age of Conversation;* Beasley, *Salons, History.* In addition to these titles, there are numerous studies of individual salons and salon women. For a survey of interpretations of the salons since the nineteenth century (albeit weighted in favor the eighteenth century), see Lilti, *Le monde des salons*, 15–58.

78. DeJean, *Tender Geographies*, 60, 71–78, 93–99. See also Erica Harth's critique of this notion ("Salon Woman Goes Public," 184–87).

79. See Beasley, *Salons, History.*

80. Alain Génetiot, *Poétique du loisir mondain, de Voiture à La Fontaine*, Lumière Classique, 14 (Paris: Champion, 1997), 488.

81. Antoine Lilti's four-part definition of the eighteenth-century salon largely applies to its seventeenth-century forebear as well: a practice of hospitality, regular meetings, a respect for the codes of civility and politeness, and a mixed-gender group. See Lilti, *Le monde des salons*, 65–66.

82. On the exclusively male cabinets and *académies* of the seventeenth century, see

Josephine de Boer, "Men's Literary Circles in Paris, 1610–1660," *PMLA* 53 (1938): 730–81.

83. For instance, going somewhat against the grain of recent scholarship, Erica Harth has argued that salons may not have been as liberating for women as some scholars have suggested, and among the reasons she cites is the fact that men were not only regular and central members of these meetings but also used them to enhance their positions within the cultural and political fields of the time. (See Harth, *Cartesian Women* and Harth, "Salon Woman Goes Public.") Owing mostly to the focus of her work, Harth understandably does not give extended consideration to the place of men within the salons, although she does cite many specific examples. Yet her argument clearly highlights the need for such an analysis.

84. See the discussion of these differences in Timmermans, *L'Accès des femmes*, 71–84.

85. Considering the century as a whole, Roger Picard identified four main types of salons: "aristocratic" (e.g., Rambouillet), "précieux" (e.g., Scudéry), "moralist" (e.g., Sablé, La Sablière, and Lafayette), and "libertine" (e.g., Lenclos). See *Les Salons littéraires et la société française, 1610–1789* (New York: Brentano's, 1943). Even if Picard's terminology is more than a little problematic and the discreetness of his categories very much open to question, his typology at least has the virtue of illustrating the diversity of salon life. More recently, Lilti too has insisted on this variety, although most of his examples concern the eighteenth century. See Lilti, *Le monde des salons*, 62–69.

86. Compare Madeleine de Scudéry and Paul Pellisson-Fontanier, *Chroniques du Samedi, suivies de pièces diverses (1653–1654)*, ed. Alain Niderst, Delphine Denis, and Myriam Maître, Sources Classiques (Paris: Champion, 2002) and the correspondence reproduced in Victor Cousin, *Madame de Sablé: Études sur les femmes illustres et la société du XVIIe siècle* (Paris: Didier, 1854) and Edouard de Barthélemy, *Les Amis de la marquise de Sablé: Recueil des lettres des principaux habitués de son salon* (Paris: E. Dentu, 1865).

87. Jean Chapelain, *Lettres de Jean Chapelain*, ed. Philippe Tamizey de Larroque, 2 vols. (Paris: Imprimerie Nationale, 1880), 1:80.

88. Harth, *Cartesian Women*, 60–63.

89. Harth, "Salon Woman Goes Public," 183.

90. For a concise statement of Lougee's argument, see especially *Le Paradis des femmes*, 149. There are several unanswered questions in Lougee's otherwise stimulating analysis. It is unclear from her discussion to what extent the salons played a specific role in the examples of hypergamy and *mésalliance* she uncovers, and connected to this is the fact she bases her statistical study of these phenomena on Somaize's highly ambiguous (and thus unreliable) *Grand dictionnaire des précieuses*.

91. On this dynamic, see Elizabeth Goldsmith, *Exclusive Conversations: The Art of Interaction in Seventeenth-Century France* (Philadelphia: University of Pennsylvania Press, 1988), 41–46.

92. Baudeau de Somaize, "Le Grand dictionnaire des précieuses," in Duchêne, *Les Précieuses*, 448.

93. Collections of salon poetry such as the *Recueils Sercy* are dominated by works authored by men. See Frédéric Lachèvre, *Bibliographie des recueils collectifs de poésies publiés de 1597 à 1700*, 4 vols (Geneva: Slatkine Reprints, 1967).

94. Viala, *Naissance de l'écrivain*, 132–37.

95. Mostly on the basis of eighteenth-century evidence, Lilti cautions against over-estimating the role of writers or literature in the salons of the ancien régime (see *Le*

monde des salons, 273). While his point about the great variety of sociable practices within salons is no doubt valid, the situation for seventeenth-century salons is unclear, at least failing an exhaustive social history of the sort he has done for the eighteenth century.

96. Thus, Roger Duchêne writes about this sort of relationship: "The women most eager to participate actively in cultural life seem to remain indebted to the masculine knowledge of the *doctes,* the Chapelains and Ménages, and these women, such as Madame de Sévigné or the comtesse de La Fayette, readily adapt to it. Since they did not have access to the culture of the *collèges* and since culture cannot be improvised, . . . they need cultural intermediaries, which is to say men taught according to tradition but capable of training the mind without overburdening them with all sorts of knowledge. They know this and do not seek to do without it but rather to take advantage of it" (*Les Précieuses ou comment l'esprit vint aux femmes* [Paris: Fayard, 2001], 90).

97. On the rivalry between Godeau and Voiture, see Emile Magne, *Voiture et l'hôtel de Rambouillet: Les Origines (1597–1635) et Les Années de gloire (1635–1648),* 2 vols. (Paris: Editions Emile-Paul Frères, 1929–30), 1:158, 202; on that between Chavaroche and Voiture, see Magne, *Voiture et l'Hôtel de Rambouillet,* 2:278; on that between Conrart and Pellisson, see Scudéry and Pellisson-Fontanier, *Chroniques,* 105–8; and on the quarrel between Chapelain and Ménage, see Georges Mongrédien, *Madeleine de Scudéry et son salon, d'après des documents inédits,* Bibliothèque Historia (Paris: Tallandier, 1946), 143–45; Barbara Krajewska, *Du coeur à l'esprit: Mademoiselle de Scudéry et ses samedis* (Paris: Kimé, 1993), 105–10.

98. The word *salonnière* appears to be a neologism created by historians and literary critics to refer to salon women. Lilti (*Le monde des salons,* 110) rejects it on the grounds that it implies an institutional structure and organization that salons never attained. Although I agree with Lilti that salons retained a measure of informality in comparison to exclusively male *académies,* I do not share his anxiety about the use of the term *salonnière* or the masculine counterpart *salonnier.*

99. One of the most dramatic success stories of this balancing act was Vincent Voiture, who secured several lucrative positions for himself but also built a solid reputation as a model for sociability and writing through the Hôtel de Rambouillet. See chapter 3.

100. I do not mean to imply that effeminacy was a threat in *all* of the salons of the period. Frequenting the *ruelles* hosted by d'Auchy or Sablé, for instance, purportedly more serious in tenor than those of Rambouillet ou Scudéry, would likely have not carried such a risk.

101. Somaize, "Les Précieuses," 527.

102. Chalesme, *L'Homme de qualité, ou les moyens de vivre en homme de bien et en homme du monde* (Paris: André Pralard, 1671), 200.

103. Quoted in Barbara Krajewska, *Mythes et découvertes: Le salon littéraire de Madame de Rambouillet dans les lettres des contemporains,* Biblio 17, 52 (Paris: Papers on French Seventeenth Century Literature, 1990), 32.

104. Charlotte de Saumaise de Chauzan de Flécelles de Brégy, *La Reflexion de la Lune sur les hommes,* ed. Constant Venesoen (Paris: Honoré Champion, 2006), 142.

105. Brégy, *La Réflexion,* 145–46.

106. Duchêne has hypothesized that Molière based his portrayal of the two valets disguised as galants on Sorel's text. See Duchêne, *Les Précieuses,* 14–22.

107. "Les Lois de la galanterie," in Duchêne, *Les Précieuses,* 313.

108. See especially Delphine Denis, *La Muse galante: Poétique de la converstion dans*

l'œuvre de Madeleine de Scudéry (Paris: Honoré Champion, 1997); Delphine Denis, *Le Parnasse galant: Institution d'une catégorie littéraire au XVIIe siècle*, Lumière Classique, 32 (Paris: Honoré Champion, 2001); Delphine Denis, "Préciosité et galanterie: Vers une nouvelle cartographie," in *Les Femmes au Grand Siècle, le Baroque, Musique et littérature: Actes du 33e Colloaue de la North American Society for Seventeeth-Century French Literature*, ed. David Wetzel, Biblio 17, 144 (Tübingen: Gunter Narr Verlag, 2002), 17–39; Alain Génetiot, *Les Genres lyriques mondains (1630–1660): Etude des poésies de Voiture, Vion d'Alibray, Sarasin et Scarron*, Histoire des Idées et Critique Littéraire, 281 (Geneva: Droz, 1990); Génetiot, *Poétique du loisir mondain;* Habib, *Galanterie française;* Alain Viala, "Introduction," in *L'Esthétique galante: Paul Pellisson, Discours sur les Œuvres de Monsieur Sarasin et autres textes,* ed. Alain Viala (Toulouse: Société de Littératures Classiques, 1989); Alain Viala, "La Littérature galante: Histoire et problématique," in *Il Seicento francese oggi: Situazione e prospettiva della ricerca,* Quaderni del Seicento Francese, 11 (Bari: Adriatica; Paris: Nizet, 1994), 101–13; Alain Viala, "D'une politique des formes: La galanterie," *XVIIe siècle* 182 (1994): 143–51; Alain Viala, " 'Les Signes Galants': A Historical Reevaluation of 'Galanterie' " *Yale French Studies* 92 (1997): 11–29; Alain Viala, "L'Eloquence galante: Une problématique de l'adhésion," in *Images de soi dans le discours: La construction de l'ethos,* ed. Ruth Amossy (Lausanne: Delachaux et Niestlé, 1999), 177–95; Viala, *La France galante.*

109. Viala conflates the honnête homme with the galant in his discussion of Méré, ignoring the terminology of honnêteté insistently used by this author. See *La France galante,* 111–41. Viala also attributes to galanterie—and excludes from honnêteté—qualities that the latter also included, especially in Méré's conception. See *La France galante,* 172.

110. *Galant* and *galanterie* have multiple meanings, and this polysemicity was widely acknowledged at the time. By far the oldest refer to sexual license and especially sexual seduction and are linked to the etymological roots *galer* (Old French for "to play" or "to play a trick") and *gale* (Old French for "amusement"). See Viala, *La France galante,* 19–39.

111. Claude Favre de Vaugelas, *Remarques sur la langue françoise utiles à ceux qui veulent bien parler et bien escrire* (Paris: Augustin Courbé, 1647), 477. Vaugelas—like many others who endeavor to define *galant* and *galanterie*—is careful to give a broad and deliberately vague definition that relies on the inexplicable *je ne sais quoi.* See the definitions of *galanterie* by Paul Pellisson, "Discours sur les Œuvres de Monsieur Sarasin," in *L'Esthétique galante: Paul Pellisson, Discours sur les Œuvres de Monsieur Sarasin et autres textes,* ed. Alain Viala (Toulouse: Société de Littératures Classiques, 1989); Madeleine de Scudéry, "De l'air galant," in *"De l'air galant" et autres conversations [1653–1684]: Pour une étude de l'archive galante,* ed. Delphine Denis, Sources Classiques, 5 (Paris: Champion, 1998), 49–57; Méré, *OC,* 1:18–19; and Dominique Bouhours, *Les Entretiens d'Ariste et d'Eugène,* ed. Bernard Beugnot and Gilles Declercq, Sources Classiques, 47 (Paris: Honoré Champion, 2003), 418. Alain Viala has argued that this reliance on the sublime has a strategic value for the social group most responsible for promoting this ideal, a group of wealthy bourgeois and petty or middling noble parvenus seeking to consolidate their newly gained socioeconomic status through a collective identity in the 1650s and 1660s. (See Viala, "Les Signes Galants," 24. Viala cites Ménage, Pellisson, Sarasin, Scudéry, and La Fontaine as examples of this "group." See also Viala, "Introduction," 35 and Viala, *La France galante,* 174–202.) Making the *je ne sais quoi* the essence of galanterie provided this

group with a means of elusive and exclusive mutual recognition, but also a basis for cultural legitimacy and a sign of distinction (Viala, "L'Eloquence galante," 180).

112. Furetière, *Dictionnaire universel.*

113. The seminal works on conversation in seventeenth-century France are Goldsmith, *Exclusvie Conversations* and Christoph Strosetzki, *Rhétorique de la conversation: Sa dimension littéraire et linguistique dans la société française du XVIIe siècle,* trans. Sabine Seubert, Biblio 17, 20 (Tübingen: Papers on French Seventeenth Century Literature, 1984). On the importance of conversation in the seventeenth-century novel, see especially DeJean, *Tender Geographies.* Examples of texts that use the conversational frame are numerous and, of course, hardly unique to seventeenth-century France. Among those that are most pertinent to galanterie are Dominique Bouhours, *Les Entretiens d'Ariste et d'Eugène* (1671); Méré, *Les Conversations* (1669); Jean-François Sarasin, "S'il faut qu'un jeune homme soit amoureux" (1656); and the numerous collections of conversations by Madeleine de Scudéry.

114. Inspired in France principally by Marino, neo-Petrarchanism was less Neoplatonic in its emphasis, more sensual and less concerned with male submission to the female beloved than was Petrarchanism. But both traditions rely on a common store of topoi and rhetorical figures. See Génetiot, *Poétique du loisir mondain,* 184–211.

115. See Jean-Michel Pelous, *Amour précieux, amour galant (1654–1675): Essai sur la représentation de l'amour dans la littérature et la société mondaines* (Paris: Klincksieck, 1980), 54–56.

116. Pelous, *Amour précieux,* 44. Pelous cites Roland Barthes's famous characterization of the "intransitive state" of desire in Racinian tragedy. As Pelous rightly points out, this characterization is even more apt for galant (and neo-Petrarchan) love poetry.

117. On the aesthetic of *la douceur,* see Génetiot, *Poétique du loisir mondain,* 347–50, and Marc Fumaroli, "*Les Fées* de Charles Perrault ou De la littérature," in *Le Statut de la littérature: Mélanges offerts à Paul Bénichou* (Geneva: Droz, 1982), 153–86. About the growing resistance to traditional "masculine" oratory, Génetiot writes, in reference to Guez de Balzac: "For the grand rhetoric, violent and masculine, of the tribune is substituted a feminine eloquence of *douceur,* of reclaimed freedom, specific to the moderate style of conversation, that temperate style which is invented at the same moment in a *mondain* poetry of the years 1630–1640" (*Poétique du loisir mondain,* 434–35).

118. See Craveri, *The Age of Conversation;* Habib, *Galanterie française;* Viala, *La France galante,* 142–73.

119. Habib, *Galanterie française,* 143.

120. Habib uses her analysis of galanterie to lament its decline in contemporary French culture and to call for a return to a modified version of this amorous code. Besides a dubious interpretation of the gender politics of galanterie, her analysis also relies upon an essentialist understanding of gender (*Galanterie française,* 432) and at times blatant homophobia (44–47).

121. See Génetiot, *Les Genres lyriques mondains,* 85–110; Sophie Rollin, *Le Style de Vincent Voiture: Une esthétique galante,* Renaissance et Age Classique (Saint-Etienne: Publications de l'Université de Saint-Etienne, 2006), 107–17.

122. See Scudéry and Pellisson-Fontanier, *Chroniques,* 166–90.

123. Viala, *La France galante,* 203–25.

124. Jean-François Sarasin is a good case in point. Although some of his writings appear in the *Chroniques du Samedi* and, accordingly, adopt the requisite ideals of love elab-

orated by Sapho, other writings evince an ironic galanterie. In one of his "chansons," for instance, the poet derides Phylis for going back on her promise to "love faithfully" and concludes "Ainsi ne pensez pas / Que mon trespas / Suive votre inconstance; / Car entre nous / Aimer si constamment est le mestier des Foux" (Thus do not think / That my death / Will follow upon your inconstancy. / For just between us / Loving so faithfully is the occupation of fools). *Les Œuvres de Monsieur Sarasin* (Paris: Thomas Jolly, 1663), 90.

125. For a stimulating analysis of the satirical reinterpretations of the *Carte de Tendre*, see Jeffrey N. Peters, *Mapping Discord: Allegorical Cartography in Early Modern French Writing* (Newark: University of Delaware Press, 2004), 117–47.

126. The literary historical debate about the *précieuses* is a long story in and of itself, which, if anything, has become even more confusing over the past decade. See Denis, "Préciosité" for a useful and mostly impartial *état de la question*. Although a few recent critics (especially Myriam Maître and Roger Duchêne) have identified several meliorative uses of the noun *précieuse* applied to a women in the 1640s and 1650s (Duchêne claims this is the case for nineteen different women [*Les Précieuses*, 181]), none of these or any other women at the time adopted the term for themselves. Furthermore, the women identified as *précieuses* did not form a cohesive sociocultural group or movement, contrary to what critical use of this term implies. As Duchêne affirms (and as Maître seems to forget), "Considering only texts [from the period], there are only a handful of *précieuses* whom it is impossible to place in one category alone and even less in a 'cabale'" (Duchêne, *Les Précieuses*, 188). Given this uncertainty, it is ultimately more important to concentrate on the meanings of the *précieuse* as a satirical fiction. On these, see especially Pelous, *Amour précieux*, 307–454, and Domna C. Stanton, "The Fiction of Préciosité and the Fear of Women," *Yale French Studies* 62 (1981): 107–34.

127. See, for instance Pelous, *Amour précieux*, 404–6; Stanton, "Fiction of Préciosité"; and Maître, *Les Précieuses*, 57–121.

128. Among the most important male satirists of the *précieuses* were, besides Molière, Baudeau de Somaize, de Pure, and Saint-Evremond. Women who contributed to this satire included the Grande Mademoiselle (Mademoiselle de Montpensier), Marie-Catherine Desjardins (aka Madame de Villedieu), and Ninon de Lenclos.

129. From all accounts, Brébeuf and de Pure are among the very few writers to use the term *précieux* at midcentury. See Maître, *Les Précieuses*, 55, and Duchêne, *Les Précieuses*, 133, 136.

130. Michel de Pure, *La Prétieuse ou le mystère des ruelles*, 2 vols. (Paris: Droz, 1939), 2:158.

131. Eva Avigdor, *Coquettes et précieuses: Textes inédits* (Paris: A.-G. Nizet, 1982), 88.

132. Molière [Jean-Baptiste Poquelin], *Les Précieuses ridicules*, ed. Micheline Cuénin (Geneva: Droz, 1973), 7.

133. Duchêne, *Les Précieuses*, 19.

134. Sorel, "Les Lois," 323.

135. To the extent that this is indeed the case (and further research would be necessary to determine this, assuming that such a question can receive anything like a definitive answer), several different explanations come to mind. Perhaps, as some have suggested, the salon itself never was the utopian discursive space for women it has been portrayed to be and, instead, gave men yet another venue from which to promote their own careers and interests. See especially Harth, "Salon Woman Goes Public." Or, perhaps with time what may have been an institution founded on feminocentric interests became increasingly an-

drocentric. From all accounts, this would certainly appear to be the case in the eighteenth century, when the (male) philosophes set the agenda for salon discussions. See Dena Goodman, *The Republic of Letters: A Cultural History of the French Enlightenment* (Ithaca, NY: Cornell University Press, 1994); Lilti, *Le monde des salons;* and Russo, *La Cour et la ville.* If men dominated or came to dominate salon interactions, then effeminacy would indeed have been a less urgent concern. In a broader sense, as Muchembled has argued, the *mondain* ideal of masculinity seems to have become softer over the course of the seventeenth century, with a deliberate effort to downplay the signs of the traditional warrior ethos.

136. Gaudet, *Bibliothèque*, unpaginated preface.

137. See Frédéric Deloffre, "Introduction," in *Le Petit-Maître corrigé*, ed. Frédéric Deloffre, by Pierre de Marivaux (Geneva: Droz, 1955), 11–143.

138. On the mistreatment of women by *petits-maîtres*, see Deloffre, "Introduction," 22. On homoeroticism in the depiction of this figure, see Pierre Saint-Amand, "Le Triomphe des Beaux: Petits-maîtres et jolis hommes au dix-huitième siècle," *L'Esprit Créateur* 43, no. 3 (2003): 37–46.

139. Gaudet, *Bibliothèque*, 22–23.

140. "Impertinence *(la fatuité)* is one of those faults that is only found among the most refined peoples. It was well known to the Greeks during the great centuries of their republic. It probably originates from an abuse of politeness and wit" (*Bibliothèque*, 11).

CHAPTER 3

1. Pellisson, "Discours sur les Œuvres de Monsieur Sarasin," 67.

2. Vaugelas, *Remarques*, 478.

3. See the discussion of this question in Michèle Longino Farrell, *Performing Motherhood: The Sévigné Correspondence* (Hanover, NH: University Press of New England, 1991), 45–56.

4. For detailed biographical information on Voiture, see Rollin, *Le Style de Vincent Voiture: Une esthétique galante*, 49–71, and Emile Magne, *Voiture et l'Hôtel de Rambouillet*, vol. 1, *Les origines, 1597–1635*, vol. 2, *Les années de gloire, 1635–1648* (Paris: Emile-Paul Frères, 1929–30).

5. Chapelain, *Lettres de Jean Chapelain*, 1:578.

6. Quoted in Magne, *Voiture et l'Hôtel de Rambouillet*, 2:101 n. 3.

7. Vincent Voiture, *Œuvres de Voiture: Lettres et poésies*, ed. M. A. Ubicini (1855; Geneva: Slatkine Reprints, 1967), 2, 13.

8. Génetiot, *Poétique du loisir mondain*, 488.

9. Pinchesne elaborates on Voiture's supposedly feminine qualities thus: "His demeanor was as suave as his wit; he was without animosity or enviousness toward the works and glory of others; he judged things serenely and dispassionately and never said malicious things nor took pleasure in diminishing the reputation of anyone. He always had the convictions one must have toward religion, was charitable toward the poor, and those who knew him in his youth always found him far removed from any sort of libertinism. Although in other things he loved mockery, he never wrote anything satirical, and nothing of his is not to the advantage of those of whom he speaks" (*Œuvres de Voiture*, 1:8–9).

10. The "femininity" of Voiture's writing is also asserted by René Le Pays, who

uses the allegory of matriarchal lineage to trace literary history back to the Greeks. Le Pays begins his narrative with his own muse, whose mother was Voiture's: "The Muse Amourette is the daughter of Voiture's Muse. That lighthearted air they both have, that galant and polished character one sees in each are the convincing proof of it. It is true that her lightheartedness, galanterie, and polish are far removed from the lightheartedness, galanterie, and polish of her mother. In Voiture, all that is accompanied by a certain refinement that the Muse Amourette has not been capable of imitating. But she still is no less her daughter even though she doesn't have all her beauties and graces" (*Nouvelles œuvres,* 97–98). The feminizing effect of the mother-daughter allegory is suspended briefly when Le Pays implicitly equates his own relation to Voiture with that of a lowlier son to his more illustrious father: "The younger Cicero was the son of the father of Eloquence although he did not have the slightest glimmer of his father's eloquence. Indeed, Monseigneur, children do not always have all their father's virtue." Immediately, however, Le Pays reverts to the mother-daughter metaphor: "Voiture's Muse had many other daughters who still live and who are more blessed than my Muse. But it is presently only a matter of showing the glory of this illustrious mother. It is still so recent that one must not search for the titles elsewhere than in the memory of the *honnête gens*" (98). The father-son comparison seems to temper the feminizing effect of the mother-daughter allegory. And taken together, these competing metaphors seem to suggest the fantasy of a literary androgenesis (i.e., mothers begetting daughters are actually fathers begetting sons). In any event, Le Pays's juxtaposition of the two metaphors parallels Voiture's ambivalence toward both women and galant masculinity, as we will see.

11. See Magne, *Voiture et l'Hôtel de Rambouillet,* 2:29.

12. See Magne, *Voiture et l'Hôtel de Rambouillet,* 2:61, 183, 186.

13. Le Pays, *Nouvelles œuvres,* 98.

14. Génetiot notes that, thanks to his *charges,* Voiture was one of the wealthiest writers of his time and that he lived "nobly with ease" (*Poétique du loisir mondain,* 163). Génetiot also argues that seventeenth-century *mondain* society was not organized according to rigidly exclusive socioeconomic distinctions: "*Mondain* society can be conceived as a nexus that the bare criteria of sociological belonging or geographic locale are not sufficient to characterize . . . *mondain* society is the whole of individuals who recognize each other among themselves as belonging to it because of their innate mastery of the 'knowledge of society,' the art of behaving and conversing well in it" (*Poétique du loisir mondain,* 115).

15. In his correspondence with his friend Costar, Voiture expresses optimism about the possibility of being recognized as a noble through one's "virtuous" and "noble" actions. Commenting on a Spanish proverb ("Each is the son of his works"), he concludes: "That being the case, Monsieur, he who is born a commoner can be reborn as a gentleman and fill his life with light in spite of the obscurity of his origins" (*Œuvres de Voiture,* 2:150).

16. See Odette de Mourgues, "Voiture and the Question of Wit," *L'Esprit Créateur* 20, no. 4 (1980): 7–18, and Micheline Cuénin, "La Lettre éducatrice de la sensibilité: L'exemple de Voiture," *Revue d'Histoire Littéraire de la France* 78 (1978): 922–33.

17. Voiture, *Œuvres de Voiture,* 1:17–20. See also Magne, *Voiture et l'Hôtel de Rambouillet,* 1:27ff.

18. "I know that you do not always want to hear about my passions. But since you cannot be touched by them and since they are too insignificant to create a little feeling in you, there is no danger of you knowing that I have more esteem for you alone than all the rest of the world" (*Œuvres de Voiture,* 1:19).

19. Voiture, *Œuvres de Voiture*, 1:336–37.

20. On the masculine narcissism of Petrarchan topoi, see Lynn Enterline, *The Tears of Narcissus: Melancholia and Masculinity in Early Modern Writing* (Stanford, CA: Stanford University Press, 1995).

21. Letter 84 (*Œuvres de Voiture*, 1:250–52).

22. Worn at the waist or at the groin, ribbons, or *galants*, were a prominent accessory of fashionable masculine attire in the 1640s and 1650s. See Jacques Ruppert, *Le Costume* (Paris: Flammarion, 1996), 3:9, 7 vols.

23. These quarrels pitted Voiture against other men of letters in the emerging literary field of the period. On the quarrel of the *Suppositi* (which opposed Voiture and Chapelain), see Magne, *Voiture et l'Hôtel de Rambouillet*, 2:142–48; on the quarrel of the *muscadin* (between Voiture and Balzac), see Magne, *Voiture et l'Hôtel de Rambouillet*, 2:112–13; and on the quarrel of the Uranistes and the Jobelins (the debate between defenders of Voiture and Benserade), see Magne, *Voiture et l'Hôtel de Rambouillet*, 1:17–19.

24. Somaize, "Les Précieuses," 504.

25. See Chapelain, *Lettres de Jean Chapelain*, 1:295.

26. See, for instance Magne, *Voiture et l'Hôtel de Rambouillet*, 2:277, 280.

27. "La Pompe funèbre de Voiture à Monsieur Ménage," in *Œuvres de J.-Fr. Sarasin*, ed. Paul Festugière 2 vols. (1656; Paris: Champion, 1926), 2:442. See also Pinchesne (in Voiture, *Œuvres de Voiture*, 1:2) and "Le Portrait du pitoyable Voiture," in Gédéon Tallemant des Réaux, *Historiettes*, ed. Antoine Adam, 2 vols. (Paris: Pléiade, 1960), 1:488.

28. Tallemant des Réaux, *Historiettes*, 490.

29. Georges and Madeleine de Scudéry, *Artamène, ou le Grand Cyrus* (Institut de Littérature Française Moderne, Université de Neuchâtel), http://www.artamene.org/cyrus.xml?page=3567&=Afficher, http://www.artamene.org. 1 November 2008. See also Paul Pellisson, *Histoire de l'Académie Françoise*, 2 vols. (Paris: J. B. Coignard, 1743), 1:274–75, and Sarasin, "Pompe funèbre," 2:442.

30. Georges and Madeleine de Scudéry, *Artamène, ou le Grand Cyrus*, http://www.artamene.org/cyrus.xml?page=3567&=Afficher.

31. Pellisson, *Histoire de l'Académie Françoise*, 1:275.

32. Sarasin, "Pompe funèbre," 1:442.

33. Sorel, "Les Lois," 324.

34. "Hésionide is not one of those women who reads many different books. For, although she likes to read, only the works of Crisante and Valère appeal to her and give her material for reflection when she is alone, which does not happen often, since she is one of the society women who loves company the most" (Somaize, "Le Grand dictionnaire," 475–76).

35. Tallemant des Réaux, *Historiettes*, 1:489.

36. "About Voiture I will tell you further that the mistakes he makes against exactness of meaning through affectation shock me much more than those that escaped him through negligence or inattention. I say 'by affectation' because there are some so blatant it is not possible that he did not notice them" (Méré, *OC*, 1:108).

37. On the gendered connotations of this association, see Peters, "Boileau's Nerve," 31–32.

38. Méré distinguishes between two types of *justesse* in this *Discours* (*OC*, 1:96), but concentrates on the second, which Voiture falls short of, according to Méré. It is implied, but never stated explicitly, that Voiture is lacking in "good sense" and "solid reason."

39. Pierre Costar, *Defense des ouvrages de Monsieur de Voiture, A Monsieur de Balzac* (Paris: Thomas Iolly, 1654), 14.

40. Farrell, *Performing Motherhood*, 44.

41. "He captivated all different sorts of minds as if he had never thought to captivate each one of them: women, men of letters, courtiers, the most enlightened, the most mediocre, in serious matters, in leisure, whether he had to play his role in a serious and regimented conversation or whether, among friends and acquaintances, he had to let himself commit that innocent debauchery of the mind, those wise follies where well-planned discourse sometimes leaves room for the whimsy and jokes of poetry and where everything is in season except cold and severe reason" ("Discours sur les Œuvres de Monsieur Sarasin," 74).

42. Bouhours, *Les Entretiens*, 165.

43. "Since the nobility of thought," continues Eudoxe, "according to Hermogenes comes from the majesty of the things of which they are the images, as we have seen, their enticement, according to Demetrius, can come from the nature of the objects that capti- vate by themselves, such as flowers, light, beautiful days, and everything that touches the senses" (*La Manière de bien penser dans les ouvrages d'esprit*, ed. Suzanne Guellouz [Toulouse: Université de Toulouse-Le Mirail, 1988], 132).

44. Bouhours, *La Manière de bien penser*, 133.

45. Bouhours, *Les Entretiens*, 240.

46. Bouhours, *Les Entretiens*, 241.

47. In their recent critical edition of *Les Entretiens*, Bernard Beugnot and Gilles Declercq comment: "There is nothing of the sort about Achilles in Homer or literally about Rinaldo in *Jerusalem Delivered*; rather, these are critical interpretations by Bouhours" (*Les Entretiens*, 241 n. 18).

48. Bouhours, *Les Entretiens*, 125.

49. For a discussion of Bouhours's ambivalent relationship to the midcentury salons and their literary aesthetic, see Beasley, *Salons, History*, 66–76.

50. La Bruyère, *Les Caractères*, 83.

51. For a compelling reading of this *caractère*, see Farrell, *Performing Motherhood*, 29–36.

CHAPTER 4

1. For accounts of Scudéry's life and her salon, see Mongrédien, *Madeleine de Scud- éry;* Alain Niderst, *Madeleine de Scudéry, Paul Pellisson et leur monde*, Publications de l'Université de Rouen (Paris: Presses universitaires de France, 1976); Nicole Aronson, *Mademoiselle de Scudéry, ou, le voyage au pays de Tendre* (Paris: Fayard, 1986); and Kra- jewska, *Du coeur à l'esprit*.

2. Ever since the seventeenth century, readers and critics have speculated about the *à clef* portraits of persons, places, and events in Scudéry's novels. Beginning with Victor Cousin in the nineteenth century, a great deal of effort has been expended to reconstruct the "keys" in these two novels. (For recent studies in this vein, see especially Niderst, *Madeleine de Scudéry* and Jacqueline Plantié, *La mode du portrait littéraire en France [1641–1681]*, Lumière Classique [Paris: H. Champion, 1994]. On the limits of an *à clef* reading of Scudéry's works, see Mathilde Bombart, "Pour une seconde remise en cause des clés supposées des romans de Mademoiselle de Scudéry," *Littératures Classiques* 54 [2005]: 247–56.) If it is clear that Scudéry did indeed intend to make such allusions, many of which concern members of her own salon, it is also clear that they were in no way

meant to be "direct" or "realistic" portrayals. Instead, as Delphine Denis has noted, they are a "figuration" of the real wherein the social becomes an aesthetic experience and the literary is tied to—but not reduced to—an extratextual world. See especially Delphine Denis, "Les Samedis de Sapho: Figurations littéraires de la collectivité," in *Vie des salons et activités littéraires, de Marguerite de Valois à Mme de Staël*, ed. Roger Marchal (Nancy: Presses universitaires de Nancy, 2001), 107–15, and Delphine Denis, "Les Inventions de Tendre," *Intermédialités/Intermedialities*, no. 4 (2004): 45–66. This same dynamic is visible in the writings that directly concern the Samedis, particularly the *Chroniques du Samedi*, a rare chronicle of salon activities (Scudéry and Pellisson-Fontanier, *Chroniques*). This collection and other surviving texts (letters and poems) reveal that members of the Samedis viewed their interactions as a partial retreat from the concerns and obligations of the "real" outside world through the mediation of rituals based on fictional models.

3. Scudéry's work has attracted a great deal of attention from feminist critics over the past two decades. See the bibliography in Delphine Denis and Anne-Elisabeth Spica, eds., *Madeleine de Scudéry: Une femme de lettres au XVIIe siècle: Actes du Colloque international de Paris, 28–30 juin 2001* (Arras: Artois Presses Université, 2002), 321–40. English-language work on Scudéry owes much to the pathbreaking scholarship of Joan DeJean, particularly in *Tender Geographies*.

4. DeJean defines "tender geographies" of seventeenth-century women's writings as an "intricate analysis of the human heart formulated in tandem with a questioning of basic assumptions regarding women's social and legal status" (DeJean, *Tender Geographies*, 93).

5. This aspect of Scudéry's work is widely recognized. For recent critical work to explore Scudéry's emphasis on relationality, see Denis, *La Muse galante;* Delphine Denis, "L'Echange complimenteur: Un lieu commun du bien-dire," *Franco Italica* 15–16 (1999): 143–61; and Myriam Maître, "L'Amour, geste langagier: Préciosité et politesse chez Madeleine de Scudéry," *Franco Italica* (1999): 163–73.

6. This is evident in the main frame narratives and intercalated stories of *Le Grand Cyrus* and *Clélie*, where the narrative point of view adopts the perspectives of both male and female characters. Even stories that purport to concentrate on one character give almost equal billing to her or his love interest (e.g., Phaon in "Histoire de Sapho").

7. For reasons of accessibility, I use the recent paperback editions of *Artamène ou le Grand Cyrus*, ed. Claude Bourqui and Alexandre Gefen (Paris: Garnier-Flammarion, 2005) and *Clélie, histoire romaine*, ed. Delphine Denis (Paris: Folio, 2006) whenever passages I analyze are included in these excerpted editions. References are given in the text and are indicated by *Artamène-GF* for the Garnier-Flammarion edition of *Le Grand Cyrus* and *Clélie-F* for the Folio edition of *Clélie*. When quoting passages not included in the above editions, I use the Slatkine edition of *Le Grand Cyrus* (*Artamène ou le Grand Cyrus*, 10 vols. [Geneva: Slatkine Reprints, 1972]), indicated as *Artamène-S* in the text, and the Champion edition of *Clélie* (*Clélie, histoire romaine*, ed. Chantal Morlet-Chantalat, Sources Classiques, 5 vols. [Paris: Champion, 2001–5]), indicated as *Clélie-C*. References to Scudéry's conversation "De l'air galant" ("De l'Air") are given in the text and indicated as "De l'air." References to the translation of "Histoire de Sapho" by Karen Newman (*The Story of Sapho*, trans. Karen Newman [Chicago: University of Chicago Press, 2003]) are indicated as "Story." I have modified Newman's translation to conform to my use of key words throughout this study (i.e., *galant* instead of *gallant, captivate* instead of *please*, etc.). References to the *Chroniques du Samedi* are given in the text and indicated as *Chroniques*.

8. According to the narrator of the "Histoire de Sapho," among those who kept their distance from Sapho were "young men, merry and rash, who bragged that they could not read; they prided themselves on the sort of militant ignorance that gave them the audacity to censure what they knew nothing about. They had persuaded themselves that men of wit did nothing but talk of things they didn't understand" (*Story*, 21; *Artamène-GF*, 461).

9. On these antecedents and their influence on Scudéry's conception of love, see Maître, "L'Amour, geste langagier." On the importance of relationality in Scudéry's depiction of love, see Maître, "L'Amour, geste langagier," 166.

10. See Peters's brilliant reading of the *Carte de Tendre* in Peters, *Mapping Discord*, chap. 2.

11. On the figuration of Clélie's authority in the *Carte de Tendre*, see Peters, *Mapping Discord*, 111–14. In a different vein, see DeJean, *Tender Geographies*, 87–89.

12. See "Autour de la *Carte de Tendre*," in *Chroniques*, 285–330.

13. See Myriam Maître, "Sapho, reine de Tendre: Entre monarchie absolue et royauté littéraire," in *Madeleine de Scudéry: Une femme de lettres au XVIIe siècle* (Arras: Artois Presses Université, 2002), 179–93. Maître argues that the "republican" organizational model was not as prominent as the "monarchical" in Scudéry's and other salons of the period.

14. Expounding on the further benefits of "scrupulous modesty," Sapho states: "We wouldn't see women quarreling among themselves over a lover, putting one another down, selling their hearts like diamonds for mercenary reasons . . . because if galanterie is sometimes permitted, then those who practice it cannot be censured for being unable to prevent themselves from loving another more than they love themselves" (*Story*, 103; *De l'air*, 57).

15. At the beginning of *Clélie*, Aronce and Horace are each unaware of the other's love for the eponymous heroine but nonetheless "lived together with much friendship" (*Clélie-C*, 1:111). As the novel progresses, their friendship is severely strained, and yet this does not keep Aronce from repeatedly saving his rival's life, inspired by Clélie's influence. In the *Chroniques du Samedi*, Scudéry acts to defuse the rivalries between Isarn and Pellisson and between Conrart and Pellisson. See, for instance, *Chroniques*, 93–97, 114–21.

16. See Goodman, *The Republic of Letters*.

17. That one must be endowed with an innate superiority before one can be refined further is a constant throughout the discourses of early modern civility, as we saw in chapter 1. This notion also parallels conceptions of nobility, in spite of their evolution from the sixteenth to the seventeenth centuries. See Schalk, *From Valor to Pedigree*.

18. Scudéry and Pellisson-Fontanier, *Chroniques*, 135.

19. Furetière defines *sensibilité* as an "ability of the senses to receive impressions from objects" and in an example that clearly highlights its semantic connection with softness and sociable refinement: "There are some people with a nature so hard and brutish that they are without *sensibilité*" (Furetière, *Dictionnaire universel*).

20. See *Clélie-C*, 1:116–18; *Clélie-F*, 71–75.

21. The widespread assumption, especially in the past but still prevalent today, that mothers are more "caring" and sensitive to emotional needs than fathers is a case in point. On the rise of the emotionally sensitive man in modern Western cultures, see among others Elisabeth Badinter, *X Y, de l'identité masculine* (Paris: Editions O. Jacob, 1992), 212–27, 239–74.

22. This hierarchy goes from her "half-friends" and "new friends" to her "friends,"

"habitual friends," "solid friends," "intimate friends" *(amis particuliers)*, and finally her "tender friends" *(Clélie-C,* 1:177; *Clélie-F,* 89–90).

23. See especially the "Gazette de Tendre," *Chroniques,* 306–21.

24. Only a few critics have explicitly recognized this point, among them Maître, *Les Précieuses,* 588.

25. Speaking to the men in the conversation, she states: "Although that sort of tenderness is of much less interest for me . . . than the one I've just spoken about is for you, I gladly allow Aronce to teach you to understand yourselves if it's true that you don't know yourselves well enough" *(Clélie-C,* 1:119; *Clélie-F,* 76).

26. See Pelous, *Amour précieux,* 133–304.

27. See Peters, *Mapping Discord,* 96.

28. My thanks to Jeffrey Peters for pointing out this curious detail on the *Carte de Tendre.*

29. Likewise, in the *Chroniques du Samedi,* the male members of Scudéry's salon persistently ask her to inform them of their progress toward Tendre, and, in response, Scudéry remains enigmatic. See, for instance, *Chroniques,* 126–30.

30. Peters, *Mapping Discord,* 114.

31. See among others Peters, who reads the Carte as the "literal embodiment of the woman herself" *(Mapping Discord,* 109).

32. This is true for Phaon and Sapho *(Artamène-GF,* 524–27), Herminius and Valérie *(Clélie-C,* 3:96–98), and Plotine and Mutius *(Clélie-C,* 5:374–76).

33. Sapho repeatedly articulates this critique of men: "All men have in their hearts a natural propensity toward inconstancy so that, were I a thousand times more charming than I am, it would be imprudent of me to believe I might find one wholly faithful man" *(Story,* 67; *Artamène-S,* 10:451; *Artamène-F,* 525).

34. See Roger Duchêne, "Mlle de Scudéry, Reine de Tendre," in *Les Trois Scudéry: Actes du colloque du Havre,* ed. Alain Niderst (Paris: Klincksieck, 1993), 626, and James S. Munro, *Mademoiselle de Scudéry and the Carte de Tendre,* Durham Modern Languages Series (Durham, UK: University of Durham, 1986), 56, 82.

35. For instance, making a distinction among a "good husband," an "enticing lover" *(agréable amant),* and a "perfect honnête homme," Valérie displays a cold realism about the unequal balance of power between men and women *(Clélie-C,* 3:130). On the recognition of a social power dynamic that runs counter to the idealism expressed by the main characters in Scudéry's novels, see Munro, *Mademoiselle de Scudéry,* 81.

36. To be sure, this exploratory approach to gender and heterosocial relations generally is part of a broader logic. Maître discerns what she calls "a space of questioning, where judgment is suspended" in Scudéry's novels (Maître, *Les Précieuses,* 550).

37. This intercalated narrative is found in part 4, book 1 of *Le Grand Cyrus.* Four men in turn attempt to convince Martésie that they are each the most unfortunate in love: a lover who is separated from his beloved (Timocrate), one whose love is unrequited (Philoclès), another who grieves the passing of his beloved (Artibie), and finally a lover who is jealous (Léontidas). In the end, Martésie determines that Artibie is the most worthy of pity. See *Artamène-GF,* 228–432.

38. See especially Raymond Kiblansky, Erwin Panofsky, and Fritz Saxl, *Saturn and Melancholy: Studies in the History of Natural Philosophy, Religion, and Art* (London: Nelson, 1964), 217–40.

39. The association of genius with melancholy was famously articulated for the first time by Aristotle (or, most likely, a follower of his) in book 30 of the *Problems.* See Jen-

nifer Radden, ed., *The Nature of Melancholy* (Oxford: Oxford University Press, 2000), 55–60.

40. See especially Noémi Hepp, in Jean Jehasse et al., "A propos de la *Clélie:* Mélancolie et perfection féminine," in *Mélanges offerts à Georges Couton* (Lyon: Presses universitaires de Lyon, 1981), 166–67. Hepp also argues that the Princesse de Clèves likewise evinces this "feminine" melancholy.

41. Boileau-Despréaux, "Dialogue," 9.

42. Boileau cites Artamène's example to support his claim that the novels of Scudéry and those of her contemporaries promote nothing more than "love and softness *(mollesse)*" (Boileau-Despréaux, "Dialogue," 8).

43. Freud famously defines melancholy as the "unconscious loss of a love-object" (Radden, *The Nature of Melancholy*, 285).

44. Sigmund Freud, "Mourning and Melancholy," in Radden, *The Nature of Melancholy*, 285.

45. See *Clélie-C*, 3:99.

46. See *Story*, 76–90; *Artamène-S*, 10:471–501; *Artamène-F*, 541–57.

47. In the "Histoire de Sapho," see *Story*, 113–15; *Artamène-S*, 10:557–59. In the "Histoire d'Herminius et de Valérie," see *Clélie-C*, 3:120–22.

48. Freud, "Mourning and Melancholy," 293.

49. Freud, "Mourning and Melancholy," 292.

50. Herminius says that "the ladies have their victories and their triumphs, and they know how to wage war so well in peace time that . . . they deserve a lot of glory" (*Clélie-C*, 2:174; *Clélie-F*, 228).

51. On Scudéry's "feminization" of *la gloire*, see Chantal Morlet-Chantalat, *La Clélie de mademoiselle de Scudéry: De l'épopée à la gazette: Un discours féminin de la gloire* (Paris: Champion, 1994), 162–77, 307–18; and Hepp, "A la recherche."

52. In contrast to "normal" grief, Freud notes, perplexed, that melancholy does not "set up the economic condition for a phase of triumph after it has run its course or at least produce some slight indication of such a state" ("Mourning and Melancholy," 292).

53. Petrarch's famous pronouncement "Et ho in odio me stesso et amo altruit" (I hate myself and I love another) has been glossed repeatedly, from the early modern period onward. For a compelling analysis of this question, see Enterline, *The Tears of Narcissus*, 3.

54. On the disruption of the masculine subject produced by melancholy, see Juliana Schiesari, *The Gendering of Melancholia: Feminism, Psychoanalysis, and the Symbolics of Loss in Renaissance Literature* (Ithaca, NY: Cornell University Press, 1992) and Enterline, *The Tears of Narcissus*.

55. At the end of both *Le Grand Cyrus* and *Clélie*, the final unions of Artamène and Mandane and Aronce and Clélie, respectively, are described in exceedingly concise fashion, a striking contrast with the hundreds of pages devoted to the courtship of each couple up to that point.

56. See *Story*, 121; *Artamène-S*, 10:573; *Artamène-GF*, 572.

57. See *Artamène-S*, 10:582, 601.

58. On the function of pseudonymns in Scudéry's salon, see Denis, "Les Samedis" and Anne E. Duggan, *Salonnières, Furies, and Fairies: The Politics of Gender and Cultural Change in Absolutist France* (Newark: University of Delaware Press, 2005), 95–97.

59. See, for instance, the letter that Pellisson writes under the name of Linières, who is often ridiculed by members of Scudéry's salon ("Lettre d'Acante sous le nom de M. de Linières à Mlle Robineau," *Chroniques*, 192–95).

60. This is not to deny that there are several moments in the *Chroniques* when men of the Samedis express emotional torment, or something approaching it, as a result of what appears to be rivalry among themselves or conflict with Scudéry herself. See, for instance, the rivalry between Conrart and Pellisson at the beginning of the text and Conrart's efforts to paint a negative portrait of his rival for Scudéry, which results in her testy exchange with Pellisson (113–25). There is also the extraordinary admission by Pellisson of his own melancholic predisposition, which we might characterize as clinical depression today (252–54). Still, none of these moments make use of amorous melancholy per se.

61. On the material history of the *Chroniques du Samedi* and its meanings, see Alain Niderst, Delphine Denis, and Myriam Maître, "Introduction," in *Chroniques du Samedi*, 7–45.

62. See especially Luce Irigaray, ed., *Sexes et genres à travers les langues: Éléments de communication sexuée* (Paris: Editions Grasset, 1990), 397. This is but one of numerous differences that Irigaray observes between the discourse of men and women based on a series of field tests conducted by researchers in Italy, France, and several English-speaking countries.

CHAPTER 5

1. Quoted in Georges Mongrédien, *Le Grand Condé: L'homme et son œuvre* (Paris: Hachette, 1959), 199.

2. For biographies of the Grand Condé, see especially Pierre Duhamel, *Le Grand Condé ou l'orgueil* (Paris: Perrin, 1981); Mongrédien, *Le Grand Condé;* and Bernard Pujo, *Le Grand Condé* (Paris: Albin Michel, 1995).

3. See Maurice Lever, *Les Bûchers de Sodome* (Paris: Fayard, 1985), 210–17. For examples of police records concerning men observed (and often entraped) for sodomy, see Merrick and Ragan, *Homosexuality in Early Modern France*, 31–94. Far more information is available for such cases in the eighteenth than in the seventeenth century. See, for instance, Jeffrey Merrick, "Sodomitical Inclinations in Early Eighteenth-Century Paris," *Eighteenth-Century Studies* 30 (1997): 289–95, and Jeffrey Merrick, "Sodomitical Scandals and Subcultures in the 1720s," *Men and Masculinities* (1999): 373–92. According to Alfred Soman ("Pathologie historique: Le témoignage des procès de bestialité aux XVIe–XVIIe siècles," in *Actes du 107e Congrès national des Sociétés savantes: Section de philologie moderne et d'histoire jusqu'à 1610*, 2 vols. [Paris, 1984], 1:149–62), the texts in Ludovico Hernandez, *Les Procès de sodomie au XVIe, XVIIe, et XVIIIe siècles* (Paris: Bibliothèque des curieux, 1920) are not reliable; yet this conclusion is questioned by Michael Sibalis, "Homosexuality in Early Modern France," in *Queer Masculinities, 1550–1800: Siting Same-Sex Desire in the Early Modern World*, ed. Katherine O'Donnell and Michael O'Rourke (Basingstoke, UK: Palgrave Macmillan, 2006), 213. For a detailed example of mid-seventeenth-century trial documents relating to a prosecution for sodomy, see Jeffrey Merrick, "Chaussons in the Streets: Sodomy in Seventeenth-Century Paris," *Journal of the History of Sexuality* 15, no. 2 (2006): 167–203.

4. For accounts of the high-placed personages thought to have been "sodomites" in seventeenth-century France, see Marc Daniel, *Hommes du Grand Siècle: Etudes sur l'homosexualité sous les règnes de Louis XIII et de Louis XIV* (Paris: Arcadie, 1957); Lever, *Les Bûchers;* Didier Godard, *Le Goût de Monsieur: L'homosexualité masculine au XVIIe siècle* (Montblanc: H & O, 2002); and especially Robert Oresko, "Homosexuality and the

Court Elites of Early Modern France: Some Problems, Some Suggestions, and an Example," in *The Pursuit of Sodomy: Male Homosexuality in Renaissance and Enlightenment Europe*, ed. Kent Gerard and Gert Hekma (New York: Harrington Park Press, 1989), 105–28.

5. I wish to thank Michèle Longino for suggesting this turn of phrase to me.

6. The Grand Condé seems to have escaped this risk, although his case is truly exceptional. Even Philippe d'Orléans occasionally provoked the ire of his brother, Louis XIV, because of his sexual reputation. And at least some observers at court, notably Saint-Simon, were puzzled by the king's indulgence of his brother's activities. See Lever, *Les Bûchers*, 145–49.

7. Foucault, *The History of Sexuality*, 101. In the early-modern period, the term *sodomy* encompassed such acts as anal intercourse (heterosexual and homosexual), bestiality, cunilingus, incest, oral sex, and masturbation. On the polymorphous reference of "sodomy," see Alan Bray, *Homosexuality in Renaissance England* (London: Gay Men's Press, 1982) and Cameron McFarlane, *The Sodomite in Fiction and Satire, 1660–1750*, Between Men—Between Women (New York: Columbia University Press, 1997). While this broad usage continued to be prevalent in seventeenth-century France, my own impression (based on my own research) is that the terms *sodomie* and *sodomite* were increasingly used to designate male homosexual acts and actors.

8. Lever even casts doubt on the effectiveness of the early seventeenth-century crackdown on sexuality: "Thus, in spite of the reassertion of control by the Counter-Reformation . . . high nobles, the king himself displayed their illicit love affairs publicly, or very nearly so" (*Les Bûchers*, 142).

9. Foucault, *The History of Sexuality* (original French version, 1976).

10. Foucault, *History of Madness*. The original French edition of this work was published in 1961.

11. Foucault, *History of Madness*, 88.

12. Foucault, *History of Madness*, 88. On the chronology of "homosexuality" in Foucault's work, see Didier Eribon, *Insult and the Making of the Gay Self*, trans. Michael Lucey (Durham, NC: Duke University Press, 2004), 267–73.

13. For a useful overview of the debate about this question, see Katherine Crawford, *European Sexualities, 1400–1800* (Cambridge: Cambridge University Press, 2007), 200–206.

14. Discussing medical theories of the early modern period, Laqueur writes that "the male body, indeed, seemed equally capable of responding erotically to the sight of women as to attractive young men" (*Making Sex*, 52). By contrast, Sibalis concludes that "there is little hard evidence that the sexual interest in both women and boys manifested by some nobles and intellectuals in the sixteenth and seventeenth centuries was anything more than a cultural trope" ("Homosexuality in Early Modern France," 223). Although it is unclear precisely what Sibalis means by "cultural trope," evidence that I present in this chapter suggests that what we would now call bisexual attractions were more than motifs inherited from literary or other cultural antecedents and that these "tropes" corresponded to what is presented as the desires experienced by at least some individuals in this period.

15. For an overview of historical work on early modern French male same-sex sexuality, see Sibalis, "Homosexuality in Early Modern France."

16. Jonathan Goldberg, *Sodometries: Renaissance Texts, Modern Sexualities* (Stanford, CA: Stanford University Press, 1992), 20.

17. Foucault, *History of Madness*, 88.

18. See especially Guy Poirier, *L'Homosexualité dans l'imaginaire de la Renaissance*, Confluences-Champion, 7 (Paris: Honoré Champion, 1996), 107–61; Donald Stone, "The Sexual Outlaw in France, 1602," *Journal of the History of Sexuality* 2, no. 4 (1992): 597–608; David Teasley, "The Charge of Sodomy as a Political Weapon in Early Modern France: The Case of Henry III in Catholic League Polemic, 1585–1589," *Maryland Historian* 18 (1987): 17–30; Joseph Cady, "The 'Masculine Love' of the 'Princes of Sodom': 'Practicing the Art of Ganymede' at Henri III's Court: The Homosexuality of Henri III and His *Mignons* in Pierre de L'Estoile's *Mémoires-Journaux*," in *Desire and Discipline: Sex and Sexuality in the Premodern West*, ed. Jacqueline Murray and Konrad Eisenbichler (Toronto: University of Toronto Press, 1996), 123–54; Zorach, "The Matter of Italy"; Crawford, "Love, Sodomy, and Scandal"; Reeser, *Moderating Masculinity*, 235–65.

19. See Merrick, "The Cardinal and the Queen" and Seifert, "Eroticizing the Fronde."

20. On the early modern understanding of sodomy as both cosmic and cultural disorder, see Bray, *Homosexuality* and McFarlane, *The Sodomite*.

21. These included heterosexual anal intercourse, pederasty, bestiality, clerical concubine-keeping, abuse of a young girl by an adult man, sexual intercourse between Christians and Jews, masturbation, coitus interruptus, among other things. This multireferentiality notwithstanding, sodomy increasingly denoted male-male sex acts throughout the seventeenth and, especially, eighteenth centuries. See McFarlane, *The Sodomite*, 2–3.

22. In an earlier version of this study, I indicated that there were something on the order of seventy songs and poems about sodomy in the *Chansonnier Maurepas*. Thanks to Nicholas Hammond, though, I have since discovered that there are many more, perhaps as many as five hundred. From my more recent forays into this newly rediscovered trove I believe that my analysis is still valid.

23. Of course, it is entirely possible that just as many satirical songs and poems circulated before 1660. But it is impossible to know if the greater number of satires in the *Chansonnier Maurepas* is due to a quantitative increase in production or to more systematic and thorough preservation.

24. I use the term "sodomite" in quotation marks so as to bracket the often undecidable question as to whether the men satirized in the songs and poems I study could indeed be categorized as such.

25. The songs and poems compiled by Clairambault are known as the *Chansonnier Clairambault* and are found in the Département des Manuscrits at the Bibliothèque nationale de France.

26. Annette Keilhauer, *Das französische Chanson im späten Ancien Régime: Strukturen, Verbreitungswege und gesellschaftliche Praxis einer populären Literaturform*, Musikwissenschaftliche Publikationen, 10 (New York: Georg Olms Verlag, 1998), 162.

27. See Emile Raunié, "Préface," in *Chansonnier historique du XVIIIe siècle*, ed. Emile Raunié, 10 vols. (Paris: A. Quantin, 1879), xxxiv–xl.

28. See Paul d'Estrée, "Les Origines du Chansonnier de Maurepas," *Revue d'Histoire Littéraire de la France* (1896): 334 and Keilhauer, *Das französische Chanson*, 162.

29. I have reproduced Clairambault's annotations for all of the quotes given here and indicated them as "note in manuscript."

30. This is precisely the type of response that Robert Darnton concludes was possible among elite readers during the ancien régime (*The Forbidden Best-Sellers of Pre-Revolutionary France* [New York: W. W. Norton, 1995], 193).

31. On this "crisis," albeit from different perspectives, see Peter Burke, *The Fabrication of Louis XIV* (New Haven: Yale University Press, 1992), 125–33; Darnton, *Forbidden Best-Sellers*, 181–216; Kathryn Hoffmann, *Society of Pleasures: Interdisciplinary Readings in Pleasure and Power during the Reign of Louis XIV* (New York: St. Martin's Press, 1997), 149–58.

32. On this "crisis of representations," see Burke, *Fabrication*, 125–33.

33. Jean-Frédéric Phélypeaux comte de Maurepas, comp., *Recueil dit de Maurepas, pièces libres, chansons, épigrammes, et autres vers satiriques sur divers personnages des siècles de Louis XIV et Louis XV*, 6 vols. (Leyde: Np, 1865), 5:37–38. Those named are Biran, Grammont, La Ferté, Mailly, Mimur, Roucis, and Tilladet. On the "Confraternity" disbanded in 1682, see Merrick and Ragan, *Homosexuality in Early Modern France*, 118–24. The "Confraternity" was the subject of the first part of *La France devenue italienne*, a satirical novel clandestinely published in 1686.

34. "Chansonnier Maurepas," *Recueil de chansons, vaudevilles, sonnets, eprigrammes, eptiaphes, et autres vers Satiriques & Historiques, avec des remarques curieuses*, 12617, 12618, 12619, 12620, 12623, 12643, 12688, Fonds français (Bibliothèque nationale de France, Département des Manuscrits), MS fr. 12643, fol. 197.

35. Jacques Chausson was burned at the stake for sodomy in 1661; Achilles de Harlay was first president of the Parlement de Paris; Auguste Servien was an abbot; Charles-Belgique-Hollande de la Trimouille was a member of a well-known family of the high nobility; Henri de Turenne and Louis-Joseph de Vendôme were famous military officers; and Louis de Vermandois, the illegitimate son of Louis XIV, was implicated in the "Confraternity" scandal of 1682.

36. "He captured this city in 1697" (note in manuscript).

37. Maurepas, *Recueil dit de Maurepas*, 5:180.

38. "This is addressed to the crowd that saw the fireworks" (note in manuscript).

39. "Jean-Baptiste Lully etc." (note in manuscript).

40. "People paid a half *louis d'or* per place to see the fireworks" (note in manuscript).

41. "Chausson Bourgeois of Paris, was burned at the stake at the Place de la Grève for sodomy in 16 . . ." (note in manuscript).

42. "This is a joke, the trial was not continuing, but since Lully was a notorious sodomite, the author finds it humorous to say so in order to set up the joke that follows" (note in manuscript).

43. "The author means that Lully will soon be burned at the Place de la Grève as one of Chausson's accomplices and that the fire would please the public more than it did for the capture of Franche-Comté" (note in manuscript).

44. "Chansonnier Maurepas," MS fr. 12619, fol. 101.

45. Maurepas, *Recueil dit de Maurepas*, 4:318.

46. Maurepas, *Recueil dit de Maurepas*, 1:131.

47. "Burned at the stake at the Place de la Grève for sodomy in the year 16 . . ." (note in manuscript.

48. "François de Comminges, dubbed Knight of the Saint-Esprit in 1661" (note in manuscript).

49. Maurepas, *Recueil dit de Maurepas*, 4:245.

50. "Lully, musician" (note in manuscript). This note is in error. Jean Galbert de Campistron (1656–1723) was a playwright and poet who had collaborated with Lully and, before that, served as secretary to Vendôme.

51. Maurepas, *Recueil dit de Maurepas*, 5:52.

52. "Nose" *(nez)* is often a euphemism for penis in the seventeenth century. Although the nineteenth-century Leyden edition of the *Chansonnier Maurepas* gives only "nez" here, the original manuscript at the BNF provides the variant "vit" ("Chansonnier Maurepas," MS fr. 12619, fol. 395).

53. Maurepas, *Recueil dit de Maurepas,* 1:272. "From this song we can ascertain the inclinations of this good lord, who is very well built, with the best countenance in the world, and an ugly face, but moreover without the slightest intelligence" (note in manuscript).

54. For a discussion of the transgressive connotations attached to such a role, see Michel Rey, "1700–1750, Les Sodomites créent un mode de vie," *Cahiers Gai-Kitsch-Camp* (1994): xix–xx.

55. I borrow this definition of the "abject" from Julia Kristeva, *Pouvoirs de l'horreur* (Paris: Editions du Seuil, 1980).

56. Paul Scarron, *Poésies diverses,* ed. Maurice Cauchie, 2 vols. (Paris: Marcel Didier, 1960), 2:32.

57. "Chansonnier Maurepas," MS fr. 12620, fol. 89.

58. Maurepas, *Recueil dit de Maurepas,* 2:229.

59. Peter Stallybrass and Allon White, *The Politics and Poetics of Transgression* (Ithaca, NY: Cornell University Press, 1986), 4–5. I am indebted here to McFarlane's treatment of Stallybrass and White (see especially McFarlane, *The Sodomite,* 108, 121–22).

60. Although several figures identified as "sodomites" are attacked in other satires for reasons other than sodomy (e.g., Harlay, Vendôme, and Vermandois), Philippe d'Orléans and Lully, the most popular targets, are exclusively satirized for sodomy.

61. See especially Foucault, *History of Madness,* 88.

62. See in Maurice Lever's account the contrast between his treatment of the first half of the century (*Les Bûchers,* 99–142) and the second half (*Les Bûchers,* 189–237).

63. There are, of course, numerous examples of repression of sodomy during the first half of the century, as Lever himself recounts (see *Les Bûchers,* 99–142). One of the most famous of these is the trial of Théophile de Viau, which I discuss later in this chapter.

64. Jean Mainil, *Dans les règles du plaisir: Théorie de la différence dans le discours obscène, romanesque et médical de l'Ancien Régime* (Paris: Editions Kimé, 1996), 38.

65. See especially Trumbach, *Heterosexuality and the Third Gender,* 9. See also Randolph Trumbach, "Gender and the Homosexual Role in Modern Western Culture: The 18th and the 19th Centuries Compared," in *Homosexuality, Which Homosexuality?* ed. Dennis Altman et al. (London: GMP Publishers, 1989), 149–69 and Randolph Trumbach, "Sex, Gender, and Sexual Identity in Modern Culture: Male Sodomy and Female Prostitution in Enlightenment England," in *Forbidden History: The State, Society, and the Regulation of Sexuality in Modern Europe,* ed. John C. Flout (Chicago: University of Chicago Press, 1992), 89–106.

66. "Chansonnier Maurepas," MS fr. 12643, fol. 222. See also Maurepas, *Recueil dit de Maurepas,* 5:74–75. This poem has been attributed to Denis de Saint-Pavin.

67. "Chansonnier Maurepas," MS fr. 12688, fol. 258.

68. Maurepas, *Recueil dit de Maurepas,* 5:75.

69. "Chansonnier Maurepas," MS fr. 12619, fol. 219. "That is to say the love of women or that of boys" (note in manuscript).

70. Maurepas, *Recueil dit de Maurepas,* 1:256.

71. Lully's Italian origins were presumed to give him just such a predisposition.

Throughout the early modern period, French satirists regularly portrayed sodomy as being far more widespread in Italy than in France. It is often referred to as the *vice italien* or *mœurs italiennes*. On the ramifications of this association in the sixteenth century, see Zorach, "The Matter of Italy."

72. Maurepas, *Recueil dit de Maurepas*, 5:37–39.

73. "She was one of the ugliest, most impertinent, and oldest women in the world who was nonetheless conceited, debauched, and [who] prostituted her daughter" (note in manuscript).

74. "Brunet was a Page of the King's Music, with whom Lully was in love and who was sometimes the active partner and sometimes the passive partner with him" (note in manuscript).

75. Maurepas, *Recueil dit de Maurepas*, 2:28–29.

76. McFarlane makes a similar observation about satirical representations of sodomy in early modern England. See McFarlane, *The Sodomite*, 68.

77. These "sodomites" might also provide a useful means for defining future research into the history and representations of sodomy and the sodomite in the France of Louis XIV. For instance, even a cursory glance at the satires in the *Chansonnier Maurepas* suggests that Randolph Trumbach's justifiably seminal account of the sodomite in late seventeenth-century and early eighteenth-century England does not completely apply to the sodomite in France of the same period. If, according to Trumbach, the seventeenth-century English sodomite was thought to be attracted to both women and boys, in France he could desire women and boys, women and men, or exclusively boys and/or men. While the English sodomite changed from being a rake in the seventeenth century to being an effeminate molly in the early eighteenth century (again, according to Trumbach), the French sodomite of these same periods came in many different guises—rake, effeminate man, warrior, among others—and, arguably, did not transform from one type into another. Finally, Trumbach's argument that the late seventeenth- and early eighteenth-century English sodomite was used to distinguish between men and women at a time when this difference was increasingly blurred is very useful for understanding the function of the French sodomite, but not for the same reasons. Whereas in England the rise of the "egalitarian family" would seem to have been the culprit, in France it was perhaps much more the widely acclaimed, but no less angst-provoking cultural and civilizing authority of women.

78. Eribon, *Insult*, 72.

79. On the notion of insult as citation, see Judith Butler, *Excitable Speech: A Politics of the Performative* (New York: Routledge, 1997).

80. Butler, *Excitable Speech*, 79.

81. Furetière, *Dictionnaire universel*.

82. For instance, in a satire directed at an ambitious prelate, Maynard contrasts the public demeanor of the would-be cardinal with the mockery he endures in the *cabinet:*

On le sifle au cabinet;
et pourtant ce galand homme
pretend au premier bonnet
qui nous doit venir de Rome

[He is booed in the cabinet; / and yet this galant man / claims the first Cardinal's cap / that Rome will give us (*Poésies de François Maynard: Recueil de 1646 et choix de divers autres recueils,* ed. F. Gohin [Paris: Garnier Frères, 1927], 126; emphasis added).

83. Seventeenth-century authors often distinguish between the appropriate public and private expression of feelings. What was *bienséant* in the cabinet was not necessarily so in public, as d'Aubignac explains in reference to dramaturgical practice: "If the scene represented a military encampment, it would not be plausible for a queen to come out of her tent in order to lament her fate to the gods and to her confidant alone. These lamentations should be made in the cabinet. It is not that one cannot represent in certain places what usually doesn't happen there; but a color taken from the truth of action must be found in order to put actors in these places where afterward one can adroitly make them say and do anything one wants" (*La Pratique du théâtre. Nouvelle édition avec des corrections et des additions inédites de l'auteur, une préface et des notes,* ed. Pierre Martino [Alger: Jules Carbonel; Paris: Edouard Champion, 1927], 274) .

84. Furetière, *Dictionnaire universel.*

85. The early modern equivalent of the contemporary dyad public vs. private is public vs. particular *(particulier).* See especially, Hélène Merlin, *Public et littérature en France au XVIIe siècle* (Paris: Les Belles Lettres, 1994); Philippe Ariès and Georges Duby, gen. eds., Roger Chartier, ed., *A History of Private Life: Passions of the Renaissance,* trans. Arthur Goldhammer (Cambridge: Harvard University Press, 1989); and the very useful discussion in Beasley, *Revising Memory,* 26–31. Although *particulier* covers part of the semantic field encompassed by the modern *private,* it has other meanings as well. In addition to modern definitions (of or pertaining to a species or individual; that which is uncommon, apart, separated; a specific quality), Furetière's entry for *particulier* includes the meanings "private *(privé),* as opposed to [state] powers" and "familiar, secret."

86. To illustrate the first metaphorical meaning, for instance, Furetière provides the following sentence: "This courtier knows all the secrets of the cabinet."

87. As Schehr and Fisher point out, the metaphor of the closet has not been nearly as influential in contemporary France where homosexuality has often been constructed as a "private nonquestion" and gay liberation has been framed in decidedly less optimistic terms than in North America ("Introduction," in *Articulations of Difference: Gender Studies and Writing in French,* ed. Dominique D. Fisher and Lawrence R. Schehr [Stanford, CA: Stanford University Press, 1997], 3–4).

88. In a very suggestive study, Stewart highlights the function of secrecy as well as political and interpersonal transaction in the closet of early modern England. Although he does not argue for ambiguity per se (as I do here), he does show that the closet draws attention to secrets and relationships, and particularly secretive relationships. See Alan Stewart, "The Early Modern Closet Discovered," *Representations* 50 (Spring 1995): 76–100.

89. For an example of the tendency to accentuate tolerance, see Godard, *Le Goût de Monsieur;* for work that stresses repression see Bray, *Homosexuality* and Lever, *Les Bûchers.*

90. Godard *(Le Goût de Monsieur)* gives a far more optimistic assessement of the openness and tolerance of sodomitical reputations and behavior than does Lever *(Les Bûchers).* Godard writes that "shame, secrecy, dissimulation, clandestinity, which will be essential components of the homosexual condition in the nineteenth and twentieth centuries, are not only absent from these behaviors, but the entourage of those concerned do not even recognize that there could be grounds for remaining silent about them" (*Le Goût*

de Monsieur, 216). While it is true that those close to "sodomites" do not always refrain from mentioning their reputations, it is an exaggeration to claim that shame, secrecy, dissimulation, and clandestinity did not surround sodomy in seventeenth-century France, as my discussion of Boisrobert will demonstrate.

91. The most extensive biography of Boisrobert is that of Emile Magne, *Le Plaisant abbé de Boisrobert, fondateur de l'Académie française, 1592–1662. Documents inédits* (Paris: Mercure de France, 1909). See also Carcopino, *Boisrobert* and the excellent commentary by Maurice Cauchie in François Le Métel de Boisrobert, *Epistres en vers*, ed. Maurice Cauchie, Société des Textes Français Modernes, 2 vols. (Paris: Hachette, 1921–27). On Boisrobert's sodomitical reputation, see Dr. N. Praetorius, pseud. for Eugène Wilhelm, "Der homosexuelle Abbé Boisrobert, der Gründer des 'Académie française,'" *Zeitschrift Für Sexualwissenschaft* 9 (1922): 4–7, 33–42, and Seifert, "The Male Writer."

92. Boisrobert is not the only figure to whom Tallemant attributes sodomitical inclinations or practices. See for instance the *historiettes* devoted to Andelot, Bellegarde, César de Vendôme, Condé, Guiche, and Yvetot. However, Tallemant devotes much more attention to Boisrobert's reputation than to any of these others.

93. Charles de Saint-Evremond, "Comédie des Académistes," in *La "Comédie des Académistes" di Saint-Evremond e il contrastato esordio dell'Accademia Francese nella satira letteraria del tempo*, ed. Paolo Carile (Milan: Instituto Editoriale Cisalpino, 1969), 172.

94. "La Boscorobertine, ou Lettre de Florimond à la Belle Iris sur l'abbé ridicule," in Magne, *Le Plaisant abbé de Boisrobert*, 438.

95. Tallemant des Réaux, *Historiettes*, 1:413.

96. It is telling that Godard never mentions these two denunciations in his discussion of Boisrobert, about whom he concludes that "no one is ever scandalized; the witnesses are as relaxed as the hero himself" (*Le Goût de Monsieur*, 69).

97. On this banishment from Paris (23 January 1641–16 November 1642), see Magne, *Le Plaisant abbé de Boisrobert*, 270–74.

98. On this affair, see Magne, *Le Plaisant abbé de Boisrobert*, 319–22.

99. Gilles Ménage, *Le Parnasse alarmé* (Paris: n.p., 1649), 7.

100. François Le Métel de Boisrobert, *Response au Parnasse alarmé par l'Académie Françoise* (Paris: n.p., 1649), n.p.

101. Tallemant des Réaux, *Historiettes*, 2:322.

102. See Sedgwick's illuminating discussion of this link in *Epistemology of the Closet* (Berkeley and Los Angeles: University of California Press, 1990), 73–74.

103. DeJean contends that the trial of Théophile de Viau (1623–25) imposed an official distinction between heterosexuality and homosexuality and made the representation of homoeroticism in print taboo (*The Reinvention of Obscenity: Sex, Lies, and Tabloids in Early Modern France* [Chicago: University of Chicago Press, 2002], 46). Boirobert's reaction to Ménage's allusion in *Le Parnasse alarmé* would seem to confirm DeJean's conclusion. Still, homoerotic representations continued to circulate in manuscript form throughout the seventeenth century, as I have shown in the first section of this chapter.

104. For instance, see Boisrobert, *Epistres en vers*, 2:14.

105. Foucault, *The History of Sexuality*, 43.

106. For an incisive overview of the tensions between "differentist" and "continuist" approaches to the study of early modern same-sex sexuality (and a vigorous defense of the "continuist" position), see David M. Robinson, *Closeted Writing and Lesbian and Gay*

Literature: Classical, Early Modern, Eighteenth-Century (Burlington, VT: Ashgate, 2006), vii–xv, 3–17, 251–58.

107. Théophile formulates this famous imperative in his first-person narrative "Première journée," in *Libertins du XVIIe siècle*, ed. Jacques Prévot, Bibliothèque de la Pléiade (Paris: Gallimard, 1998), 7. For an exhaustive overview of the reception of Théophile's oeuvre, see Guido Saba, *Fortunes et infortunes de Théophile de Viau: Histoire de la critique suivie d'une bibliographie* (Paris: Klincksieck, 1997). For a general introduction to Théophile's work, see Guido Saba, *Théophile de Viau: Un poète rebelle*, Ecrivains (Paris: Presses universitaires de France, 1999).

108. See Lever, *Les Bûchers*, 108–18; Godard, *Le Goût de Monsieur*, 40–59; and especially DeJean, *Reinvention of Obscenity*, 29–55.

109. To date, critics have mostly skirted around the question of Théophile's representation of a nonnormative sexual persona in spite of the acknowledgment of homoeroticism in a few of his poems and the allegations of sodomy made by prosecutors during his trial. The two most authoritative accounts of Théophile's life and trial (Frédéric Lachèvre, *Le Libertinage devant le Parlement de Paris. Le procès du poète Théophile de Viau [11 juillet 1623–1er septembre 1625]* [Paris: H. Champion, 1909] and Antoine Adam, *Théophile de Viau et la libre pensée française en 1620* [Geneva: Slatkine, 1966]) acknowledge these accusations but either discount them (Lachèvre) or downplay them (Adam). (I return to the treatment of sodomy in Lachèvre's and Adam's work later.) DeJean's illuminating work on Théophile's trial ("Une Autobiographie en procès: L'affaire Théophile de Viau," *Poétique*, no. 48 [1981]: 431–48 and *Reinvention of Obscenity*, 29–55) does not have as its goal to examine the sexual "selves" portrayed in the poet's work. Lever and Godard offer brief biographical accounts of Théophile's friendship with Jacques Vallée Des Barreaux but do not consider Théophile's writings. Leonard Hinds explores the rhetorical strategy of Théophile during his trial, but like DeJean does not set out to analyze the poet's representation of a sexual persona per se. I wish to acknowledge my debt to these scholars, each of whom, in a different way, has provided crucial insights for my own reflection on Théophile.

110. The immediate instigation for Théophile's trial was the allegation that he had participated in the publication of the *Parnasse des poètes satyriques* (1622), which included texts considered to be "impieties and blasphemies" (Lachèvre, *Le Libertinage*, 1:132). In the course of the trial, the prosecution actually spent less time on the texts from the *Parnasse* attributed to Théophile than on other matters.

111. Prosecutors interrogated Théophile on (what were perceived to be) Epicurean tendencies in his writings and concentrated specifically on his paraphrase of Plato's *Phaedo*, excerpts from his play *Pyrame et Thisbé*, his idiosyncratic first-person narrative *Première journée*, and selected verse. Two poems in particular attracted the attention of the prosecutors: the chanson "Approche, approche ma dryade!" with the refrain "Et tu me bransleras la pique" (Claire Gaudiani, *The Cabaret Poetry of Théophile de Viau: Texts and Traditions* [Tübingen: Narr, 1981], 88–90) and his so-called sodomite sonnet ("Philis, tout est . . . tu, je meurs de la vérole") (*Œuvres poétiques*, ed. Guido Saba, Classiques Garnier [Paris: Bordas, 1990], 358). Théophile repeatedly denied authorship of these poems and never acknowledged the "libertine" verse attributed to him during his lifetime (or subsequently). On the attribution of these poems, see Lachèvre, *Le Libertinage* and Gaudiani, *The Cabaret Poetry*.

112. *Parnasse des poètes satyriques*, 2. If, as DeJean has astutely observed, this "vow" does not specify the gender of the poet's partner (*Reinvention of Obscenity*, 47–48), at least

some readers at the time assumed that it referred to male same-sex sodomy. In his deposition for Théophile's trial, Louis Sageot declared that "he had heard people attribute to the said Théophile a sonnet in which, complaining of syphilis that he had had, he vowed to God only to have carnal knowledge of boys, but did not remember who had told him that" (Lachèvre, *Le Libertinage*, 1:255). That Sageot's knowledge of the sonnet is secondhand indicates that the "vow" in the final line of sonnet was understood to refer to male same-sex sodomy, at least in some circles (Sageot had ties to Garasse and, indirectly, to the prosecution).

113. Lachèvre, *Le Libertinage*, 1:501 (27 August 1625). In response, Théophile contested the basis for the question: "Responded 'yes' and that it was concerning a woman, and does not know for whom he wrote it" (Lachèvre, *Le Libertinage*, 1:501).

114. For accounts of Théophile's trial, see Lachèvre, *Le Libertinage* and Adam, *Théophile de Viau*. See also the engaging studies by DeJean ("Une Autobiographie en procès"; *Reinvention of Obscenity*, 29–55) and Hinds, "'Honni soit qui mal y pense.'"

115. DeJean, "Une Autobiographie en procès," 431.

116. DeJean, *Reinvention of Obscenity*.

117. Christian Jouhaud, *Les Pouvoirs de la littérature: Histoire d'un paradoxe* (Paris: Gallimard, 2000), 67.

118. Jouhaud, *Les Pouvoirs de la littérature*, 44–46. Throughout his careeer as a writer and until the end of his life, Théophile was connected with some of the highest-placed nobles of his day. Much of his poetry was composed while in the service of either the duc de Candale or the duc de Montmorency, and his panegyrical verse attests that his pen was pressed into the service of these and other nobles. Jouhaud shows that Guez de Balzac resisted the constraints that came with being an "écrivain courtisan" and even accused Théophile of bearing reponsibility for his arrest and imprisonment (43–45). Jouhaud also argues that Balzac was one of many seventeenth-century writers who professed submission to the political powers of their time in order to carve out an autonomous space for literary production.

119. In addition to the texts I will be discussing here and the "sodomite sonnet," at least two of Théophile's "libertine" (or "cabaret") poems contain homoerotic elements: "A un marquis" (Gaudiani, *The Cabaret Poetry*, 63) and "Au marquis de Boukinquan" (Gaudiani, *The Cabaret Poetry*, 103–4). In addition, several of Théophile's poems ostensibly addressed to women were originally written for men. See Adam, *Théophile de Viau*, 99. Furthermore, in a number of his poems, the gender of the lovers is ambiguous (Claire Gaudiani, "The Androgynous Vision in the Love Poetry of Théophile de Viau," *Papers on French Seventeenth Century Literature* 11 [1979]: 132). In spite of the predominance of heterosexual desire in both his "libertine" and his conventional love poetry, we should recall that same-sex and different sex desires were not assumed to be incompatible, as I have already demonstrated.

120. DeJean, *Reinvention of Obscenity*, 46.

121. Halperin, *How to Do*, 41.

122. Eribon, *Insult*, 100.

123. *Les Œuvres poétiques du sieur Théophile* (1621) and *Œuvres du sieur Théophile, seconde partie* (1623).

124. DeJean, "Une Autobiographie en procès," 436. In his attack, Garasse notes the irony of the name *Théophile* (Greek for "lover of God") given that the poet is quite the opposite, in his opinion. He also compares the poet to two historical "Théophiles" from Constantinople whose attempts to seize power were narrowly averted. As Merlin notes,

Garasse's use of the name *Théophile* is antonomastic; it equates the name with a quality (Hélène Merlin, "Théophile de Viau: Moi libertin, moi abandonné," in *La Liberté de pensée: Hommage à Maurice Laugaa*, Licorne, 61 [Poitiers: UFR Langues Littératures, 2002], 125). See also DeJean, "Une Autobiographie en procès," 436–37.

125. Quoted in Merlin, "Théophile de Viau," 124.

126. Viau, *Œuvres poétiques*, 7.

127. Théophile de Viau, *Œuvres complètes*, ed. Guido Saba, 4 vols., Poeti e prosatori francesi (Paris; Roma: Libr. A. G. Nizet; Edizioni dell'Ateneo, 1978–87), 4:46.

128. Merlin, "Théophile de Viau," 135. Similarly, DeJean states that "the free-thinker wants to be attacked for exhibiting his status as a victim: in other words, it is the realization of Théophile's dream to find himself *in carcere*" ("Une Autobiographie en procès," 446).

129. Hinds, "'Honni soit qui mal y pense,'" 437.

130. Lachèvre, *Le Libertinage*, 1:255–56.

131. Lachèvre, *Le Libertinage*, 1:466.

132. See Lachèvre, *Le Libertinage*, 1:481–82.

133. Lachèvre, *Le Libertinage*, 1:466 In his "Apologie au roi" (1625), Théophile recounts this "confrontation" in some detail. He explains what Sageot told about his friendship with the priest Voisin, one of Théophile's chief accusers, and claims that Sageot's deposition had been manipulated by the priest (Prévot, *Libertins*, 125): "[Sageot] did not deny that he had been a disciple of Father Voisin in his younger years, confessed that from their first meeting they had maintained a very close friendship, and a confidence that they have never broken off, that they had communicated with each other about their accusations against me, and that Father Voisin had urged him to testify." As in the court record, Théophile contends that he had compromising knowledge about Sageot, which he used in his rebuttal: "The obligation to criticize him lead me to declare some of his vices, which made him cry on cross-examination . . . I modestly told some of the secrets of his life, entirely capable of weakening his testimony" (125). It is not difficult to deduce that Théophile is insinuating a sodomitical relationship between Voisin and Sageot based on the descriptions here (note the reference to a "very close friendship" [*amitié très étroite*] and the word "vices" [*infamies*] and especially the subsequent banishment of Voisin by Louis XIII on suspicions of sodomy [Lachèvre, *Le Libertinage*, 1:496, 506, 521–24]).

134. "La Plainte de Théophile à son ami Tircis," "Theophilus in carcere," and "Apologie de Théophile" are three of the thirteen texts written during the poet's imprisonment. Each was published first separately and then together in the *Recueil de toutes les pièces faites par Theophile, depuis sa prise jusques à present* (1625).

135. The initial publication of this poem late in 1623, without Théophile's knowledge or consent, was likely the version read by Garasse for his *Apologie du Père F. Garassus* (January 1624). Théophile's friends published the poem in a new edition of the *Nouveau recueil de diverses poésies du sieur Théophile la plus part faites durant son Exil* (1624), but their version omits a critical passage (see below). The manuscript version was the object of court proceedings on 16 June 1624. A third version of the poem was published in the 1625 *Recueil de toutes les pièces faites par Théophile, depuis sa prise jusques à présent*, a collection authorized by Théophile. See Mario Roques, "Autour du procès de Théophile: Histoire d'une variante," in *Mélanges d'histoire littéraire de la Renaissance offerts à Henri Chamard* (Paris: Nizet, 1951), 285–93.

136. Scholars do not agree about the identity of "Tircis." Lachèvre contends that he is Jacques Vallée Des Barreaux (Lachèvre, *Le Libertinage*, 191). Adam disagrees and sug-

gests he is Théophile's past patron, the duc de Candale (Adam, *Théophile de Viau*, 368). Bavarel-Croissant notes difficulties with the hypotheses of both Lachèvre and Adam (Marie-Françoise Baverel-Croissant and Jacques Vallée Des Barreaux, *La Vie et les œuvres complètes de Jacques Vallée Des Barreaux [1599–1673]*, Libre Pensée et Littérature Clandestine [Paris: Honoré Champion, 2001], 26–31).

137. The 1625 version of the poem includes "Punissant" here. This, however, is illogical, as numerous critics have noted. In the "Apologie de Théophile," the poet quotes "En souffrant" (Prévot, *Libertins*, 68). Georges de Scudéry's 1632 edition of Théophile's works, likely based on a manuscript, substitutes "Permettant" (Roques, "Autour du procès," 291–92).

138. Prévot, *Libertins*, 29.

139. Adam, *Théophile de Viau*, 378 n. 1.

140. Théophile de Viau, "Plainte de Théophile à un sien amy. Pendant son absence" (n.p., 1623), 7.

141. Quoted in Roques, "Autour du procès," 286–87.

142. See Adam, *Théophile de Viau*, 378 n. 1, and Viau, *Œuvres complètes*, 4:10–11 n. 80.

143. Roques, "Autour du procès," 287.

144. "Response de Tircis à la plainte de Théophile prisonnier" (Paris: n.p., 1623) Lachèvre assumes that the author of this pamphlet is Des Barreaux (*Le Libertinage*, 1:222–26). Adam gives convincing arguments to the contrary (*Théophile de Viau*, 368–71).

145. Viau, "Plainte de Théophile," 12.

146. The author writes: "You injustly accuse Rome of *permitting* it" (emphasis added).

147. Prévot, *Libertins*, 56–57.

148. Prévot, *Libertins*, 4.

149. Prévot, *Libertins*, 63.

150. It might be argued that this sleight of hand parallels a curious variant introduced by Théophile in his quotation of verses 75–80. In this rendition here, "Un plaisir naturel" (v. 75) of the original and all subsequent printed editions (including the edition supervised by Théophile's friends in 1625) becomes "Des plaisirs innocents." While it is impossible to prove his intentions, the effect of this variant is to emphasize the multiplicity of the poet's pleasures at the expense of reference to a single transgression (i.e., sodomy) and to underscore a moralistic distinction (with the adjective "innocents") in place of the vaguely Epicurean "naturel." The passage from the "Plainte de Théophile" as quoted in the "Apologie" reads:

> Des plaisirs innocents où mes esprits enclins
> Ne laissent point de place à des désirs malins,
> Ce divertissement qu'on doit permettre à l'homme,
> Et que Sa Sainteté ne punit pas à Rome:
> Car la nécessité que la police suit
> En souffrant ce péché ne fait pas peu de fruit.
> (Prévot, *Libertins*, 68)

151. The distinction among thought, word, and action is a commonplace of Jesuit theology at the time. Contrary to what Théophile implies, Vasquez did not specialize in casuitry, but his notoriety as a theologian made him an easy target for enemies of the Je-

suits in France, including those in "libertine" circles. The reference here to Vasquez and especially the examples Théophile provides are obviously ironic. My thanks to Jacob Schmutz for information on Vasquez.

152. Viau, *Œuvres poétiques*, 298–338. Several poems from the beginning of Théophile's career depict a seemingly intimate friendship with Roger du Plessis de Liancourt and present some of the topoi that are further developed here. See "Contre l'hiver" (*Œuvres poétiques*, 45–49), "Stances" (*Œuvres poétiques*, 74), "Philandre sur la maladie de Tircis" (*Œuvres poétiques*, 373–74), "A Monsieur de Liancourt" (*Œuvres poétiques*, 389–93). See also Saba, *Théophile de Viau*, 33–35. On friendship in sixteenth-century France, see Marc D. Schachter, *Voluntary Servitude and the Erotics of Friendship: From Classical Antiquity to Early Modern France* (Burlington, VT: Ashgate, 2008). For an overview of friendship among male writers and scholars in seventeenth-century France, see Philippe-Joseph Salazar, "Herculean Lovers: Towards a History of Men's Friendship in the 17th Century," *Thamyris* 4, no. 2 (1997): 249–66. And for a later period but with many insights applicable to the early seventeenth century, see Jeffrey Merrick, "Male Friendship in Pre-Revolutionary France," *GLQ* 10, no. 3 (2004): 407–32.

153. The identification of Tircis as Des Barreaux has never been definitively established, as Adam notes (*Théophile de Viau*, 391 n. 4), yet most editors of Théophile's work seem convinced of it (see Viau, *Œuvres complètes*, 3:151 n. 63).

154. This comparison is made clear retrospectively, at the end of Ode IV, when Tircis recounts a dream he had of the poet's persecution and death. The initial words of comfort and advice the poet gives to Cygnus (that time blunts all passions and that his judgment could have spared him love for Phaethon) thus apply to Tircis.

155. See Alan Bray, "Homosexuality and the Signs of Male Friendship in Early Modern England," in *Queering the Renaissance*, ed. Jonathan Goldberg (Durham, NC: Duke University Press, 1994), 40–61, and Alan Bray, *The Friend* (Chicago: University of Chicago Press, 2003).

156. On this tension in "De l'amitié," see Marc D. Schachter, "'That Friendship Which Possesses the Soul': Montaigne Loves La Boétie," *Journal of Homosexuality* 41, nos. 3–4 (2001): 5–21.

157. One might think of Judith Butler's now classic work on performativity, for instance. See Judith Butler, *Gender Trouble: Feminism and the Subversion of Identity* (New York: Routledge, 1990).

158. Viau, *Œuvres complètes*, 4:lv.

159. Baverel-Croissant and Des Barreaux, *La Vie*, 25.

160. Of the twenty-four Latin letters, seven are addressed to Des Barreaux (2, 7, 12, 13, 16, 17, 21), more than to any other recipient. Significant references to Des Barreaux occur in three other letters (5, 8, 9). And the very first Latin letter is from Des Barreaux to Théophile, the only one not by the poet.

161. Viau, *Œuvres complètes*, 4:149.

162. Viau, *Œuvres complètes*, 4:lv.

163. Tallemant des Réaux, *Historiettes*, 2:933 n. 7.

164. Lachèvre, *Le Libertinage*, 1:553.

165. See Godard, *Le Goût de Monsieur*, 51, 58–59. Initially, Lever is a bit more circumspect than Godard ("Perhaps, after all, Théophile . . . only had a platonic passion for Des Barreaux. But his correspondence leaves no doubt that he loved him deeply" [110]). Then a few pages later he cites passages from the correspondence in order to equate Théophile and Des Barreaux with Oscar Wilde and Alfred Douglas (117).

166. Tallemant des Réaux, *Historiettes*, 2:29.

167. See Lachèvre, *Le Libertinage*, 1:206, 223 (letters from Des Barreaux to Théophile) and Lachèvre, *Le Libertinage*, 1:501 (letter by Théophile, addressee unspecified). In an account written after Théophile's release from prison, Garasse also refers to Latin letters by Des Barreaux before the poet's arrest: "This young man, being thus with Théophile every day, acquired a very bad reputation for himself. And when Théophile was taken to the Châtelet, escaping to England, after his [Théophile's] execution in effigy, there were found among his papers Latin letters from Des Barreaux that were sufficient to inflict on him the same punishment as his uncle [Geoffroy Vallée, who was burned at the stake for atheism in 1574], if the court had not taken into consideration his youth" (Prévot, *Libertins*, 133).

168. Bray, *The Friend*, 316. The intensity and exclusivity of their friendship did not preclude female love interests. In Letter 1 (addressed to Théophile), Des Barreaux mentions that he has fallen in love with a "tender virgin" but also asserts: "For me, everything is going rather well, as well as possible without you" (*Œuvres complètes*, 4:149). And in Letter 17, Théophile evokes the beauty of "Caliste" and asks Des Barreaux to remind her of their past love. But then he turns to his addressee and states: "If anyone tries to keep me from those who are bound to me by a friendship so sweet and so divine, may he be found guilty of violating nature" (*Œuvres complètes*, 4:175).

169. Bray, *The Friend*, 218–19. In Letter 9, addressed to his friend Luillier, Théophile states: "He knows full well of the affection and respect I have for the marvelous beauty of his body and soul" (*Œuvres complètes*, 4:161).

170. Bray speaks of an asymmetry between the signs of sodomy and friendship in early modern Europe. "The asymmetry of friendship to 'sodomy' necessarily lay in a critical difference. 'Sodomy' signified enormously, but it did so in the measure of how little it referred to a datum that could actually be verified or refuted. It was that that made its implications so suggestive. Friendship both signified and referred. Its terms were not, could not, be held apart from the difficult distinctions that shaped those boundaries and limits. Its ethics recognized them, and its conventions negotiated them through rather difficult and dangerous demands" (*The Friend*, 276).

171. Michel Foucault, "De l'amitié comme mode de vie," in *Dits et écrits, 1954–1988*, ed. Daniel Defert and François Ewald, 4 vols., Bibliothèque des Sciences Humaines (Paris: Gallimard, 1994), 4:163.

CHAPTER 6

1. These memoirs are not to be confused with his *Mémoires pour servir à l'histoire de Louis XIV*, first published in 1727. The *Mémoires* to which I refer in this chapter are the *Mémoires de l'abbé de Choisy habillé en femme* and not the former.

2. Only the Marquis d'Argenson mentions Choisy's cross-dressing, although based on accounts provided by the Abbé himself at the end of his life, rather than his own observations. See Geneviève Reynes, *L'Abbé de Choisy, ou, l'ingénu libertin* (Paris: Presses de la Renaissance, 1983), 323 n. 5. To date, no other contemporary references to Choisy's cross-dressing have been found.

3. For biographies of Choisy, see Reynes, *L'Abbé de Choisy* and Dirk Van der Cruysse, *L'Abbé de Choisy, androgyne et mandarin* (Paris: Fayard, 1995).

4. One could speculate, for instance, that Choisy's accounts of cross-dressing

were largely fictional. Van der Cruysse counters that allusions to political and personal events prove the authenticity of the *Mémoires* (*L'Abbé de Choisy*, 101), although I find it difficult to understand how "authenticity" of any sort can be affirmed in the absence of confirmation by other sources.

5. See Julia Prest, *Theatre under Louis XIV: Cross-Casting and the Performance of Gender in Drama, Ballet, and Opera* (New York: Palgrave Macmillan, 2006), 130–37.

6. Joseph Harris, *Hidden Agendas: Cross-Dressing in Seventeenth-Century France*, Biblio 17, 156 (Tübingen: Gunter Narr Verlag, 2005), 18.

7. Harris, *Hidden Agendas*, 48.

8. Harris, *Hidden Agendas*, 42.

9. Sylvie Steinberg, *La Confusion des sexes: Le travestissement de la Renaissance à la Révolution* (Paris: Fayard, 2001), 123.

10. See Foucault, *History of Madness*, 44–77. Although Foucault devotes scant attention to gendered "deviance," Albistur and Armogathe extend his analysis to speak of a "great confinement" of women during the second half of the seventeenth century in France. See Maïté Albistur and Daniel Armogathe, *Histoire du féminisme français* (Paris: Des femmes, 1977), 1:195–200.

11. Mitchell Greenberg, *Baroque Bodies: Psychoanalysis and the Culture of French Absolutism* (Ithaca, NY: Cornell University Press, 2001), 123.

12. Georges Mongrédien, "Introduction," in *Mémoires de l'abbé de Choisy: Mémoires pour servir à l'histoire de Louis XIV. Mémoires de l'abbe de Choisy habillé en femme*, ed. Georges Mongrédien, by François-Timoléon de Choisy (Paris: Mercure de France, 1966), 12.

13. See Greenberg, *Baroque Bodies*, 111–59; Annette Runte, "Die Geometrie adligen Geschlechtertausches: Vormoderne Travestie im höfischen Raum des französischen Absolutismus am Beispiel Abbé de Choisy," *Forum Homosexualität und Literatur*, no. 40 (2002): 9–33; Henri Castanet, "Le Transformisme de M. l'Abbé de Choisy ou logique de la féminisation dans la perversion," *Information psychiatrique* 75, no. 7 (1999): 743–84; Pierrick Brient, "Le Désaveu du féminin chez l'abbé de Choisy," *Adolescence* 57 (2006): 711–18.

14. See especially Butler, *Gender Trouble*, 128–49. Butler argues for the relevance of drag in the following way: "In imitating gender, drag implicitly reveals the imitative structure of gender itself—as well as its contingency" (137).

15. Frédéric Charbonneau, "Sexes hypocrites: Le théâtre des corps chez Jean-Jacques Bouchard et l'abbé de Choisy," *Études Françaises* 34, no. 1 (1998): 120.

16. Dominique Bertrand, "Fictions et mémoires de l'androgynie: Les écritures croisées de l'abbé de Choisy," in *L'un(e) miroir de l'autre*, ed. Alain Montandon et al., Cahiers de recherches du CRLMC (Clermont-Ferrand: Université Blaise-Pascal, 1998), 164.

17. Elizabeth Guild, "'Le Moyen de faire de cela un grand homme': The Abbé de Choisy and the Unauthorized Body of Representation," *Romanic Review* 85, no. 2 (1994): 181.

18. Stephen Whittle, "Foreword," in *The Transgender Studies Reader*, ed. Susan Stryker and Stephen Whittle (New York: Routledge, 2006), xi.

19. Susan Stryker, "(De)Subjugated Knowledges: An Introduction to Transgender Studies," in *The Transgender Studies Reader*, ed. Susan Stryker and Stephen Whittle (New York: Routledge, 2006), 10.

20. As I write, widespread use of the term *transgender* is itself barely ten years old (see Whittle, "Foreword," xi; Stryker, "[De]Subjugated Knowledges," 5–6; Jay Prosser,

Second Skins: The Body Narratives of Transsexuality, Gender and Culture [New York: Columbia University Press, 1998], 176) as are its political and theoretical underpinnings. The newness of this field should not, of course, be the basis for an accusation of anachronism since concepts and terms articulated in one period can theorize antecedent manifestations of the phenomena they describe.

21. Laqueur's hypothesis about the one-sex model is derived from early modern medicine elaborated from Aristotelian and especially Galenic thought and posits an analogy between the male and female bodies where the female is an imperfect version of the male. See Laqueur, *Making Sex,* 63–113.

22. See Park and Nye, "Destiny Is Anatomy"; Winfried Schleiner, "Early Modern Controversies about the One-Sex Model," *Renaissance Quarterly* 53, no. 1 (2000): 180–91; Janet Adelman, "Making Defect Perfection: Shakespeare and the One-Sex Model," in *Enacting Gender on the English Renaissance Stage,* ed. Viviana Comensoli and Anne Russell (Urbana: University of Illinois Press, 1999), 23–52.

23. Laqueur discusses François Poullain de la Barre, whose protofeminist writings date from the 1670s, as an illustration of "the turn to biology when an old ordering of man and woman collapses" (*Making Sex,* 155).

24. Laqueur, *Making Sex,* 138–39.

25. Joan DeJean has made this observation about the "Histoire de la Marquise-Marquis de Banneville," and her insight is certainly valid for the *Mémoires* as well. See Joan DeJean, *Ancients against Moderns: Culture Wars and the Making of a Fin de Siècle* (Chicago: University of Chicago Press, 1997), 122. Laqueur's contention that there was no link between gender and personhood in the early modern period has as a corollary his claim that sex lacked ontological status (*Making Sex,* 139). However, Katharine Park and Robert Nye counter that "metaphysical distinctions had an ontological status for [Renaissance natural philosophers] that gave rise to palpable physical differences" (Park and Nye, "Destiny Is Anatomy," 55).

26. See, for instance, David Kates's biography of the eighteenth-century crossdresser, the Chevalier d'Eon. Kates argues at the outset that since "there is simply no indication that d'Eon hates his own body or that he wanted, or even imagined he would be better off with, the body of a woman," the chevalier was not a "transsexual" or even a "transvestite." See Gary Kates, *Monsieur d'Eon Is a Woman: A Tale of Political Intrigue and Sexual Masquerade* (Baltimore: John Hopkins University Press, 2001), xxii.

27. Leslie Feinberg has opened the way for such historical work with hir (and the possessive adjective is Feinberg's) *Transgender Warriors: Making History from Joan of Arc to Dennis Rodman* (Boston: Beacon Press, 1996). However, Feinberg does not mention Choisy.

28. See for instance Van der Cruysse, *L'Abbé de Choisy,* 50–55; Harris, *Hidden Agendas,* 221; Guild, "Le Moyen de Faire de Cela un Grand Homme," 187.

29. Van der Cruysse, *L'Abbé de Choisy,* 50.

30. Reynes, *L'Abbé de Choisy,* 58–59.

31. Whittle, "Foreword," xi.

32. When referring to Choisy (as either the historical figure or the narrative voice of his *Mémoires*), I will alternate, by paragraphs, between the masculine and the feminine. With this practice, I attempt to approximate Choisy's own ambivalently gendered narrative voice. I recognize that this practice will be jarring for readers, especially at first. However, I hope that it will reproduce in some small way the shifting and unstable existence that Choisy attempts to communicate in his writings.

33. For further information about the publication history of the *Mémoires,* see Choisy, *Mémoires,* 525–27.

34. For a discussion of the various hypotheses about the chronology of the "Comtesse des Barres" and the "Madame de Sancy" episodes, see Van der Cruysse, *L'Abbé de Choisy,* 102–3.

35. Van der Cruysse, *L'Abbé de Choisy,* 413.

36. Choisy, *Mémoires,* 522. Subsequent pages references will be given in the text.

37. Van der Cruysse, *L'Abbé de Choisy,* 413–14.

38. Van der Cruysse notes that there are many details in "La Comtesse des Barres" that are difficult to verify, such as the existence and the ownership of the Château de Crespon, and also expresses skepticism about the authenticity of the seduction scene with La Grise. See *L'Abbé de Choisy,* 148.

39. In point of fact, the short fragment about his stint as an actress in Bordeaux also recounts a transition back to masculinity, which makes a third instance.

40. Prosser, *Second Skins,* 130–31.

41. See, for example, Joseph Harris, "Stealing Beauty: The Abbé de Choisy's Appropriation of the Feminine," in *Possessions: Essays in French Literature, Cinema and Theory,* ed. Julia Horn and Lynsey Russell-Watts, Modern French Identities, 24 (Oxford: Peter Lang, 2003), 121–34, and Guild, "Le Moyen de Faire de Cela un Grand Homme."

42. Critics have often noted with astonishment that Choisy was able to assume his feminine personas with little or no opposition from official or unofficial sources, leading some to speculate that his accounts exaggerate his own cross-dressing or downplay the pressure he may have felt not to do so or that the public felt constrained by political necessity not to make a scandal of it. See for instance Reynes, *L'Abbé de Choisy,* 75–77. It should also be noted that the impunity with which Choisy was seemingly able to cross-dress flouted the severe legal penalties for transvestism in this period. See Steinberg, *La Confusion des sexes,* 25–54.

43. Within the transgender community, there is considerable debate about both the nature and the appropriate responses to the feeling of noncorrespondence between gender identity and biological sex. Where some strive to transition and thus to "pass," others advocate for the right to live in an ambiguous middle ground between or beyond genders. See Kate Bornstein, "Gender Terror, Gender Rage," in Stryker and Whittle, *The Transgender Studies Reader,* 236–43.

44. As Jay Prosser has astutely observed, this premise runs counter to many poststructuralist theories of the body, and most famously Judith Butler's: "[B]ecause the [transsexual] subject speaks of the imaginary body as more real or more sensible, I argue that this phenomenon illustrates the materiality of the bodily ego rather than the phantasmatic status of the sexed body: the material reality of the imaginary and not, as Butler would have it, the imaginariness of material reality. That the transsexual's trajectory centers on reconfiguring the body reveals that it is the ability to feel the bodily ego in conjunction and conformity with the material body parts that matters in a transsexual context; and that sex is perceived as something that must be changed underlines its very un-phantasmatic status" (Prosser, *Second Skins,* 43–44).

45. Greenberg, *Baroque Bodies,* 139–40.

46. See Prosser, *Second Skins,* 78–79.

47. A few pages before this allusion, Choisy, while describing a simpler outfit (a dress over a *jupon*), states: "I didn't put on *haut-de-chausses* anymore; I thought I looked more like a woman that way, and I wasn't afraid of being cold since it was summer" (433).

Whether or not Choisy was motivated by a preoccupation with *outward* resemblance in this instance is difficult to determine: would the *haut-de-chausses* really have been visible under the two layers of clothing? Whatever the case, Choisy frames her decision as one of personal judgment ("I thought" [*il me semblait*]), which again focuses on her own body image.

48. The "corps" that Choisy describes here would seem to be a corset (or stay), an undergarment used to correct posture, rather than a bodice, an outer garment providing an upright stiffness prized by aristocrats in the seventeenth and eighteenth centuries. See Daniel Roche, *The Culture of Clothing: Dress and Fashion in the "Ancien Régime,"* trans. Jean Birrell (Cambridge: Cambridge University Press, 1994), 122–23.

49. Choisy repeats this claim at the beginning of the "Madame de Sancy" episode: "People saw the top of my shoulders that had been kept quite white by the great care I'd had taken of them my whole life. Every evening I washed my neckline and my upper bosom with calf water and cream of sheep's feet, thanks to which my skin was soft and white" (434).

50. Quoted in Isabelle Billaud, "'Une âme de femme dans un corps d'homme': La représentation du travesti dans les *Mémoires de l'abbé de Choisy*," *Lumen: Selected Proceedings from the Canadian Society for Eighteenth-Century Studies = Travaux choisis de la Société canadienne d'étude du dix-huitième siècle* 23 (2004): 137.

51. Prosser, *Second Skins*, 68.

52. Earlier, Madame Gaillot, a friend of the comtesse, tells her essentially the same thing: "Few ladies resemble you . . . and one has to be as beautiful as you are to have so little need of external remedies. Your mirror suffices and tells you continually that you have everything by yourself" (502).

53. Frédéric Charbonneau observes that "the parallelism between the episodes creates the impression that we are dealing with a succession of *commedia dell'arte* performances, improvised from a single framework: sumptuous settling in, at Bourges or the Faubourg Saint-Marceau; double cross-dressing of Choisy and his 'mistresses,' Charlotte and Roselie; scenes of exhibitionism, carnivalesque marriages, debonnaire priests, venal aunts" ("Sexes hypocrites," 119).

54. See Reynes, *L'Abbé de Choisy*, 152–54.

55. See Maître, *Les Précieuses*, 207, 438–39.

56. Greenberg, *Baroque Bodies*, 137–38.

57. Some feminists have leveled precisely this critique at MTF (male-to-female) transgendered persons (see, for example, Janice G. Raymond, "Sappho by Surgery: The Transsexually Constructed Lesbian-Feminist," in Stryker and Whittle, *The Transgender Studies Reader*, 131–43), which in turn has provoked a countercritique (see, among others, Carol Riddell, "Divided Sisterhood: A Critical Review of Janice Raymond's *The Transsexual Empire*," in Stryker and Whittle, *The Transgender Studies Reader*, 144–58, and Gayle Rubin, "Of Catamites and Kings: Reflections on Butch, Gender, and Boundaries," in Stryker and Whittle, *The Transgender Studies Reader* 471–80).

58. In each episode, two girls are befriended/seduced in succession; one in each of them is cross-dressed by Choisy (Roselie in "La Comtesse des Barres" and Babet in "Madame de Sancy"); one in each of them is a naive ingenue (La Grise in "La Comtesse des Barres," and Babet in "Madame de Sancy"); Choisy pretends to be married to each of them, etc.

59. Harris has remarked that "Choisy is attracted to young girls in their early teens, those who are on the borderline between childhood and maturity and whom he can introduce to the world of adult femininity" ("Stealing Beauty," 130).

60. Speaking of Mlle de La Grise after her marriage, Choisy writes: "I didn't think about her anymore. A married woman was nothing for me any longer; the sacrament instantly wiped away all her charms" (*Mémoires*, 517). See also 521.

61. Greenberg, *Baroque Bodies*, 145.

62. Describing a bed scene with Mlle de La Grise, Choisy affirms: "It is such sweet pleasure to deceive the eyes of the public" (*Mémoires*, 503).

63. See Nicholas Hammond, "All Dressed Up . . . : L'Abbé de Choisy and the Theatricality of Subversion," *Seventeenth-Century French Studies* 21 (1999): 170, and Greenberg, *Baroque Bodies*, 147.

64. By a sort of mutual agreement, both Choisy / Madame de Sancy *and* Charlotte / Monsieur de Maulny suspend the reality of their biological sex when they are together: "When Charlotte entered the cabinet, I put a wig on her to imagine she was a boy. From her end, she had no difficulty imagining I was a woman. And thus, contented, we both had much pleasure together" (*Mémoires*, 446).

65. "I acted as a girl for five months on the stage of a big city; everyone was deceived; I had lovers to whom I gave small favors, very reserved about the big ones" (*Mémoires*, 431–32).

66. See *Mémoires*, 453–55. Reynes speculates that Choisy is the author of this song, which counts no fewer than twelve stanzas, is composed in an elegant style, and includes many of the motifs of the *Mémoires* (praise of the Abbé's beauty, for instance). See Reynes, *L'Abbé de Choisy*, 157–58.

67. The scene occurs in the enigmatic (because brief and fragmentary) section entitled "Les Intrigues de l'abbé avec les petites actrices Montfleury et Mondory" (*Mémoires*, 471–473). See especially 472.

68. See *Mémoires*, 477.

69. Choisy writes that "he was as handsome as a prince and knew it too" (*Mémoires*, 483). The chevalier pursues the comtesse des Barres and even makes a proposal of marriage, which the comtesse refuses. Choisy explains this reaction not via a sexual incompatibility but rather by the chevalier's personality and presumed motivation: "He acted very passionate at first, but I didn't care for his pretenses and believed that he only found me beautiful because I was rich" (484).

70. See Greenberg, *Baroque Bodies*, 142.

71. Greenberg entertains the possibility that the bed scene with Mlle de La Grise might indeed be seen as a realization of the unconscious desire for lesbian transgression that (supposedly) existed at the time. But he shuts down this possibility just as quickly as he evokes it because, in his reading, Choisy is a man: "It is this desire for [sexual and in particular lesbian] transgression that Choisy both realizes and at the same time undermines; despite a first level of sexual violation that is scandalous in its own right (the perverse seduction of a young virgin), the more pernicious, inarticulable threat of lesbianism, although suggested, is held off, by heterosexual recuperation: 'she' is really a 'he'" (Greenberg, *Baroque Bodies*, 145).

72. At the end of "Madame de Sancy" he returns to his apartment at the Palais du Luxembourg to keep it from being given to another noble. Although he does not specify it, Choisy presumably is in masculine garb once there. He then resumes gambling and, by his own account, loses the wherewithal to "faire la belle" (469). At the end of the short fragment about his "intrigues" with the actresses Montfleury and Mondory, Choisy abandons cross-dressing and takes up gambling while traveling in Italy after Mlle de Mondory fails to reciprocate his affections (473). And, at the end of "La Comtesse des Barres," it is

pressure from Choisy's relatives that forces him to stop playing a "a role they had toler-ated because of extreme youth" (522). He then travels to Venice whereupon he com-mences gambling. Whether or not these three endings are three separate events or three versions of the same event has been the subject of considerable speculation by Choisy's biographers. See Reynes, *L'Abbé de Choisy*, 182–83, and Van der Cruysse, *L'Abbé de Choisy*, 170.

73. For a synthesis of the arguments in favor of a collaboration by Choisy, Lhéritier, and Perrault, see Joan DeJean, "Introduction," in Choisy, et al., *Histoire de la Marquise-Marquis de Banneville*, vii–xviii. To my mind, all of the arguments *for* a collaboration with Perrault or Lhéritier or both are highly circumstantial and do not take sufficient ac-count of the arguments *against* it. Although Choisy and Perrault were fellow members of the informal "Académie du Luxembourg" and although the editor of the *Mercure galant* claimed that "La Belle au bois dormant" (one of Perrault's fairy tales) was by the same person as the "Histoire de la Marquise-Marquis de Banneville" (a puzzling attribution that has caused much speculation among scholars), it should also be remembered that Perrault never claimed authorship of the *Histoires ou contes du temps passé* (1697), which was attributed to his son, Pierre Darmancour. (This fact is the basis for the continuing controversy about whether Perrault was actually the author of "his" fairy tales.) Jacques Chupeau has speculated that Perrault may have used this attribution to further dissimu-late his authorship of *Histoires ou contes du temps passé* (Jacques Chupeau, "Notice," in *Nouvelles du XVIIe siècle*, ed. Raymond Picard, Jean Lafond, and Jacques Chupeau, Bib-liothèque de la Pléiade [Paris: Gallimard, 1997], 1672). The arguments in favor of a col-laboration with Lhéritier are even more tenuous and center on her supposed contacts with the *Mercure galant* and her authorship of "Marmoisan," a novella about a woman who as-sumes her brother's identity to save her father's honor. Besides the fact that Lhéritier pub-lished frequently in the *Mercure galant*, it is unclear what sort of contacts she may have had with the editor of that periodical and even less so that she was the young woman of the 1695 preface who introduces herself as the author of the "Histoire de la Marquise-Marquis de Banneville." Her story "Marmoisan," which Lhéritier explicitly acknowl-edges as her own, follows the literary conventions of cross-dressing far more closely than the novella I analyze here. It should also be noted that "Histoire de la Marquise-Marquis de Banneville" would represent a considerable departure, both in tone and in content, for Perrault and especially for Lhéritier, who uses her fictional texts to advocate for a highly traditional conception of gendered and sexual behavior, her protofeminist positions on women's writing notwithstanding. Admittedly this in no way definitively resolves the question about collaboration. However, most recent critics consider that Choisy was if not the sole author at least the primary collaborator. It should not be forgotten that he is the only one of the three to make explicit references to the story (without, to be sure, claiming authorship per se [see *Mémoires*, 436–37 and 471]) and that there are many par-allels between this text and the *Mémoires de l'abbé de Choisy habillé en femme*, which, not insignificantly, were penned long after the novella (see Van der Cruysse, *L'Abbé de Choisy*, 346–49).

74. Another allusion to the novella is found in the "Madame de Sancy" episode ("a little story . . . that spoke of a man of quality who wanted to be a woman because he was handsome" [436]). Madame de Sancy's neighbors assume that this character (Prince Sionad and not the hero/ine) is none other than Choisy/Sancy and even offer to ask that her/his name be published. However, Choisy/Sancy cautions them against this: "Society

is very mean-spirited, and it's so rare to see a man wanting to be a woman that one is often exposed to malicious jokes" (437).

75. The preface does not appear in the longer 1696 edition of the novella and, thus, is not included in Joan DeJean's edition. See "Histoire de la Marquise-Marquis de Banneville," in *Nouvelles du XVIIe siècle*, ed. Jean Lafond, Jacques Chupeau, and Raymond Picard, Bibliothèque de la Pléiade (Paris: Gallimard, 1997), 971–72. Subsequent references to this edition are designated as "Histoire" (Pléiade).

76. Choisy, "Histoire" (Pléiade), 971.

77. Of course, a more complex reading might be envisioned if one accepted the hypothesis of collaborative authorship with Charles Perrault or Marie-Jeanne Lhéritier de Villandon or both.

78. Choisy, "Histoire" (Pléiade), 971.

79. Choisy, "Histoire" (Pléiade), 971–72.

80. François-Timoléon de Choisy, Marie-Jeanne L'Héritier de Villandon, and Charles Perrault, *The Story of the Marquise-Marquis de Banneville*, ed. Joan DeJean, trans. Steven Rendall (New York: Modern Language Association, 2004), 60. The corresponding quote in the French original is found in François-Timoléon de Choisy, Marie-Jeanne L'Héritier de Villandon, and Charles Perrault, *Histoire de la Marquise-Marquis de Banneville*, ed. Joan DeJean, Texts and Translations (New York: Modern Language Association of America, 2004), 58. Subsequent references are given in the text. The first reference is to this English translation and the second, in brackets, to this edition of the French original.

81. See DeJean, *Ancients against Moderns*, 119–20, and Joseph Harris, "Novel Upbringings: Education and Gender in Choisy and La Fayette," *Romanic Review* 97, no. 1 (2006): 3–14.

82. See Harris, *Hidden Agendas*, especially 18–20, 153–76.

83. Marjorie Garber has famously argued that cross-dressing can indicate "a category crisis elsewhere, an irresolvable conflict or epistemological crux that destabilizes comfortable binarity, and displaces the resulting discomfort on to a figure that already inhabits, indeed incarnates the margin" (*Vested Interests: Cross-Dressing and Cultural Anxiety* [New York: Routledge, 1992], 17). On the uses of cross-dressing to express anxieties about questions other than sex and gender, see Harris, *Hidden Agendas*.

84. See the example of the eponymous heroine in Lhéritier's "Marmoisan," who, as a cross-dressed solidier, evokes the ridicule (if not suspicions) of her companions on the battlefield by insisting on keeping her clothes clean. See Catherine Velay-Vallantin and Marie-Jeanne L'Héritier de Villandon, *La fille en garçon*, ed. Catherine Velay-Vallantin, Classiques de la Littérature Orale (Carcassonne: GARAE/Hésiode, 1992), 39–41.

85. See 5 [5] and 11 [11]. It should be noted that these descriptions of Mariane's beauty are far more precise and stereotypically literary than the allusions to the beauty of the comtesse des Barres and Madame de Sancy in the *Mémoires*.

86. Thus, I only partially agree with Harris' conclusion: "Whatever 'real' body the Little Marquise has is mediated through her fantasized bodily self which is at once a symbolic, cultural construct and the object of her imaginary identification" (Harris, *Hidden Agendas*, 217). To be sure, Mariane possesses a body image at odds with her sexed body. And yet, the narrative makes clear that her body nonetheless at least partially corresponds to her body image as well.

87. Choisy, *Mémoires*, 505.

88. See 27–28 [26–27]. For other descriptions of the seductive effect of Mariane's beauty, see 7 [7].

89. Among other things, the comtesse d'Aletref has him learn to carry his body as a girl, has his ears pierced, and has him wear a corset. See 18–21 [17–20].

90. See Harris, *Hidden Agendas*, 51, 129–38.

91. Most of the additions to the 1696 version of the novella consist of scenes that describe reactions to Mariane's beauty. These additions are indicated in the notes of Jacques Chupeau's edition "Histoire" (Pléiade), 1681–1700.

92. In this sense, I disagree with DeJean's assertion (conflating gender with sexuality, it should be noted) that "in the world of 'Histoire de la marquise-marquis de Banneville,' sexuality is simultaneously an *état*, something that can be recreated at will, and a *condition*, something fixed at birth. Identity can be performative and stable at the same time" (*Ancients against Moderns*, 122). Although there is an undeniable performative aspect to Mariane's and Bercour's reciprocal assumption of each other's "sexe," the narrative and indeed both Mariane's and Bercour's statements indicate that it is not a matter of conscious "will" but rather a motivation that is more deeply ingrained and to a certain extent unconscious. Thus, I do not concur with DeJean's further contention that this narrative is one of "gender bending," which as she uses that term implies a willful play with the signs of gender, equivalent in many ways to drag. See *Ancients against Moderns*, 122 and "Introduction," xix–xxi.

93. However, Mariane's uncle does know that she is a man, but he is unaware that Bercour is a woman. After the death of Madame de Banneville, he consents to the marriage thinking that what he thinks is a same-sex couple will allow his children to inherit the Petite Marquise's fortune.

94. See Harris, *Hidden Agendas*, 166–76.

95. The narrative subtly but carefully prepares this conclusion from the very first encounter between Mariane and Bercour. Although the hero/ine "felt nothing" (26 [26]) for all the suitors she attracted, upon seeing Bercour "she felt something she had never felt before, a certain delicate and profound joy that passes from the eyes to the heart, and in which lies all the happiness of life" (30 [29]). Later, she tells him: "My dear Marquis, you are made for me. All other men displease me; I cannot bear them. When they come to tell me that they love me, I feel an invincible repugnance for them, and everything about you, dear Marquis, charms me" (47 [46]). Retrospectively, it is clear that she only feels desire when the object is male and the relation heterosexual. The desire that Bercour feels for Mariane is likewise heterosexual, but again unwittingly so.

96. This passage appears in an addition found in the 1723 version of the novella and is published as "Appendix A" in DeJean's edition (64–65 [62–63]).

AFTERIMAGE

1. This engraving is one of twelve executed by Bosse as adaptations of work by Jean de Saint-Igny and entitled "La Noblesse française à l'église." See Bibliothèque Nationale de France, "Abraham Bosse," http://expositions.bnf.fr/bosse/feuille/html/index_mode.htm. For further information on Bosse, see André Blum, *Abraham Bosse et la société française au dix-septième siècle* (Paris: A. Morancé, 1924) and Sue Welsh Reed, *French Prints from the Age of the Musketeers* (Boston: Museum of Fine Arts, Boston, 1998), 21–28.

2. At the outset of her now-classic study, Butler contends that *"gender* is not a noun, but neither is it a set of free-floating attributes . . . within the inherited discourse of the metaphysics of substance, gender proves to be performative—that is, constituting the identity it is purported to be. In this sense, gender is always a doing, though not a doing by a subject who might be said to preexist the deed. . . . There is no gender identity behind the expressions of gender; that identity is performatively constituted by the very 'expressions' that are said to be its results." And at the end of her book, she writes: "[W]hen the subject is said to be constituted, that means simply that the subject is a consequence of certain rule-governed discourses that govern the intelligible invocation of identity" (Butler, *Gender Trouble*, 24–25, 145).

3. "If women, subjected to a labour of socialization which tends to diminish and deny them, learn the negative virtues of self-denial, resignation and silence, men are also prisoners, and insidiously victims, of the dominant representation" (Bourdieu, *Masculine Domination*, 49).

4. Judith Butler, *Undoing Gender* (New York: London: Routledge, 2004), 10.

5. Bourdieu asks, rhetorically, "[D]o not the invariants which, beyond all the visible changes in the position of women, are observed in the relations of domination between the sexes require one to take as one's privileged object the historical mechanisms and institutions which, in the course of history, have continuously abstracted these invariants from history?" (*Masculine Domination*, 4)

Bibliography

Adam, Antoine. *Théophile de Viau et la libre pensée française en 1620*. Geneva: Slatkine, 1966.

Adams, Rachel, and David Savran, eds. *The Masculinity Studies Reader*. Keyworks in Cultural Studies. Malden, MA: Blackwell, 2002.

Adelman, Janet. "Making Defect Perfection: Shakespeare and the One-Sex Model." In *Enacting Gender on the English Renaissance Stage*, edited by Viviana Comensoli and Anne Russell, 23–52. Urbana: University of Illinois Press, 1999.

Albistur, Maïté, and Daniel Armogathe. *Histoire du féminisme français*. Paris: Des femmes, 1977.

Alcover, Madeleine. *Poullain de La Barre: Une aventure philosophique*. Biblio 17. Tübingen: Papers on French Seventeenth Century Literature, 1981.

Arditi, Jorge. *A Genealogy of Manners: Transformations of Social Relations in France and England from the Fourteenth to the Eighteenth Century*. Chicago: University of Chicago Press, 1998.

Ariès, Philippe, and Georges Duby, gen. eds., Roger Chartier, ed. *A History of Private Life: Passions of the Renaissance*. Translated by Arthur Goldhammer. Cambridge: Harvard University Press, 1989.

Aronson, Nicole. *Mademoiselle de Scudéry, ou, le voyage au pays de Tendre*. Paris: Fayard, 1986.

Ashe, Fidelma. *The New Politics of Masculinity: Men, Power, and Resistance*. New York: Routledge, 2007.

Aubignac, François Hédelin d'. *La Pratique du théâtre. Nouvelle édition avec des corrections et des additions inédites de l'auteur, une préface et des notes*. Edited by Pierre Martino. Algiers: Jules Carbonel; Paris: Edouard Champion, 1927.

Avigdor, Eva. *Coquettes et précieuses: textes inédits*. Paris: A.-G. Nizet, 1982.

Baader, Renate. *Dames de lettres: Autorinnen des preziösen, hocharistokratischen und "modernen" Salons (1649–1698): Mlle de Scudéry, Mlle de Montpensier, Mme d'Aulnoy*. Romanistische Abhandlungen. Stuttgart: J. B. Metzlersche Verlagsbuch, 1986.

Backer, Dorothy Anne Liot. *Precious Women*. New York: Basic Books, 1974.

Badinter, Elisabeth. *X Y, de l'identité masculine*. Paris: Editions O. Jacob, 1992.

Barker, Nancy Nichols. *Brother to the Sun King—Philippe, Duke of Orléans*. Baltimore: Johns Hopkins University Press, 1989.

Barthélemy, Edouard de. *Les Amis de la marquise de Sablé: Recueil des lettres des principaux habitués de son salon*. Paris: E. Dentu, 1865.

Baverel-Croissant, Marie-Françoise, and Jacques Vallée Des Barreaux. *La Vie et les œuvres complètes de Jacques Vallée Des Barreaux (1599–1673)*. Libre Pensée et Littérature Clandestine. Paris: Honoré Champion, 2001.

Beasley, Faith E. *Revising Memory: Women's Fiction and Memoirs in Seventeenth-Century France*. New Brunswick, NJ: Rutgers University Press, 1990.

Beasley, Faith E. *Salons, History, and the Creation of Seventeenth-Century France: Mastering Memory*. Burlington, VT: Ashgate, 2006.

Bellegarde, Abbé Morvan de. *Réflexions sur le ridicule, et sur les moyens de l'éviter, où sont représentez les differens Caracteres & les Mœurs des Personnes de ce Siècle*. Paris: Jean Guignard, 1698.

Benserade, Isaac de. *Iphis et Iante, Comédie*. Edited by Anne Verdier, Christian Biet, and Lise Leibacher-Ouvrard. Vijon: Lamsaque, 2000.

Bertrand, Dominique. "Fictions et mémoires de l'androgynie: Les écritures croisées de l'abbé de Choisy." In *L'un(e) miroir de l'autre*, edited by Alain Montandon et al. Cahiers de recherches du CRLMC, 149–66. Clermont-Ferrand: Université Blaise-Pascal, 1998.

Bibliothèque Nationale de France. "Abraham Bosse." http://expositions.bnf.fr/bosse/feuille/html/index_mode.htm.

Billaud, Isabelle. "'Une âme de femme dans un corps d'homme': La représentation du travesti dans les *Mémoires de l'abbé de Choisy*." *Lumen: Selected Proceedings from the Canadian Scoeity for Eighteenth-Century Studies = Travaux choisis de la Société canadienne d'étude du dix-huitième siècle* 23 (2004): 133–49.

Bitton, Davis. *The French Nobility in Crisis, 1560–1640*. Stanford, CA: Stanford University Press, 1969.

Blum, André. *Abraham Bosse et la société française au dix-septième siècle*. Paris: A. Morancé, 1924.

Boer, Josephine de. "Men's Literary Circles in Paris, 1610–1660." *PMLA* 53 (1938): 730–81.

Boileau-Despréaux, Nicolas. "Dialogue des héros de roman." In *Œuvres complètes de Boileau: Dialogues, Réflexions critiques, Œuvres diverses*, edited by Charles-H. Boudhors, 7–54. Paris: Société Les Belles Lettres, 1960.

Boileau-Despréaux, Nicolas. *Satires, Épîtres, Art poétique*. Edited by Jean-Pierre Collinet. Poésie/Gallimard. Paris: Gallimard, 1985.

Boisrobert, François Le Métel de. *Epistres en vers*. Edited by Maurice Cauchie. 2 vols. Société des Textes Français Modernes. Paris: Hachette, 1921–27.

Boisrobert, François Le Métel de. *Response au Parnasse alarmé par l'Académie Françoise*. Paris: n.p., 1649.

Bombart, Mathilde. "Pour une seconde remise en cause des clés supposées des romans de Mademoiselle de Scudéry." *Littératures Classiques* 54 (2005): 247–56.

Bordo, Susan. *The Flight to Objectivity: Essays on Cartesianism and Culture*. Albany: State University of New York Press, 1987.

Bornstein, Kate. "Gender Terror, Gender Rage." In *The Transgender Studies Reader*, edited by Susan Stryker and Stephen Whittle, 236–43. New York: Routledge, 2006.

"La Boscorobertine, ou Lettre de Florimond à la Belle Iris sur l'abbé ridicule." In Emile Magne, *Le Plaisant abbé de Boisrobert, fondateur de l'Académie française, 1592–1662. Documents inédits*, 408–43. Paris: Mercure de France, 1909.

Bouhours, Dominique. *Les Entretiens d'Ariste et d'Eugène*. Edited by Bernard Beugnot and Gilles Declercq. Sources Classiques, 47. Paris: Honoré Champion, 2003.

Bouhours, Dominique. *La Manière de bien penser dans les ouvrages d'esprit*. Edited by Suzanne Guellouz. Toulouse: Université de Toulouse-Le Mirail, 1988.

Bourdieu, Pierre. *La Domination masculine*. Paris: Seuil, 1998. Translated as *Masculine Domination* by Richard Nice (Stanford, CA: Stanford University Press, 2001).

Bray, Alan. *The Friend*. Chicago: University of Chicago Press, 2003.

Bray, Alan. "Homosexuality and the Signs of Male Friendship in Early Modern England." In *Queering the Renaissance*, edited by Jonathan Goldberg, 40–61. Durham, NC: Duke University Press, 1994.

Bray, Alan. *Homosexuality in Renaissance England*. London: Gay Men's Press, 1982.

Brégy, Charlotte de Saumaise de Chauzan de Flécelles de. *La Réflexion de la Lune sur les hommes*. Edited by Constant Venesoen. Paris: Honoré Champion, 2006.

Breitenberg, Mark. *Anxious Masculinity in Early Modern England*. Cambridge Studies in Renaissance Literature and Culture, 10. Cambridge: Cambridge University Press, 1996.

Brient, Pierrick. "Le Désaveu du féminin chez l'abbé de Choisy." *Adolescence* 57 (2006): 711–18.

Burke, Peter. *The Fabrication of Louis XIV*. New Haven: Yale University Press, 1992.

Burke, Peter. *The Fortunes of the Courtier: The European Reception of Castiglione's Cortegiano*. University Park: Pennsylvania State University Press, 1996.

Bury, Emmanuel. *Littérature et politesse: L'invention de l'honnête homme, 1580–1750*. Paris: Presses universitaires de France, 1996.

Bussy-Rabutin, Roger de. *Lettres*. 2 vols. Paris: Delaulne, 1697.

Butler, Judith. *Excitable Speech: A Politics of the Performative*. New York: Routledge, 1997.

Butler, Judith. *Gender Trouble: Feminism and the Subversion of Identity*. New York: Routledge, 1990.

Butler, Judith. *Undoing Gender*. New York: Routledge, 2004.

Cady, Joseph. "The 'Masculine Love' of the 'Princes of Sodom': 'Practicing the Art of Ganymede' at Henri III's Court: The Homosexuality of Henri III and His *Mignons* in Pierre de L'Estoile's *Mémoires-Journaux*." In *Desire and Discipline: Sex and Sexuality in the Premodern West*, edited by Jacqueline Murray and Konrad Eisenbichler, 123–54. Toronto: University of Toronto Press, 1996.

Caillières, Jacques de. *Traitté de la fortune des gens de qualité, et gentilhommes particuliers. Divisé en deux parties*. Paris: Louis Chamhoudry, 1658.

Callewaert, Staf. "Bourdieu, Critic of Foucault: The Case of Empirical Social Science against Double-Game-Philosophy." *Theory, Culture and Society* 23, no. 6 (2006): 73–98.

Carcopino, Jérôme. *Boisrobert*. Paris: Elvire Choureau et Georges Blaizot, 1963.

Carroll, Stuart. *Blood and Violence in Early Modern France*. Oxford: Oxford University Press, 2006.

Carter, Philip. *Men and the Emergence of Polite Society, Britain 1660–1800*. Women and Men in History. New York: Longman, 2001.

Castanet, Henri. "Le Transformisme de M. l'Abbé de Choisy ou logique de la féminisation dans la perversion." *Information psychiatrique* 75, no. 7 (1999): 743–84.

Castiglione, Baldassarre. *The Courtier*. Translated by George Anthony Bull. New York: Penguin, 1976.

La Catégorie de l'honnête dans la culture du XVIe siècle. Saint-Etienne: Institut d'études de la Renaissance et de l'âge classique, 1985.

Chalesme. *L'Homme de qualité, ou les moyens de vivre en homme de bien et en homme du monde*. Paris: André Pralard, 1671.

"Chansonnier Maurepas." *Recueil de chansons, vaudevilles, sonnets, eprigrammes, eptiaphes, et autres vers Satiriques & Historiques, avec des remarques curieuses.* 12617, 12618, 12619, 12620, 12623, 12643, 12688. Fonds français. Bibliothèque nationale de France, Département des Manuscrits.

Chapelain, Jean. *Lettres de Jean Chapelain.* Edited by Philippe Tamizey de Larroque. 2 vols. Paris: Imprimerie Nationale, 1880.

Charbonneau, Frédéric. "Sexes hypocrites: Le théâtre des corps chez Jean-Jacques Bouchard et l'abbé de Choisy." *Études Françaises* 34, no. 1 (1998): 107–22.

Charron, Pierre. *De la sagesse.* Edited by Barbara de Negroni. Corpus des œuvres de philosophie de langue française. Paris: Fayard, 1986.

Chartier, Roger. "Distinction et divulgation: La civilité et ses livres." In *Lectures et lecteurs dans la France d'Ancien Régime,* 45–86. Paris: Seuil, 1987.

Choisy, François-Timoléon de. "Histoire de la Marquise-Marquis de Banneville." In *Nouvelles du XVIIe siècle,* edited by Jean Lafond, Jacques Chupeau, and Raymond Picard, 971–88. Bibliothèque de la Pléiade. Paris: Gallimard, 1997.

Choisy, François-Timoléon de. *Mémoires de l'abbé de Choisy: Mémoires pour servir à l'histoire de Louis XIV. Mémoires de l'abbe de Choisy habillé en femme.* Edited by Georges Mongrédien. Paris: Mercure de France, 2000.

Choisy, François-Timoléon de, Marie-Jeanne L'Héritier de Villandon, and Charles Perrault. *Histoire de la Marquise-Marquis de Banneville.* Edited by Joan DeJean. Texts and Translations. New York: Modern Language Association, 2004.

Choisy, François-Timoléon de, Marie-Jeanne L'Héritier de Villandon, and Charles Perrault. *The Story of the Marquise-Marquis de Banneville.* Edited by Joan DeJean. Translated by Steven Rendall. New York: Modern Language Association, 2004.

Chupeau, Jacques. "Notice." In *Nouvelles du XVIIe siècle,* edited by Raymond Picard, Jean Lafond, and Jacques Chupeau, 1671–80. Bibliothèque de la Pléiade. Paris: Gallimard, 1997.

Cicero, Marcus Tullius. *De Officiis.* Translated by Walter Miller. Loeb Classical Library, 30. Cambridge: Harvard University Press, 1997.

Clarke, Stanley. "Descartes's 'Gender'." In *Feminist Interpretations of René Descartes,* edited by Susan Bordo, 82–104. University Park: Pennsylvania State University Press, 1999.

Coignet, Cédric. "Une masculinité en crise à la fin du XVIIième siècle? La critique de l'efféminé chez La Bruyère." *Genre & Histoire,* no. 2 (Printemps, 2008). http://genrehistoire.fr/document.php?id=249.

Colletet, Guillaume. *Poësies diverses.* Paris: L. Chamhoudry, 1656.

Conley, John J. *The Suspicion of Virtue: Women Philosophers in Neoclassical France.* Ithaca, NY: Cornell University Press, 2002.

Connell, R. W. *Masculinities.* Berkeley and Los Angeles: University of California Press, 1995.

Costar, Pierre. *Defense des ouvrages de Monsieur de Voiture, A Monsieur de Balzac.* Paris: Thomas Iolly, 1654.

Cousin, Victor. *Madame de Sablé: Études sur les femmes illustres et la société du XVIIe siècle.* Paris: Didier, 1854.

Cowart, Georgia. "Of Women, Sex, and Folly: Opera under the Old Regime." *Cambridge Opera Journal* 6, no. 3 (1994): 205–20.

Craveri, Benedetta. *The Age of Conversation.* Translated by Teresa Waugh. New York: New York Review Books, 2005.

Crawford, Katherine. *European Sexualities, 1400–1800*. Cambridge: Cambridge University Press, 2007.

Crawford, Katherine. "Love, Sodomy, and Scandal: Controlling the Sexual Reputation of Henry III." *Journal of the History of Sexuality* 12, no. 4 (2003): 513–42.

Crawford, Katherine. *Perilous Performances: Gender and Regency in Early Modern France.* Harvard Historical Studies. Cambridge: Harvard University Press, 2004.

Crawford, Katherine. "The Politics of Promiscuity: Masculinity and Heroic Representation at the Court of Henry IV." *French Historical Studies* 26, no. 2 (2003): 225–52.

Crawford, Katherine. "Privilege, Possibility, and Perversion: Rethinking the Study of Early Modern Sexuality." *Journal of Modern History* 78 (2006): 412–33.

Cuénin, Micheline. "La Lettre éducatrice de la sensibilité: l'exemple de Voiture." *Revue d'Histoire Littéraire de la France* 78 (1978): 922–33.

Daniel, Marc. *Hommes du Grand Siècle: Etudes sur l'homosexualité sous les règnes de Louis XIII et de Louis XIV.* Paris: Arcadie, 1957.

Darnton, Robert. *The Forbidden Best-Sellers of Pre-Revolutionary France.* New York: W. W. Norton, 1995.

DeJean, Joan. *Ancients against Moderns: Culture Wars and the Making of a Fin de Siècle.* Chicago: University of Chicago Press, 1997.

DeJean, Joan. "Une Autobiographie en procès: L'affaire Théophile de Viau." *Poétique* 48 (1981): 431–48.

DeJean, Joan. "Introduction." In François-Timoléon de Choisy, Marie-Jeanne L'Héritier de Villandon, and Charles Perrault, *Histoire de la Marquise-Marquis de Banneville*, edited by Joan DeJean, vii–xxvi. Texts and Translations. New York: Modern Language Association of America, 2004.

DeJean, Joan. *The Reinvention of Obscenity: Sex, Lies, and Tabloids in Early Modern France.* Chicago: University of Chicago Press, 2002.

DeJean, Joan. *Tender Geographies: Women and the Origins of the Novel in France.* New York: Columbia University Press, 1991.

Deloffre, Frédéric. "Introduction." In Pierre de Marivaux, *Le Petit-Maître corrigé*, edited by Frédéric Deloffre, 11–143. Geneva: Droz, 1955.

Denis, Delphine. "L'Echange complimenteur: Un lieu commun du bien-dire." *Franco Italica* 15–16 (1999): 143–61.

Denis, Delphine. "Les Inventions de Tendre." *Intermédialités/Intermedialities* 4 (2004): 45–66.

Denis, Delphine. *La Muse galante: Poétique de la converstion dans l'œuvre de Madeleine de Scudéry.* Paris: Honoré Champion, 1997.

Denis, Delphine. *Le Parnasse galant: Institution d'une catégorie littéraire au XVIIe siècle.* Lumière Classique, 32. Paris: Honoré Champion, 2001.

Denis, Delphine. "Préciosité et galanterie: vers une nouvelle cartographie." In *Les Femmes au Grand Siècle, le Baroque, Musique et littérature: Actes du 33e Colloaue de la North American Society for Seventeeth-Century French Literature*, edited by David Wetzel. Biblio 17, 144, 17–39. Tübingen: Gunter Narr Verlag, 2002.

Denis, Delphine. "Les Samedis de Sapho: Figurations littéraires de la collectivité." In *Vie des salons et activités littéraires, de Marguerite de Valois à Mme de Staël*, edited by Roger Marchal, 107–15. Nancy: Presses universitaires de Nancy, 2001.

Denis, Delphine, and Anne-Elisabeth Spica, eds. *Madeleine de Scudéry: Une femme de lettres au XVIIe siècle: Actes du Colloque international de Paris, 28–30 juin 2001.* Arras: Artois Presses Université, 2002.

Dens, Jean-Pierre. *L'Honnête homme et la critique du goût: Esthétique et société au XVIIe siècle.* French Forum Monographs. Lexington, KY: French Forum, 1981.

d'Estrée, Paul. "Les Origines du Chansonnier de Maurepas." *Revue d'Histoire Littéraire de la France,* vol. 3 (1896), 332–45.

Dewald, Jonathan. *Aristocratic Experience and the Origins of Modern Culture: France, 1570–1715.* Berkeley and Los Angeles: University of California Press, 1993.

Digby, Tom, ed. *Men Doing Feminism.* New York: Routledge, 1998.

DiPiero, Thomas. *Dangerous Truths and Criminal Passions: The Evolution of the French Novel, 1569–1791.* Stanford, CA: Stanford University Press, 1992.

Duchêne, Roger. "Mlle de Scudéry, Reine de Tendre." In *Les Trois Scudéry: Actes du colloque du Havre,* edited by Alain Niderst, 625–32. Paris: Klincksieck, 1993.

Duchêne, Roger. *Les Précieuses ou comment l'esprit vint aux femmes.* Paris: Fayard, 2001.

Duggan, Anne E. *Salonnières, Furies, and Fairies: The Politics of Gender and Cultural Change in Absolutist France.* Newark: University of Delaware Press, 2005.

Duhamel, Pierre. *Le Grand Condé ou l'orgueil.* Paris: Perrin, 1981.

Elias, Norbert. *The Civilizing Process.* Translated by Edmund Jephcott. Oxford: Blackwell, 1994.

Enterline, Lynn. *The Tears of Narcissus: Melancholia and Masculinity in Early Modern Writing.* Stanford, CA: Stanford University Press, 1995.

Eribon, Didier. *Insult and the Making of the Gay Self.* Translated by Michael Lucey. Durham, NC: Duke University Press, 2004.

Faret, Nicolas. *L'Honnête homme ou l'art de plaire à la cour.* Edited by Maurice Magendie. Geneva: Slatkine Reprints, 1970.

Farrell, Michèle Longino. *Performing Motherhood: The Sévigné Correspondence.* Hanover, NH: University Press of New England, 1991.

Feinberg, Leslie. *Transgender Warriors: Making History from Joan of Arc to Dennis Rodman.* Boston: Beacon Press, 1996.

Ferguson, Gary. "Masculinity, Confession, Modernity: François de Sales and the Penitent Gentleman." *L'Esprit Créateur* 43, no. 3 (2003): 16–25.

Ferrand, Jacques. *Traité de l'essence et guérison de l'amour ou De la mélancolie érotique (1610).* Edited by Gérard Jacquin and Eric Foulon. Paris: Anthropos, 2001.

Fisher, Dominique D., and Lawrence R. Schehr. "Introduction." In *Articulations of Difference: Gender Studies and Writing in French,* edited by Dominique D. Fisher and Lawrence R. Schehr, 1–17. Stanford, CA: Stanford University Press, 1997.

Fitelieu. *La Contre-mode.* Paris: Louys de Hevqveville, 1642.

Fletcher, Jonathan. *Violence and Civilization: An Introduction to the Work of Norbert Elias.* Cambridge: Polity Press, 1997.

Ford, Philip, and Paul White, eds. *Masculinities in Sixteenth-Century France.* Cambridge: Cambridge French Colloquia, 2006.

Foucault, Michel. "De l'amitié comme mode de vie." In *Dits et écrits, 1954–1988,* edited by Daniel Defert and François Ewald, 4:163–67. Bibliothèque des Sciences Humaines. Paris: Gallimard, 1994.

Foucault, Michel. *History of Madness.* Edited by Jean Khalfa. Translated by Jonathan Murphy and Jean Khalfa. New York: Routledge, 2006.

Foucault, Michel. *The History of Sexuality: An Introduction.* Translated by Robert Hurley. New York: Vintage, 1978.

La France devenue italienne avec les autres désordres de la cour. In *Histoire amoureuse des Gaules,* edited by Paul Boiteau. Paris: Jannet, 1858.

Bibliography

Franko, Mark. *Dance as Text: Ideologies of the Baroque Body*. Cambridge: Cambridge University Press, 1993.

Freccero, Carla. *Queer/Early/Modern*. Durham, NC: Duke University Press, 2006.

Freud, Sigmund. "Mourning and Melancholy." In *The Nature of Melancholy*, ed. Jennifer Radden, 283–94. Oxford: Oxford University Press, 2000.

Fumaroli, Marc. "*Les Fées* de Charles Perrault ou De la littérature." In *Le Statut de la littérature: Mélanges offerts à Paul Bénichou*, 153–86. Geneva: Droz, 1982.

Furetière, Antoine. *Dictionnaire universel*. 1690. Marsanne: Redon, 1999. CD-ROM.

Garber, Marjorie. *Vested Interests: Cross-Dressing and Cultural Anxiety*. New York: Routledge, 1992.

Gardiner, Judith Kegan, ed. *Masculinity Studies and Feminist Theory: New Directions*. New York: Columbia University Press, 2002.

Garlick, Steve. "The Beauty of Friendship: Foucault, Masculinity and the Work of Art." *Philosophy and Social Criticism* 28, no. 5 (2002): 558–77.

Gaudet, Charles. *Bibliothèque des petits-maîtres*. Paris: Chez la petite Lolo, Marchande de Galanteries, à la Frivolité, 1762.

Gaudiani, Claire. "The Androgynous Vision in the Love Poetry of Théophile de Viau." *Papers on French Seventeenth Century Literature* 11 (1979): 121–36.

Gaudiani, Claire. *The Cabaret Poetry of Théophile de Viau: Texts and Traditions*. Tübingen: Narr, 1981.

Gerzan, François du Soucy de. *La Conduite du courtisan: Dedié à Mr de Bassompierre*. Paris: Iean Bessin, 1646.

Génetiot, Alain. *Les Genres lyriques mondains (1630–1660): Etude des poésies de Voiture, Vion d'Alibray, Sarasin et Scarron*. Histoire Des Idées et Critique Littéraire, 281. Geneva: Droz, 1990.

Génetiot, Alain. *Poétique du loisir mondain, de Voiture à La Fontaine*. Lumière Classique, 14. Paris: Champion, 1997.

Gibson, Wendy. *Women in Seventeenth-Century France*. New York: St. Martin's Press, 1989.

Godard, Didier. *Le Goût de Monsieur: L'homosexualité masculine au XVIIe siècle*. Montblanc: H & O, 2002.

Goldberg, Jonathan. *Sodometries: Renaissance Texts, Modern Sexualities*. Stanford, CA: Stanford University Press, 1992.

Goldsmith, Elizabeth. *Exclusive Conversations: The Art of Interaction in Seventeenth-Century France*. Philadelaphia: University of Pennsylvania Press, 1988.

Goldsmith, Elizabeth. *Publishing Women's Life Stories in France, 1647–1720: From Voice to Print*. Burlington, VT: Ashgate, 2001.

Goodman, Dena. *The Republic of Letters: A Cultural History of the French Enlightenment*. Ithaca, NY: Cornell University Press, 1994.

Gordon-Seifert, Catherine E. "Strong Men—Weak Women: Gender Representation and the Influence of Lully's 'Operatic Style' on French *Airs Sérieux* (1650–1700)." In *Musical Voices of Early Modern Women: Many-Headed Melodies*, edited by Thomasin Lamay, 135–67. Women and Gender in the Early Modern World. Burlington, VT: Ashgate, 2005.

Goulet, Anne-Madeleine. *Poésie, musique et sociabilité au XVIIe siècle: Les Livres d'airs de différents auteurs publiés chez Ballard de 1658 à 1694*. Paris: H. Champion, 2004.

Grande, Nathalie. *Stratégie de romancières: De "Clélie" à la "Princesse de Clèves" (1654–1678)*. Paris: H. Champion, 1999.

Greenberg, Mitchell. *Baroque Bodies: Psychoanalysis and the Culture of French Absolutism.* Ithaca, NY: Cornell University Press, 2001.

Guild, Elizabeth. "'Le Moyen de faire de cela un grand homme': The Abbé de Choisy and the Unauthorized Body of Representation." *Romanic Review* 85, no. 2 (1994): 179–90.

Habib, Claude. *Galanterie française.* Paris: Gallimard, 2006.

Halperin, David M. *How to Do the History of Homosexuality.* Chicago: University of Chicago Press, 2002.

Halperin, David M. *What Do Gay Men Want? An Essay on Sex, Risk, and Subjectivity.* Ann Arbor: University of Michigan Press, 2007.

Hammond, Nicholas. "All Dressed Up: L'Abbé de Choisy and the Theatricality of Subversion." *Seventeenth-Century French Studies* 21 (1999): 165–72.

Harris, Joseph. *Hidden Agendas: Cross-Dressing in Seventeenth-Century France.* Biblio 17, 156. Tübingen: Gunter Narr Verlag, 2005.

Harris, Joseph. "Novel Upbringings: Education and Gender in Choisy and La Fayette." *Romanic Review* 97, no. 1 (2006): 3–14.

Harris, Joseph. "Stealing Beauty: The Abbé de Choisy's Appropriation of the Feminine." In *Possessions: Essays in French Literature, Cinema and Theory,* edited by Julia Horn and Lynsey Russell-Watts, 121–34. Modern French Identities, 24. Oxford: Peter Lang, 2003.

Harth, Erica. *Cartesian Women: Versions and Subversions of Rational Discourse in the Old Regime.* Ithaca, NY: Cornell University Press, 1992.

Harth, Erica. "The Salon Woman Goes Public . . . or Does She?" In *Going Public: Women and Publishing in Early Modern France,* edited by Elizabeth C. Goldsmith and Dena Goodman, 179–93. Ithaca, NY: Cornell University Press, 1995.

Hekman, Susan J., ed. *Feminist Interpretations of Michel Foucault.* University Park: Pennsylvania State University Press, 1996.

Hepp, Noémi. "A la recherche du mérite des dames." In *Destins et enjeux du XVIIe siècle,* edited by Yves-Marie Bercé, 109–17. Paris: Presses universitaires de France, 1985.

Hepp, Noémi. "A propos de la *Clélie:* Mélancolie et perfection féminine." In Jean Jehasse et al., *Mélanges offerts à Georges Couton,* 161–68. Lyon: Presses universitaires de Lyon, 1981.

Hernandez, Ludovico. *Les Procès de sodomie au XVIe, XVIIe, et XVIIIe siècles.* Paris: Bibliothèque des curieux, 1920.

Hinds, Leonard. "'Honni soit qui mal y pense' I: Avowals, Accusations, and Witnessing in the Trial of Théophile de Viau." *Papers on French Seventeenth Century Literature* 27, no. 53 (2000): 435–44.

Hoffmann, Kathryn. *Society of Pleasures: Interdisciplinary Readings in Pleasure and Power during the Reign of Louis XIV.* New York: St. Martin's Press, 1997.

Irigaray, Luce, ed. *Sexes et genres à travers les langues: Éléments de communication sexuée.* Paris: Editions Grasset, 1990.

Jardine, Alice, and Paul Smith, eds. *Men in Feminism.* New York: Methuen, 1987.

John of Salisbury. *Frivolities of Courtiers and Footprints of Philosophers.* http://www.constitution.org/salisbury/policrat123.htm.

Jouhaud, Christian. *Les Pouvoirs de la littérature: Histoire d'un paradoxe.* Paris: Gallimard, 2000.

Juvenel de Carlincas, Félix. *Le Portrait de la Coquette, ou la Lettre d'Aristandre à Timagène.* Paris: Sercy, 1659.

Kates, Gary. *Monsieur d'Eon is a Woman: A Tale of Political Intrigue and Sexual Masquerade.* Baltimore: John Hopkins University Press, 2001.

Keilhauer, Annette. *Das französische Chanson im späten Ancien Régime: Strukturen, Verbreitungswege und gesellschaftliche Praxis einer populären Literaturform.* Musikwissenschaftliche Publikationen, 10. New York: Georg Olms Verlag, 1998.

Kiblansky, Raymond, Erwin Panofsky, and Fritz Saxl. *Saturn and Melancholy: Studies in the History of Natural Philosophy, Religion, and Art.* London: Nelson, 1964.

Koch, Erec R. "Cartesian Corporeality and (Aesth)Ethics." *PMLA* 121, no. 2 (2006): 405–20.

Krais, Beate. "The Gender Relationship in Bourdieu's Sociology." *SubStance* 93 (2000): 53–67.

Krajewska, Barbara. *Du coeur à l'esprit: Mademoiselle de Scudéry et ses samedis.* Paris: Kimé, 1993.

Krajewska, Barbara. *Mythes et découvertes: le salon littéraire de Madame de Rambouillet dans les lettres des contemporains.* Biblio 17, 52. Paris: Papers on French Seventeenth Century Literature, 1990.

Kristeva, Julia. *Pouvoirs de l'horreur.* Paris: Editions du Seuil, 1980.

La Bruyère, Jean de. *Les Caractères de Théophraste traduits du grec avec Les Caractères ou les Mœurs de ce siècle.* Edited by Robert Garapon. Paris: Garnier Frères, 1962.

Lachèvre, Frédéric. *Bibliographie des recueils collectifs de poésies publiés de 1597 à 1700.* 4 vols. Geneva: Slatkine Reprints, 1967.

Lachèvre, Frédéric. *Le Libertinage devant le Parlement de Paris: Le procès du poète Théophile de Viau (11 juillet 1623–1er septembre 1625).* Paris: H. Champion, 1909.

LaGuardia, David. *Intertextual Masculinities in French Renaissance Literature: Rabelais, Brantôme, and the Cent Nouvelles Nouvelles.* Burlington, VT: Ashgate, 2008.

Laqueur, Thomas. *Making Sex: Body and Gender from the Greeks to Freud.* Cambridge: Harvard University Press, 1990.

Le Hir, Marie-Pierre. "Cultural Studies Bourdieu's Way: Women, Leadership, and Feminist Theory." In *Pierre Bourdieu: Fieldwork in Culture,* edited by Nicholas Brown and Imre Szeman, 123–44. Lanham, MD: Rowman and Littlefield, 2000.

Le Pays, René. *Nouvelles œuvres, suivies du Dialogue de l'Amour et de la raison.* Edited by Albert de Bersaucourt. Collection des chefs-d'œuvre méconnus. Paris: Editions Bossard, 1925.

Le Roux, Nicolas. *La Faveur du roi: Mignons et courtisans au temps des derniers Valois.* Epoques. Seyssel: Champ Vallon, 2001.

Lever, Maurice. *Les Bûchers de Sodome.* Paris: Fayard, 1985.

Lilti, Antoine. *Le Monde des salons: Sociabilité et mondanité à Paris au XVIIIe siècle.* Paris: Fayard, 2005.

Lloyd, Genevieve. *The Man of Reason: "Male" and "Female" in Western Philosophy.* Minneapolis: University of Minnesota Press, 1984.

Long, Kathleen P., ed. *High Anxiety: Masculinity in Crisis in Early Modern France.* Sixteenth Century Essays and Studies. Kirksville, MO: Truman State University Press, 2002.

Lougee, Carolyn C. *Le Paradis des femmes: Women, Salons, and Social Stratification in Seventeenth-Century France.* Princeton, NJ: Princeton University Press, 1976.

Louis, Marie-Victoire. "Bourdieu: Défense et illustration de la domination masculine." *Les Temps modernes* 604 (May–July 1999): 325–58.

Lovell, Terry. "Thinking Feminism with and against Bourdieu." *Feminist Theory* 1, no. 1 (2000): 11–32.

Magendie, Maurice. *La Politesse mondaine et les théories de l'honnêteté en France au XVIIe siècle, de 1600 à 1660.* 2 vols. Paris: Félix Alcan, 1925.

Magne, Emile. *Le Plaisant abbé de Boisrobert, fondateur de l'Académie française, 1592–1662. Documents inédits.* Paris: Mercure de France, 1909.

Magne, Emile. *Voiture et l'Hôtel de Rambouillet.* Vol. 1, *Les origines, 1597–1635;* vol. 2, *Les années de gloire, 1635–1648.* Paris: Emile-Paul Frères, 1929–30.

Mainil, Jean. *Dans les règles du plaisir: Théorie de la différence dans le discours obscène, romanesque et médical de l'Ancien Régime.* Paris: Editions Kimé, 1996.

Maître, Myriam. "L'Amour, geste langagier: Préciosité et politesse chez Madeleine de Scudéry." *Franco Italica* (1999): 163–73.

Maître, Myriam. *Les Précieuses: Naissance des femmes de lettres en France au XVIIe siècle.* Lumière Classique, 25. Paris: Champion, 1999.

Maître, Myriam. "Sapho, reine de Tendre: Entre monarchie absolue et royauté littéraire." In *Madeleine de Scudéry: Une femme de lettres au XVIIe siècle,* 179–93. Arras: Artois Presses Université, 2002.

Mathieu, Nicole-Claude. "Bourdieu ou le pouvoir auto-hypnotique." *Les Temps modernes* 604 (May–July 1999): 286–324.

Maurepas, Jean-Frédéric Phélypeaux comte de, comp. *Recueil dit de Maurepas, pièces libres, chansons, épigrammes, et autres vers satiriques sur divers personnages des siècles de Louis XIV et Louis XV.* 6 vols. Leyde: n.p., 1865.

Maynard, François de. *Poésies de François Maynard: Recueil de 1646 et choix de divers autres recueils.* Edited by F. Gohin. Paris: Garnier Frères, 1927.

McFarlane, Cameron. *The Sodomite in Fiction and Satire, 1660–1750.* Between Men—Between Women. New York: Columbia University Press, 1997.

McLaren, Margaret A. *Feminism, Foucault, and Embodied Subjectivity.* Albany: State University of New York Press, 2002.

Mennell, Stephen. *Norbert Elias: An Introduction.* Dublin: University College Dublin Press, 1998.

Merlin, Hélène. *Public et littérature en France au XVIIe siècle.* Paris: Les Belles Lettres, 1994.

Merlin, Hélène. "Théophile de Viau: Moi libertin, moi abandonné." In *La Liberté de pensée: Hommage à Maurice Laugaa,* 123–36. Licorne, 61. Poitiers: UFR Langues Littératures, 2002.

Merlin, Hélène. "Les Troubles du masculin en France au XVIIe siècle." In *Le Masculin: Identité, Fictions, Dissémination,* edited by Horacio Amigorena and Frédéric Monneyron, 11–57. Paris: L'Harmattan, 1998.

Merrick, Jeffrey. "The Cardinal and the Queen: Sexual and Political Disorders in the Mazarinades." *French Historical Studies* 18, no. 3 (1994): 667–99.

Merrick, Jeffrey. "Chaussons in the Streets: Sodomy in Seventeenth-Century Paris." *Journal of the History of Sexuality* 15, no. 2 (2006): 167–203.

Merrick, Jeffrey. "Male Friendship in Pre-Revolutionary France." *GLQ* 10, no. 3 (2004): 407–32.

Merrick, Jeffrey. "Sodomitical Inclinations in Early Eighteenth-Century Paris." *Eighteenth-Century Studies* 30 (1997): 289–95.

Merrick, Jeffrey. "Sodomitical Scandals and Subcultures in the 1720s." *Men and Masculinities* (1999): 373–92.

Merrick, Jeffrey, and Bryant T. Ragan, eds. *Homosexuality in Early Modern France: A Documentary Collection*. New York: Oxford University Press, 2001.

Mesnard, Jean. "'Honnête homme' et 'honnête femme' au XVIIe siècle." In *Présences féminines: Littérature et société au XVIIe siècle français*, edited by Ian Richmond and Constant Venesoen, 36, 15–46. Biblio 17. Paris: Papers on French Seventeenth Century Literature, 1987.

Ménage, Gilles. *Le Parnasse alarmé*. Paris: n.p., 1649.

Méré, Antoine Gombaud chevalier de. "Divers propos." *Revue d'Histoire Littéraire de la France* (1922–26), 1922: 83–98, 214–24; 1923: 80–89, 380–83, 520–29; 1924: 490–96; 1925: 68–78, 432–56; 1926: 596–601.

Méré, Antoine Gombaud chevalier de. *Lettres de Monsieur le Chevalier de Méré*. 2 vols. Paris: Denis Thierry, 1682.

Méré, Antoine Gombaud chevalier de. *Oeuvres complètes du chevalier de Méré*. Edited by Charles-H. Boudhors. 3 vols. Paris: F. Roches, 1930.

Modleski, Tania. *Feminism without Women: Culture and Criticism in a Postfeminist Age*. New York: Routledge, 1991.

Moi, Toril. "Appropriating Bourdieu: Feminist Theory and Pierre Bourdieu's Sociology of Culture." *New Literary History* 22, no. 4 (1991): 1017–47.

Molière [Jean-Baptiste Poquelin]. *The Misanthrope and Other Plays*. Translated by Donald Frame. New York: Signet Classics, 2005.

Molière [Jean-Baptiste Poquelin]. *Oeuvres complètes*. Edited by Robert Jouanny. 2 vols. Classiques Garnier. Paris: Garnier frères, 1962.

Molière [Jean-Baptiste Poquelin]. *Les Précieuses ridicules*. Edited by Micheline Cuénin. Geneva: Droz, 1973.

Mongrédien, Georges. *Le Grand Condé: L'homme et son œuvre*. Paris: Hachette, 1959.

Mongrédien, Georges. "Introduction." In François-Timoléon de Choisy, *Mémoires de l'abbé de Choisy: Mémoires pour servir à l'histoire de Louis XIV. Mémoires de l'abbe de Choisy habillé en femme*, edited by Georges Mongrédien, 9–22. Paris: Mercure de France, 2000.

Mongrédien, Georges. *Madeleine de Scudéry et son salon, d'après des documents inédits*. Bibliothèque Historia. Paris: Tallandier, 1946.

Montaigne, Michel de. *Les Essais de Michel de Montaigne*. Edited by Pierre Villey. 3 vols. Paris: Presses universitaires de France, 1965.

Montandon, Alain. *Bibliographie des traités de savoir-vivre en Europe*. Clermont-Ferrand: Association des publications de la Faculté des lettres et sciences humaines de Clermont-Ferrand, 1995.

Moriarty, Michael. *Taste and Ideology in Seventeenth-Century France*. Cambridge Studies in French. Cambridge: Cambridge University Press, 1988.

Morlet-Chantalat, Chantal. *La Clélie de Mademoiselle de Scudéry: De l'épopée à la gazette: Un discours féminin de la gloire*. Paris: Champion, 1994.

Mossuz-Lavau, Janine. "Dominants et dominées." *Magazine littéraire* 369 (October 1998): 58.

Motley, Mark. *Becoming a French Aristocrat: The Education of the Court Nobility, 1580–1715*. Princeton, NJ: Princeton University Press, 1990.

Moulton, Ian. *Before Pornography: Erotic Writing in Early Modern England*. Studies in the History of Sexuality. New York: Oxford University Press, 2000.

Mourgues, Odette de. "Voiture and the Question of Wit." *L'Esprit Créateur* 20, no. 4 (1980): 7–18.

Muchembled, Robert. *L'Invention de l'homme moderne: Sensibilités, mœurs et comportements collectifs sous l'Ancien Régime*. Paris: Fayard, 1988.

Muchembled, Robert. *La Société policée: politique et politesse du XVIe au XXe siècle*. Paris: Seuil, 1998.

Munro, James S. *Mademoiselle de Scudéry and the Carte de Tendre*. Durham Modern Languages Series. Durham, UK: University of Durham, 1986.

Nagle, Jean. *La Civilisation du cœur: Histoire du sentiment politique en France, du XIIe au XIXe siècle*. Paris: Fayard, 1998.

Niderst, Alain. *Madeleine de Scudéry, Paul Pellisson et leur monde*. Publications de l'Université de Rouen. Paris: Presses universitaires de France, 1976.

Niderst, Alain, Delphine Denis, and Myriam Maître. "Introduction." In Madeleine de Scudéry and Paul Pellisson-Fontanier, *Chroniques du Samedi, suivies de pièces diverses (1653–1654)*, edited by Alain Niderst, Delphine Denis, and Myriam Maître, 7–45. Sources Classiques. Paris: Champion, 2002.

Nye, Robert A. *Masculinity and Male Codes of Honor in Modern France*. New York: Oxford University Press, 1993.

Oresko, Robert. "Homosexuality and the Court Elites of Early Modern France: Some Problems, Some Suggestions, and an Example." In *The Pursuit of Sodomy: Male Homosexuality in Renaissance and Enlightenment Europe*, edited by Kent Gerard and Gert Hekma, 105–28. New York: Harrington Park Press, 1989.

Park, Katharine, and Robert Nye. "Destiny Is Anatomy." *New Republic*, 18 February 1991, 53–57.

Le Parnasse des poètes satyriques, ou dernier recueil des vers piquans et gaillards de nostre temps. N.p.: n.p., 1622.

Pasquier, Nicolas. *Le Gentilhomme*. Paris: Iean Petit-Pas, 1611.

Paster, Gail Kern. *The Body Embarrassed: Drama and the Disciplines of Shame in Early Modern England*. Ithaca, NY: Cornell University Press, 1993.

Paster, Gail Kern. *Humoring the Body: Emotions and the Shakespearean Stage*. Chicago: University of Chicago Press, 2004.

Pekacz, Jolanta K. *Conservative Tradition in Pre-Revolutionary France: Parisian Salon Women*. The Age of Revolution and Romanticism: Interdisciplinary Studies, 25. New York: Peter Lang, 1999.

Pellisson, Paul. "Discours sur les Œuvres de Monsieur Sarasin." In *L'Esthétique galante: Paul Pellisson, Discours sur les Œuvres de Monsieur Sarasin et autres textes*, edited by Alain Viala, 51–74. Toulouse: Société de Littératures Classiques, 1989.

Pellisson, Paul. *Histoire de l'Académie Françoise*. 2 vols. Paris: J. B. Coignard, 1743.

Pelous, Jean-Michel. *Amour précieux, amour galant (1654–1675): Essai sur la représentation de l'amour dans la littérature et la société mondaines*. Paris: Klincksieck, 1980.

Peters, Jeffrey N. "Boileau's Nerve, or the Poetics of Masculinity." *L'Esprit Créateur* 43, no. 3 (2003): 26–36.

Peters, Jeffrey N. "Is Alceste a Physiognomist? Toward a Masculinity of Reference in the Seventeenth Century." In *Entre Hommes: French and Francophone Masculinities in Culture and Theory*, edited by Todd W. Reeser and Lewis C. Seifert, 87–114. Newark: University of Delaware Press, 2008.

Peters, Jeffrey N. *Mapping Discord: Allegorical Cartography in Early Modern French Writing*. Newark: University of Delaware Press, 2004.

Picard, Roger. *Les Salons littéraires et la société française, 1610–1789*. New York: Brentano's, 1943.

Plantié, Jacqueline. *La mode du portrait littéraire en France (1641–1681)*. Lumière Classique. Paris: H. Champion, 1994.

Poirier, Guy. *L'Homosexualité dans l'imaginaire de la Renaissance*. Confluences-Champion, 7. Paris: Honoré Champion, 1996.

Poullain de La Barre, François. *Three Cartesian Feminist Treatises*. Edited by Marcelle Maistre Welch. Translated by Vivien Bosley. Chicago: University of Chicago Press, 2002.

Praetorius, Dr. N. [Eugène Wilhelm]. "Der homosexuelle Abbé Boisrobert, der Gründer des 'Académie française'." *Zeitschrift für Sexualwissenschaft* 9 (1922): 4–7, 33–42.

Prest, Julia. *Theatre under Louis XIV: Cross-Casting and the Performance of Gender in Drama, Ballet and Opera*. New York: Palgrave Macmillan, 2006.

Prévot, Jacques, ed. *Libertins du XVIIe siècle*. Bibliothèque de la Pléiade. Paris: Gallimard, 1998.

Prosser, Jay. *Second Skins: The Body Narratives of Transsexuality*. Gender and Culture. New York: Columbia University Press, 1998.

Pujo, Bernard. *Le Grand Condé*. Paris: Albin Michel, 1995.

Pure, Michel de. *La Prétieuse ou le mystère des ruelles*. 2 vols. Paris: Droz, 1939.

Quintilian, Marcus Fabius. *The Institutio Oratoria of Quintilian*. Translated by Harold Edgeworth Butler. 4 vols. Cambridge: Harvard University Press, 1976.

Radden, Jennifer, ed. *The Nature of Melancholy*. Oxford: Oxford University Press, 2000.

Ranum, Orest. "Judicial Virtue and Masculinity: The Image of the Judge in the 1660s." In *Curiosité: Etudes d'histoire de l'art en l'honneur d'Antoine Schnapper*, edited by Antoine Schnapper, Olivier Bonfait, Véronique Gérard Powell, and Philippe Sénéchal, 75–82. Paris: Flammarion, 1998.

Raunié, Emile. "Préface." In *Chansonnier historique du XVIIIe siècle*, edited by Emile Raunié, 1:i–xcviii. 10 vols. Paris: A. Quantin, 1879.

Raymond, Janice G. "Sappho by Surgery: The Transsexually Constructed Lesbian-Feminist." In *The Transgender Studies Reader*, edited by Susan Stryker and Stephen Whittle, 131–43. New York: Routledge, 2006.

Reed, Sue Welsh. *French Prints from the Age of the Musketeers*. Boston: Museum of Fine Arts, Boston, 1998.

Reeser, Todd W. *Moderating Masculinity in Early Modern Culture*. North Carolina Studies in the Romance Languages and Literatures, 283. Chapel Hill: UNC Department of Romance Languages, 2006.

Reeser, Todd W., and Lewis C. Seifert. "Oscillating Masculinity in Bourdieu's *La Domination masculine*." *L'Esprit Créateur* 43, no. 3 (2004): 87–97.

Reichardt, Rolf. "Der Honnête homme zwischen höfischer und bürgelicher Gesellschaft. Seriell-begriffsgeschichtliche Untersuchungen von Honnêteté-Traktaten des 17. und 18. Jahrhunderts." *Archiv für Kulturgeschicte* 69 (1987): 341–70.

"Response de Tircis à la plainte de Théophile prisonnier." Paris: n.p., 1623.

Rey, Michel. "1700–1750, Les Sodomites créent un mode de vie." *Cahiers Gai-Kitsch-Camp* 24 (1994): xi–xxxiii.

Reynes, Geneviève. *L'Abbé de Choisy, ou, l'ingénu libertin*. Paris: Presses de la Renaissance, 1983.

Richards, Jennifer. "'A Wanton Trade of Living?' Rhetoric, Effeminacy, and the Early Modern Courtier." *Criticism* 42, no. 2 (2000): 185–206.

Richelet, Pierre. *Dictionnaire français*. 1680. Marsanne: Redon, 1999. CD-ROM.

Riddell, Carol. "Divided Sisterhood: A Critical Review of Janice Raymond's *The Trans-*

sexual *Empire.*" In *The Transgender Studies Reader,* edited by Susan Stryker and Stephen Whittle, 144–58. New York: Routledge, 2006.

Robinson, David M. *Closeted Writing and Lesbian and Gay Literature: Classical, Early Modern, Eighteenth-Century.* Burlington, VT: Ashgate, 2006.

Roche, Daniel. *The Culture of Clothing: Dress and Fashion in the "Ancien Régime."* Translated by Jean Birrell. Cambridge: Cambridge University Press, 1994.

Rollin, Sophie. *Le Style de Vincent Voiture: Une esthétique galante.* Renaissance et Age Classique. Saint-Etienne: Publications de l'Université de Saint-Etienne, 2006.

Roques, Mario. "Autour du procès de Théophile: Histoire d'une variante." In *Mélanges d'histoire littéraire de la Renaissance offerts à Henri Chamard,* 285–93. Paris: Nizet, 1951.

Rosso, Corrado. "L'Honnête homme dans la tradition italienne et française." In *Actes de New Orleans,* 105–23. Biblio 17, 5. Paris: Papers on French Seventeenth Century Literature, 1982.

Rousseau, Jean-Jacques. *Lettre à d'Alembert sur son article Genève.* Edited by Marc Launay. Paris: Garnier-Flammarion, 1967.

Rubin, Gayle. "Of Catamites and Kings: Reflections on Butch, Gender, and Boundaries." In *The Transgender Studies Reader,* edited by Susan Stryker and Stephen Whittle, 471–80. New York: Routledge, 2006.

Runte, Annette. "Die Geometrie adligen Geschlechtertausches: Vormoderne Travestie im höfischen Raum des französischen Absolutismus am Beispiel Abbé de Choisy." *Forum Homosexualität und Literatur,* no. 40 (2002): 9–33.

Ruppert, Jacques. *Le Costume.* 7 vols. Paris: Flammarion, 1996.

Russo, Elena. *La Cour et la ville de la littérature classique aux Lumières: L'invention de soi.* Paris: Presses universitaires de France, 2002.

Russo, Elena. "Sociability, Cartesianism, and Nostalgia in Libertine Discourse." *Eighteenth-Century Studies* 30, no. 4 (1997): 383–400.

Saba, Guido. *Fortunes et infortunes de Théophile de Viau: Histoire de la critique suivie d'une bibliographie.* Paris: Klincksieck, 1997.

Saba, Guido. *Théophile de Viau: un poète rebelle.* Ecrivains. Paris: Presses universitaires de France, 1999.

Saint-Amand, Pierre. "Le Triomphe des Beaux: Petits-maîtres et jolis hommes au dix-huitième siècle." *L'Esprit Créateur* 43, no. 3 (2003): 37–46.

Saint-Evremond, Charles de. "Comédie des Académistes." In *La "Comédie des Académistes" di Saint-Evremond e il contrastato esordio dell'Accademia Francese nella satira letteraria del tempo,* edited by Paolo Carile. Milan: Instituto Editoriale Cisalpino, 1969.

Salazar, Philippe-Joseph. "Herculean Lovers: Towards a History of Men's Friendship in the 17th Century." *Thamyris* 4, no. 2 (1997): 249–66.

Sarasin, Jean-François. *Œuvres de J.-Fr. Sarasin.* Edited by Paul Festugière. 2 vols. Paris: Champion, 1926.

Sarasin, Jean-François. *Les Œuvres de Monsieur Sarasin.* Paris: Thomas Jolly, 1663.

Sarasin, Jean-François. "La Pompe funèbre de Voiture à Monsieur Ménage." In *Œuvres de J.-Fr. Sarasin,* edited by Paul Festugière, 2:437–60. 2 vols. 1656; Paris: Champion, 1926.

Scarron, Paul. *Poésies diverses.* Edited by Maurice Cauchie. 2 vols. Paris: Marcel Didier, 1960.

Schachter, Marc D. "'That Friendship Which Possesses the Soul': Montaigne Loves La Boétie." *Journal of Homosexuality* 41, nos. 3–4 (2001): 5–21.

Bibliography

Schachter, Marc D. *Voluntary Servitude and the Erotics of Friendship: From Classical Antiquity to Early Modern France.* Burlington, VT: Ashgate, 2008.

Schalk, Ellery. *From Valor to Pedigree: Ideas of Nobility in France in the Sixteenth and Seventeenth Centuries.* Princeton, NJ: Princeton University Press, 1986.

Schiesari, Juliana. *The Gendering of Melancholia: Feminism, Psychoanalysis, and the Symbolics of Loss in Renaissance Literature.* Ithaca, NY: Cornell University Press, 1992.

Schleiner, Winfried. "Early Modern Controversies about the One-Sex Model." *Renaissance Quarterly* 53, no. 1 (2000): 180–91.

Scholar, Richard. *The Je-Ne-Sais-Quoi in Early Modern Europe: Encounters with a Certain Something.* Oxford: Oxford University Press, 2005.

Scodel, Joshua. *Excess and the Mean in Early Modern English Literature.* Princeton, NJ: Princeton University Press, 2002.

Scudéry, Georges de. "Le Pousseur de Beaux Sentiments." In *Poésies choisies de Messieurs Bensserade, Boisrobert, Bertault, de Marigny, de Lafemas, Boileau, de Montereuil, de Francheville, Testu, Petit, Loret, Le Bret, Bardou, et de plusieurs autres,* 411. Paris: Charles de Sercy, 1665.

Scudéry, Georges de, and Madeleine de Scudéry. *Artamène, ou le Grand Cyrus.* Institut de Littérature Française Moderne, Université de Neuchâtel. http://www.artamene.org.

Scudéry, Georges de, and Madeleine de Scudéry. *Artamène ou le Grand Cyrus.* 10 vols. Geneva: Slatkine Reprints, 1972.

Scudéry, Georges de, and Madeleine de Scudéry. *Artamène ou le Grand Cyrus.* Edited by Claude Bourqui and Alexandre Gefen. Paris: Garnier-Flammarion, 2005.

Scudéry, Madeleine de. *Clélie, histoire romaine.* Edited by Chantal Morlet-Chantalat. 5 vols. Sources Classiques. Paris: Champion, 2001–5.

Scudéry, Madeleine de. *Clélie, histoire romaine.* Edited by Delphine Denis. Paris: Folio, 2006.

Scudéry, Madeleine de. *"De l'air galant" et autres conversations (1653–1684): Pour une étude de l'archive galante.* Edited by Delphine Denis. 1653–84. Sources Classiques, 5. Paris: Champion, 1998.

Scudéry, Madeleine de. "De l'air galant." In *"De l'air galant" et autres conversations (1653–1684): Pour une étude de l'archive galante,* edited by Delphine Denis, 49–57. Sources Classiques, 5. Paris: Champion, 1998.

Scudéry, Madeleine de. *The Story of Sapho.* Translated by Karen Newman. Chicago: University of Chicago Press, 2003.

Scudéry, Madeleine de, and Paul Pellisson-Fontanier. *Chroniques du Samedi, suivies de pièces diverses (1653–1654).* Edited by Alain Niderst, Delphine Denis, and Myriam Maître. Sources Classiques. Paris: Champion, 2002.

Sedgwick, Eve Kosofsky. *Between Men: English Literature and Male Homosocial Desire.* Gender and Culture. New York: Columbia University Press, 1985.

Sedgwick, Eve Kosofsky. *Epistemology of the Closet.* Berkeley and Los Angeles: University of California Press, 1990.

Seifert, Lewis C. "Eroticizing the Fronde: Sexual Deviance and Political Disorder in the *Mazarinades.*" *L'Esprit Créateur* 35, no. 2 (1995): 22–36.

Seifert, Lewis C. "The Male Writer and the 'Marked' Self in Seventeenth-Century France: The Case of the Abbé de Boisrobert." *EMF: Studies in Early Modern France* 9: The New Biographical Criticism (2004): 125–42.

Seifert, Lewis C. "Masculinity in *The Princess of Clèves.*" In *Approaches to Teaching Lafayette's The Princess of Clèves,* edited by Faith Beasley, 60–67. Approaches to

Teaching World Literature. New York: Modern Language Association of America, 1998.

Seifert, Lewis C. "Pig or Prince? Murat, d'Aulnoy and the Limits of 'Civilized' Masculinity." In *High Anxiety: Masculinity in Crisis in Early Modern France*, edited by Kathleen P. Long, 183–210. Sixteenth Century Essays and Studies. Kirksville, MO: Truman State University Press, 2002.

Sibalis, Michael. "Homosexuality in Early Modern France." In *Queer Masculinities, 1550–1800: Siting Same-Sex Desire in the Early Modern World*, edited by Katherine O'Donnell and Michael O'Rourke, 211–31. Basingstoke, UK: Palgrave Macmillan, 2006.

Silverman, Kaja. *Male Subjectivity at the Margins.* New York: Routledge, 1992.

Smith, Gretchen Elizabeth. *The Performance of Male Nobility in Molière's Comédies-Ballets: Staging the Courtier.* Burlington, VT: Ashgate, 2005.

Smith, Pauline. *The Anti-courtier Trend in Sixteenth-Century French Literature.* Geneva: Droz, 1966.

Solnon, Jean-François. *La Cour de France.* Paris: Fayard, 1987.

Somaize, Baudeau de. "Le Grand dictionnaire des précieuses." In Roger Duchêne, *Les Précieuses ou comment l'esprit vint aux femmes,* 414–548. Paris: Fayard, 2001.

Soman, Alfred. "Pathologie historique: Le témoignage des procès de bestialité aux XVIe–XVIIe siècles." In *Actes du 107e Congrès national des Sociétés savantes: Section de philologie moderne et d'histoire jusqu'à 1610,* 1:149–61. 2 vols. Paris, 1984.

Sorel, Charles. "Les Lois de la galanterie." In Roger Duchêne, *Les Précieuses ou comment l'esprit vint aux femmes,* 311–26. Paris: Fayard, 2001.

Stallybrass, Peter, and Allon White. *The Politics and Poetics of Transgression.* Ithaca, NY: Cornell University Press, 1986.

Stanton, Domna C. *The Aristocrat as Art: A Study of the Honnête Homme and the Dandy in Seventeenth- and Nineteenth-Century French Literature.* New York: Columbia University Press, 1980.

Stanton, Domna C. "The Fiction of Préciosité and the Fear of Women." *Yale French Studies* 62 (1981): 107–34.

Steinberg, Sylvie. *La Confusion des sexes: Le travestissement de la Renaissance à la Révolution.* Paris: Fayard, 2001.

Stewart, Alan. "The Early Modern Closet Discovered." *Representations* 50 (Spring 1995): 76–100.

Stone, Donald. "The Sexual Outlaw in France, 1602." *Journal of the History of Sexuality* 2, no. 4 (1992): 597–608.

Strosetzki, Christoph. *Rhétorique de la conversation: Sa dimension littéraire et linguistique dans la société française du XVIIe siècle.* Translated by Sabine Seubert. Biblio 17, 20. Tübingen: Papers on French Seventeenth Century Literature, 1984.

Stryker, Susan. "(De)Subjugated Knowledges: An Introduction to Transgender Studies." In *The Transgender Studies Reader,* edited by Susan Stryker and Stephen Whittle, 1–17. New York: Routledge, 2006.

Stuurman, Siep. *François Poulain de la Barre and the Invention of Modern Equality.* Cambridge: Harvard University Press, 2004.

Surkiss, Judith. "No Fun and Games Until Someone Loses an Eye: Transgression and Masculinity in Bataille and Foucault." *Diacritics* 26, no. 2 (1996): 18–30.

Tallemant des Réaux, Gédéon. *Historiettes.* Edited by Antoine Adam. 2 vols. Paris: Pléiade, 1960.

Bibliography

Teasley, David. "The Charge of Sodomy as a Political Weapon in Early Modern France: The Case of Henry III in Catholic League Polemic, 1585–1589." *Maryland Historian* 18 (1987): 17–30.

Timmermans, Linda. *L'Accès des femmes à la culture (1598–1715): Un débat d'idées de Saint François de Sales à la Marquise de Lambert.* Paris: Champion, 1993.

Traister, Bryce. "Academic Viagra: The Rise of American Masculinity Studies." *American Quarterly* 52, no. 2 (2000): 274–304.

Trumbach, Randolph. "Gender and the Homosexual Role in Modern Western Culture: The 18th and the 19th Centuries Compared." In *Homosexuality, Which Homosexuality?* edited by Dennis Altman et al., 149–69. London: GMP Publishers, 1989.

Trumbach, Randolph. *Heterosexuality and the Third Gender in Enlightenment London.* Vol. 1 of *Sex and the Gender Revolution.* Chicago: University of Chicago Press, 1998.

Trumbach, Randolph. "Sex, Gender, and Sexual Identity in Modern Culture: Male Sodomy and Female Prostitution in Enlightenment England." In *Forbidden History: The State, Society, and the Regulation of Sexuality in Modern Europe*, edited by John C. Flout, 89–106. Chicago: University of Chicago Press, 1992.

Van der Cruysse, Dirk. *L'Abbé de Choisy, androgyne et mandarin.* Paris: Fayard, 1995.

Van Krieken, Robert. *Norbert Elias.* New York: Routledge, 1998.

Vaugelas, Claude Favre de. *Remarques sur la langue françoise utiles à ceux qui veulent bien parler et bien escrire.* Paris: Augustin Courbé, 1647.

Velay-Vallantin, Catherine, and Marie-Jeanne L'Héritier de Villandon. *La fille en garçon.* Classiques de la Littérature Orale. Carcassonne: GARAE/Hésiode, 1992.

Viala, Alain. "D'une politique des formes: La galanterie." *XVIIe siècle* 182 (1994): 143–51.

Viala, Alain. "L'Eloquence galante: Une problématique de l'adhésion." In *Images de soi dans le discours: la construction de l'ethos*, edited by Ruth Amossy, 177–95. Lausanne: Delachaux et Niestlé, 1999.

Viala, Alain. *La France galante: Essai historique sur une catégorie culturelle, de ses origines jusqu'à la Révolution.* Les Litteraires. Paris: Presses universitaires de France, 2008.

Viala, Alain. "Introduction." In *L'Esthétique galante: Paul Pellisson, Discours sur les Œuvres de Monsieur Sarasin et autres textes*, edited by Alain Viala. Toulouse: Société de Littératures Classiques, 1989.

Viala, Alain. "La Littérature galante: Histoire et problématique." In *Il Seicento francese oggi: Situazione e prospettive della ricerca*, 101–13. Quaderni del Seicento Francese, 11. Bari: Adriatica; Paris: Nizet, 1994.

Viala, Alain. *Naissance de l'écrivain: Sociologie de la littérature à l'âge classique.* Le Sens Commun. Paris: Editions de Minuit, 1985.

Viala, Alain. "'Les Signes Galants': A Historical Reevaluation of 'Galanterie.'" *Yale French Studies* 92 (1997): 11–29.

Viau, Théophile de. *Œuvres complètes.* Edited by Guido Saba. Poeti e prosatori francesi. 4 vols. Paris: Nizet, 1978–87.

Viau, Théophile de. *Œuvres poétiques.* Edited by Guido Saba. Classiques Garnier. Paris: Bordas, 1990.

Viau, Théophile de. "Plainte de Théophile à un sien amy. Pendant son absence." N.p., 1623.

Vienne, Philibert de. *Le Philosophe de Court.* Edited by Pauline M. Smith. Textes Littéraires Français. Geneva: Droz, 1990.

Vincent, Thierry. *L'Indifférence des sexes: Critique psychanalytique de Bourdieu et de l'idée de domination masculine.* Strasbourg: Arcanes, 2002.

Voiture, Vincent. *Œuvres de Voiture: lettres et poésies.* Edited by M. A. Ubicini. 1855; Geneva: Slatkine Reprints, 1967.

Waller, Margaret. "The Emperor's New Clothes: Display, Cover-Up and Exposure in Modern Masculinity." In *Entre Hommes: French and Francophone Masculinities in Theory and Culture,* edited by Todd W. Reeser and Lewis C. Seifert, 115–42. Newark: University of Delaware Press, 2008.

Whitehead, Stephen M., and Frank J. Barrett, eds. *The Masculinities Reader.* Cambridge: Polity; Malden, MA: Blackwell, 2001.

Whittle, Stephen. "Forward." In *The Transgender Studies Reader,* edited by Susan Stryker and Stephen Whittle, xi–xvi. New York: Routledge, 2006.

Wilkin, Rebecca. "Descartes, Individualism, and the Fetal Subject." *differences* 19, no. 1 (2008): 96–127.

Wilkin, Rebecca. *Women, Imagination, and the Search for Truth in Early Modern France.* Burlington, VT: Ashgate, 2009.

Wintroub, Michael. "Words, Deeds, and a Womanly King." *French Historical Studies* 28, no. 3 (2005): 387–413.

Zanger, Abby. "Lim(b)Inal Images: 'Betwixt and Between' Louis XIV's Martial and Marital Bodies." In *From the Royal to the Republican Body: Incorporating the Political in Seventeenth- and Eighteenth-Century France,* edited by Sara E. Melzer and Kathryn Norberg, 32–63. Berkeley and Los Angeles: University of California Press, 1998.

Zorach, Rebecca. "The Matter of Italy: Sodomy and the Scandal of Style in Sixteenth-Century France." *Journal of Medieval and Early Modern Studies* 28, no. 3 (1998): 581–609.

Index

abjection, 14–15, 166
Académie Française, 175, 176
Adam, Antoine, 185, 204, 289n109,
  291–92n136, 292n144, 293n153
affectation, 110
affectivity: gender and, 119; male body
  and, 146; men and, 123–24. *See also*
  melancholy; *tendresse*
aggression: civilizing process and, 8–9,
  256n19; galanterie and, 89; honnêteté
  and, 9
agrément, 44, 112, 260n27, 261n32
air galant (Scudéry, Madeleine de):
  definition of, 118; men and, 118–19;
  men vs. women in, 120–22; power in,
  121–25; *tendresse* and, 127; women and,
  120
Alcibiades, 30, 38, 50
Alexander the Great, 30, 38
Aligre, Marie d', 90
Amadis de Gaule, 104
anagnorisis, 239–41
Angennes, Julie d', 105
"Apologie de Théophile" (Viau), 189,
  193–96, 292n37, 292n150
Aragonais, Jeanne, 90
Arditi, Jorge, 258n2, 259n7
Argenson, Marc-René de Voyer de
  Paulmy d', 160, 214, 294n2
Ariosto, Ludovico, 103–4
aristocracy: benefits of absolutism for, 75;
  curialization of, 74–75; emasculation
  of, 75; honnêteté and, 38; ideal of, un-
  der Henri III, 73; pacification of, and
  Louis XIV, 8, 75
Artamène ou le Grand Cyrus (Scudéry,
  Madeleine de), 11, 70, 108–9, 117,

118–19, 120, 122, 123–24, 132, 135,
  138–39, 141–42, 145, 277n6, 278n8,
  278n14, 279n33, 279n37, 280n55. *See
  also* Scudéry (Madeleine de)
art de plaire, 11, 25–26, 41, 45, 87
Art poétique (Boileau), 55
ataraxia, 26
Aubignac, Abbé François Hédelin d', 81,
  92
Auchy, Charlotte des Ursins, d', 79
Augustus (Gaius Julius Caesar Octa-
  vianus), 30
authorship, 17, 186, 192, 289–90nn110–12,
  232–33, 273–74n10, 300n73

Badinter, Elizabeth, 278n21
Balzac, Jean-Louis Guez de: career of,
  290n118; Voiture and, 108, 110–11, 115,
  271n117, 275n23; writer in Rambouillet's salon, 81
bardache, 164, 171
Barthes, Roland, 271n116
Baudelaire, Charles, 184
Baverel-Croissant, Marie-Françoise,
  291–92n136
Beasley, Faith, 78, 257n25, 276n49, 287n85
bel esprit, 89
Bellegarde, Abbé Jean-Baptiste Morvan
  de, 63–64
Benedicti, Jean, 67, 264n29
Bertrand, Dominique, 209
Beugnot, Bernard, 276n47
bienséances, 25, 27, 33, 78
biography, 17
body: in Cartesian dualism, 252n5; cross-
  dressing and constructivist readings of,
  209; Foucault on, in seventeenth

body (*continued*)
century, 12–14, 257n28; as nature, 237–40; one-sex vs. two-sex model and, 211, 253n7, 296n25; poststructuralist vs. transgender theories of, 210, 297n44; theatricality of, 223–27, 298n52; transformation of, 220–21, 298nn48–49; in transgender studies, 210. *See also* body image; female body; male body; material body

body image: "Histoire de la marquisemarquis de Banneville," 233, 239, 240; material body and, 219, 239–40; *Mémoires de l'Abbé de Choisy habillé en femme* and, 218–21, 222, 298n47; sentient experience and, 220; transgender and, 219–20

Boer, Josephine de, 267–68n82

Boileau-Despréaux, Nicolas: *Art poétique*, 55; DeJean on, 265n43; "Dialogue des héros de roman," 70–71, 119, 135, 265nn43–44; on galant homme, 65–66; on Scudéry (Madeleine de), 70–71, 92, 119, 120, 135, 265nn43–44, 280n42; quartier du Temple and, 160; *querelle des femmes* and, 168

Boisrobert, Abbé François Le Métel de, 173–81; *Epistres en vers*, 178; Godard on, 288n96; Ménage and, 178–79; Ninon de Lenclos and, 177; reputation as sodomite, 15, 153, 156, 173–81; "Response au Parnasse alarmé," 178–79; Richelieu and, 175, 177; Saint-Evremond on, 176; scandals about sodomy of, 177–79; scholarship on, 288n91; secrecy about sodomy of, 179–80; Tallemant on, 175, 176–79, 288n91; women and, 176

Bordo, Susan, 252n5

Bosse, Abraham, 246–50, 302n1

Bossy, Michel-André, 266n46

Bouhours, Dominique: cross-gendered ideal of, 112–13; salons and, 276n49; on Voiture, 111–14;

Bourdieu, Pierre: Foucault and, on power, 13, 14; on masculinity, 5–7, 17, 59, 80, 249, 250, 254n11, 255nn12–13, 255n15, 257n31, 258n36, 303n3, 303n5

Bray, Alan, 201, 204–5, 282n7, 283n20, 287n89, 294n170

Brébeuf, Georges de, 272n129

Brégy, Charlotte de Saumaise de Chauzan de Flécelles de, 84, 91

Breitenberg, Mark, 68, 255n15

Brunet (page de la musique du Roi), 169, 171, 286n74

Buckingham, George Villiers, Duke of, 55–56

Burke, Peter, 161

Bury, Emmanuel, 258n2, 259n7

Bussy-Rabutin, Roger de, 24–25

Butler, Judith, 209, 246, 250, 286n79, 293n157, 295n14, 297n44, 303n2

cabinet: closet and, 174, 180–81; conversation and, 174; definition of, 173; intimacy and, 174; *particulier* and, 174; privacy and, 173; secrecy and, 174–75

Caesar, Julius, 29, 38–40, 152, 262n53

Caillières, Jacques de, 8, 29–30, 77–78

Campistron, Jean Galbert de, 164, 284n50

canon, 18

Carlincas, Félix Juvenel de, 66

Carte de Tendre (Scudéry, Madeleine de): DeJean on, 278n11; female authority and, 121; figuration of Woman, 131; interpretation and, 131; men and women in, 131; Peters on, 121, 131, 272n125, 275n37, 278nn10–11, 279n28, 279n31; satires of, 92; *tendresse* and, 127, 129–32

Cartesianism, 252–53n5

Castiglione, Baldassare: conduct literature and, 8; on effeminacy, 72; embraced by seventeenth-century France, 74; on moderation, 72; rejected by sixteenth-century France, 72; on *sprezzatura*, 28, 63; on subservience to prince, 76; source for honnêteté, 23, 24, 34

casuistry, 195

Certain, Marie-Françoise, 169, 171

Chalesme, 83

Chansonnier Clairambault, 283n25

Chansonnier Maurepas: composition of, 159; contents of, 158, 283n22; events and persons in, 160. *See also* satires of "sodomites"

Chapelain, Jean, 79, 82, 99, 109, 269n97, 275n23

Charbonneau, Frédéric, 209, 298n53

Charron, Pierre, 61

Chartier, Roger, 256n17, 259n7

Chausson, Jacques, 153, 162, 163, 164, 167, 284n35, 284n41, 284n43, 284n47

Chavaroche, Jean de, 81

Choisy, Abbé François-Timoléon de, 207–45; as author of "Histoire de la marquise-marquis de Banneville," 233, 300n73; autobiography and, 215–16; Bertrand on, 209; Charbonneau on, 209, 298n53; cross-dressing and, 14, 15–16, 207–45, 297n42; d'Argenson on, 294n2; on effeminacy of Philippe d'Orléans, 76, 267n68; gambling and, 232; Guild on, 209–10; "Histoire de la marquise-marquis de Banneville," 207, 210, 232–45, 300–301nn74–75, 301n85, 302nn91–92, 302n95; interpretations of cross-dressing by, 209–10; Mémoires de l'abbé de Choisy habillé en femme, 207, 210, 213–32, 233, 244–45, 297n38, 297n47, 298nn48–49, 298n52, 298n53, 298–99nn58–60, 299n64, 299n69, 299–300nn71–72; on men's vs. women's writing, 234–35; one-sex vs. two-sex model and, 211; on friendship, 229–30; pathologizing interpretation of, 209; performative interpretation of, 209–10; public reaction to cross-dressing by, 297n42; Reynes on, 212–13, 297n42, 299n66, 299–300n72; subjectivity and, 227; subversiveness of writings by, 209; as transgender, 210–32; as transsexual, 212–13; transitions to femininity by, 244–45; Van der Cruysse on, 212, 294nn3–4. See also "Histoire de la marquise-marquis de Banneville"; Mémoires de l'abbé de Choisy habillé en femme

Christina (Queen of Sweden), 84, 91

Chroniques du Samedi (Scudéry, Madeleine de), 11, 90–91, 117, 118, 121, 125, 126, 127, 132, 142–47, 278n15, 279n29, 280–81nn59–61. See also Scudéry (Madeleine de)

Chupeau, Jacques, 300n73

Cicero, Marcus Tullius, 24, 26, 98

civility: dominance and, 8; essentialism of, 278n17; gender and, 7–9; intersubjectivity and, 9; masculinity and, 7–12; men and, 7–8. See also galanterie; honnêteté; salons; sociability

civilizing process: aggression and, 8–9, 256n19; gender and, 8, 120; honnêteté and, 21; masculine subjectivity and, 8–9. See also Elias, Norbert

Clairambault, Pierre, 159, 160, 283n25, 283n28

Clarke, Stanley, 252n5

Clélie (Scudéry, Madeleine de), 11, 70, 117, 118, 122–23, 126–34, 135–38, 139–41, 145, 278n15, 278–79n22, 279n25, 279n32, 280n50, 280n55. See also Scudéry (Madeleine de)

closet, 174, 180–81, 287n87

Colletet, Guillaume, 62

commerce du monde, le. See social exchange

Comminges, François Guitaut de, 164, 284n48

Confraternity scandal of 1682, 161, 167, 170, 284n33, 284n35

Conrart, Valentin, 90

conversation: cabinet and, 174; galanterie and, 87; in honnêteté, 39, 41, 43, 260n26; salons and, 79–81, 83; Scudéry (Madeleine de) on, 117, 118, 120, 123; in seventeenth-century France, 271n113, 271n117; Voiture and, 98, 100, 101, 102; women and, 10, 24, 27, 78

Conversations, Les (Méré), 38–40, 47–48, 261n39

coquets, 84

Corneille, Pierre, 3, 223

Costar, Pierre, 108, 110–11, 274n15

courtiers: critiques of, in the Middle Ages, 71–72; effeminacy of, 71–77; soft ideal for, during seventeenth century, 74; women and, 77

courtly love, 44–47, 87, 89, 91, 103, 129, 119

Courtin, Antoine de, 74

Cousin, Victor, 276n2

Cowart, Georgia, 265n40

Craveri, Benedetta, 10
Crawford, Katherine, 253n6, 257n32, 282n13
Créquy, François, chevalier de, 166
cross-dressing: attitudes toward, in early modern France, 208; Choisy and, 207–45, 297n42; condemnation of men and, 208; Garber on, 301n83; gender norms and, 208, 236; interpretations of Choisy's, 208–9; masculine dominance and, 12, 15–16; public reactions to Choisy's, 297n42; in seventeenth-century fiction, 235–36, 239–41
Cuénin, Micheline, 103
Cureau de la Chambre, Marin, 68
Cygnus, 197–98

Darmancour, Pierre, 300n73
Darnton, Robert, 160, 283n30
Declercq, Gilles, 276n47
decorum, 24
DeJean, Joan: on Boileau, 265n43; on the *Carte de Tendre*, 278n11; on Choisy, 296n25, 300n73, 301n75, 302n92; on salon writing, 78; on seventeenth-century novel, 271n113; on "tender geography," 118, 277n4; on Théophile de Viau, 186–87, 196, 288n103, 289n109, 289n112, 290n114, 291n128
della Casa, Giovanni, 9
Deloffre, Frédéric, 273n138
Denis, Delphine, 86, 272n126, 277n2, 277n5, 280n58
Dens, Jean-Pierre, 258n2
Des Barreaux, Jacques Vallée, 15, 197–206, 289n109, 291n136, 292n144, 293n153, 293n160, 293n165, 294nn167–68
Descartes, René, 3, 252–53n5
des Loges, Marie Bruneau, 79
des Ursins, Marie-Félice, 197
Dewald, Jonathan, 255–56n16
"Dialogue des héros de roman" (Boileau), 70–71, 119, 135, 265nn43–44
DiPiero, Thomas, 256n17
Discours de la justesse (Méré), 110
Discours de la vraïe Honnesteté (Méré), 30, 53

Doctrine curieuse des beaux esprits de ce temps, La (Garasse), 182
dominance: abjection and, 14; civility and, 8; masculine habitus and, 5; masculinity and, 2; as struggle, 5. *See also* dominated masculinity; masculine dominance; masculine subjectivity
dominated masculinity, 5–7, 9
Donneau de Visé, Jean, 99
douceur, 88, 100, 113, 271n117
Duchêne, Roger, 95, 269n96, 269n106, 272n126
Du Saix, Antoine, 72–73

effeminacy: appearance as sign of, 64; Bellegarde on, 63–64; Castiglione on, 72; causes of, 67–71; concupiscence as cause of, 67; continuity of, 58; contradictions exposed by, 71; courtiers and, 71–77; critiques of, in the Middle Ages, 71–72; definition of, 58–59; erotomania as cause of, 68; excess as sign of, 60–61; extravagance as sign of, 63; Faret on, 63, 64; fashion and, 61, 65, 268n15; female principle and, 60; femininity and, 58–59, 65; galanterie and, 89–91; hard masculinity contrasted with, 61; Henri III and, 73, 74; heterosexuality and, 67, 68–70, 85, 264n28; in "Histoire de la marquise-marquis de Banneville" (Choisy), 242–44; homosexuality and, 66–67, 243–44, 264n28; homosociality and, 67; humoral medicine on, 68–69; La Bruyère on, 65; lack and, 61; language as sign of, 65–66; love as cause of, 69–70; male body and, 58, 62, 63–65; male-female sociability and, 10; misogyny and, 60; moderation and, 61, 72, 73; *mollesse* as signifier of, 61–62; mollitude as cause of, 67; narcissism as sign of, 63–64; novels as cause of, 70–71; ostentatiousness as sign of, 65; as perspective on masculinity, 59; *petits-maîtres* and, 96–97; *précieuses* and, 93–96; relation to dominant masculinity, 59; salons and, 77–86; Scudéry on, 118, 119, 147; sex/gender system and, 97; sexual intercourse as cause of,

68–69; signs of, 60–67; soft masculinity
and, 59; softness as sign of, 61; staging
of, 58; terms for, in early modern
France, 71, 265–66n45; Voiture and,
108–15; women and, 61, 63, 64, 69–71
Elias, Norbert, 9, 21, 74, 256nn18–19. *See
also* civilizing process
enjouement, 87, 100, 127, 136, 138, 142
Enterline, Lynne, 140, 275n20, 280n54
Eon de Beaumont, Charles-Geneviève-
Louis-Auguste-André-Timothée d',
296n26
Epistres en vers (Boisrobert), 178
Eribon, Didier: on gay self, 181, 165–86,
187, 201; on insults, 156–57, 172

Faret, Nicolas, 7, 9, 24, 61, 64, 176, 263n15
fashion, 33–34, 55, 57, 61, 65, 108, 246–50,
263n15
fat, 64, 140, 273n140
Feinberg, Leslie, 296n27
female body: grotesque, 169, 171; honnêteté and, 43–44; one-sex gender
model and, 211, 253n7; sexualized,
168
female principle, 42, 53, 60, 118
femininity: Choisy's transitions to,
244–45; effeminacy and, 58–59, 65;
galanterie and, 87; in *Mémoires de
l'abbé de Choisy habillé en femme*,
225–27; masculinity vs., in *tendresse*,
127–38; melancholy and, 135. *See also*
women
feminism, 2–3
Femmes savantes, Les (Molière), 61–62
Ferrand, Jacques, 68
Fisher, Dominique D., 287n87
Fitelieu, sieur de Rodophe et du Montour
de, 65, 69–70
Flaubert, Gustave, 184
Foucault, Michel: on body and sexuality in
seventeenth century, 12–14; Bourdieu
and, on power, 13, 14, 257n31; gender
and, 13; on "great confinement,"
295n10; on homosexuality as nineteenth-century invention, 181, 185; on
male friendship, 205, 206; masculinity
and, 13; masculinity studies and,

257n30; on meanings of homosexuality
in early modern period, 153–55, 180,
282n7; past vs. present sexualities and,
258n33; on sodomy in seventeenth century, 155, 156, 167, 257n26
Franco, Mark, 253n6
Freccero, Carla, 257n32
Freud, Sigmund, 137, 139, 140, 219,
280n43, 280n52
friendship: as marriage, 204; Choisy and,
227–32, 298nn58–59; love vs., 132–33;
Scudéry (Madeleine de) on, 124, 127,
129–33, 278–79n22. *See also* male
friendship; Viau, Théophile de
Fronde, 67, 92, 158, 160, 165
Furetière, Antoine: on *cabinet*, 173, 174;
on *galanterie*, 87; on *honnêteté*, 22; on
particulier, 287n85

galant (ribbon), 275n22
galanterie, 11; *art de plaire* in, 87; *bel esprit*
in, 89; conversation in, 87; definitions
of, 87, 270nn110–11; *douceur* in, 88,
271n117; *enjouement* in, 87; femininity
and, 87; Furetière on, 87; gender and,
86–91; Habib on, 88–89; heterosexuality in, 87; heterosociality in, 87–89; homosociality in, 89; honnêteté compared
to, 40, 87; as ideal, 86; *je ne sais quoi* in,
87, 270–71n111; libertine, 91–92; male
role-playing in, 89; male self-display
in, 89–90; masculinity and, 86–91; neo-
Petrarchanism in, 87, 89; Pelous on, 88,
271n116; rivalry among men and,
89–91; scholarship on, 86, 88; Scudéry
(Madeleine de) on, 118–25; soft masculinity and, 86, 88–89, 91; *suavitas* in,
88; submission of men to women in,
121–22; *tendresse* and, 126, 127; Vaugelas on, 87, 270n111; Viala on, 86, 91,
259n7, 270nn109–11. *See also* galant
homme; Voiture, Vincent
galant homme, 11; honnête homme compared to, 40–41, 87; as posture in
Voiture's writing, 103–7; tender masculinity compared to, 118; Voiture as
model for, 98–103. *See also* galanterie;
Voiture, Vincent

Garasse, François, 182–83, 188, 189–96, 289–90n112, 290–91n124, 291n135, 294n167
Garber, Marjorie, 301n83
Gaston d'Orléans, 99
Gaudet, Charles, 96, 97, 263n13
Génetiot, Alain, 78, 86, 100, 271n114, 271n117, 274n14
gender: affectivity and, 119; *air galant* and, 118–25; authorship and, 17, 232–33, 273–74n10; biological sex and, 211, 230, 236–37; blurring of, as ideal, 112–13, 118; body and, 210; *Carte de Tendre* and, 127, 129–32; Cartesianism and, 3; as category of analysis, 4, 8, 17; civility and, 7–9; civilizing process and, 8, 120; Elias and, 8–9; Foucault and, 13; galanterie and, 86–91; honnêteté and, 11, 23–56; as linguistic mark, 245; melancholy and, 134–42; as nature, 234–37; neo-Petrarchanism and, 87; one-sex model of, 211, 253n7, 296n21; passing as a, 215; performativity of, 209–10, 224–25, 246, 248, 303n2; as play, 142–47; relationality and, 119; salons and, 10, 11, 12, 80, 118, 142–47; sexuality and, 169, 185, 232; sodomy and, 167–73; *tendresse* and, 127; two-sex model of, 211. *See also* Choisy, Abbé François-Timoléon de; cross-dressing; effeminacy; femininity; masculinity; men; Méré, Antoine Gombaud de; Scudéry (Madeleine de); transgender; Voiture, Vincent; women
gender binary, 3, 5, 17, 110, 112, 211
gender dysphoria, 212
gendered habitus, 5–6
gender identity, 211, 213, 216, 219, 233, 237, 239, 297n43, 303n2
gender norms, 8, 208, 209, 225, 236
gender trouble, 159, 168
Gérard, Armand de, 25
Gerzan, François du Soucy de, 76–77
Girac, Paul de, 108, 110
Girard, René, 45
Glaber, Raoul, 71
gloire, 139–41

Godard, Didier, 185, 204, 287nn89–90, 288n96, 289n109, 293n165
Godeau, Antoine, 79, 81, 269n97
Goffman, Irving, 186
Goldberg, Jonathan, 156
Goldsmith, Elizabeth, 268n91, 271n113
Goodman, Dena, 125, 273n135
Gordon-Seifert, Catherine, 265n40
Goussault, Jacques, 9, 25
Grand Condé (Louis II de Bourbon): Louis XIV and, 152; sodomy and, 152, 154, 281n2
Grand dictionnaire des précieuses (Somaize), 80, 82–83, 108, 268n90
great confinement (Foucault), 154, 295n10
Greenberg, Mitchell, 209, 219, 226, 228, 299n71
Guild, Elizabeth, 209–10

Habib, Claude, 10, 86, 88–89, 256n24, 271n120
habitus, 5, 253n7. *See also* gendered habitus, masculine habitus
Halperin, David: on effeminacy, 67, 264n28; on gay abjection, 14, 15, 258n35; on history of sexuality, 257n30, 257n32; on sexual subjectivity vs. sexual identity, 181, 185–86
hard masculinity, 61
Harlay, Achilles de, 162, 284n35, 285n60
Harris, Joseph, 208, 236, 239, 298n59, 301n84, 301n86
Harth, Erica, 78, 79–80, 252n5, 267n78, 268n83, 272n135
Henri III: aristocratic ideal under, 72, 76; effeminacy and, 72, 74; pamphlets about, 158, 160, 165, 166
Hepp, Noémi, 135, 259n3, 280n40
heterosexuality; Choisy and, 16, 229–30, 231–32, 241–42, 302n95; effeminacy and, 67, 68, 69, 85, 264n28; galanterie and, 87; homosociality and, 42, 48–49; honnêteté and, 42, 46–47, 50–53; invention of, 155; *petit-maître* and, 96; sodomy and, 157, 158, 168–70, 172, 173, 282n7, 283n21; *tendresse* and, 128; Viau and, 191, 288n103, 290n119. *See also* heterosociality; love; marriage

heterosociality: civilizing process and, 10; galanterie and, 87–89; honnêteté and, 41–53; masculine submission and, 10; Scudéry on, 118, 132. *See also* salons

Hinds, Leonard, 188, 289n109

"Histoire de la marquise-marquis de Banneville" (Choisy): acquisition of gender identity in, 237; anagnorisis in, 239–41; authorship of, 232–33, 300n73; autobiographical pretense of, 233; beauty of heroine in, 301n85; body image vs. anatomical sex in, 239–40; cited in *Mémoires de l'abbé de Choisy habillé en femme*, 300–301n74; correspondence between body and gender in, 237; DeJean on, 296n25, 300n73, 301n75, 302n92; effeminacy in, 242–44; gender as nature in, 234–37; gender vs. heterosexual desire in, 242; Harris on, 301n86; heroine's coquettishness in, 237; heterosexual desire in, 241–42, 302n95; homoeroticism in, 241–44; interpretations of, 302n92; literary convention in, 236; marriage in, 241; parallels with *Mémoires de l'abbé de Choisy habillé en femme*, 244; performativity of gender in, 302n92; plot of, 235–36; recognition of gendered beauty in, 238; same-sex desire in, 243–44; sexuality as nature in, 237–42, 302n95; sexuality in *Mémoires de l'abbé de Choisy habillé en femme* and, 244; similarity to *La Princesse de Clèves*, 236; variants of, 301n75, 302n91

homme formaliste, 32–33

homoeroticism: censorship of, 288n103; Choisy and, 231, 241–44; Orgon and, 2; Sorel on, 85; Viau and, 184, 204, 288n103, 289n109. *See also* homosexuality; male same-sex desire; sodomy

homosexuality: effeminacy and, 66–67, 264n28; masculinity and, 151–52; masculinity and, in seventeenth-century France, 153–55; sodomy vs., 175. *See also* homoeroticism; homosociality; male same-sex desire; sodomy

homosociality: galanterie and, 89–91; heterosexuality and, 42, 48–49; honnêteté and, 42, 47–52, 262n48, 262n53; in salons, 85–86; male same-sex desire and, 50–52. *See also* female principle; salons

honestus, 24

honnête femme, 22, 259n3, 259n6

honnête homme: as courtly lover, 42, 44–47; Faret on, 9, 10; galant homme compared to, 40–41, 87; happiness as objective of, 25, 53; honnête femme compared to, 22, 259n3, 259n6; tender masculinity compared to, 118; women as model for, 42–44. *See also* honnêteté

honnête masculinity. *See* honnête homme; honnêteté

honnêteté: adaptability in, 54; aggression and, 9; Alcibiades as model of, 50; aristocracy in, 35–36, 38; *art de plaire* in, 25–26, 41; *ataraxia* in, 26; *bienséances* in, 25, 27, 33; Buckingham as model of, 55–56; Caesar as model of, 38–40, 262n53; Castiglione as source for, 23, 24, 34; civilizing process and, 21; context for development of, 22, 256n17, 259n7; conversation in, 39, 41, 43, 260n26; corporeality in, 55–56; counterexamples of, 31–36; courtier and, 37–38; court life and, 35, 37–38; elusiveness of, 23; Epicureanism in, 26; evolution of, 25, 260n16; fashion and, 33–34, 55, 57; female body in, 43–44; female principle in, 42, 53; femininity and, 22; galanterie compared to, 40; gender and, 21; heterosexuality and, 42, 46–47, 50–53; heterosociality in, 41–52; *homme formaliste* and, 32–33; homoeroticism and, 45–46; homosociality in, 42, 45–46, 47–53, 262n48, 262n53; *honnêtes gens* and, 35; *juste milieu* as goal in, 27–28; *justesse* in, 260; *le grand monde* in, 37–38; *le monde* in, 33; *le provincial* and, 33–34; male same-sex desire in, 49–53; masculine dominance and, 56; masculinity and, 22, 46–47; *mérite* in, 35–36; models for, 29, 36–41; moderation and women in, 43; Moriarty on, 36, 38, 261n33; professional men and, 34–36; relationality of, 3,

honnêteté (*continued*)
30–31; relationship to other masculine types in, 23; rivalry in, 44–45, 63; scholarship on, 21, 258n2; sexuality and, 42; social exchange (*le commerce du monde*) in, 44–45; sources of, 24; *sprezzatura* in, 28; Stanton on, 9, 24, 39, 42, 46, 258n2, 259n3, 259n10, 260n18, 262n59; Stoicism in, 26; theatricality in, 53–54; universality of, 34; *virtù* in, 26; warriors and, 31, 38–40; women and, 22, 41–52, 260n27. *See also* honnête femme; honnête homme; Méré, Antoine Gombaud de
humoral medicine: effeminacy in, 68–69; male body in, 68–69, 253–54n7; moderation of men and women in, 28
hyperbole, 104

inclination, 130
insults, 156–57, 172
intersubjectivity, 9
Irigaray, Luce, 146, 281n62
Isarn, Samuel, 126, 144

je ne sais quoi: definition of, 54; galanterie and, 87, 270–71n111; honnêteté and, 11, 23, 53–56, 248
Jouhaud, Christian, 184, 290n118
juste milieu: elusiveness of, 28; honnêteté and, 27–28; men vs. women and, 27–28
justesse, 110, 260n25

Kates, David, 296n26
Kiblansky, Raymond, 134
Koch, Erec, 252n5
Kristeva, Julia, 285n55

La Bruyère, Jean de, 9, 21, 114–15
La Chétardie, Joachim Trotti de, 9, 25
Lachèvre, Frédéric, 185, 204, 268n93, 289nn109–11, 290n114, 291–92n136, 292n144
La Contamine, Philippe Bouvet de, 153, 167
Lafayette, Marie-Madeleine Pioche de La Vergne de, 4, 218, 268n85
La Fontaine, Jean de, 81, 160, 270n111

Lambert, Anne-Thérèse de Marguenat de Courcelles de, 223, 233
language: effeminacy and, 65–66; men's, 89; *précieuses* and, 95; women's, 66, 88, 271n117; *See also* Bouhours, Dominique; men's writing; Méré, Antoine Gombaud de; Voiture, Vincent; women's writing
Laqueur, Thomas, 211, 253n7, 282n14
La Reynie, Gabriel Nicolas de, 160
La Rochefoucauld, François VI de, 9, 22, 81
La Sablière, Marguerite Hessein de, 81, 268n85
La Trimouille, Charles-Belgique-Hollande de, 162, 164–65, 284n35, 285n53
Laugaa, Maurice, 187
Le Gendre, Marie, 90
Lenclos, Anne (Ninon) de, 177
Le Pays, René, 70, 102, 265n39, 273n10
Le Petit, Claude, 167
L'Étoile, Pierre de, 158
Lever, Maurice, 167, 185, 204, 282n8, 285nn62–63, 287nn89–90, 289n109, 293n165
Lhéritier de Villandon, Marie-Jeanne, 232–33, 300n73
Liancourt, Roger du Plessis de, 293n152
Lignières, François Payot de, 152
Lilti, Antoine, 267n74, 267n81, 268n85, 268–69n96, 269n98
Lois de la galanterie, Les (Sorel), 85–86, 95
Longino, Michèle (Farrell), 111, 273n3, 276n51, 282n5
Lougee, Carolyn, 80, 268n90
Louis XIII, 99, 178, 183, 291n133
Louis XIV: Confraternity scandal of 1682 and, 161, 284n35; courtiers of, 161; gender trouble and reign of, 168; Grand Condé and, 152; illegitimate daughters of, 159; masculinity of, 3, 76, 253n6; pacification of nobility and, 8, 75; Philippe d'Orléans and, 76, 170, 282n6; in satires of "sodomites," 169; scholarship on masculinity of, 253n6; sodomy and reign of, 158–73, 286n77
love: as cause of effeminacy, 69–70;

friendship vs., 132–33; *gloire* and, 139–41; melancholy and, 135–37; Scudéry (Madeleine de) on, 123–24, 132–33; *tendresse* and, 128–29; women's authority over, 123–24. *See also* heterosexuality; homosexuality; male friendship

Lully, Jean-Baptiste, 162, 163, 170, 171, 172, 284nn42–43, 284n50, 285n60, 285n71, 286n74

Magendie, Maurice, 258n2
Magne, Emile, 269n97, 275n23, 288n91
Mainil, Jean, 168
"Maison de Sylvie, La" (Viau), 197–202
Maître, Myriam, 92, 121, 272n126, 278n13
male body: affectivity and, 146; effeminacy and, 58, 62, 63–65; habitus and, 5, 255n13; history of, 2, 253n7; honnêteté and, 55–56; humoral medicine and, 68–69, 253–54n7; in *Mémoires de l'abbé de Choisy habillé en femme*, 219; one-sex gender model and, 211, 253n7; in salon of Scudéry (Madeleine de), 146; salons and, 85
male friendship: Bray on, 201, 204–5, 294n170; Des Barreaux and Viau, 197–206, 289n109, 291n136, 292n144, 293n153, 293n160, 293n165, 294nn167–68; Foucault on, 205–6; Liancourt and Viau, 293n152; male same-sex desire and, 201; Montaigne on, 201; signs of, 201; topoi of, 202–3; Viau's ideal of, 199–201
male same-sex desire: effeminacy and, 243–44; friendship and, 201, 203–6; homosociality and, 50–53; in honnêteté, 49–53. *See also* homoeroticism; homosexuality; homosociality; sodomy
Malherbe, François de, 81
marginality: canon and, 18; Louis XIV and, 253n6; masculinity and, 1–2, 6–7, 9, 10, 12–14, 21, 59, 60, 93–94, 208, 249, 255n14; sodomy and, 156
markedness, 1, 13, 17, 21, 253–54n7
"Marmoisan" (Lhéritier), 300n73, 301n84
marriage: Choisy on, 229–30, 241–42, 299n60, 299n64; friendship as, 204; salons and, 80; Scudéry on, 117, 122, 134, 138

masculine dominance: Bourdieu on, 5–7; cross-dressing and, 12, 15–16; effeminacy and, 75, 77, 91; honnêteté and, 26, 28, 31, 47, 56, 248; marginality and, 13, 14; pornography and, 168; Scudéry (Madeleine de) and, 134; sodomy and, 12–15; *sprezzatura* and, 28; submission and, 6–7; Voiture and, 102
masculine habitus, 5–7
masculine subjectivity: abjection and, 14–15; Bourdieu on, 5–7; Breitenberg on, 255n15; Choisy and, 227; civility and, 8–10; markedness and, 17; *précieuses* and, 92; Scudéry (Madeleine de) and, 118, 125; sodomy and, 157, 181, 185–86
masculine submission: civilizing process and, 10; masculine domination and, 6–7; in salons, 79–80, 121–22, 142–47
masculinity: anxiety about salons and, 96; civility and, 7–12; constraints on, 4, 8–10; crises of, 6, 255n15; Descartes and, 252–53n5; dominance and, 2, 5–7, 14, 26, 28, 31, 47, 75, 77, 91, 102, 134, 168, 248; dominant vs. dominated positions in, 5–7; galanterie and, 86–91; gender binary and, 3, 5, 17, 110, 112, 211; homosexuality and, 151–52; homosexuality and, in seventeenth-century France, 153–55; humoral medicine and, 69; marginality and, 1–2, 6–7, 9, 10, 12–14, 21, 59, 60, 93–94, 208, 249, 255n14; markedness and, 1, 13, 17, 21, 253–54n7; melancholy and, 134–42; multiplicity of, 6, 17; past vs. present, 205–6, 250; *précieuses* and, 92–95; in salons, 11–12, 77–91; war and, 9. *See also* Choisy, Abbé François-Timoléon de; dominated masculinity; effeminacy; femininity; galant homme; gender; hard masculinity; heterosexuality; heterosociality; homosociality; honnête homme; honnêteté; male body; male friendship; male same-sex desire; masculine dominance; masculine habitus; masculine subjectivity; men; men's

masculinity (*continued*)
  writing; Méré, Antoine Gombaud de;
  moderation; Scudéry (Madeleine de);
  sodomy; soft masculinity; tender masculinity; Viau, Théophile de; Voiture,
  Vincent; women
masculinity studies: crisis model and,
  255n14; Foucault and, 257n30; purview
  of, 2–3; relation to feminism of, 2–3;
  scholarship on seventeenth-century
  France, 3, 251–52n4; scholarship on sixteenth-century France, 251n4; women's
  writing in seventeenth-century France
  and, 3
material body, 219, 221, 239–40
Maurepas, Jean-Frédéric Phélypeaux de,
  159
Maynard, François, 286n82
Mazarin, Jules, 67, 76, 158, 160, 165, 166,
  267n68
mazarinades, 67, 158
McFarlane, Cameron, 285n59, 285n76
melancholy: attacks on use by Scudéry
  (Madeleine de), 135; desire and, 141; *enjouement* vs., 136; Freud on, 137, 138,
  140; gender and, 135; genius as trait of,
  279–80n39; *gloire* and, 139–41; happiness and, 141–42; interiority and, 137;
  literary tradition of, 134, 140–41; lost
  object in, 137–39; love and, 135–37;
  masculine ideals and, 139; masculinity
  and, 134–42; narrative closure and, 141;
  paradoxical nature of, 136; pleasure
  and, 136; prominence in writing of
  Scudéry (Madeleine de), 134; Scudéry's
  heroes and, 137–38; Scudéry's heroines
  and, 138–39; sociability and, 136;
  women and, 135
*Mémoires de l'abbé de Choisy habillé en
  femme* (Choisy): body image in,
  219–21; Charbonneau on, 298n53;
  clothing in, 220, 225, 297–98n47; conventional femininity in, 225–27; coquettishness in, 226; criticism of cross-
  dressing in, 223; cross-dressing as
  childhood habit in, 216; end of cross-
  dressing in, 232, 299–300n72; episodes
  of, 214–15; exhibitionism in, 228–29;

female rite of passage in, 228; fluid sexual desires in, 230–32; friendship with
  girls in, 227–32, 298nn58–59; gender of
  narrator in, 213, 223, 245; Greenberg
  on, 209, 219, 226, 228, 299n71; Harris
  on, 236, 239, 298n59; heterosexual vs.
  homosexual desires in, 231, 299n71;
  historical authenticity of, 215, 297n38;
  Lafayette in, 218; male body in, 219;
  marriage in, 229–31, 299n60, 299n64;
  men and beauty in, 217; mentoring of
  girls in, 227–28; narcissism in, 217, 221;
  parallels with "Histoire de la marquise-
  marquis de Banneville," 244; publication history of, 213–14; recognition of
  gender in, 221–23, 298n52; sexuality in,
  228–32, 299n69; sexuality in "Histoire
  de la marquise-marquise de Banneville" and, 244; theatricality in,
  223–27, 298n52; transformation of
  body in 220–21, 298nn48–49; transgender autobiography and, 215–16; transitional subjectivity in, 215–16, 232,
  244–45; Van der Cruysse on, 214,
  297n38, 299–300n60. *See also* Choisy,
  Abbé François-Timoléon de; transgender
men: affectivity of, 123–24; anxiety about
  salons and, 96; Brégy on, in salons, 84;
  Christina of Sweden on, in salons, 84;
  condemnation of cross-dressing by,
  208; *coquets,* 84; courtier and honnêteté,
  31–36; dangers of salons for, 83; domination of, 303n3; emotional torment of,
  in Scudéry's salon, 281n60; fashion
  and, 246–50; *homme formaliste* and
  honnêteté, 32–33; infidelity of, 133,
  279n33; *le provincial* and honnêteté,
  33–34; neglect of role in salons, 78; *petits-maîtres,* 96–97; *pousseur de beaux
  sentiments,* 57–58, 84; *précieuses* and,
  92–95; *précieux,* 71, 93–94, 265–66n45,
  272n129; professional, and honnêteté,
  34–36; rivalry and, 124–25, 269n97;
  role-playing in galanterie, 89; salons
  and, 77–86; satire of, and salons,
  83–86; Sorel on, in salons, 85–86; submission to women in salons, 79,

121–22, 142–47; warrior and honnêteté, 31, 38–40; and women in *air galant*, 120–22; and women in honnêteté, 46–47; writing of, and salons, 81–82. *See also* courtiers; effeminacy; galant homme; galanterie; honnête homme; honnêteté; masculinity; male friendship; men's writing; Scudéry (Madeleine de); Voiture, Vincent

Ménage, Gilles: Boisrobert and, 178–80, 288n103; Sarasin on, 67; Scudéry and, 81, 82, 269n97, 270n111

ménage à trois, 51–53

men's writing, 99, 234–35

Méré, Antoine Gombaud, chevalier de, 21–56; on *bienséances*, 260n24; *Discours de la justesse*, 110; *Discours de la vraïe Honnesteté*, 30, 53; female principle and, 118; homosociality and, 262nn48–49, 262nn52–53; influence in eighteenth century, 25; on *justesse*, 260nn25–26, 275n38; *Les Conversations*, 38–40, 47–48, 261n39; master of honnêteté, 28–29, 33, 46–47; phallic privilege and, 147; scholarship on, 258n2, 262n59, 270n109; theoretician of honnêteté, 23; on Viau, 49, 262n55; on Voiture, 275n36; on women, 262n50; writings of, 259n8. *See also* honnête homme; honnêteté

Merlin, Hélène, 186–87, 196, 287n85, 290–91n124

Merrick, Jeffrey, 281n3, 293n152

Mesnard, Jean, 22, 259n3, 259n6

metrosexual, 57–58

Misanthrope, Le (Molière), 63, 226

misogyny, 60, 171–72

moderation: as aristocratic ideal under Henri III, 73; Castiglione on, 72; Cicero on, 24; effeminacy and, 61, 72–74; honnêteté and, 53, 260n26, 260–61n28; Reeser on, 257n30, 263n3; and women in honnêteté, 28, 43. *See also justesse; juste milieu*

Molière [Jean-Baptiste Poquelin]: honnêteté and, 21; *Le Misanthrope*, 63, 226; *Les Femmes savantes*, 61–62; *Les Précieuses ridicules*, 85, 93–95, 269n106; *Le*

Tartuffe, 1–2; on *précieuses*, 272n128; portrayal of marquis, 66, 265n45

mollesse, 61–62

mollitude, 67, 264n29

Mongrédien, Georges, 209

Montaigne, Michel de, 9, 23, 24, 201, 263n6, 293n156

Montandon, Alain, 259n6

Montpensier, Anne Marie Louise d'Orléans de, 272n128

Moriarty, Michael, 36, 38, 261n33

Motley, Mark, 266n57

Moulton, Ian, 68

Mourgues, Odette de, 103

Muchembled, Robert, 74, 255–56nn16–17, 258n2, 266n58, 272–73n135

Munro, James S., 279n35

neo-Petrarchanism, 87, 89, 91, 103–7, 119, 271n114

Neoplatonism, 91, 119, 198, 199

Nepos, Cornelius, 50

nobility. *See* aristocracy

Nye, Robert, 255–56n16, 296n25

Orléans, Philippe d'. *See* Philippe d'Orléans

Ovid, 65

paideia, 24

Panofsky, Erwin, 134

Park, Katharine, 296n25

"Parnasse alarmé, Le" (Ménage), 178

Parnasse des poètes satyriques, Le, 183

particulier, 287n85

Pascal, Blaise, 21

Pasquier, Nicolas, 62, 66

Paster, Gail Kern, 264–65n30

pastoral novel, 119

Paulmy, Jacques, 153, 167

Pellisson, Paul: on galanterie, 270n111; on Sarrasin, 276n41; on Voiture, 98, 109, 111; Scudéry (Madeleine de) and, 81, 90–91, 142, 143–45, 146, 269n97, 277n2, 278n15, 280n59, 281n60

Pelous, Jean-Michel, 88, 92, 271n116

performativity: gender and, 209–10, 224–25, 246, 248; transgender and, 210

Perrault, Charles, 168, 232–33, 300n73
Peters, Jeffrey: on Boileau, 55; on the
    Carte de Tendre, 121, 131, 272n125,
    275n37, 278nn10–11, 279n28, 279n31;
    on physiognomy and masculinity,
    254n7, 265n30
petit-maître, 11, 96–97, 273n138
Petrarch, Francesco, 42, 140, 280n53. *See
    also* neo-Petrarchanism
Phaethon, 197–98
Philippe d'Orléans (brother of Louis
    XIV): Choisy and, 231; effeminacy of,
    76, 267n68; Louis XIV and, 76, 282n6;
    satires about sodomy of, 161–62, 163,
    170, 282n60; sodomy and, 153
phobic enchantment, 166–67
Picard, Roger, 268n85
Pinchesne, Martin, 99–101, 273n9
"Plainte de Théophile à son ami Tircis,
    La" (Viau), 189–92, 291n135, 292n137,
    292n150
plaire, 260n18
Plato, 23, 50, 85
poetic melancholy, 134
Polyeucte (Corneille), 223
polysemicity, 106
Poullain de la Barre, François, 168, 252n5,
    296n23
pousseur de beaux sentiments, 57–58, 84, 93
power: *air galant* and, 121–25; Bourdieu
    and Foucault on, 13, 14
précieuses: debates about, 272n126;
    Duchêne on, 95, 269n106, 272n126; ef-
    feminacy and, 93–95; language and, 95;
    Maître on, 92, 272n126; masculine sub-
    jectivity and, 92; men and, 92–95;
    Pelous on, 92; Stanton on, 92, 272n126;
    Voiture and, 108
Précieuses ridicules, Les (Molière), 85,
    93–95, 269n106
précieux, 71, 93–94, 265–66n45, 272n129
Prest, Julia, 208
preterition, 193, 196, 197
Prétieuse, La (Pure), 93
Princesse de Clèves, La (Lafayette), 236
privacy, 173, 287n85
professional men, 34–36
Prosser, Jay, 215, 216, 297n44

provincial, le, 33–34
Pseudo-Aristotle, 135
Pure, Abbé Michel de, 93, 272n129

querelle des femmes, 159, 168
Quintillian, Marcus Fabius, 24

Racine, Jean, 3, 160
Rambouillet, Catherine de Vivonne, mar-
    quise de: salon hostess, 81, 117; salon
    of, 79, 268n85, 269n100; Voiture and
    salon of, 98, 99, 100, 101, 102, 103, 104,
    105, 106, 115
Reeser, Todd, 254–55n11, 257n30, 260n26,
    260–61n28, 263n3
Reichardt, Rolf, 258n2, 259n6
"Response au Parnasse alarmé" (Bois-
    robert), 178–79
Rey, Michel, 285n54
Reynes, Geneviève, 212–13, 297n42,
    299n66, 299–300n72
Richards, Jennifer, 266n48
Richelet, Pierre, 22, 261n32
Richelieu, Armand Jean du Plessis de, 3,
    15, 175, 176, 177, 178
rivalry: among men in galanterie, 86,
    89–91; among men in salons, 269n97,
    281n60; honnêteté and, 44–45, 63;
    Scudéry (Madeleine de) on,
    124–25
Robinson, David M., 288–89n106
Rollin, Sophie, 103
Roques, Mario, 191
Rousseau, Jacques, 69, 265n36
ruelles. See salons
Ruppert, Jacques, 275n22
Russo, Elena, 25, 258n2, 260n16, 262n58,
    273n135

Saba, Guido, 203–4, 289n107
Sablé, Madeleine de Souvré, marquise de,
    79
Sageot, Louis Forest, 188–89, 193, 196,
    289–90n112, 291n133
Saint-Amand, Pierre, 273n138
Saint-Evremond, Charles de, 176
Saint-Igny, Jean de, 302n1
Saintot, Anne, 103–4

Saint-Simon, Louis de Rouvroy de, 76, 221, 282n6

Salazar, Philippe-Joseph, 293n152

Salisbury, John of, 72

salonnière, 269n98

salons: anachronism of term, 267n74; anxiety about men and, 96; Brégy on men in, 84; Christina of Sweden on men in, 84; conflict between male writers in, 81–82; conversation in, 79–81; court and, 78; dangers for men in, 83; distinction conferred by, 80; Duchêne on, 269n96; effeminacy and, 77–86; feminocentric culture of, 78, 82; Harth on, 78, 79–80, 252n5, 267n78, 268n83, 272n135; homoeroticism in, 85–86; homosociality in, 85–86; male body and, 85; male writer and hostess in, 81–82; marriage and, 80; men in, 77–86, 121–22, 142–47, 269n97; men's writing and, 81–82; mimetic rivalry and, 86; motivation for men in, 82–83; neglect of men's role in, 78–79; rivalries between men in, 269n97, 281n60; satire of men in, 83–86; Scudéry (Georges de) on men in, 57–58, 84; Sorel on men in, 85–86; scholarship on, 267n77; submission of men to women in, 79–80, 121–22, 142–47; terms for, 77; varieties of, 268n85; Voiture and, 98–99, 114–15; women and, 78; women's writing and, 78. *See also* Scudéry (Madeleine de)

Sarasin, Jean-François, 67, 81, 90, 98, 108, 109, 111, 114–15, 270n111, 271n124, 276n41

satire, 163

satires of "sodomites": abjection in, 166; ambivalence in, 167–68; as aggression, 163–65; as insults, 172–73; Brunet in, 169, 171, 286n74; Campistron in, 164, 284n50; Certain in, 169, 171; Chausson in, 163, 164, 167, 284n35, 284n41, 284n43, 284n47; Confraternity of 1682 in, 161; connection between gender and sexuality in, 169; Créquy in, 166; descriptions of sex acts in, 161; during reign of Louis XIV, 157–73; fluidity of object choice in, 170; gender trouble and, 159, 168; heterosexual masculine norm and, 172; heterosexual vs. homosexual acts in, 168–69; humor in, 165–66; in *Chansonnier Maurepas*, 158–73; La Trimouille in, 164–65, 285n53; Louis XIV in, 169; Lully in, 162, 163, 170, 171, 172, 284nn42–43, 284n50, 285n60, 285n71, 286n74; misogyny in, 171–72; motivation for, 160; Philippe d'Orléans in, 161–62, 163, 170, 282n60; phobic enchantment and, 166–67; political turmoil and, 158; sexuality of Louis XIV and Philippe d'Orléans in, 170; themes in, 162–64; Vendôme in, 162, 166, 284n35–36, 285n60

Saxl, Fritz, 134

Scarron, Paul, 165–66

Schachter, Marc, 293n152, 293n156

Schalk, Ellery, 261n34

Schehr, Lawrence R., 287n87

Schiesari, Juliana, 140, 280n54

Scholar, Richard, 54, 259n9

science du monde, la, 78

Scipio (Publius Cornelius Scipio Africanus Major), 32–33

Scodel, Joshua, 260n26

Scudéry, Georges de, 70; on men in salons, 57–58, 84

Scudéry, Madeleine de, 11, 117–47; *à clef* portraits in works of, 276–77n2; affectivity and, 119, 123–24; affectivity in salon of, 146; *Artamène ou le Grand Cyrus*, 11, 70, 108–9, 117, 118–19, 120, 122, 123–24, 132, 135, 138–39, 141–42, 145, 277n6, 278n8, 278n14, 279n33, 279n37, 280n55; attacks on, 70–71, 104, 119, 120, 135; *Chroniques du Samedi*, 11, 90–91, 117, 118, 121, 125, 126, 127, 132, 142–47, 278n15, 279n29, 280–81nn59–61; *Clélie*, 11, 70, 117, 118, 122–23, 126–34, 135–38, 139–41, 145, 278n15, 278–79n22, 279n25, 279n32, 280n50, 280n55; courtly love and, 91, 119, 129; Denis on, 277n2, 277n5, 280n58; female principle and, 118; *galanterie* and, 118–25; gender and, 117–47; gendered role-playing in salon of, 142–47;

Scudéry, Madeleine de (*continued*)
heterosociality and, 118, 132; *inclina-tion*, 130; Journée des madrigaux, 90–91; Maître on, 121, 278n13; male body in salon of, 146; male desire in salon of, 145–46; male vs. female characters in works of, 277n6; masculine subjectivity and, 118, 125; melancholy in salon of, 145; men's emotional torment in salon of, 281n60; neo-Petrarchanism and, 12, 119; Neoplatonism and, 119; on conversation, 117, 118, 120, 123; on effeminacy, 118, 142; on female authority, 121–25; on friendship, 124, 126, 127, 129–32, 278–79n22; on love, 123–24, 132–33; on male desire, 122, 141; on male rivalry, 124; on marriage, 117, 122, 134, 138; on men's infidelity, 279n33; on men's speech, 123–24; on sociability, 117, 127, 136; on women's freedom, 122; on women's modesty, 122–23, 278n14; on women's refining influence, 125; on women's role in society, 122–23; Pellisson and, 142,143–45, 146; Queen of Tendre, 121, 145; relation of novels to salon of, 142; salon of, 12, 79, 81, 82, 90–91, 117–18, 121, 125, 126, 127, 132, 134, 142–47, 277n2; soft masculinity and, 125; *tendresse* in salon of, 144–45, 279n29; typology of personalities and, 125. *See also air galant; Carte de Tendre;* melancholy; tender masculinity; *tendresse*
secrecy, 174, 179, 180–81
Sedgwick, Eve Kosofsky, 42, 45, 47, 52, 174, 228n102
sensibilité, 126
Servien, Auguste, 162, 284n35
sex/gender system, 2, 14, 17, 97, 209, 250
sexual identity, 185
sexuality: as nature, 237–42, 302n95; Choisy and, 227–32; fluidity of object choice, 155, 170–71, 230–32, 282n14; Foucault on, in seventeenth century, 12–14; honnêteté and, 42; past vs. present, 181, 257n32, 258n33. *See also* heterosexuality; homoeroticism; homosex-

uality; male same-sex desire; sodomy
sexual subjectivity, 15, 156, 157, 185, 186
Sibalis, Michael, 281n3, 282nn14–15
Silverman, Kaja, 255n14
Smith, Pauline, 266n50
sociability: effeminacy and male-female, 10; melancholy and, 136; Scudéry on, 117, 123, 125, 136; Voiture and, 100. *See also* civility; galanterie; heterosociality; homosociality; honnêteté; salons
social exchange (*le commerce du monde*): honnêteté and, 44–45; Scudéry on, 120; Voiture and, 100
Socrates, 23, 29, 30, 50
sodomy: as "Italian vice," 191; during the reign of Louis XIV, 158–73, 286n77; early modern meanings of, 282n7, 283n21; gender and, 167–73; Grand Condé and, 152; heterosexuality and, 157, 158, 168–70, 172, 173, 282n7, 283n21; homosexuality vs., 175; masculine dominance and, 12–15; masculine subjectivity and, 157, 181, 185–86; masculinity and, in seventeenth-century France, 151–206; representation in early modern England and France, 286n77; repression of, 154, 155, 157, 167–68, 175, 282n8 285n63, 287n89; scholarship on, 175, 281–82nn3–4; Sibalis on, 281n3, 282nn14–15. *See also* Boisrobert, Abbé François Le Métel de; satires of "sodomites"; Viau, Théophile de
soft masculinity, 59, 86, 88–89, 91
Somaize, Baudeau de, 80–81, 82–83, 108, 109, 268n90, 272n128
Soman, Alfred, 281n3
Sorel, Charles, 85–86, 91, 92, 95, 109, 269n106
sprezzatura, 24, 28, 63
Stallybrass, Peter, 166
Stanton, Domna C.: on honnêteté, 9, 24, 39, 42, 46, 258n2, 259n3, 259n10; on the *je ne sais quoi*, 262n59; on *plaire*, 260n18; on the *précieuses*, 92, 272n126
Steinberg, Sylvie, 208, 297n42

Stewart, Alan, 287n88
Stoicism, 26, 61
Strosetzki, Christoph, 271n113
suavitas, 88
syllepsis, 104
symbolic violence, 258n36

Tallemant des Réaux, Gédéon: on Boisrobert, 175, 176–79, 180, 288n92; on
Viau, 204, 205; on Voiture, 108, 109;
satires of "sodomites" by, 158
Tartuffe, Le (Molière), 1–2
tender masculinity: definition of, 120; *tendresse* and, 128–34. *See also* Scudéry
(Madeleine de); *tendresse*
tendresse: air galant and, 127; definition of,
126; elusiveness of, 134; femininity vs.
masculinity in, 127–38; friendship and,
126, 127, 132–33; gender and, 127; heterosexuality and, 128; libertine
galanterie and, 128; love and, 128–29;
refining influence of, 129. *See also*
Scudéry (Madeleine de); tender masculinity
Théophile de Viau. *See* Viau, Théophile
de
"Theophilus in carcere" (Viau), 189,
192–93
Traister, Bryce, 255n15
transgender: anachronism and, 211–12,
295–96n20; autobiographies by, 215;
body image and, 218–21, 222, 233, 240,
298n47; Choisy as, 210–13; Choisy's
writings and, 16; definition of, 210;
feminist critiques of, 298n57; gender
identity vs. embodied sex and, 211–12,
213, 216, 219, 233, 237, 239, 297n43;
performativity and, 210; recognition by
others and, 221–22; skin and, 221;
transformation of body and, 220; transitioning and, 211–12, 215, 219, 221; vs.
poststructuralist theories of body, 210,
297n44. *See also* Choisy, Abbé
François-Timoléon de; "Histoire de la
marquise-marquis de Banneville"; *Mémoires de l'abbé de Choisy habillé en
femme;* transsexual
transgender studies, 210, 212

transsexual, 212, 213, 215, 216, 219–20,
296n26, 297n44
Trumbach, Randolph, 168, 286n77
Turenne, Henri de, 162, 284n35

urbanus, 24

Van der Cruysse, Dirk, 212, 214,
294nn3–4, 297n34, 297n38,
299–300n72
Vasquez, Gabriel, 195, 292–93n151
Vaugelas, Claude Favre de, 87, 98,
270n111
Vendôme, Louis-Joseph de, 162, 166,
284n35–36, 285n60
Venette, Nicolas, 168
Vermandois, Louis de, 162, 284n35,
285n60
Viala, Alain, 86, 91, 259n7, 270nn109–111
Viau, Théophile de, 14, 15, 49, 157,
181–206; Adam on, 185, 204, 289n109,
291–92n136, 292n144, 293n153; ambiguity of, during trial, 188–89; "Apologie au Roi," 291n133; "Apologie de
Théophile," 189, 193–96, 292n37,
292n150; career of, 290n118; censorship
and, 184; DeJean on, 186–87, 196,
288n103, 289n109, 289n112, 290n114,
291n128; Des Barreaux and, 197–206,
289n109, 291n136, 292n144, 293n153,
293n160, 293n165, 294nn167–68;
Garasse and, 182–83, 188, 189–96,
289–90n112, 290–91n124, 291n135,
294n167; Godard on, 289n109,
293n165; Greek mythology used by,
197; Hinds on, 188, 289n109; heterosexuality and, 191, 288n103, 290n119; homoerotic poetry by, 290n119; honnêteté
and, 49; interpretation of friendship
with Des Barreaux, 204–6; Jouhaud on,
184, 290n119; Lachèvre on, 185, 204,
268n93, 289nn109–11, 290n114,
291–92n136, 292n144; "La Maison de
Sylvie," 197–202; "La Plainte de
Théophile à son ami Tircis," 189–92,
291n135, 292n137, 292n150; Latin letters of, 202–5, 293n160; Liancourt and,
293n152; male friendship and, 197–206,

Viau, Théophile de (*continued*)
293n152; Méré on, 49, 262n65; Merlin
on, 186–87, 196, 290–91n124; modernity of, 182; on casuistry, 195; *Parnasse
des poètes satyriques* and, 183; persona
of, 186–88; preterition and, 193, 196,
197; prison writings of, 182, 186–202;
pseudonym of, 186–87; Saba on, 203;
Sageot and, 188–89, 193, 196,
289–90n112, 291n133; self-defense of,
184; sexual persona of, 156, 181–206,
289n109; sodomite sonnet of, 183,
289–90n112; "Theophilus in carcere,"
189, 192–93; topoi of male friendship
and, 202–3; trial of, 182–85,
289–90nn110–13, 291n133
Vienne, Philibert de, 73
Villedieu, Madame de (Marie-Catherine
Desjardins), 4, 272n128
virtù, 26
Voiture, Vincent, 98–116; ambivalence toward women, 107; as example for
women, 102; as model of galanterie,
98–103; Balzac and, 108, 110–11, 115,
271n117, 275n23; Bouhours on, 111–14;
bourgeois origins of, 102–3; conversation and, 98, 100, 101, 102; Costar on,
110–11; demeanor of, 273n9; dominance over women, 102; Donneau de
Visé on, 99; *douceur* and, 100, 113; effeminacy and, 108–15; *enjouement* and,
100; fashion and, 108; female principle
and, 118; "feminine" quality of writing
by, 101–2, 110–12, 273–74n10;
galanterie and, 98–116; galant homme
as posture for, 103–7; hyperbole used
by, 104; insincerity and, 109; *justesse*
and, 110; *la belle raillerie* and, 100; La
Bruyère on, 114–15; *le commerce du
monde* and, 100; Le Pays on, 102,
273–74n10; Longino (Farrell) on, 111,
273n3, 276n51; member of Rambouillet's salon, 81; men's writing and, 99;
Méré on, 110, 275n36, 275n38; neo-Petrarchanism and,103–7, 119; Pellisson
on, 98, 109, 111; personal nature of
writing by, 98–99, 110; Pinchesne on,

99–101, 273n9; polysemicity used by,
106; *précieuses* and, 108; quarrels among
men of letters and, 275n23; reception
of, 107–16; salons and, 98–99, 114–15;
Sarasin on, 108; satires about, 108–10;
Scudéry (Madeleine de) on, 108–9; sociability and, 100; social position of,
274nn14–15; Somaize on, 108, 275n34;
syllepsis used by, 104; Tallemant des
Réaux on, 108, 109; *tendresse* and, 126;
Vaugelas on, 98; women and, 100–102,
107–10, 114–15
volupté, 62

Waller, Margaret, 263n15
war, 29, 31, 38–40, 139–40. *See also*
Fronde; Wars of Religion
warrior, 31, 38–40
Wars of Religion, 157–58, 160
White, Allon, 166
Wilde, Oscar, 184
Wilkin, Rebecca, 252n5
writing. *See* men's writing; women's writing
women: *air galant* and, 120; arbiters of
honnêteté, 43; as cause of effeminacy,
69–71; as model for honnête homme,
42–44; as superego for men, 125; Boisrobert and, 176; conversation and, 10,
24, 27, 78; courtiers and, 77; dominated
masculinity and, 5–7; domination of,
303n3; *douceur* and, 271n117; Elias on,
256n18; freedom of, 122; historical positions of, 303n5; honnêteté and, 22, 27,
41–52; marriage and, 122; melancholy
and, 135; moderation and, in honnêteté,
43; modesty and, 122–23, 278n14;
petits-maîtres and, 96–97; power over
men of, 121–25; refining influence of,
118–25; role in society of, 122–23; role
of, compared to men in honnêteté,
46–47; salons and, 78–91; scholarship
on seventeenth-century French, 4,
16–17; sodomy and, 167–72; submission of men to, in salons, 79–80,
121–22, 142–47; Voiture and, 100–102,
107–10, 114–15. *See also* female prin-

ciple; femininity; heterosociality; women's writing

women's writing: Choisy on, 234–35; in seventeenth century, 4, 16–17, 265n43, 277n4, 300n73; La Bruyère on, 115; sa-lons and, 78; Voiture's writing as, 101–2, 110–12, 273–74n10. *See also* Scudéry (Madeleine de)

Zanger, Abby, 253n6, 267n69